AF702608

The Rise and Fall of the Bund in Poland. 1944–1949

Studies in Jewish History and Memory

Edited by

Lucyna Aleksandrowicz-Pędich

Sławomir Jacek Żurek

Volume 18

Martyna Rusiniak-Karwat

The Rise and Fall of the Bund in Poland. 1944–1949

Translated by Małgorzata Sochańska-Kumor

PETER LANG

Berlin · Bruxelles · Chennai · Lausanne · New York · Oxford

Bibliographic information published by the Deutsche Nationalbibliothek
The Deutsche Nationalbibliothek lists this publication in the Deutsche Nationalbibliografie; detailed bibliographic data is available online at http://dnb.d-nb.de.

Library of Congress Cataloging-in-Publication Data
LCCN: 2025024158

Cover image courtesy of Adam Lis.

Proofreading by Alina Nowobilska

The project is financed from state budget funds granted by the Minister of Science under the Program Doskonała nauka II
Doskonała Nauka II – Wsparcie monografii naukowych - MONOG/SP/0017/2023/01

Ministerstwo Nauki i Szkolnictwa Wyższego

ISSN 2364-1975
ISBN 978-3-631-93636-8 (Print)
ISBN 978-3-631-93637-5 (E-PDF)
ISBN 978-3-631-94001-3 (E-PUB)
DOI 10.3726/b23015

© 2025 Peter Lang Group AG, Lausanne (Switzerland)
Published by Peter Lang GmbH, Berlin (Germany)

info@peterlang.com

All rights reserved.
All parts of this publication are protected by copyright. Any utilization outside the strict limits of the copyright law, without the permission of the publisher, is forbidden and liable to prosecution. This applies in particular to reproductions, translations, microfilming, and storage and processing in electronic retrieval systems.

This publication has been peer reviewed.

www.peterlang.com

Contents

Introduction

Poland is our homeland, here lies our future.[1]

In the autumn of 1944, in the Polish lands liberated from German occupation by the Red Army, life began to slowly revive, both politically (the establishment of the so-called Lublin Poland) and socially. This also applied to the Jewish community that survived the Holocaust. Jewish political activists began to resume the work of pre-war institutions and create new ones. These included the Central Committee of Jews in Poland (CKŻP) and local Jewish committees, the Society for the Protection of Health at the CKŻP (TOZ), the Organisation for the Development of Industry, Crafts and Agriculture among the Jewish Population (ORT) and the Jewish Theatre. At the same time, political life was flourishing once again on the so-called 'Jewish Street'.[2] One of the parties that re-emerged in a country recovering from the ravages of war and brought together the few Jews who had survived the Holocaust, both in Poland and abroad, was the *Yidisher algemeyner arbeter bund*, the All-Jewish Workers' Union, commonly known as the Bund. The party was established in 1897 and remained operational in Poland until 1949.

This monograph is dedicated to the activities of the 'Polish' Bund[3] in the years 1944–1949, within the borders of post-Yalta Poland. In the Second Polish Republic (1918–1939), the Bund was one of the largest and best-organised political groups operating in the Jewish community.[4] The party did not cease its activities

1 Archives of the Jewish Historical Institute (hereinafter AŻIH), the Bund collection, unsorted files, Michał Szuldenfrei, political speech delivered during the First National Conference of the Bund in Łódź, 16–17 June 1945.

2 The term 'Jewish Street' was already used during the Second Polish Republic by the Jewish community to distinguish the Polish political scene from the activities of the political parties among Jews in shtetls and in Jewish quarters of large towns and cities, including elections to the Jewish religious councils.

3 The term 'Polish' Bund was not used by the Bundists themselves in post-war Poland. It is a term I created and is synonymous with the term 'Bund' in Poland after the war. This term is intended to indicate where the Bundists initiated their activities and the existence of the committees, in contrast to the activities of Bundists from Poland after the war within the Representation of the Polish Bund in America and in Western European countries.

4 The high level of support for the Bund in the Jewish community was demonstrated, for example, by the results of the parliamentary elections in 1928, when it received 80,300 votes out of 556,000 votes cast for Jewish lists, placing it third, behind the Union of National Jewish Parties and the All-Jewish Electoral Bloc.

even after the outbreak of World War II in the German-occupied territories. Underground Bund committees were established in the ghettos, including the Central Committee in the Warsaw Ghetto, which, in addition to party activities and the publication of underground press, provided material assistance to members of organisations affiliated with the Bund. Jewish socialists also participated in the Warsaw Ghetto Uprising.[5]

Bund representatives held seats in municipal councils. In 1919, for example, there were 160 Bundist councillors, including: 5 in Łódź, 7,872 votes and 5 councillors in Warsaw (about 20% of the Jewish vote), 2,416 votes and 5 councillors in Lublin, 2,036 votes and 5 seats in Tomaszów Mazowiecki, and 577 votes and 7 councillors in Maków Mazowiecki. In December 1922, elections for the second Sejm were held, in which the Bundists won 81,473 votes (information from: *Di geshikhte fun bund,* vol. IV, ed. S. Dubnov-Erlich, J. Sh. Hertz, Kh. Sh. Kazdan, E. Scherer, Nyu york 1972, pp. 33, 36). As the economic crisis worsened, the Bund, which focused on the problems of the working class, gained more and more support. In 1936, the Bund emerged as the strongest Jewish party in the municipal council elections in Łódź and in the elections for the board of the Jewish Religious Council in Warsaw. In Łódź, the Bund was one of the parties that enjoyed significant support among the Jewish population from the time Poland gained its independence. An example of this is the fact that in the 1919 municipal council elections, it received 25% of the Jewish vote and won five council seats. In 1923, it obtained 21% of the Jewish vote; in 1927–5 council seats; in 1934–3 council seats and in 1936 as much as 48% of the Jewish votes earning 6 seats. In 1938, the Bund won 11 seats. Overall, during one term, 75 Bund representatives sat on the Łódź City Council (information from: P. Samuś, "The Bund Organization in Łódź, 1898–1939," in: *Jewish Politics in Eastern Europe: The Bund at 100,* ed. J. Jacobs, foreword by F. Tych, New York 2001, pp. 106–107; R. M. Shapiro, *The Polish Kehile Elections of 1936: A Revolution Re-Examined*, New York 1988, p. *passim*; J. Tomaszewski, "Niepodległa Rzeczpospolita," in: *Najnowsze dzieje Żydów w Polsce w zarysie (do 1950 roku)*, ed. J. Tomaszewski, Warsaw 1993, pp. 228, 231). For more on the history of the Bund in the years 1918–1939, see also: J. Jacobs, "The Bund in Vilna, 1918–1939," *Polin* 2013, vol. 25; B. Johnpoll, *The Politics of Futility. The General Jewish Workers Bund of Poland (1917–1943)*, New York 1967; E. Nowogródzki, *The Jewish Labor Bund in Poland 1915–1939. From its Emergence as an Independent Political Party Until the Beginning of World War II,* tr. M. Nowogrodzki, Rockville 2001 (Polish edition: E. Nowogródzki, *Żydowska Partia Robotnicza BUND w Polsce w latach 1915–1939,* tr. P. Sawicka, Warsaw 2005).

5 See, e.g.: *En Direct du Ghetto. La presse clandestine juive dans le ghetto de Varsovie*, ed. D. Blatman, Paris 2005; *Idem*, *For Our Freedom and Yours. The Jewish Labour Bund in Poland 1939–1949*, London–Portland 2003; *Idem*, "The Bund at the Beginning of the German Occupation of Poland," *Gal-Ed* 1993, no. XIII; Johnpoll, *op. cit.*; B. Goldstein, *Finf yor in varshever geto*, Nyu york 1947; *Archiwum Ringelbluma.*

As far as the Bundists in the USSR during World War II are concerned, the fates of two pre-war party leaders have been documented: Victor Alter and Henryk Erlich, who were held captive in Soviet prisons.[6] In 2017 and 2018, I published articles on the situation of members of Bundist organisations in the USSR and their attempts to engage in party activities under Soviet supervision.[7] Thanks to the fact that these articles were published in English, they gained recognition and appreciation of researchers as well as the children and subsequent generations of families with Bundist roots outside Poland.

The post-war activities of the Bund would not have been possible without the engagement of young socialists, who were seen as the hope for the continued existence of the party on the political scene. This refers to the activities of two organisations affiliated with the Bund – the youth organisation *Yugnt bund 'tsukunft'* ('Future' Youth Union; hereinafter Tsukunft) and the children's organisation SKIF or *Sotsyalistisher kinder-farband* (Socialist Children's Union, hereinafter Skif). Both organisations cooperated more closely with the Bund than in the past. In this book, I focus exclusively on describing the activities of the Bund. The organisations affiliated with it require a separate study in order to emphasise their independence in the political arena, as was the case prior to 1939, including their strong critical stance towards the political situation in Poland at the time and their refusal to engage in self-criticism and to continue working within the communist movement.

Konspiracyjne Archiwum Getta Warszawy. vol. XVI: *Prasa getta warszawskiego: „Bund" i „Cukunft"*, p. I: *„Bund"*, intr., ed. M. Rusiniak-Karwat, p. II: *„Cukunft"*, intr., ed. A. Jarkowska-Natkaniec, Warsaw 2016; M. Rusiniak-Karwat, „Bund," in: *Encyklopedia getta warszawskiego. Wybrane hasła*, ed. M. Ferenc, Warsaw 2024, pp. 48–58.

6 M. Hułas, "Polskie starania o uwolnienie Wiktora Altera i Henryka Erlicha," *Kwartalnik Historii Żydów* 2020, no. 274, pp. 397–424; G. Pickhan, „'That Incredible History of the Polish Bund Written in a Soviet Prison': The NKVD Files on Henryk Erlich and Wiktor Alter," *Polin* 1997, vol. X, pp. 247–272; Sh. Redlich, *War, Holocaust and Stalinism. A Documented Study of the Jewish Anti-Fascist Committee in the USSR*, Luxemburg 1995; D. Urzyńska, "Kontakty Adama Ciołkosza z przywódcami Bundu Wiktorem Alterem i Henrykiem Erlichem," *Biuletyn Żydowskiego Instytutu Historycznego* 1999, no. 3 (191), pp. 12–22.

7 The articles were written as part of the grant I received from the National Science Centre to work on the Soviet authorities' policy towards the Jewish socialists – the Jewish Workers' Party, the Bund – in the years 1939–1957. See: M. Rusiniak-Karwat, "Bundists under Soviet Occupation: The Case of Matwiej Bernstein," *Studia Polityczne* 2017, no. 3 (45), pp. 141–151; *Idem*, "Bundists in the Soviet Union during World War II," in: *Bundist Legacy after the Second World War "Real" Place versus "Displaced" Time*, Series: Free Ebrei, Vol. 1, ed. V. Pinto, Leiden–Boston 2018, pp. 7–17.

The aim of the monograph is to shed light on the little-known and often overlooked activities of the Bund in post-war reality, in which the pre-war party leaders at all levels of its organisational structures were missing, as well as the interest in the party's programme among the surviving Jewish proletariat, which had helped shape it before the war. Contrary to Marek Edelman's statements – repeated many times in his numerous speeches – that the Bund almost ceased to exist and meant nothing after World War II, that it was exclusively a social movement born out of nostalgia for the past,[8] I will show the activity of the Bund as a political party – decimated, but still alive, which, in the new reality, tried to modify its political programme and make its presence felt on the so-called 'Jewish Street', i.e. within the Presidium of the CKŻP, and in Jewish committees as well as on the broader Polish political scene. I will show the evolution of the party's programme, which occurred as a result of the tragic consequences of the war, and present a new interpretation of the three main ideological pillars of the Bund, on which it was founded from the beginning of its existence, and their significance for Bundists in the post-war era:

- *doykeyt* (hereness);
- *mishpokhedikeyt* (familiariness);
- *yidishkeyt* (Jewishness, whatever is related to the Yiddish language and culture).

Over the past half-century, a number of monographs and articles have been published on various aspects of Jewish community life in Poland between 1944 and 1949.[9] Only a few contain information about the Bund, and most address only

8 For more, see, i.a.: M. Rusiniak-Karwat, „Marek Edelman – socjalista i strażnik pamięci. Narodziny legendy (1944–1949)," *Studia Polityczne* 2013, no. 32, pp. 281–298.

9 See, i.a.: N. Aleksiun, *Dokąd dalej? Ruch syjonistyczny w Polsce (1944–1950)*, Warsaw 2002; Y. Bauer, *Flight and Rescue. Brichah, The Organised Escape of Jewish Survivors of Eastern Europe, 1944–1948*, New York 1970; idem, *Out of Ashes. The Impact of American Jews on Post-Holocaust European Jewry*, Pergamon Press 1989; N. Bażanowska, *To był mój dom. Żydowski Dom Dziecka w Krakowie w latach 1945–1957*, Kraków 2011; G. Berendt, „Zjednoczenie Syjonistów Demokratów 'Ichud' – 'z biało-niebieskimi sztandarami w morzu czerwonych sztandarów'," in: *Między emigracją a trwaniem. Syjoniści i komuniści żydowscy w Polsce po Holocauście*, ed. A. Grabski, G. Berendt, Warsaw 2003; D. Flisiak, *Działalność syjonistów-rewizjonistów w Polsce w latach 1944/1945–1950*, Lublin 2020; A. Grabski, *Żydowski ruch kombatancki w Polsce w latach 1944–1949*, Warsaw 2002; *idem, Działalność komunistów wśród Żydów w Polsce (1944–1949)*, Warsaw 2004; *idem, Lewica przeciwko Izraelowi. Studia o żydowskim lewicowym antysyjonizmie*, Warsaw 2008; *idem, Centralny Komitet*

selected issues, such as Natalia Aleksiun's book,[10] which describes the relations between the representatives of various Zionist factions, Bundists and communists, shown mainly by the Presidium of the CKŻP. Similarly, August Grabski also explores, in his books, the Jewish communist milieu within the CKŻP. He examines the attitude toward the Bund, among other things, and evaluates the process of the Bund's self-dissolution from the perspective of a Jewish communists.[11] Many works concerning this period contain only select pieces of information about the Bund. An example of this is the album published in 2012 by the Katowice branch of the Institute of National Remembrance, which is a follow-up to the exhibition of the same title. It presents the life of the Jewish community in Upper Silesia until 1949, including the political activities of the various Jewish political parties, mainly the Zionists.[12] The existence of the Bund is mentioned in three sentences, one of which downplays the importance of the party (stating that the Bund did not enjoy support in the Silesian Province).[13] Among the rich iconographic material, there were also no photographs or documents regarding the activities of the Bund's Provincial Committee in Katowice. This is different in the case of the Polish-English

Żydów w Polsce (1944–1950). Działalność polityczna, Warsaw 2015; M. Grynberg, *Żydowska spółdzielczość pracy w Polsce w latach 1945–1949,* Warsaw 1986; K. Kersten, *Polacy – Żydzi – Komunizm. Anatomia półprawd 1939–1968,* Warsaw 1992; A. Lech, K. Radziszewska, A. Rykała (ed.), *Społeczność żydowska i niemiecka w Łodzi po 1945 roku,* Łódź 2010; K. Kaczyńska, *"Orać zagon lepszej doli?" Żydowskie rolnictwo w Polsce w latach 1945–1950,* Warsaw 2021; E. Koźmińska-Frejlak, *Po Zagładzie. Praktyki asymilacyjne Ocalałych jako strategie zadomawiania się w Polsce (1944/45–1950),* Warsaw 2022; J. Mieczkowski, *Żydzi, Niemcy i Ukraińcy na Pomorzu Zachodnim w latach 1945–1956. Liczba, położenie i działalność polityczna,* Szczecin 1994; J. Nalewajko-Kulikov, *A Citizen of Yiddishland. Dovid Sfard and the Jewish Communist Milieu in Poland,* tr. P. Glasser, Berlin 2020; A. Namysło, *Utracone nadzieje. Ludność żydowska w województwie śląskim/katowickim w latach 1945–1970 / Lost Hopes. Jews in the Silesian/Katowickie Voivodship in Years 1945–1970,* Katowice 2012; L. Olejnik, *Polityka narodowościowa Polski w latach 1944–1960,* Łódź 2003; J. Schatz, *The Generation. The Rise and Fall of Jewish Communists in Poland,* Berkeley–Los Angeles–Oxford 1991; B. Szaynok, *Ludność żydowska na Dolnym Śląsku 1945–1950,* Wrocław 2000; *idem, Z historią i Moskwą w tle. Polska a Izrael 1944–1968,* Warsaw 2007; *Jewish Presence in Absence. The Aftermath of the Holocaust in Poland, 1944–2010,* eds. F. Tych. M. Adamczyk-Garbowska, tr. G. Dąbkowski, J. Taylor-Kucia, Jerusalem 2014.

10 N. Aleksiun, *Dokąd dalej? Ruch syjonistyczny,* Warsaw 2002, sub-chapter: „Obóz syjonistyczny a komuniści żydowscy i Bund na forum CKŻP", pp. 245–266.

11 Grabski, *Działalność komunistów wśród Żydów*; *Idem, Centralny Komitet Żydów w Polsce.*

12 Namysło, *Utracone nadzieje. Ludność żydowska.*

13 Ibid., p. 114.

album by Anna Grużlewska, which illustrates the life of the Jewish community in the post-war Dzierżoniów County. Thanks to the photographs and their captions, we can learn not only facts about the activities of the Bund and Tsukunft but also the names of the key activists of Bund organisations in Lower Silesia.[14]

Until the late 1990s, few researchers focused on the history of the Bund in post-war Poland. The issue was first raised in a collective work published on the occasion of the party's 100th anniversary[15] (The Polish version was edited by Jürgen Hensel and Feliks Tych, the English version by Jack Jacobs).[16] The Polish volume includes articles by David Engel, Bożena Szaynok and Natalia Aleksiun, and covers selected aspects of the Bund's activities between 1944 and 1949. The main issues addressed are the party's political programme and its relationships with other political groups on the 'Jewish Street'. They do, however, omit the Bund's social, cultural, and material activities, as well as the party's post-war operations, the structure of its committees and affiliated organisations.[17] The earlier period of the Bund's history was presented in more detail. The research was filled with information, which was incredibly useful especially for historians and political scientists from Poland and abroad. In recent years, there has been a growing interest in the history and historiography of Jewish socialists. Most of the works focus on the period before 1939.[18] The history of the Bund, from its

---

14 A. Grużlewska, *Polska Jerozolima. Fenomen żydowskiego osiedla w powiecie dzierżoniowskim. 1945–1950 / Polish Jerusalem. The Phenomenon of the Jewish Settlement in the County of Dzierżoniów. 1945–1950,* Dzierżoniów 2019.

15 *Bund. 100 lat historii 1897–1997,* ed. F. Tych, J. Hensel, Warsaw 2000.

16 *Jewish Politics in Eastern Europe: The Bund at 100,* ed. J. Jacobs, New York 2001.

17 D. Engel, *Bund po Holocauście; pomiędzy odnową a samolikwidacją,* pp. 289–303; N. Aleksiun, *Bund a syjoniści w Polsce po drugiej wojnie światowej,* pp. 325–345; B. Szaynok, „Bund i komuniści żydowscy w Polsce po 1945 r.," in: *Bund. 100 lat historii. 1897–1997,* ed. F. Tych, J. Hensel, Warsaw 2000, pp. 305–324. The English language edition contains two essays, one by David Engel and one by Natalia Aleksiun: D. Engel, "The Bund after the Holocaust: Between Renewal and Self-Liquidation," pp. 213–226; N. Aleksiun, "Where was there a Future for Polish Jewry? Bundist and Zionist Polemics in Post-World War II Poland," pp. 227–243, in: *Jewish Politics in Eastern Europe.*

18 See, e.g.: R. Gechtman, "The Debates on the National and Jewish Question in the Second International and the Jewish Labor Bund, 1889–1914," in: *Rebels Against Zion. Studies on the Jewish Left Anti-Zionism,* ed. A. Grabski, Warsaw 2011; A. Grabski, *Lewica przeciwko Izraelowi. Studia o żydowskim lewicowym antysyjonizmie,* Warsaw 2008; S. Bergman, "Przyczynki do historii Bundu," *Biuletyn Żydowskiego Instytutu Historycznego* 1992, nos 2–3 (162–163); J. Jacobs, "Bundist Anti-Zionism in Interwar Poland," *Tel Aviver Jahrbuch für Deutsche Geschichte* 2005, vol. 33; *Idem,* "The Bund in Vilna, 1918–1939," *Polin* 2013, vol. 25; B. Johnpoll, *The Politics of Futility. The General Jewish Workers Bund of Poland (1917–1943),* New York 1967; G. Pickhan, *„Gegen den Strom"*

founding until 1944, has also been documented by the Bundists themselves.[19]

Only parts of Daniel Blatman[20] and David Slucki's books have been devoted to the history of the Bund in post-war Poland.[21] These studies deal with the narrowly presented history of the party leadership, focusing on issues related to the political programme and the contacts between the Bund's representatives in Poland and Bundist organisations abroad. However, these studies lack a characterisation of the entire political environment. Furthermore, the image of the Bund in Poland presented in both publications is that of the Bund operating outside of Poland. It perceived the 'Polish' Bund as a defeated organisation unable to adapt to the new reality and some of its activists who joined the Polish Workers' Party (PPR) and later to the Polish United Workers' Party (PZPR), as traitors to the party's ideals.

In both studies, the authors relied primarily on documents from the 'Western' Bund.[22] In the case of Daniel Blatman, also those in the Archives of Modern Records (AAN) in Warsaw. The publications did not previously use unknown

---

der Allgemeine Jüdische Arbeiterbund „BUND" in Polen 1918–1939, Stuttgart–München 2001; *idam*, "Uwagi o Bundzie," *Kwartalnik Historii Żydów* 2003, no. 1 (205); J. D. Zimmerman, *Poles, Jews and the Politics of Nationality, 1892–1914*, Madison 2004; F. Wolff, *Neue Welten in der Neuen Welt. Die transnationale Geszichte des Allgemeinen Jüdischen Arbeiterbundes 1897–1947*, Köln–Weimar–Wien 2014 (English edition: *Yiddish Revolutionaries in Migration. The Transnational History of the Jewish Labour Bund*, tr. L. Balhorn, J.-P. Herrmann, Leiden–Boston 2021); M. Trębacz, *Izrael Lichtenstein. Biografia żydowskiego socjalisty*, Łódź 2016; M. Kozłowska, *Świetlana przyszłość? Żydowski Związek Młodzieżowy Cukunft wobec wyzwań międzywojennej Polski*, Kraków 2016.

19 J. Sh. Hertz, *Der bund in bilder. 1897–1957*, Nyu york 1958; idem, *Di geshikhte fun Bund in lodzh*, Nyu york 1958; *Di geshikhte fun bund*, vols. I–III, ed. G. Aronson, S. Dubnov-Erlich, J. Sh. Hertz, E. Nowogrodzki, Kh. Sh. Kazdan, E. Scherer, Nyu york 1960–1966; *Di geshikhte fun bund*, vol. IV, ed. S. Dubnov-Erlich, J. Sh. Hertz, Kh. Sh. Kazdan, E. Scherer, Nyu york 1972; *Di geshikhte fun bund*, vol. V, Nyu york 1981; E. Nowogródzki, *The Jewish Labor Bund in Poland 1915–1939*. Memoirs of Bernard Goldstein were published in English translation from Yiddish: *Twenty Years with the Jewish Labor Bund. A Memoir of Interwar Poland Poland*, tr., ed. M. S. Zuckerman, Indiana 2016 (title of the original: *Tsvantsik yor in varshever 'bund': 1919–1939*, New York 1960).

20 D. Blatman, *For Our Freedom and Yours. The Jewish Labour Bund in Poland 1939–1949*, London 2003 (242 pages).

21 D. Slucki, *The International Jewish Labor Bund after 1945. Toward a Global History*, New Brunswick–New Jersey–London 2012, Chapter Two: "On the Ruins of the Old World. The Bund in Central and Eastern Europe", sub-chapter: "Between Fascism and Communism", pp. 56–74 (265 pages in total).

22 I will use the term 'Western' Bund when referring to the Bundist organisations established after the war in France, Great Britain and the USA in order to avoid repetition and listing all these countries every single time.

documents concerning the party's activities, which are held in the Archives of the Jewish Historical Institute and in the Institute of National Remembrance. Also, not all Bund press titles and its affiliated organisations were used in the previously mentioned studies. David Slucki did not use a single document or press title in Polish in his work due to his lack of knowledge of the language. He considered the main goal of his work to be the description of Bund organisations after the war, who were scattered all over the world.[23]

When I began working on my thesis, I felt obliged to show the entire political environment of the Bund in post-war Poland in order to portray the final stage of the Jewish socialist movement in Poland – which is also one of the last chapters in the history of Jews in our lands. To this end, in addition to reading newspapers, literature and conducting archival research, I made use of the accounts of several of the last participants in the political events of 1944–1949, who lived and were active within the Jewish community.

One of the problems faced in this research was the attempt to reconstruct the least known final period of the Bund's activity. To achieve this involves analysing the party's activities, presenting its scope and structure, membership, programme and its implementation, and evaluating its achievements, significance and position within the Jewish community, from its revival in 1944 (since the founding of the party's Lublin Committee) until the Bund's self-dissolution in January 1949. This is a portrayal of the Bund seen from within the Jewish community, mainly including the party members themselves. Presenting an assessment of the Bund's environment by Polish political groups requires extensive press and archival research and a different approach to the question, which is not the subject of my research and would not change the image of the Bund's activities after 1945.

By revealing the 'final chapter' of the history of Jewish socialists in Poland, I intend to show, above all, how the party's ideology evolved among the Bundists, how the values that were fundamental to the movement before the war were re-evaluated, for example regarding national and cultural autonomy, and how

23 A collection of essays dedicated to the post-war Bund titled *Bundist Legacy after the Second World War "Real" Place versus "Displaced" Time* was edited by Vincenzo Pinto. It is part of the series: *Free Ebrei*, vol. 1, Leiden–Boston 2018. The volume contains an article penned by Bożena Szaynok titled "Bund and Jewish Fraction of the Polish Workers' Party in Poland after 1945," pp. 18–38. The monograph dedicated to the Bund in Sweden is also worthy of attention, see: H. Blomqvist, *Socialism på jiddisch: judiska Arbeter Bund i Sverige*, Stockholm 2020 (English version: *Socialism in Yiddish: The Jewish Labor Bund in Sweden*, tr. H. Blomquist, P. (H.) Glasser, Södertörn 2022).

the party, which dominated the 'Jewish Street', before the war, dealt with its actual marginalisation in the new post-war reality. Marginalisation was caused by the decimation of the Jewish community during the Holocaust and, at the same time, the increased importance of Zionist ideology and national sentiment in the context of rebuilding their own Jewish state in the Land of Israel. The traditional, pre-war Bund's programme had to face a new approach to the foundations of its ideology. More and more Jews in Poland and abroad thought that if they were dying as a nation, they could live as a nation. For this, it is necessary to create their own Jewish state, where Jews would feel at home and not as strangers scattered across the diaspora. On the other hand, Bund activists recognised that the Polish government was drifting towards the Soviet model and moving away from democratic principles. This was the reason for the different decisions of Bund members, who either accepted the monopolistic position of the PZPR or remained loyal to tradition and the social democratic model. After the self-dissolution of the party, they could choose to emigrate or decide to suspend their political activity.

In my book, I not only analyse the political programme and describe the political contacts within the Jewish community in post-war Poland but also focus on the relationship with the Bundist environment abroad. It seems important to demonstrate the shift in the attitude of Bundists' towards emigration, as well as towards the creation of a unified Bundist organisation, bringing together organisations scattered all over the world through the establishment of the Co-ordinating Committee of Bundist and Affiliated Jewish Socialist Organizations in Various Countries. Before the war, this was impossible due to the pursuit of national and cultural autonomy in their country of residence.

The primary sources used in my work include documents created by the Bund, which are held in Polish archives (Archives of the Jewish Historical Institute, Archives of Modern Records [AAN], Archives of the Institute of National Remembrance [AIPN] in Warsaw, Łódź, Kraków, Szczecin, and Wrocław, State Archives in Wrocław [AP Wrocław]), foreign archives (Yad Vashem Archives in Jerusalem, Diaspora Archives in Tel Aviv, YIVO Archives in New York, the so-called 'Bund Archives'), as well as documents produced by individual committees and branches of the CKŻP or other institutions cooperating with Jewish socialists (Archives in London: the National Archives which contain information on cooperation, with, among others, the Labour Party in the United Kingdom[24]).

24 My heartfelt gratitude goes to the Lanckoroński Foundation from Brzezie, thanks to which I was able to conduct research in archives and libraries in London in the spring of 2007.

I managed to find a rich 'legacy' left behind by the Bundists. It consists of minutes from meetings of the organisational committee, correspondence, photographs and memoirs of members who were active Bundists in post-war Poland. For many years, these materials lay in the Archives of the Jewish Historical Institute in Warsaw, wrapped in gray paper with an annotation: "to be destroyed." In the late 1990s, they were partially recovered and sorted by August Grabski. Thanks to the courtesy of the management of the ŻIH Archives, Agnieszka Reszka and Monika Taras, I was able to study these materials in detail and thus enrich our knowledge of the party's history between 1944 and 1949. In order to use the party's documentation, I organised it (according to a geographical and chronological system) and arranged it in folders stored in 24 boxes (5 linear metres of files). After the Polish version of my book was written (in autumn of 2016), the files were divided into archival units. Therefore, referring to the Bund records from the JHI Archives, I use the notation: "the Bund, unsorted files."

In addition to documents, I also used the press published in Polish and Yiddish by the Bund in Poland and in the West, as well as the press organs of other political groups, including Jewish and CKŻP. When analysing articles or documents produced by the party and its affiliated organisations, I frequently encountered difficulties in identifying the participants of the events simply because their authors often wrote in the passive voice: "it was decided," "it was carried out," "it was organised," or the subject of sentences was the party itself, e.g. "the Central Committee or the Bund municipal committee has decided." Another problem was the identification of first names, because even in most of the organisation's membership lists, they are mainly listed by their surnames, without the initials of their first names.

I structured the book on a problem-based chronological order, presenting in the following chapters the issues and events related to the reconstruction, activities, and main problems addressed by the party. The book consists of seven chapters, which in turn consist of subsections that address specific issues that require expansion. In these, I try to establish a chronology and identify three stages of the existence of the Bund in Poland:

I. Autumn 1944–1946 – rebuilding of party life and structures (in 1946, the majority of the Bund committees were established). I will present these issues in Chapters One to Three;
II. 1947–first half of 1948 – the period of 'relative stabilisation'. 1947 was mainly characterised by the organisation and the celebration of the party's 50th anniversary. I will discuss these issues in Chapters Four to Six;

III. Second half of 1948–January 1949 – the decline of the party and the beginning of the unification with PPR, which resulted in acts of 'self-criticism' of some Bundists and the party's self-dissolution. These issues are presented in Chapter Seven.

In the first chapter, titled "Reviving the Bund," I will describe the process of rebuilding the party in the initial period of its existence after the end of World War II (autumn 1944–1946). As I have already mentioned, most of committees were established across Poland at that time. In this chapter, I will present an outline of the party's structure, indicating the differences in relation to the period before 1939, as well as the differences between the individual committees. I will analyse the revised political programme of the Bund, adapted to the new realities. I will also attempt to characterise the composition of the Bund's Central Committee elected in 1945–1946, and to identify and present the four programme options existing within the party, which differ in their approach to the concept of continued existence.

In Chapters Two and Three, I will discuss the Bund's cooperation with other political organisations and the attitude of its members to the political realities of the so-called 'Lublin Poland'. In Chapter Two, I will present the Bund's activity on the so-called 'Jewish (political) Street', in the departments and Presidium of the CKŻP, as well as in local Jewish committees, highlighting the conflict areas between the Bundists and other political groups (milieus). This was evident in the Bundist press and in the Jewish Communist and Zionists press. The Bundists criticised not only the programmes but also the press, which, in their opinion, was supposed to be free from politics and free from favouring one party over another. This applied to the following publications issued by the Culture and Propaganda Department of the CKŻP, such as *Dos naye lebn* and *Biuletyn Żydowskiej Agencji Prasowej* (Bulletin of the Jewish Press Agency).

In Chapter Three titled "The Bund on the 'Polish (political) Street'",[25] I will show the Bund's attitude toward the Polish political parties of the time, especially the Polish Socialist Party (PPS), which it supported, and its cooperation with the Polish Workers' Party (PPR). I will attempt to identify regional differences regarding these issues in the various towns and cities where the Bund was active. I will present the involvement of Jewish socialists in major political campaigns of

25 'Polish (political) Street' – I will use this term when referring to the Bund's activities among Polish political groups, including the State National Council (KRN) and the Legislative Sejm, instead of using the descriptive term 'Polish political scene'. This term is analogous to the term 'Jewish Street'.

the time, including participation in the pre-election campaign in 1946 (conducted, among others, in the party press and during committee meetings concerning the referendum) and in the elections to the Legislative Sejm in January 1947, in which the Bund ran jointly with the PPS on the 'democratic bloc' list.[26] Also the speeches by the representative of the Jewish socialists, Dr Michał Szuldenfrei,[27] will be analysed, specifically during the sessions of the State National Council (KRN), concerning the participation of the Jewish community in reinstating order in Poland.

In Chapter Four, I will analyse the various forms of the Bund's activity in post-war Poland, using a problem-based approach. I will pay particular attention to the new meaning and understanding of the term *mishpokhedikeyt* ('familiariness') by the Bundists. For the majority of the party members, the Committee's leadership became a substitute for the family lost, in addition to the party comrade, as a consequence of the war and the Holocaust. In this chapter, I will also highlight the party's efforts to improve the material situation of its members. I will present various forms of social assistance (creating job opportunities in cooperatives and providing material aid) for party members and supporters. I will also describe other forms of party activity, including participation in May Day celebrations and party anniversaries.

No party can exist without a mass medium, which after the war was the press,[28] so I will analyse the Bund's journalistic activities, including the publication of *Biuletyn Bundu*, *Głos Bundu*, and *Folkstsaytung*. In addition to material aid and propaganda campaigns actions, the Bund tried to rebuild its structures by appealing to its long history and tradition. The reconstruction of the party's archives and commemoration of the heroism of Bundists, as well as members of Tsukunft and Skif who perished during the Holocaust, was supposed to help in

---

26 'Democratic bloc' – a bloc of political parties and political groups formed around the Polish Workers' Party (PPR) and supporting its policies. It included the so-called reborn Polish Socialist Party (PPS), the People's Party (SL), and the Democratic Party (SD).

27 See: Biography.

28 Another means of information was the radio. The Bund did not have its own radio station or programme. Information about the party's activities could be heard on radio programmes aired in Yiddish from 1945 by the Radio Division within the Department of Culture and Propaganda at the CKŻP. These broadcasts could also be heard outside of Poland. Their content of the broadcasts included propaganda information about the political activity of Jews in Poland. In the case of the Bund, they covered national congresses, the party's 50th anniversary and its dissolution (see: AŻIH, CKŻP. Department of Culture and Propaganda, ref. 303/XIII/68–112).

this endeavour. This was the scope of activity primarily of the Historical Commission, established by the Bund's Central Committee. I will use the description of the Commission's activities – which involved commemorating the fate of Polish Jews during the war and the German occupation, and the participation of the Bund representatives in, among other things, the events such as the anniversary of the Warsaw Ghetto Uprising or the liquidation of the ghetto, to present – the process of shaping the Bund's image of the fight against Nazi Germany.

The fifth chapter titled "The Bund versus Zionism" will be dedicated to one of the key elements of Bundist ideology – anti-Zionism. The change in the Bund's attitude toward Zionism and their opinion of this socio-political movement, as expressed in the press show a process of revision of one of the main views of Jewish socialists towards the Jewish state, which formed the basis of the Bund's ideology before 1939. The weakening of the Bundists' struggle with the ideology of Zionism, for example, through their support for the emigration of Jews from Poland and in their official stance toward the state of Israel, established in 1948. This demonstrates that in the new reality, the main ideas to which they had been faithful since the beginning of their political movement can and should be revised.

In Chapter Six, I will present the relationship between the 'Polish' Bund and the 'Western' Bund, using the example of contacts with communities in the USA, France (Paris), and the United Kingdom (London), which were created mainly by Bund members – emigrants from Poland before and after the outbreak of World War II, as well as representatives of the so-called *landsmanshaftn*, i.e. regional associations. I will analyse the origin and background of the difficult cooperation between Bundists who were party members in Poland before 1939, but had to operate in different countries after the war. In 1948, this led to a conflict due to the policies of the Polish authorities and had to end with a break in contact of the 'Polish' Bund from the World Bund Coordinating Committee, which was established in 1947.

In Chapter Seven, I will present the process of the Bund's dissolution, i.e. the final stage of the party's existence in Poland, which officially began in April 1948 during the National Bund Conference in Wrocław and lasted until 16 January 1949. I will analyse the dissolution of local committees and attempts by some of their own comrades to indoctrinate Bundists in the Stalinist spirit, so that in the situation that arose, they would 'self-criticise' their previous activities and renounce their ideals and join the PPR and later the PZPR. I will show the different attitudes of the Bund members in the party leadership towards the situation that had arisen. To conclude the chapter, I will analyse the activities of the Bund Liquidation Commission, whose tasks included the settlement of the affairs of the party and its affiliated organisations (vacating the party's premises, producing inventories of their equipment and disposing of the party's documents). The liquidation process was completed by the end of June 1949.

The book concludes with appendices containing copies of documents on the Bund's core programme in post-war Poland, biographies of the leading party activists and affiliated organisations as well as photographs depicting the activities of Jewish socialists.

Finally, I would like to thank everyone who kindly supported me with advice at various stages of the book's creation. I would like to thank Professor Grzegorz Nowik, Professor Grzegorz Mazur, and the late Professor Jerzy Holzer for their many valuable comments, as well as Professor Grzegorz Berendt for reviewing the Polish edition of the book. I would like to thank the reviewers of the Polish edition, Dr Magdalena Semczyszyn[29] and Dr Bartosz Kaliski,[30] for their words of appreciation as well as valuable insights and suggestions, which have been included in the English version. I would also like to thank my colleagues and the management at the Institute of Political Studies at the Polish Academy of Sciences. A big thank you goes to Dr August Grabski, Dr Magdalena Kozłowska, Aleksandra Król and Dr Zbigniew Palski. And last but not least, I owe a debt of gratitude to my family, especially my husband Karol and my son Juliusz, for their support and understanding.

29 Review published in *Polish-Jewish Studies* 2021, no. 2, pp. 413–419 (Polish version), pp. 424–430 (English version).

30 Review: B. Kaliski, „Związek nasz bratni," *Nowe Książki* 2018, no. 1, pp. 83–84.

Chapter One
Reviving the Bund

In the autumn of 1944, representatives of the Bund in Poland, who during World War II belonged to the underground Bund committees, in the Warsaw, Częstochowa, Łódź and Piotrków Trybunalski ghettos, as well as in Warsaw on the so-called 'Aryan side', in areas occupied by Nazi Germany,[31] decided to come out of hiding after the war and continue their activities legally in newly reborn Poland. The Bund members returning to Poland from the USSR, with General Zygmunt Berling's Army[32], as well as those from territories that were outside of Poland's borders after the war, such as the Vilna region (e.g. Grzegorz (Grisha) Jaszuński[33] came from there to Lublin), also began rebuilding the party as early as the summer of 1944. Initially, the two groups operated separately.

Despite the destruction of party offices, documents, and, above all, the decimation of party ranks, the Bund members who had survived the Holocaust attempted to rebuild party structures similar to those before 1939 and to re-establish party committees in the cities and towns where Jews lived. There were also sceptics among the surviving party members who doubted the possibility of rebuilding the party. The post-war leadership lacked the pre-war Bund leaders, including Victor Alter and Henryk Erlich, who died in Soviet prisons, Shmul Zygielbojm,[34] who committed suicide in London in May 1943, Józef Portnoy[35] and Vladimir Kosovsky[36] who died in exile in New York in 1941, as well as many others who perished in ghettos, Nazi German camps, and in the USSR.

---

31 For more information on the Bund's underground in various locations, see, i.a.: The Archives of Modern Records (hereafter: AAN), General Jewish Labour Bund in Poland. Central Committee (hereafter: the Bund), ref. 30-III-1-5 and 30-IV-20 vol. I–II; Blatman, *For Our Freedom and Yours*, pp. 35–68, 90–120.

32 The Polish First Army (Polish: Pierwsza Armia Wojska Polskiego), also known as Berling's Army, was created on 29 July 1944, in the USSR, from the previously existing Polish First Corps in the USSR, as a part of the Polish People's Army (Ludowe Wojsko Polskie). Organisationally subordinated to the Supreme Command of the Polish Army, and operationally subordinated to the commanders of the Red Army fronts. It ended its combat trail in May 1945 by reaching the Elbe river bank and storming Berlin with some of its units.

33 See: Biography.

34 See: Biography.

35 See: Biography.

36 See: Biography.

The years 1944–1946 are the first stage of the Bund's existence in Poland after World War II, because it is precisely this period that can be distinguished as a time of trial for the reconstruction and continuation of the Bund's life in People's Poland.[37]

Setting up the Lublin Committee (24 September 1944). The onset of post-war activities

Lublin was the first place where the Bundists and Holocaust survivors who were active in the party arrived from the USSR territories. It was here that the Bund's organisational committee was established on 24 September 1944, consisting of Dr Shlomo Herszenhorn,[38] Dr Michał Szuldenfrei,[39] and Grzegorz Jaszuński.[40] It is worth noting that Herszenhorn and Szuldenfrei were also officials of the Polish Committee of National Liberation (PKWN) as representatives of the Jewish community in Poland.[41]

The first Bund conference in so-called 'Lublin Poland' was organised in Lublin in November 1944 by a group of Bundists who had arrived from behind the new eastern border. During the meeting, Bund members discussed the country's political situation and outlined the party's political path in the new political

37 People's Poland (Polska Ludowa) the colloquial name of the Polish state between 1944 to 1989, which until 1952 officially bore the official name Rzeczpospolita Polska (Republic of Poland). The announcement of the *Manifesto of the Polish Committee of National Liberation* (PKWN) on 22 July 1944 is considered to be the beginning of the People's Republic of Poland (PRL). From that point on, the construction of a state system based on an alliance with the USSR began, in which power was gradually seized by the communists, which led to the unification of the workers' parties and the establishment of a system with the leading role of the Polish United Workers' Party (PZPR).

38 See: Biography.

39 See: Biography.

40 At the same time, other Jewish organisations were established in Lublin, e.g. the Provisional Central Committee of Polish Jews, which later transformed into the Central Committee of Jews in Poland. For more information, see, i.a.: J. Adelson, „W Polsce zwanej Ludową," in: *Najnowsze dzieje Żydów w Polsce w zarysie (do 1950 roku)*, ed. J. Tomaszewski, Warsaw 1993, pp. 424–427; L. Dobroszycki, *Survivors of the Holocaust in Poland. A Portrait Based on Jewish Community Records 1944–1947*, New York 1994, pp. 3–7.

41 This was also written about by D. Engel ("The Bund After the Holocaust: Between Renewal and Self-Liquidation," in: *Jewish Politics in Eastern Europe: The Bund at 100*, ed. J. Jacobs, New York 2001, pp. 215–217).

conditions. The aim was to strive for unity of the labour movement, to reject the "legalism" of the Polish Government-in-Exile in London, to cooperate primarily with the Polish Socialist Party (PPS) and the Polish Workers' Party (PPR), and to establish contact and merge with Bundists in other cities and towns in Poland.[42] It was decided that the PPS would be the main political ally, as it had been in the pre-war period. To this end, a representative of the Jewish socialists, Dr Michał Szuldenfrei, joined the PPS parliamentary faction in the State National Council (KRN).[43]

The next Bund meetings took place in Lublin at the beginning of 1945. The first was on 14 January, followed by another on 8 February 1945. Among those who took part were Grisha (Grzegorz) Jaszuński and Dr Michał Szuldenfrei from the USSR, and Leon Feiner,[44] Salo Fiszgrund,[45] and Bernard Goldstein,[46] who had travelled from Warsaw in January. In order to enable the terminally ill Feiner (one of the ardent supporters of the Bund's revival), to participate in the discussions, they were held in the hospital where he was undergoing treatment. At the February meeting, a resolution was passed, in which it was decided, among other things:

> [...] to immediately undertake the unification of all [Bund's – author's note] centres throughout Poland based on the political platform of, (a) Aligning Poland's foreign policy with a close and sincere alliance with the USSR, (b) Adherence to the July Manifesto, (c) Support for the actions of the State National Council (KRN) and the Provisional Government, (d) Commitment to the unity of the labour movement in Poland and (e) Full cooperation with Polish democracy while distancing ourselves from the 'government' in exile in London. The CK [Central Committee of the Bund – author's note] calls on all members and sympathizers of the Bund, both in the country and on emigration, to unite within a single Bund organisation based on this political platform.[47]

The post-war period of the Bund's activities in the People's Republic of Poland was primarily characterised by efforts to deal with the new situation related to the de facto marginalisation of the party, which in the 1930s had been the largest

42 *Biuletyn Bundu* 1945, no. 1, pp. 11–14

43 „Zebranie 'Bundu' w Lublinie", *Biuletyn Żydowskiej Agencji Prasowej* 1945, no. 6/16, f. 1–2.

44 See: Biography.

45 See: Biography.

46 See: Biography.

47 „Rezolucja CK Bundu," *Biuletyn Bundu* 1945, no. 1, p. 16.

force on the 'Jewish Street'.[48] In the post-war period, in addition to the old slogans of the fight for socialism, the international brotherhood of all proletarians and oppressed, who were striving 'Jewish Street' – as well as Bundist (also outside Poland) decided to commemorate the history of the movement and the events of the recent war, including the Holocaust and the Warsaw Ghetto Uprising.[49]

The Bund taught Jewish workers to think and feel not in terms of alienation but in terms of being citizens of the country. It taught them to bind their fate with the fate of their country. But it also taught the Jewish masses that in the country where they reside, the country to which they sacrifice their toil, sweat, and blood, they should demand their rights and fight for those rights.[50]

Conferences and nationwide party conventions – developing a programme. Integration of the environment

The resolutions of the first conventions and meetings in Lublin were often repeated by the Bund members during subsequent plenary meetings, conferences, or congresses, as is evidenced by the First Nationwide Conference of the Bund, held on 16–17 June 1945 in Łódź. It was attended by forty-four delegates from centres such as Lublin, Warsaw, Łódź, Częstochowa, Piotrków Trybunalski, and Przemyśl. Among the delegates were Dr Shlomo Herszenhorn, Szefner,[51] Sioma Temczyn,[52] Liber Brener (who survived the war under German occupation),[53] Perlsztejn,[54] Weksler,[55] Michał Szuldenfrei, and Salo Fiszgrund. They had different experiences of the party's wartime fate, underground activities, work in the ghettos and on the 'Aryan side', as well as exile and labour camps in the USSR. It should be added that

48 On the history of the Bund and its significance in the political and social life of the Jewish community, see, i.a.: E. Nowogródzki, *The Jewish Labor Bund in Poland 1915–1939. From its Emergence as an Independent Political Party Until the Beginning of World War II,* transl. by M. Nowogrodzki, Rockville 2001.

49 For more information on this topic, see: F. Wolff, "The Collateral Prisoner. A Bundist Holocaust Survivor between Nazi Perpetrators, Anti-Communism and British World Politics," *The International of Communist Studies* 2011, no. 24, pp. 88–89.

50 „Dr Michał Szuldenfrei. Przewodniczący CK Bundu w Polsce, poseł na Sejm, 50 lat Bundu (1897–1947)," *Głos Bundu* 1946, nos 2–3, p. 1.

51 First name could not be found.

52 See: Biography.

53 See: Biography.

54 First name could not be found.

55 First name could not be found.

from the beginning, Bund members repatriated from the USSR (M. Szuldenfrei, S. Herszenhorn et al.) played a vital role in organising the party's activities before those who had survived the Holocaust under German occupation joined in. The aim of the conference was to define the party's political line, which after the war, the members themselves referred to more often as an organisation than a party.[56]

During the meeting, national and internal organisational issues were discussed. The following guidelines for the party were:

1. Solidarity with the Polish workers' movement. It was emphasised that: "Our place is in the democratic camp. Cooperation with the Polish working class."[57]
2. Combating anti-Semitism,
3. Freedom to emigrate and opposition to emigrationism,[58]
4. Fighting against Zionism,
5. Participation in the economic reconstruction of the country.

The resolution emphasised, among other things, that: "The conference considers it necessary to fight emigrationism as an ideology that presents emigration as the only solution to the current situation of the Jewish population in Poland." It emphasised that emigration "[...] discourages the Jewish population from working and fighting for a better tomorrow in their own country."[59] The conclusion read:

> The conference [...] took a firm stance on the political issue, decisively distancing itself from the so-called London orientation and aligned itself with the orientation of the State National Council and its policy of sincere friendship with the Soviet Union.[60]

---

56 *Biuletyn Bundu* 1945, no. 2, pp. 1–14.

57 Archives of the Jewish Historical Institute (hereinafter: AŻIH), the Bund, files n., documents relating to the first national conference of the Bund in Łódź held on 16–17 June 1945.

58 Emigrationism, this term used by the Bundists to describe the mass emigration of Jews from Poland to Palestine and subsequently to the State of Israel, which was strongly opposed by Jewish socialists. They believed that everyone had the right to choose their destination, which did not necessarily have to be the Jewish state. This opposition was rooted in their broader political vision, which sought to integrate Jews into the societies they lived in rather than encouraging their departure to a nationalistic, religiously defined homeland. For a more detailed explanation, see: Chapter Five entitled "The Bund versus Zionism."

59 AŻIH, the Bund, files n., documents relating to the first national conference of the Bund in Łódź held on 16–17 June 1945.

60 AŻIH, the Bund, files n., documents relating to the first national conference of the Bund in Łódź held on 16–17 June 1945.

One of the main issues of the conference was to answer the question: should the party exist in its decimated ranks and, consequently, consider the point of existence of a party without the Jewish masses.[61] In his report, Dr Michał Szuldenfrei emphasised that:

> Maintaining the historical continuity of the Bund is not driven by an unrealistic reverence for the beautiful tradition of what has passed. It stems from a sense of social duty and responsibility. We continue to spin this golden thread that has stretched since the founding of the Bund – we spin this golden thread, loyal to our Bundist oath of "life-and-death loyalty to the Bund."[62]

The discussion among the leaders of the Bund about the purpose of the party (organisation) after the Holocaust dominated other issues. Ignacy Falk[63] (one of the leaders of the party in post-war Poland) justified the existence of the movement as follows: "[…] wherever there is even the smallest settlement of Jewish workers, there will be a Bund!"[64] It was optimistically believed that they would be the "pioneers in rebuilding a new Jewish life."[65] This was stated by Luba Bielicka-Blum,[66] widow of Abrasha Blum, one of the leading activists in the Underground Bund Committee in the Warsaw Ghetto.[67]

The following issues were raised in internal party matters:

- Material assistance (Grzegorz Jaszuński),
- Attracting youth to the party (Felenberg[68]),
- Increasing and strengthening contacts with the provinces (Ignacy Falk and Liber Brener),
- Teaching the Jewish language (Yiddish) to children,
- Intensive cooperation with the Jewish Committees (sections of the Central Jewish Committee in Poland) with the presence of its own representatives in various departments existing within the framework of the Central Committee as well as in local authorities (in municipal councils).

---

61 „Tsu der yidisher bafelkerung in poyln," *Folkstsayung* 1946, no. 1, p. 2.

62 AŻIH, the Bund, files n., documents relating to the first national conference of the Bund in Łódź held on 16–17 June 1945: political report by Michał Szuldenfrei.

63 See: Biography.

64 AŻIH, the Bund, files n., documents relating to the first national conference of the Bund in Łódź held on 16–17 June 1945.

65 Ibid.

66 See: Biography.

67 *Biuletyn Bundu* 1945, no. 2, pp. 1–14.

68 First name could not be found.

For the first time, the establishment of a Historical Commission within the Central Committee of the Bund was discussed: "The Central Committee of the Bund should create a Commission to compile materials concerning our role and work in the ghettos and on the 'Aryan' side."[69] The proposal was put forward by David Klin[70] who survived the occupation mainly in Warsaw, where he was active in the Bund underground committee. Additionally, a membership fee of 20 zlotys per month was introduced.

During the conference, after the elections, the composition of the first post-war Central Committee of the Bund was established, including: Dr Michał Szuldenfrei as chairman, Dr Shlomo Herszenhorn as vice-chairman, Salo Fiszgrund as first secretary, Ignacy Falk – as second secretary, and members: Grzegorz Jaszuński, Leyb Pudłowski[71] from Łódź, and Liber Brener from Częstochowa.[72]

Four resolutions were passed: a political resolution, a resolution on anti-Semitism, a resolution on emigration, and a resolution on the activities of the Jewish Committees.[73] These resolutions set the direction for the party's programme. The political theses presented at the conference were repeated many times during party meetings and disseminated in the Bund press, e.g. in an article by Yudl Kersz, titled "Tsu der yidisher bafelkerung in poyln (To the Jewish Society in Poland)"[74] published in *Folkstsaytung* (February 1946, issue 1).[75]

---

69 AŻIH, the Bund, files n., ibid.

70 See: Biography.

71 See: Biography.

72 YIVO Archives, ref. RG 1458 – Roman Blitt Collection, Folder 5, Roman Blit's letter from 29 July 1945.

73 AŻIH, the Bund, files n., documents relating to the first national conference of the Bund in Łódź held on 16–17 June 1945.

74 See: Biography.

75 Y. Kersz, „Tsu der yidisher bafelkerung in poyln. Derklerung fun der bundisher fraktsye baym tsentral-komitet fun yidn in poyln," *Folkstsaytung* 1946, no. 1, p. 2. Dr Michał Szuldenfrei, in a letter to Emanuel Scherer, praised the high level of the conference, emphasising: "The discussion at the congress was of a high standard. And yet each of the participants was reminded of their thoughts and feelings of those old pre-war party congresses, they were reminded of the thoughts and feelings of those who led those congresses, who were their soul, who set the right tone and direction. Not a single member of the old pre-war party leadership was present at this congress. [...] The theses of the ideological-political report and the resolutions based on them were adopted by an overwhelming majority of the congress, against only a few votes. This firm stance of the congress was then also expressed in the election of the Central Committee. Even against the proposals of the outgoing party leadership, those who spoke out against the main theses of the report in any

The speeches at the First National Conference of the Bund were very different from those delivered during the National Bund Congress in Łódź (6–7 July 1946), which took place shortly after the murder of Bundist Fishke Nejman[76] in Łódź, and after the Kielce pogrom.[77] The murder was never solved, and the perpetrators

way were voted out. The worker delegates in particular, did not want to allow any of these comrades into the Central Committee. The Central Committee was elected exclusively from among members with a unified ideological stance. This position of the congress was primarily a documentation of the firm will to maintain 'the Bund' as a party, it was an expression of deep attachment to the party, its rich tradition, and its entire intellectual and militant legacy. Following this line, set out by the convention, the party continues to strive to unite the Jewish workers around the tried and tested banner of 'the Bund', to protect the unity of the Bund movement, the principles of socialism and the entire tradition of 'the Bund'" (quoted from YIVO Archives, ref. RG 1478 Supplement 2 – Scherer Collection, File 70).

76 Fishke (Feliks) Nejman (Najman) (1917–24 June 1946, Łódź) spent the war in the Soviet Union, from where he returned to Łódź in the autumn of 1945 as a second lieutenant in the 1st Tadeusz Kościuszko Infantry Division. After the war, he was a member of the Bund's Łódź Committee. He began studying at the Faculty of Social Sciences at the University of Łódź. His biography also included a period of service in the Security Office (UB). He planned to emigrate to Sweden, where his girlfriend was waiting for him, and from there to the United States. He was shot in the bathroom, with a shot to the back of the head, in an apartment on Mielczarskiego Street in Łódź, where he lived with Bund member Włodzimierz Szer. His death was widely reported throughout Poland, and the perpetrators were never found. His obituary was published on the front page of *Folkstsaytung* (June 1946, no. 4). For more information on Fishke Nejman, see: AŻIH, the Bund, files n., correspondence with the Łódź Committee; ŻIH (Jewish Historical Institute), Documentation Department, photographs related to the Bund, Łódź Committee; J. Sh. Hertz, *Di geshikhte fun bund in lodzh*, Nyu york 1958, p. 470; W. Szer, *Do naszych dzieci. Wspomnienia*, Warsaw 2013, pp. 198, 208–209; „Zamordowanie Feliksa Nejmana," *Biuletyn Żydowskiej Agencji Prasowej* 1946, no. 68/178, f. 2; M. Trębacz, „Gutman – Nejman – Stupaj. Żydowskie życie w powojennej Łodzi na przykładzie wybranych biografii," in: *Druga Rzeczpospolita i nie tylko. Ludzie, środowiska, idee*, ed. J. Pietrzak, Łódź 2016, pp. 207–213.

77 On the subject of the mood among Jews in Poland and the state of security, see, e.g.: A. Cała, *Ochrona bezpieczeństwa fizycznego Żydów w Polsce powojennej. Komisje Specjalne przy Centralnym Komitecie Żydów w Polsce*, Warsaw 2014; A. Rykała, *W reakcji na powojenną przemoc antysemicką. Samoobrona Żydów w Łodzi – uwarunkowania społeczno-polityczne i przestrzenne*, Łódź 2020; *Pogromy Żydów na ziemiach polskich w XIX i XX wieku*, vol. 4: *Holokaust i powojnie (1939–1946)*, ed. A. Grabski, Warsaw 2019. The Kielce Pogrom took place on 4 July 1946. For more information on the pogrom, see, e.g.: J. Tokarska-Bakir, *Pod klątwą. Społeczny portret pogromu kieleckiego*, 2 volumes, Warsaw 2018.

were never found, but Nejman's death had a significant impact on the psyche of Jewish socialists and was linked to the atmosphere of the Kielce pogrom. Nejman was a member of the Łódź Bund Committee, which had many plans for the future.

> This death shook the community. An ordinary Jew, not a public figure of any kind, was not safe in his own home and was murdered in broad daylight in the largest Polish city at the time. Does it, therefore, make sense to stay in this country, to start a family here, to raise children?[78]

The so-called fascists, primarily the National Armed Forces (NSZ)[79] were blamed for the murder, in line with the prevailing atmosphere in the country.

Nejman's funeral was a political demonstration: ten thousand people gathered at the funeral procession, which was led by officers[80] of the Polish People's Army, representatives of the Bund, followed by representatives of the PPS with banners and delegations of the PPR with wreaths, the Brotherhood of Students from the University of Łódź, and representatives of Skif and Tsukunft as well as various Jewish organisations (including Zionist ones) operating in Poland. In addition to representatives of the Bund, such as Dr Michał Szuldenfrei from the Central Committee of the Bund and Tsukunft, who also spoke at the grave. Representatives of the Łódź Jewish Committee, PPS, PPR, the Brotherhood of Students from the University of Łódź, and the rectorate of the University of Łódź, also spoke. Nejman was buried with military honours at the Jewish cemetery in Łódź.[81]

After Nejman's murder, there was a clear change in the Bundists' attitude toward the prospects of Jewish life in post-war Poland. The party's attitude towards emigration from Poland changed. A clear dispute emerged between the participants of the National Congress of the Bund in Łódź (6–7 July 1946), and the members of the party's leadership on the fundamental issue of whether to live in Poland or to emigrate from it. The congress participants emphasised that if the PPS (Polish Socialist Party) and PPR (Polish Workers' Party) did not take decisive action against anti-Semitism, the Bund would cease to participate in the construction of a Jewish *yishuv* (settlement) in Poland. This negative stance

78 Szer, *op. cit.*, p. 209.

79 B. Mark, „Der mord un der zelbstmord," *Dos naye lebn* 1946, no. 22, p. 3.

80 "While in Łódź, I saw the funeral of Security Office Lieutenant Najman in the street. He was killed by the underground. The funeral was big, with social and military delegations in attendance" (quoted from P. Hecht, "Serce zostało w Piotrkowie," in: *Losy żydowskie. Świadectwo żywych*, vol. III, ed. M. Turski, Warsaw 1996, p. 152).

81 B., "Der letster veg fun Fishke Nejman. Di leviye fun tragish-umgekumenem tuer fun 'Bund'," *Dos naye lebn* 1946, no. 22, p. 8; "Pogrzeb Feliksa Najmana," *Biuletyn Żydowskiej Agencji Prasowej* 1946, no. 70/180, f. 2.

was evident in the statements by Perelsztejn,[82] a party representative from Lower Silesia, who stated that "there is no future for a Jewish settlement in Poland."[83] Shaya Szechatow[84] emphasised that assistance is necessary for the Jewish community during their emigration from Poland. Pinkus Wołkowicz[85] from the Łódź Committee expressed himself pessimistically and bluntly: "Afn beys-oylem vet nisht onshteyn keyn yidisher yishev" ("No Jewish settlement will ever arise in a cemetery"). The word "cemetery" could refer to both the graves of comrades murdered during the German occupation and Nejman's grave.

During this period, various factions within the party can be distinguished, differing in their attitude to the prospects for the future of the Bund. Two fundamental options clashed: the first supported maintaining a presence on the 'Jewish Street', while the second advocated for dissolving the party and emigrating from Poland (Ignacy Falk). Within the first faction, three smaller groups emerged:

1. Those advocating a merger with the PPS (represented by Michał Szuldenfrei),
2. Those opting for close cooperation with the PPR (Leyb Pudłowski),
3. Supporters of maintaining an independent presence on the 'Jewish Street' (a group led by Salo Fiszgrund).[86]

The lack of a unified position in such a small group, I believe, influenced the future, not only of each of them but of the party as a whole.

Regardless of disputes and disagreements about the future, Bund members, apart from competing with other parties for influence among Jewish workers, focused on cooperation with other Jewish organisations gathered under the CKŻP in order to revive and save Jewish culture, including the language of Jews from Poland and, more broadly, from Central and Eastern Europe.

Formation of committees – distribution, number of members, party leaders

After the re-establishment of the Bund, was the party's activities slowly picked up again, before doubts about its purpose arose a few years later. The first months after

82 Most likely Izrael Perelsztejn.

83 AŻIH, the Bund, files n., National Congress of the Bund in Łódź held on 6–7 July 1946, protocol from the convention, resolutions made during the convention, including the one related to the pogrom in Kielce.

84 See: Biography.

85 See: Biography.

86 AAN, Zachariasz, ref. 476/28, f. 155.

the war were still characterised by great enthusiasm, which turned into scepticism as emigration became more and more common. This is evident, for example, in the number of the Bund members during various periods of activity, although this data is incomplete. Not all committees kept records or lists of members. Szymon Zachariasz,[87] a representative of the Jewish PPR faction within the CKŻP, stated in reports on the Bund's activities that in 1946 – which in post-war Poland should be considered the best year for Jewish socialists – the party had 1,500 members.[88]

It should be noted that not everyone who considered themselves a Bund member and attended party meetings could join the party, just as not everyone who submitted a membership declaration was accepted as a member. Throughout the post-war period of the Bund's activities in the PRL, 2,956 party membership cards were issued.[89] During the Łódź conference in 1945, the following membership numbers were reported: Łódź – 106, Częstochowa – 41, Warsaw – 30, Lublin – 30, Piotrków Trybunalski – 15, Tarnów – 30, Kraków – 23, Płock – 5. In total, about 320 Bund members. From the minutes of the National Congress of the Bund held in July 1946, we know about 2,250 members belonged to the party and these figures differ from those recorded by Zachariasz (1,500 people).[90]

The number of in 1945 is proof of the inaccuracy of the data. None of the cities in Lower Silesia are listed. We know from the archives that in Dzierżoniów, as early as 1945, there was a committee that was of great importance for the Jewish

87 Szymon Zachariasz (1900–1970), member of the Zionist Left from 1916–1918, member of the Polish Communist Party from December 1918, and member of the Central Committee of the Communist Party of Poland in the years 1927–1938. During World War II, he stayed in the USSR, where he was active in the Union of Polish Patriots, among other organisations. After the war, he was a member of the Presidium of the CKŻP. In the years 1948–1964, he was a member of the Central Commission for Party Control at the Central Committee of the United Polish Workers' Party (KC PZPR) – information from: A. Grabski, *Działalność komunistów wśród Żydów w Polsce (1944–1949)*, Warsaw 2004, p. 69.

88 AAN, PPR KC Secretariat, ref. 295/VII-149, f. 19, Characteristics of the activities of the various parties and organisations included in the Jewish committees.

89 List of party membership cards issued. AŻIH, the Bund, files n., The data does not reflect the actual number of Bund members. The number 2,956 is an overestimate. The list includes the number of Bund members of its youth organisation, Tsukunft. Some party members received duplicate membership cards with new numbers. Moreover, not everyone who considered themselves Bundists or Tsukunft members after the war and participated in meetings actually registered as a member.

90 AŻIH, the Bund, files n., documents relating to the National Congress of the Bund in Łódź held on 6–7 July 1946.

yishuv in post-war Poland, including the Bund. At large number of Bundists lived there at the time. Katowice, whose representative was present at the conference, and Przemyśl, where an organisational cell existed at the time, were also missing from the list.[91]

In the summer of 1946, according to information from the June issue of *Folkstsaytung*, there were 19 committees,[92] including those in Łódź (Central Committee), Kraków, Tarnów, Lublin, Białystok, Włocławek, Częstochowa, Szczecin, and in Lower Silesia in Dzierżoniów (a provincial committee until the end of 1946, then a district committee), Bielawa (Dzierżoniów district), Wałbrzych, Kłodzko, Ludwikowice, Nowa Ruda, Kamienna Góra, Boża Góra, Jelenia Góra, Ząbkowice Śląskie, Niemcza, Legnica, and Piotrków. The article in *Folkstsaytung* emphasised that "a new Jewish kibbutz is being built in Lower Silesia. Repatriates from the Soviet Union are now heading there."[93] In Upper Silesia, there was one committee in Katowice which included other cities and towns in the region, including Sosnowiec, Bytom, Zabrze, Bielsko, Opole, and Będzin.[94]

It is also difficult to determine the duration of the committees' existence because not all of them kept records. Some of them existed for too short of a time, and many communities, especially in Lower Silesia, were only a 'transit point' in emigration to Western Europe and Palestine. The migration of Bund members to other (larger) Jewish communities was caused not only by their departure from Poland but also by the lack of financial resources to continue the committee's work. The residual activity of the committees' was also justified by their small membership numbers. The main source for the reconstruction of the life of the individual committees is the correspondence of the Central Committee of the Bund and the information published in *Folkstsaytung* under the column *Fun partey-lebn* ("From the life of the party") and, from July 1946 onwards, in *Głos Bundu* in the section: "From the life of the party." Due to lack of space, only a few committees were mentioned in each newspaper article.

The structure of the post-war Bund was similar to that of the Jewish committees operating within the framework of the CKŻP. The Bund was divided into: the Central Committee, which included a chairman, Vice-Chairman,

91 Ibid.

92 In total, 40 local Bund committees were in operation in Poland (see: ibid.).

93 I. Falk, "Dos repatratsye-problem," *Folkstsaytung* 1946, no. 4, p. 2.

94 *Fun partey-lebn*, p. 6. We know that in 1946, a Bund Committee existed in Gdańsk. Due to the lack of information, we do not know how many members it had, what sort of activities it used to run or for how long (see: G. Berendt, *Żydzi na gdańskim rozdrożu (1945–1950)*, Gdańsk 2000, p. 112).

first and second secretary, and a treasurer. It was supported by the Historical Commission, and the Economic Council was responsible for cooperatives (in later years, there was also a Bund Presidium). It was in charge of the Provincial Committees and the District and County Committees at the local level, which were subordinate to them.[95]

The structure of individual committees depended on their size and the financial resources they had at their disposal. In general, each committee consisted of a chairman, a secretary, and a treasurer. The committees often had workers' canteens or restaurants (e.g. in Częstochowa), and hostels for youth and repatriates. One of these hostels was located in Warsaw at 2 Skaryszewska Street, where the Bund committee was initially based, later they moved to 40 Targowa Street, apartment no. 7. Additionally, the committees would run orphanages, such as the one in Tarnów.[96]

The Łódź group can be used as an example of a well-organised Bund committee. It was one of the largest at that time; according to data from *Folkstsaytung* (February 1946), the party had 250 members. The Bund was organised here into nine local groups. Among other things, there was a drama club, a council for repatriates, and a cultural centre which included a reading room, a library, an orchestra, and a choir.[97]

The Bund's Warsaw Committee also had a complex structure. At a meeting held on 24 May 1946, it was decided to establish the following departments within this committee: Repatriation, Culture, Productivity, Economic Affairs, and a Finance Commission.[98]

Another well-organised branch was the Białystok committee, which housed the party's Białystok Committee Archive.[99] Both the differences in the number of members and the impermanence of structures in some local committees make it difficult to establish a uniform structure and model the scope of activity of party cells apart from the basic one.

---

95 AŻIH, the Bund, files n.

96 *Kh[awer] Yankev Pat tsu gast bay undz. Varshe, fun partey-lebn. Tarnov*; M. Frejdeles, "Fun partey-lebn, Tschenstokhov," *Folkstsaytung* 1946, no. 1, pp. 4, 7; *Fun partey-lebn. Varshe*, ibid., nos 2–3, p. 6; *Yidishe arbeter unter di royte fener fun Bund. Varshe*, ibid., p. 8.

97 Bono, *Fun partey-lebn. Lodzh*, ibid., no. 1, p. 7.

98 AŻIH, the Bund, files n., protocols from the meetings of the Bund Warsaw Committee in 1946.

99 Ibid., Białystok, Protocol no. 3 from 8 July 1945 regarding the activities of the Białystok Committee, including instructions for establishing the party archives.

Objectives and tasks of the committees. Working in the committees

In the initial period of the Bund's revival after the end of the war (until the end of 1946), one of the primary goals of each of the committees was to establish a system of regular weekly party meetings (on Wednesdays in Warsaw at the beginning of 1946 and mainly on Fridays in Łódź). The purpose of the meetings was to integrate the Bundist community and to provide information about the activities of, among others, the Bund's Central Committee, by reading the *Circulars* sent by the Committee and organising visits of its members. Another form of (propaganda) activity was the distribution of reports from the Central Committee to local committees, the publication of press materials to share information about the party's activities and the production of bulletins in party offices.[100]

At the same time, they intended to mark their presence on the 'Jewish Street' by participating in May Day celebrations as well as through their activity in the area of operation of the cells of the Central Committee of Polish Jews. Academies also organised party clubs on the occasion of the May Day celebrations. In most towns, Bundists marched in the parades with Bund banners together with the PPR and PPS.[101]

An effort was made to maintain good political relations with the PPS and PPR, and with the Bund abroad. Correspondence was conducted with Bund committees operating in the West, and representatives of the American Bund were welcomed during their visits to Poland. An example of this is the visit of Yankev Pat from the New York committee, who travelled around the country and met with Bund members. Around 200 Bundists came to meet him in Łódź. On 17 December 1945, Charles Zimmerman from the USA was also a guest in Łódź.[102]

100 Ibid., correspondence between committees.

101 „Di arbet in der lodzher bundisher organizatsye,“ *Folkstsaytung* 1946, nos 2–3, p. 8.

102 Charles Zimmerman (1896–1983) was the deputy chairman of the JLC in America and a member of the Bund. He travelled Europe in 1945 and 1946 as a representative of the JLC visited, i.e. Poland in order to acquaint himself with the political situation and start a cooperation with the representatives of non-communist trade unions and labour and Sweden to take part in the Swedish Trade Union Congress (information from: Bono [Winer], "Fun partey-lebn. Lodzh," *Folkstsaytung* 1946, no. 1, p. 7; "Kh.[aver] Sharl Zimerman," *Folkstsaytung* 1946, no. 1, p. 8; "Kh. [aver] y. pat in lodzh," *Folkstsaytung* 1946, nos 2–3, p. 4; H. Blomqvist, *Socialism in Yiddish*, p. 32; http://www.yivoarchives.org/index.php?p=collections/controlcard&id=34156 [access: 10 August 2024]).

One of the Bund's activities was to commemorate fallen comrades by erecting monuments and organising memorial services (such as those held in Piotrków Trybunalski,[103] Lublin, and Łódź). In Przemyśl and Łódź, memorial services were held in honour of Artur Zygielbojm[104] and on the first anniversary of the death of Leon Feiner.[105] The anniversary of the Warsaw Ghetto Uprising was also commemorated.[106]

The Bund committees set themselves the main goal of providing social assistance to their members and their families. The care was mainly provided to repatriates from the USSR living in Lower Silesia and Szczecin, where transports from the East were mainly directed. Efforts were made to help them build a new life: dining halls and boarding houses were established at the committees. Smaller committees were also supported in their activities. The Bund members' cultural development was also taken care of by creating reading rooms and libraries where Jewish and Polish newspapers were available. Literary evenings were also held there.

In order to improve the material situation of the Bund members, the party tried to organise jobs for them immediately after the war, for example, by establishing shoemaking and tailoring cooperatives, either independently or in cooperation with Jewish committees. From articles published in *Folkstsaytung* we know that, by June 1946, such cooperatives existed in Łódź ('Igłax', 'Przyszłość', 'Wygoda', 'Malarz', a weavers' cooperative), Wrocław, Wałbrzych, Dzierżoniów, Zagórze (a tailoring cooperative established with the help of the Dzierżoniów committee), and Legnica.[107]

The revival of the Bund in post-war Poland, as I mentioned earlier, collapsed after the murder of Fishke Nejman and the Kielce pogrom. After these events, it was often pointed out in the pages of *Folkstsaytung* and *Głos Bundu*: "[…] despite the complicated situation, we continue the life of our political party, the party's

103 „Fun partey-lebn. Pietrkov," *Folkstsaytung* 1946, no. 4, p. 6.

104 *Shmuel (Artur) Zigielbojm. 13 May 1943–1946*, ibid., nos 2–3, p. 3 (information on the course of a memorial meeting in honour of Comrade Artur); „Fun partey-lebn Pshemysl," ibid., no. 4, p. 6; „Akademia żałobna ku czci działacza 'Bundu' Artura Zygielbojma," *Biuletyn Żydowskiej Agencji Prasowej* 1946, no. 50/170, ff. 2–3.

105 „Fun kh[aver] dr leon fayner," *Folkstsaytung* 1946, no. 1, p. 8.

106 "Fun partey-lebn. Varshe," ibid., nos 2–3, p. 6.

107 Nejman, "Di arbets-kooperativn. A meglekhkeyt fun a produktiver ekzistents," *Folkstsaytung* 1946, no. 4, p. 2.

cultural life is still developing."[108] In one of the earlier issues of *Głos Bundu*, the author emphasised:

> Despite the difficult situation of the Jewish population, in defiance of the terror of an anti-Semitic and fascist reaction, the ideological personnel of the Bund in the newly established centres of Jewish life show great vitality and organisational verve. [...] Oblivious of the mood of panic and fear fostered by the Zionists [sic!], we shall continue working for the benefit of the Jewish workers.[109]

These words, as well as the statement by Zbigniew Mitzner, which was reprinted in the first issue of *Głos Bundu* (August 1946, originally published in *Robotnik*), did not prove convincing enough and did not stop the exodus of Jews from Poland, including Bund members.[110] The party press drew attention to the fact that:

> We wish to remind you and urge you to constantly and systematically spread the belief within Jewish society that Poland is not Kielce, that Poland is socialism, that Poland is equality and freedom, that Poland stands for what the workers' parties want, what the PPS wants, and not what the Polish heirs of Hitler want.[111]

Political programme in the new reality

An important event in the post-war life of Polish Jews was the Kielce pogrom, which resulted in the loss of life. For the Bund, it was the end of an era – what they had been painstakingly trying to rebuild had suddenly collapsed. The pogrom and the prevention of similar situations were often written about in the party press.[112]

In addition, under the new conditions and after numerous victims among the Bund members (both under German and Soviet occupation) brought about by the war, the canon of Bund heroes changed in the early post-war years. Those who gave their lives while working underground in the ghettos during the Warsaw Ghetto Uprising, – including young people from the ranks of Skif and Tsukunft, as well as those who died of natural causes due to health reasons. One of the sombre dates in the Bund's calendar was the anniversary of the death of two Bund pioneers and leaders who died in New York in the autumn of 1941:

---

108 „Do ludności żydowskiej," *Głos Bundu* 1947, no. 1 (5), p. 1.

109 „Z życia partii," *Głos Bundu* 1946, nos 2–3, p. 10.

110 Z. Mitzner, „Socjalizm mądrych," *Głos Bundu* 1946, no. 1, p. 1.

111 Ibid.

112 „Vu iz der oysveg?," *Folkstsaytung* 1946, no. 6, p. 1.

Józef Portnoy ("Noyekh") and Vladimir Kosovsky. These anniversaries were commemorated in autumn at their symbolic graves in Jewish cemeteries.[113]

Another symbol of a martyr's heroic death was Shmul 'Artur' Zygielbojm, whose self-sacrifice was widely reported in the newspapers, which also commemorated him: "[...] and his memory will remain in the hearts of millions of good and noble people fighting for a better world, once and for all forever free of German criminals."[114] The anniversary of the death of Leon Feiner ('Mikołaj'), who died in 1945, was also commemorated, emphasising his participation in the underground struggle of the Bund.[115]

Another hero was already mentioned Fishke Nejman, murdered in Łódź in 1946. At the end of 1946, a monument was unveiled on his grave at the Jewish cemetery, and speeches were given by Ignacy Falk, Pinkus Wołkowicz, and Gershon Fogel.[116]

Efforts continued to be made to implement slogans analogous to the pre-war ones: *doykayt* (here-ness), *khavershaft* (brotherhood), and *eynikayt* (unity). At the same time, the issues of cooperation with other organisations were increasingly raised:

> The Bund's task is an active fight for conditions that allow for unrestrained national-cultural development. It is imperative to oppose the mood of disbelief and pessimism, as well as the harmful slogans of abandoning the countries where Jews have resided for centuries, in favour of utopian theories of "solving the Jewish question" in Palestine. Based on the libertarian ideals of the working class in every country, the Bund continues to see the possibility of national-cultural existence for the Jewish masses. At the same time, cooperation with other centres of Jewish life is essential, grounded in the fight against anti-Semitism and discrimination and the struggle for a national-creative culture for the Jewish masses. The Bund, together with other genuinely progressive elements, must fight to sustain and develop creative Jewish life in Poland.[117]

The early days of the Bund were characterised by the party's main objectives in the post-war reality. Present at the first meetings in Lublin, they had an influence on what was happening in the party throughout the entire existence of the Bund in Poland and were part of the central leadership.

113 „W piątą rocznicę," *Głos Bundu* 1946, nos 2–3, p. 1.

114 J. Beluch-Beloński, „Wspomnienie o Arturze Zygielbojmie," ibid., 1947, no. 7 (11), p. 3.

115 „Życie społeczne i organizacyjne. Akademia ku czci tow. L. Fajnera," ibid., no. 4 (8), p. 8.

116 „Życie społecznej i partyjne. Łódź," ibid., no. 1 (5), p. 8. See: Biographical note – Fogel (Fogiel) Gershon Mordka.

117 „Dokończenie sprawozdania z VIII Zjazdu Bundu w Polsce," ibid., no. 4 (8), p. 6. A speech delivered by Shmuel Hurwicz during the 8th Bund convention in February 1947.

Chapter Two
The Bund on the 'Jewish Street'

The Central Committee of Jews in Poland as a space of inter-party disputes[118]

The Central Committee of Jews in Poland (CKŻP) was established in November 1944 in Lublin. It consisted of a network of provincial and local Jewish committees. In 1946, it included nineteen departments, among them Propaganda and Culture, Regional Associations, Repatriation, Emigration, and Youth Affairs. Positions in the Central Committee and Jewish committees were allocated based on the balance of power between members of the PPR faction at the CKŻP (essentially the PPR), the Bund, and Zionist organisations.[119] Representatives of

118 On the subject of relations within the CKŻP, and between Jewish parties, see from the perspective of Zionist parties in: N. Aleksiun, *Dokąd dalej? Ruch syjonistyczny w Polsce (1944–1950),* Warsaw 2002, pp. 245–266; N. Aleksiun, "Where was there a Future for Polish Jewry? Bundist and Zionist Polemics in Post-World War II Poland," in: *Jewish Politics in Eastern Europe*, pp. 227–243.

119 In the first half of 1946, the composition of the CKŻP was as follows: PPR faction (6 persons): **Marek Bitter**, Julian Łazebnik, Bernard Mark, Michał Mirski, Szymon Zachariasz, Paweł Zelicki; Ichud (a Zionist-Social-Democratic party active in Poland between 1944–1949; 4 persons): **Emil Sommerstein** (chairman of the CKŻP), Mendel Kossower, Dr Herman Parnas, Eng. **Abram Rozenman**; the Bund (4 persons): Ignacy Falk, Leo Finkelsztein, **Salo Fiszgrund**, Dr Shlomo Herszenhorn; Poale Zion Left (a Communist-Zionist party; 3 persons): Dr **Adolf Berman**, Szymon Rozenberg, Hersh Wasser; Poale Zion Right (3 persons): barrister Fishel Hercberg, Prof. **Józef Sack**, Henryk Szner; Union of Jewish Partisans (2 persons): **Hersh Smolar**, barrister Anatol Wertheim; Hehalutz (Hebr. pioneer; a non-partisan Zionist youth organisation with a pioneering character, that prepared Jewish youth for work in Palestine. It was dissolved in January 1950.) (1): Tuwia Borzykowski; Hashomer Hatsair (Hebr. Young Guardian, a Jewish scouting organisation before WWII, in 1944 a Zionist Communist party was established under the same name, engaged primarily in the illegal emigration from Poland to Palestine; 1 person): Michał Bruchański; Jewish Combat Organisation (1 person): Stefan Grajek. Bolded names are members of the CKŻP Presidium in the first half of 1946, with J. Łazebnik as a Secretary General (information from: *Zarys działalności Centralnego Komitetu Żydów w Polsce. Za okres od 1 stycznia do 30 czerwca 1946 r.*, Warsaw 1947, pp. 5–6). After the war, the Jewish Combat Organisation (ŻOB) in Poland was

the three parties – Agudah, the Folkists, and the Revisionists, which were not legalised after the war, were excluded from the CKŻP leadership.[120]

Within the framework of the CKŻP, political organisations competed with each other to occupy a dominant position. The Communists strove to make the committees a tool for rebuilding Jewish life in Poland and for promoting communist ideology in confrontation with other groups, and for uniting all Jews under the banner of the PPR. According to the Zionists, the committees were meant to facilitate the emigration of Jews from Poland. For the Communists, the committees were merely provisional and temporary organisational structures of Jewish life, while the Bundists believed that it would be a lasting structure, the role of which they perceived in accordance with their concept of the national and cultural autonomy of Jews in Poland. Despite the assumption of joint representation of the Polish Jewish community towards the authorities of the People's Republic of Poland, the different assumptions of the Communists, Bundists, and Zionists created a field of permanent and irresolvable conflict of interests and objectives.

The Bund's programme was not approved by the Communists, who formally also supported the reconstruction of the *yishuv* in Poland (*nusekh poyln,* Yiddish, the Polish option). However, mainly due to Lenin's and Stalin's criticism of this concept, they were opposed to all forms of Jewish national autonomy.[121] The Communists strived to rebuild the life of the Jewish community in Poland on the basis of equal rights and the granting of rights to establish their own cultural

no longer an organisation conducting any planned activities but rather a group of people connected by social ties. The ŻOB was represented in the CKŻP for moral and propaganda reasons (information from: A. Grabski, M. Rusiniak, "Język żydowski jako przedmiot sporów politycznych wśród polskich Żydów (1944–1949)," in: *Jidyszland – polskie przestrzenie*, ed. E. Geller, M. Polit, Warsaw 2008, p. 266).

120 Agudah (Agudes, heb. a union) – an Orthodox party whose legal activities were not permitted by the communist authorities after the war. It was mainly active within Jewish religious congregations. On the existence and activities of the CKŻP, see, e.g.: D. Engel, "The Reconstruction of Jewish Communal Institutions in Postwar Poland: The Origins of the Central Committee of Polish Jews, 1944–1945," *East European Politics Societies* 1996, vol. X, no. 1, pp. 85–107; G. Berendt, "Życie od nowa. Instytucje i organizacje żydowskie (1944–1950)," in: *Następstwa zagłady Żydów. Polska 1944–2010,* ed. F. Tych, M. Adamczyk-Garbowska, Lublin, 2012, pp. 191–214; J. Nalewajko-Kulikov, *Obywatel Jidyszlandu. Rzecz o żydowskich komunistach w Polsce,* Warsaw 2009, pp. 160–172.

121 *W. i. lenin un i. w. stalin kegn „bund"*, ed. Sz. Ogórski, Minsk 1933.

institutions but without institutional separation of Jews as a national minority, which the representatives of the Bund could not agree.[122]

In order to realise their ideological goals, the Bundists tried after the war to rebuild their position as the largest Jewish party on the 'Jewish Street' that they held during the Second Republic but lost due to the Holocaust.[123] In the new post-war reality, they could not come to terms with the progressive marginalisation of the Bund's role among the Jewish masses. On the one hand, in the wake of the Holocaust, the idea of emigrating to Palestine and building their own state became extremely attractive, and on the other hand, the PPR, as the dominant party in power, attracted those who were active and eager to advance their careers. In this situation, the Bundists constantly tried to prove to themselves and others that their position had not changed compared to the pre-war period. Like other parties, including mainly the communists, representatives of the Bund sought to gain control over the structures of the CKŻP and its local committees.

This atmosphere and the attitude of the Bundists towards Zionists is revealed in the account of Dr Moshe Ishay, a representative of the Jewish Agency in Stockholm. In January 1946, he travelled to Poland to establish a representation in Warsaw and organise the emigration of Jews. To this end, he wanted to meet with representatives of the CKŻP. As a Zionist and an outsider, he saw the Committee as follows:

> The Central Committee [of Jews in Poland] is not our ally. [...] On 10 January, I visited the Central Committee. It consists of representatives of [several – author's note] parties. Zionist parties constitute half, if not the majority, of the Committee. However, internal matters are managed in such a way that the foundation is built on our two enemies, [Paweł – author's note] Zelicki and [Marek – author's note] Bitter, along with their assistants, the two Bundists: [Shlomo – author's note] Herszenhorn and Dr [Michał – author's note] Szuldenfrei. As he has himself told me, the latter, a lawyer from Kraków, has a son in Palestine, but this does not stop him from holding such a position regarding the matter in question.
>
> Since I arrived, they have been avoiding contact, even though I introduced myself as a representative of the Jewish Agency. They have yet to respond to the request from our people to invite me officially as the Jewish Agency's representative to a committee session or even to a meeting. Nor have I received a return visit from them.[124]

122 A. Grabski, „Żydzi a polskie życie polityczne (1944–1949)," in: *Następstwa zagłady Żydów*, pp. 174–175.

123 M. Trębacz, „Bund – Międzynarodówka – PPS. Historia współzależności," *Biuletyn Instytutu Pamięci Narodowej* 2011, no. 7 (128), p. 29.

124 *Stosunki polsko-izraelskie (1945–1967). Wybór dokumentów*, selected and edited by Sz. Rudnicki, M. Silber, Warsaw 2009, p. 81 (*25 January 1946 – Excerpts from a*

In line with their ideological principles, the representatives of the Bund sought to prevent the emigration of Jews from Poland by all available means, competing with socialist parties and organisations in this respect. The CKŻP, as well as the Presidium meetings, was the main place of inter-party disputes, where representatives of individual parties tried to push through a point of view in line with their own ideology.[125]

It was not only a place of ideological disputes resulting from the difference in political programmes but also different visions of post-war Poland and where the Jewish community would be placed in it. During the meetings, the pre-war rivalry over dominance on the 'Jewish Street' continued. It was a clash of different political views, each wanting to have a dominant influence on the Committee and its activities in Poland and abroad. The Presidium meetings were also a place for expressing one's own political views and for interparty debates.

The most pronounced axis of conflict was evident between the Zionists and the Bundists, centring around the idea of emigration as opposed to the reconstruction of the Jewish community in Poland. The dispute between the Bundists and the Communists concerned the scope of the proposed autonomy for the Jewish community, on the one hand, and the differences in tradition and the PPR dependence on the party's current political guidelines on the other. The Bund faction in the CKŻP often denied all statements made by representatives of the PPR faction, as well as the position of representatives of Zionist organisations. Sometimes, minor issues of everyday life were argued over, such as small differences in subsidies allocated to various Jewish organisations in post-war Poland. These two virtually irresolvable axes of conflict meant that the Bund was in constant dispute with the other main Jewish political groups in Poland. While the conflict with the Zionists – albeit fundamental – diminished as both legal and illegal emigration progressed, the dispute with the Communists (especially as the Zionists' influence waned) remained, taking on the role of a fundamental conflict.

During the meetings of the Presidium, the decision-making body of the CKŻP, various issues related to the activities of the central office and local committees were discussed, including health care for children and the elderly and

letter from the representative of the Jewish Agency in Poland Dr. M. Ishai (Stockholm) to the Jewish Agency (Jerusalem) on the organisation of the representative office in Poland and on emigration).

125 See: Protocols of the Presidium from 1945–1948, AŻIH, Archives of the Presidium and Secretariat of the Central Committee of Jews in Poland 1945–1950 (from now on: Archives of the Presidium and Secretariat), ref. 303/I/7–34.

financial issues. From 1945 to the spring of 1948, the Bund, during the deliberations of the CKŻP – regardless of the fundamental dispute with the Zionist parties, which it accused of hindering the work of the Jewish committee in the reconstruction of the Jewish community in Poland,[126] almost always criticised the representatives of the PPR faction.[127]

The Bund faction in the CKŻP Presidium included Salo Fiszgrund, Shlomo Herszenhorn (January 1946 he was replaced temporarily by Leo Finkelsztejn[128] for the duration of the visit of the CKŻP delegation to the United States[129]), Michał Szuldenfrei, Shaya Szechatow, Gershon Fogel, and Ignacy Falk.

In order to illustrate the essence of the conflicts between representatives of the Bund and representatives of other parties, it is necessary to present the main points of contention. Until mid-1948, Ignacy Falk and Salo Fiszgrund were the most vocal critics among the Bundists in the Presidium. They placed a strong emphasis on the assistance of the CKŻP's in the development of the Jewish community in Poland, including the organisation of proper living conditions for repatriates arriving from the Soviet Union.[130]

Ignacy Falk regularly reported on the activities of the Repatriation Department, of which he was the head. As befits a Bund member, his statements included many demands aimed at improving the work of the Department and, above all, increasing the assistance provided to repatriates in organising their lives in Poland. He criticised the Zionists for their efforts to turn Poland into a transit point for Jewish repatriates.[131]

At numerous meetings, the Bund faction fought against the accession of the CKŻP to the World Jewish Congress (WJC),[132] which was considered an

---

126 Y. Kersz, "Eynhayt un di yidishe komitetn," *Folkstsaytung* 1946, nos 2–3, p. 5.

127 N. Aleksiun, *Dokąd dalej? Ruch syjonistyczny w Polsce (1944–1950)*, Warsaw 2002, pp. 245–249.

128 Leo Finkelsztejn (1885 – 29 July 1950), writer and journalist associated with the Bund. He spent the Second World War in the USSR and returned from there in 1946 in a very bad physical condition. At the beginning of 1947, he left for the USA as a representative of the Bund and, to the dissatisfaction of the Bund members, he did not return to Poland (information from: Dina, "Leo Finkelsztejn," *Unzer tsayt* 1951, no. 9, p. 22).

129 AŻIH, CKŻP. Archives of the Presidium and Secretariat, ref. 303/I/14, Protocol no. 4, from 24 January 1946, f. 18.

130 See. e.g. *ibid*, ref. 303/I/14–16, protocols from March-June 1946.

131 See. e.g. *ibid.*, ref. 303/I/11, Protocol no. 33, from 9 May 1946, f. 114–116; Protocol no. 39, from 27 May 1946, f. 135.

132 For more information, see.: Chapter Five: "The Bund versus Zionism".

outpost of Zionism. They also opposed the participation of CKŻP delegates in conferences organised by the WJC. The actions of Zionists, and especially of Communists, were heavily criticised. Salo Fiszgrund repeatedly stated that any success in cooperation with Congress would "undermine the prestige and authority of the CKŻP." In other words, he was convinced that any co-operation with the Congress would destroy the idea of creating and developing the national-cultural autonomy of the Jewish community in Poland. He advocated to end the negotiations on the CKŻP's accession to the European Secretariat because "joining the WJC would undermine the prestige of the CKŻP as the representation of Polish Jewry, and the Jewish community would be exploited as a tool in discussing Zionist issues."[133]

The representative of the PPR faction in the CKŻP, Julian Łazebnik,[134] tried to exploit this antagonism to discredit the Bund's double-dealing. During the previous discussions, he demanded from Fiszgrund that "[…] the Bund in Poland explain its position in relation to its party comrades abroad."[135]

Other contentious issues included emigration, the safety of the Jewish population, Jewish children, and their emigration to other countries.[136] During Presidium meetings, Salo Fiszgrund called for unanimity in votes and when making fundamental decisions, although he and his party colleagues did not adhere to this themselves. The Bund faction opposed the election of a new CKŻP representative to replace Emil Sommerstein[137], who had emigrated to the USA in 1946. Bund representatives Salo Fiszgrund, Shlomo Herszenhorn, Shaya Szechatow,

---

133 AŻIH, Archives of the Presidium and Secretariat, ref. 303/I/22, Protocol no. 101, from 9 July 1947, f. 205.

134 Julian (Joel) Łazebnik (1904 Warsaw – 1981) associated with the communist movement from 1921. During World War II, he was in the USSR where he was an active member of the Union of Polish Patriots (ZPP) in Tashkent. He returned to Poland in September 1946. He served as Secretary General of the CKŻP. After the liquidation of the CKŻP, he was a member of the Board of the Social-Cultural Association of Jews in Poland (TSKŻ) (information from: Grabski, *Działalność komunistów wśród Żydów*, p. 308).

135 AŻIH, Archives of the Presidium and Secretariat, ref. 303/I/20, Protocol no. 101, from 9 July 1947, f. 207.

136 More information in Chapter Five: "The Bund versus Zionism."

137 Emil Sommerstein (1883–1957) a lawyer by profession. In the Second Polish Republic, he was a member of the Zionist Organisation in Poland. During the war, he was imprisoned in Soviet labour camps. He was the head of the Organising Committee of Polish Jews in the USSR at the Union of Polish Patriots (ZPP). He headed the War Compensation Ministry at the Polish Committee of National Liberation (PKWN).

and Gershon Fogel (the latter two replacing Ignacy Falk and Leo Finkelsztejn during their visit to the USA) were opposed to the existence of the chairman's position and to Adolf Berman's candidacy.[138] For this reason, they did not take part in the election of the chairman in February 1947.[139]

In November and December 1946, disputes arose in the Presidium regarding Jewish representation in the 1947 elections to the Legislative Sejm. Representatives of all political organisations agreed only on the issue of Jewish support for the 'democratic bloc'. The Bund decided to put forward their candidates on the PPS lists. Others supported the proposal by Szymon Zachariasz (PPR faction), who demanded that the representation of Jews in the Sejm should be a representation of the CKŻP, and that candidates would be put forward by the CKŻP as an integral part of the 'democratic bloc'. It would be easier to exercise control over a candidate not affiliated with the PPR, and nominated by the CKŻP.[140] This option was supported by Adolf Berman (Poale Zion Left), Michał Bruchański[141] (Hashomer Hatsair), Prof. Józef Sack[142] and Julian Łazebnik. The Communists

---

Member of the KRN and 1st Chairman of the CKŻP (information from: Grabski, *Działalność komunistów wśród Żydów*, p. 2).

138 Adolf (Abraham) Berman (1906 Warsaw – 1978 Israel), brother of Jakub Berman. Until 1925, he studied at the Philosophy and Humanities Department of the Warsaw University, where he received a doctorate in philosophy in 1931. From 1926, he was a member of Poale Zion Left. During the occupation, he was, i.a. director of the Centos and one of the founders of the Anti-Fascist Bloc in the Warsaw Ghetto. After leaving the ghetto in the autumn of 1942, he was a member of the Jewish National Committee on the 'Aryan' side and secretary of the Council to Aid Jews 'Żegota'. After the war, he was a member of the KRN. In the years 1947–1949, he was the chairman of the CKŻP. In 1947, he was an MP to the Polish Legislative Sejm. In 1950, he emigrated to Israel, where he continued to be active in political parties, i.a., in the Left-Socialist Mapam and Maki (information from: B. Temkin-Berman, *Dziennik z podziemia*, introduction, edited and annotated by A. Grupińska, P. Szapiro, Warsaw 2000, pp. 226–235).

139 AŻIH, Archives of the Presidium and Secretariat, ref. 303/I/20, Protocol no. 18, from 6 February 1947, f. 97–99.

140 Ibid., pp. 198–202.

141 Michał Bruchański (1914 – ?), teacher by profession, head of the Youth Division of the CKŻP, member of Hashomer Hatsair (information from: AŻIH, Archive of the Personnel Department of the Central Committee of Jews in Poland (1945) 1946–1950, ref. 303/III/19 – employees personal records).

142 Józef Sack (1899–1965 Israel), during the war he was a member of the Jewish National Committee. In 1944, he fought in the Warsaw Uprising as a member of the Jewish Combat Organisation unit of the People's Army. After the war, he was the

knew that there would be no place for their representative on the list of the 'democratic bloc', as had previously been the case among the members of the State National Council (KRN).

Zachariasz's option was rejected by the Bund. According to I. Falk, the CKŻP would also monopolise political life, and it would be challenging to express different political views. In addition to the Bund, the PPR faction also faced opposition from the Ichud representatives. Falk and Fiszgrund advocated the establishment of an Inter-Party Coordination Committee in the CKŻP, which would, among other things, conduct an election campaign. During heated discussions about the elections, the Bund representatives defended party autonomy. Zachariasz's proposal was in line with the philosophy of national unity and may have been one of the first steps toward the PPR faction gaining control of Jewish parties.[143]

During these discussions, in relation to the proposal supported by the Communists and part of the Zionist left, Fiszgrund countered with the possibility of the CKŻP developing into a political organisation (according to its principles, the CKŻP should not be involved in politics). This was an absurd argument, considering the party key in the selection of members, for example, of the CKŻP Presidium.[144] Ultimately, two representatives of the Jewish community were elected to the 'democratic bloc' list: Michał Szuldenfrei on the PPS list and Józef Sack on the PPR list.[145]

After the election, during a Presidium meeting in February 1947, representatives of the Communists and other organisations accused the Bund members of having contributed to the reduction of Jewish representation in the Sejm due to their different views on this issue.[146] According to August Grabski, the accusation seems debatable, if only because of the small number of Jews remaining in Poland, who were no longer a significant minority with a large electorate as they had during the interwar period.[147]

Chairman of Poale Zion Hitachdut, Vice-Chairman of CKŻP and MP to the Legislative Sejm (information from: A. Grabski, *Żydowski ruch kombatancki w Polsce w latach 1944–1949*, Warsaw 2002, p. 186).

143 E.g. AŻIH, Archives of the Presidium and Secretariat, ref. 303/I/19, Protocol no. 98, from 27 November 1946, f. 62–66.

144 Ibid., ref. 303/I/19, Protocol no. 101, from 2 December 1946, f. 76–78.

145 Grabski, *Działalność komunistów wśród Żydów*, p. 201.

146 AŻIH, Archives of the Presidium and Secretariat, ref. 303/I/20, Protocol no. 18, from 6 February 1947, f. 101–106.

147 Grabski, *Działalność komunistów wśród Żydów*, p. 201.

Representatives of the Bund faction in the CKŻP also unsuccessfully opposed any form of cooperation between the Committee and Jewish Religious Congregations,[148] let alone unification with them. Fiszgrund emphasised that this would jeopardize the Committee's secular character, which instead of being a secular organisation, would become a substitute for the pre-war Jewish Religious Communities[149] (which was based on religious principles), contrary to the party's secular programme.

The Committee focused on the situation of Jewish children in post-war Poland and the organisation of education with arguments about the superiority of Yiddish over Hebrew and Polish. On the language issue, the Bund members stuck to their traditional position, as Fiszgrund's statement shows:

> In our committees, both the Central and Provincial ones, officials consistently use the Polish language. In fact, upon entering a Jewish Committee, one gets the impression of being in a Polish institution. This absurd practice must end. It is necessary to remind the committees that the official language in our institutions is the Jewish language.[150]

The Bund representatives believed that Jewish children, being the hope for the Jewish settlement (*yishuv*) in Poland, should remain there, while the Zionists believed that all orphans, especially those in Polish families, belonged to the Jewish settlement in Palestine.[151] Salo Fiszgrund was not opposed to the idea of

148 Jewish Religious Congregations (formerly Jewish Religious Associations). From June 1946, they were the equivalent of the Jewish Religious Communities operating in Poland until 1939. They guaranteed freedom of religious practice, religious education for youth in yeshivas, children in Talmud Torah schools, and assistance in religious emigration. The associations also oversaw the military rabbinate. The Central Authority – the Organisational Committee – was based in Warsaw and oversaw regional congregations. By 1947, there were 80 regional religious congregations in five districts: Warsaw, Łódź, Kraków, Katowice, and Wrocław. At the National Congress of Delegates of Jewish Religious Congregations in Poland, on 9–10 August 1949, the congregations merged to form the Union of Mosaic Faith in Poland, with Rabbi Shulim Treistman as its chairman (information from: J. Adelson, "W Polsce zwanej Ludową," in: *Najnowsze dzieje Żydów w Polsce w zarysie (do 1950 roku)*, ed. J. Tomaszewski, Warsaw 1993, pp. 429–433).

149 AŻIH, Archives of the Presidium and Secretariat, ref. 303/I/20, Protocol no. 3, from 19 January 1948, f. 19; Protocol no. 17 from 1 March 1948, f. 123–125.

150 AŻIH, Archives of the Presidium and Secretariat, ref. 303/I/16, Protocol no. 4, from 13–14 July 1946, f. 63.

151 A. Grabski wrote on this subject in: „Działalność Frakcji PPR w CKŻP (jesień 1944 r. – czerwiec 1946 r.," in: A. Grabski, G. Berendt, *Między emigracją a trwaniem.*

children, but he was in favour of the freedom to choose the country, as well as for the children to go straight to their final destination country, even if it was Palestine.[152]

In the spring of 1946, the Presidium plenum considered sending 1,000 Jewish orphaned children to Sweden. The report noted:

> Comrade Fiszgrund speaks out decisively against the project. There is no basis for sending children abroad; we do not know how they will be treated there or in what spirit they will be raised. The proposal should not be accepted. Instead, financial aid should be requested locally. [Mendel – author's note] Kossower, referring to Comrade Fiszgrund's speech, reads from an American newspaper a report and an interview with Comrade Fiszgrund conducted by members of the press. As a result, the Swedish Government blocked the children's entry into Sweden, allegedly based on the Central Committee's decision in this matter. According to the speaker, such an initiative should be welcomed, and 1,000 orphans should be sent away.[153]

In yet another situation, when eight children were kidnapped from the Children's Home in Świder, representatives of the Bund demanded an investigation:

> Dr [Shlomo – author's note] Herszenhorn does not know who organised the abduction of the children, but his suspicions point toward Hashomer Hatsair. It is absolutely necessary to determine the whereabouts of the group of eight from Świder.[154]

All statements were aimed at preventing the relocation of Jewish children who had survived the Holocaust from Poland. They were mainly sent to Palestine by Zionist organisations.

The commemorations of subsequent anniversaries of the Warsaw Ghetto Uprising were also a subject of dispute. In 1948, the Bundists accused the Zionists of turning the event into a Zionist demonstration.[155]

The nature of the tone of statements made by representatives of the Bundist faction in the Presidium changed after the summer holiday of 1948. After this period, Fiszgrund's statements became more subdued, at the same time, he seems

---

Syjoniści i komuniści żydowscy w Polsce po Holocauście, Warsaw 2003, pp. 67–77.

152 AŻIH, CKŻP. Archives of the Presidium and Secretariat, ref. 303/I/17, Protocol no. 73, from 17 September 1946, f. 130.

153 Ibid., ref. 303/I/15, Protocol no. 37, from 21 May 1946, f. 125.

154 Ibid., ref. 303/I/20, Protocol no. 21, from 17 February 1947, f. 116.

155 Ibid., ref. 303/I/25, Protocol no. 57, from 16 June 1948, f. 136–143. For more about the commemoration of the anniversaries of the Warsaw Ghetto Uprising, see: Chapter Four: „Forms of the Party's Operation" and sub-chapter "The Historical Commission at the Bund Central Committee and the Bundists' Involvement in Shaping the Image of Anti-Nazi Resistance."

to have spoken much less frequently and been more conciliatory. He returned to issues related to historical policy, commemorating sites of the Holocaust and organising Social Courts to pursue Jewish wartime collaborators.[156] He spoke less often on ideological issues matters, and the repercussions of the Bund's April conference in Wrocław were visible in his behaviour.[157] Even then, he recognised signs of the end of the party. This is probably why he noticed positive actions from the representatives of the PPR faction in the CKŻP. For example, he praised the participation of the CKŻP delegation at the European Jewish Culture Conference in Paris, stating that the PPR faction presented itself positively compared to other delegations. After the dissolution of the Bund in January 1949, Fiszgrund participated in the deliberations of the Presidium of the CKŻP from among the former members of the Bund. However, he no longer represented the position of the defunct party; instead, his views were closer to the politically dominant views of the PPR representatives, who were the main decision-makers during the proceedings.

The Bund's activity in the structures of the CKŻP was an attempt at democracy. The CKŻP itself was a miniature (with the exception of a few pre-war parties) of the political spectrum of the 'Jewish Street' in Poland. It resembled the political life in the PRL until the dissolution of the PSL (Polish People's Party) as an opposition party. Both substitutes for democratic structures ended their lives with the similarity of Polish political life to the Soviet model.

The Bundists and the activities of local Jewish committees

Jewish committees were established in all towns with a significant Jewish population. As with the CKŻP, the composition of the committees reflected the influence of various Jewish parties and was based on party affiliation. From June 1946, the following proportions were maintained throughout the country. PPR faction – 6 representatives, the Ichud Union of Democratic Zionists and the Bund – 4 representatives each, Poale Zion Right and Poale Zion Left – 3 representatives each, and Hashomer Hatsair – 1 representative.[158] The Presidium of each committee consisted of 7 members. According to the party quota system, there were 2 members from the PPR, 2 from Poale Zion Left, 1 from Poale Zion Right,

156 On Social Courts affiliated with the CKŻP, see.: A. Żbikowski, *Sąd Społeczny przy CKŻP. Wojenne rozliczenia społeczności żydowskiej w Polsce*, Warsaw 2014.

157 See: Chapter Seven: „The process of the Bund liquidation," sub-chapter: „Conference – Wrocław (April 1948) and Łódź (October 1948)."

158 P. Wieczorek, „Żydzi wałbrzyscy po II wojnie światowej," *Kwartalnik Historii Żydów* 2004, no. 3, p. 380.

1 from the Bund, and 1 from Ichud.[159] As you can see, the PPR representatives held a dominant position both in the central and local committees.

At the highest level, which was the Presidium of the Committee, and in the provincial or local committees, similar to the central level, activists representing different political organisations competed with each other and argued over ideology, sometimes preventing closer cooperation within the committees. One of the main reasons for this was the appointment of leadership positions in the local committees, as the representatives of each party aspired to have their representatives serve as the chairman. This was due to political rivalry for influence and control over the work of the committee. In general, the party with the most members in a given area had the deciding vote in the local committee. However, there were exceptions, such as the Provincial Jewish Committee in Lower Silesia in Dzierżoniów (from 1945 to the spring of 1946) and later in Wrocław. This way, the authorities of the Provincial Jewish Committee in Lower Silesia found themselves under the control of the Communists, who did not constitute a majority in the region but dominated in Wrocław.[160] In Jelenia Góra, a representative of the Bund held the position of Productization Department officer and was also a member of the presidium of the local Jewish Committee in Jelenia Góra.[161]

According to Noah Lasman, who returned to Poland from the USSR after the war and was a proponent of Zionism, the situation in the local committees was as follows:

> They [Jewish committees – author's note] represented authorities who believed that the place for Polish Jews was in Poland and that their mass emigration would be a disgrace. The Jewish Committees were led by pre-war Communists and Bundists, who sought to rebuild Jewish cultural life in Poland and understood that it would be challenging to achieve this if the remaining Jewish population were to leave.[162]

This report reflects one of the previous points of contention between the Zionists, Bundists, and Communists, although official reports on the activities of the individual local Bund committees reveal little or nothing about inter party conflicts. – These are only revealed in accounts from later years. A report from Lower Silesia is vague:

159 I. Białostocki, „Wojewódzki Komitet Żydów Polskich w Szczecinie (1946–1950)," *Biuletyn Żydowskiego Instytutu Historycznego* 1969, nos 71–72, p. 88.

160 G. Berendt, „Życie od nowa. Instytucje i organizacje żydowskie (1944–1950)," in: *Następstwa zagłady Żydów*, p. 200.

161 „Życie społeczne i partyjne. Jelenia Góra," *Głos Bundu* 1947, no. 1 (5), p. 8.

162 N. Lasman, *Wspomnienia z Polski*, Warsaw 1997, p. 59.

> In all localities, our organisations are adequately represented in the Jewish Committees. In some Committees, our comrades hold positions as chairpersons, their deputies, or members of the Presidium.[163]

In the autumn of 1946, the Szczecin Provincial Jewish Committee had a Bund representative, Abram Sobol.[164] The Częstochowa Jewish Committee was established on the initiative of the Bundist, Liber Brener. According to him, the work and division of responsibilities were organised on sound principles:

> All these matters are handled solely by our comrades, a few Jewish comrades from the PPR, and a representative of Jewish artisans. The Zionists remain on the sidelines.[165]

In Dzierżoniów, as in other cities, there was a party mosaic, which implied the emergence of conflicts. One of the main points of contention was the issue of rebuilding the Jewish community in Poland. In this town, the fight against the Zionists, which the Bundists waged together with the Communists, overshadowed other disputes, which by no means meant that they agreed on all issues. In the autumn of 1946, a conflict arose between the PPR and the Bund over the establishment of the Bund's own cooperatives.[166]

The fact that the representatives of each party looked after the interests of their organisation is evidenced by the words of Dina Schein, for example. After the war, when she joined the Bund in Wałbrzych, she was delegated by the party to work in the local Wałbrzych Jewish Committee. Her tasks, entrusted to her by the leadership of the Wałbrzych Bund, were to look after the interests of the Bund and to control the activities of other political groups.[167]

In addition to providing information on the activities of the local Jewish committee, the representatives of the Bund in these committees were tasked with looking after the interests of the party, e.g. in the distribution of funds to Jewish organisations in the respective city or town and with doing work for the Jewish community. Efforts were also made to ensure that the Bundists working in the

163 „Z życia partyjnego. Na Dolnym Śląsku," *Głos Bundu* 1946, [no. 1], p. 8.

164 „Z życia partii. Szczecin," ibid., nos 2–3, p. 10. See: Abraham Sobol's biographical note.

165 L. Brener, „Dzieje żydowskiego osiedla po wyzwoleniu," ibid., August 1946, [no. 1], p. 8.

166 B. Szaynok, „Żydzi w Dzierżoniowie (1945–1950)," in: *Dzierżoniów – wiek miniony. Materiały pokonferencyjne*, eds. S. Ligarski, T. Przerwa, Wrocław 2007, p. 28.

167 Dina Schein, née Hiziger-Tajtelbaum (1922, Nowy Sącz – 2018 Israel); interviewed by M. Rusiniak-Karwat, in May 2008 in Rishon Letsiyon (Israel).

Jewish committee were not reduced when the committees were cut back.[168] In addition, working in the committee brought material benefits in the form of social assistance, where there was a percentage-based allocation for different work groups, such as the Warsaw Jewish Committee. Social assistance was received by employees of all Jewish institutions.[169] These were, therefore, tangible benefits in the post-war years of hardship and poverty.

In many committees, there was a constant struggle over positions and ensuring that representatives from each political group were dismissed proportionally as part of the reductions. Such issues were discussed in the plenary sessions of the Presidium of the CKŻP, because all the local committees were unable to reach a consensus. When in the autumn of 1947, all committees were required to reduce their staff and maintain proportional representation due to poor financial conditions in Przemyśl:

> […] the Presidium of the CKŻP passed a motion proposed by Ignacy Falk to establish the following composition for the Jewish Committee: 2 the Bund, 2 Ichud, 2 PPR, 1 Poale Zion Left, and 1 Poale Zion Right.[170]

In this way, the larger parties would be able to make smaller reductions. Also during the meetings of the Presidium of the CKŻP, representatives of the Bund criticised the activities of other parties within the committees:

> Citizen Falk declares that after the establishment of the Provincial Committee in Katowice based on a party spectrum principle, the Provincial Committee does not allow the Bund representatives to cooperate within the Committee. He demands that the CKŻP issue an appropriate instruction to ensure that two representatives of the Bund are included in the Committee.[171]

Sometimes, in the fight for committee positions, the members of the Bund also made accusations against representatives of other parties. This was the case in Szczecin in March 1947, when a Bund representative made the following statement: "[…] that Zionist representatives should not be responsible for the Cultural

168 AŻIH, the Bund, file n., Protocol no. 20 from the meeting of the Warsaw Bund Committee 4 November 1946.

169 AŻIH, Provincial Jewish Committee in Warsaw. 1945–1949, file n., Protocol from the Presidium meeting, Warsaw, 6 December 1948.

170 AŻIH, Archives of the Presidium and Secretariat, ref. 303/I/22, Protocol no. 82, from 16 October 1947, f. 69.

171 Ibid., ref. 303/I/11, Protocol no. 13, from 22 February 1946, f. 48.

Department of the Jewish Committee in Szczecin as, in fact, they are not Polish citizens but Palestinians."[172]

Disputes within the committees did not only concern the allocation of positions but also the day-to-day business. When the Jewish Committee for Palestine in Combat was established in 1948 in Tarnów, where the Zionists had the most influence, an open conflict broke out between the Zionists and the Bundists. However these disputes did not prevent the establishment of theatre groups or sports teams. Nor did they prevent Zionist-socialists from marching in the May Day parade with the Bundists; e.g. members of Poale Zion Left joined the Bund and Trade Unions when they were not allowed to participate in the parade with the PPR group, under their own banner.[173]

Similar situations also occurred in the Provincial Jewish Committee in Łódź. Various parties competed for dominance not only within the committees but also in cooperatives. Representatives of the PPR faction, and Zionists, opposed the Bund's creation of a Socialist Union of Craftsmen. They believed that the association would increase the influence of socialist groups in Łódź. In this case, they were supported by the PPR in Łódź. The Communists, knowing about the Bundists' plans, created the Union of Jewish Craftsmen in Poland, which was supposed to unite all craftsmen, but under the leadership of the PPR. The Communists behind-the-scenes manoeuvring led to the rejection by the Łódź administrative authorities of the Bund's application to create the Socialist Union of Craftsmen.

In another instance, members of the PPR, together with the Bundists, jointly opposed the initiatives of Zionist organisations when they advocated increasing aid to the kibbutzim.[174] Ideological disputes were also of little importance when it came to joint cultural or educational campaigns together with the PPR faction.

---

172 Lavon Institute, Labour Archives, IV-407-1-231 B, Minutes of the Inter-Party Covenant Committee at the Provincial Committee of Jews in Poland in Szczecin, 18 March 1947 (information from: N. Aleksiun, "Where was there a Future for Polish Jewry? Bundist and Zionist Polemics in Post-World War II Poland," pp. 227–243, in: *Jewish Politics in Eastern Europe*, p. 239).

173 J. Kwiek, „Dzieje ludności żydowskiej w Tarnowie po II wojnie światowej," *Kwartalnik Historii Żydów* 2005, no. 3, pp. 363–364.

174 Kibbutz (Hebr., grouping, gathering) – a cooperative community in Palestine. After WWII, this was the name given to centres organised by Zionist parties, where Jews prepared to work on the land and emigrate to the emerging Jewish state (L. Olejnik, "Wojewódzki Komitet Żydowski w Łodzi – powstanie i główne kierunki działalności (1945–1950)," *Biuletyn Żydowskiego Instytutu Historycznego* 1998, no. 3, pp. 11–12).

For example, in Częstochowa and Piotrków Trybunalski, when Bundist Ignacy Samsonowicz[175] gave lectures in Polish on the topic "For Our Freedom and Yours" and "Pages from the History of the Jewish Resistance Movement in Poland."[176]

The fight against anti-Semitism and the general psychosis caused by the Kielce pogrom, which threatened the development of the Jewish community in Poland, also remained a unifying cause. During a meeting of Jewish workers in Wałbrzych, which was convened on 6 August 1946 by the Wałbrzych District Jewish Committee, representatives of the Bund, the PPR faction, and the PPS, all took turns to speak. They unanimously condemned the pogrom in Kielce and the spread of anti-Semitism and unanimously passed a resolution condemning anti-Semitism, advocating for the right to legal emigration, the right to live in Poland, and increasing productivisation.[177]

The Bund in the Lower Silesian Provincial Jewish Committee, did not remain on the sidelines of the main conflict with the Zionists regarding emigration. In disputes, sometimes over minor issues, the Bund was generally opposed to both the actions of the Zionists and the PPR faction. The controversies that concerned the kibbutzim were, the display of Zionist flags in the Committee's headquarters, the removal of removing Zionist symbols, and the issues of security. The Bund representatives rejected many joint resolutions.[178]

Bundists generally rejected everything related to Palestine as the future Jewish state. When the CKŻP passed a resolution on the events in Palestine in January 1948, the Provincial Committee in Lower Silesia organised a rally in Wrocław on 18 February 1948 in support of Palestine in Combat. There were no Bund

---

175 See: Biography.

176 „Życie społeczne i organizacyjne. Nasi korespondenci piszą: Częstochowa," *Głos Bundu* 1947, no. 4 (8), p. 8.

177 Productivisation, or 're-specialisation', aimed at retraining Jewish survivors and reshaping the vocational structure of the Jewish community in Poland after 1945. Its goals extended beyond merely rebuilding the lives of Holocaust survivors; it sought a profound transformation in the occupational composition of the Jewish population. The effort was designed to distance the community from pre-war stereotypes of Jews as traders and profiteers. Through initiatives such as establishing cooperatives, Jewish representatives sought to demonstrate their active participation in Poland's post-war economic reconstruction (information from: M. Grynberg, *Żydowska spółdzielczość pracy w Polsce w latach 1945–1949*, Warsaw 1986, p. *passim*. AAN, Bund, ref. 30/IV/23, vol. II, k. 105–109, Minutes of the meeting of Jewish workers in the city of Wałbrzych from 6 August 1946, convened by the District Jewish Committee in Wałbrzych).

178 Szaynok, *Ludność żydowska na Dolnym Śląsku*, pp. 160–161.

members among the crowds gathered, as they boycotted the event. A similar situation occurred in Legnica. In Dzierżoniów, however, Bund representatives participated in a pro-Palestinian rally organised by the Dzierżoniów Municipal Jewish Committee.[179]

In addition to their involvement in local Jewish committees, Bundists could be found in many different Jewish organisations, such as the Warsaw Landsmanshaft. Election matters in these organisations and candidacies from among the Bund members were discussed at Bund committee meetings.[180]

The activities of the Bund representatives in all structures of local Jewish committees and in affiliated organisations reflected – albeit with occasional exceptions – the party's political agenda. This approach was directed not only toward implementing key programming goals, but also toward achieving a dominant influence over the Jewish community in Poland.

CKŻP press organs: *Dos naye lebn* and *Biuletyn Żydowskiej Agencji Prasowej* [Bulletin of the Jewish Press Agency]

In the first years after the war, newspapers and periodicals, along with radio, were the main means of information and opinion-forming. At the plenary session of the Presidium of the CKŻP on 18 March 1945, Jonas Turkow[181] requested funds for publishing newspapers. During the next Presidium session four days later, a resolution was passed to launch an inter-party weekly titled *Dos naye lebn* (Yid.: 'new life'). This publication was a socio-political magazine, reflecting the needs and dynamics of the Jewish community in post-war Poland.

The *Dos naye lebn*'s printing house and editorial office were initially located in Łódź at 32 Narutowicza Street. The first issue of the paper was published on 10 April 1945.[182] Similar to the composition of the CKŻP, the journalists were also selected according to the representation of various Jewish parties and

179 Ibid., pp. 162–163.

180 AŻIH, Bund, files n., Protocol no. 31 from the convention of the Warsaw Bund Committee, 26 March 1947.

181 Jonas Turkow (1898 Warsaw – 1988 Tel Aviv), actor, director, documentary filmmaker. One of the CKŻP members until his departure from Poland 1946 (information from: *Polski słownik judaistyczny*, vol. II, eds. Z. Borzymińska, R. Żebrowski, Warsaw 2003, pp. 746–747).

182 On the origins of *Dos naye lebn* – see: J. Korzeniowski, "*Dos naye lebn* – pierwsza gazeta żydowska w PRL," *Biuletyn Żydowskiego Instytutu Historycznego* 1981, no. 3 (119), pp. 53–61.

communities. Grzegorz Jaszuński was appointed as a journalist on behalf of the Bund. Leo Finkelsztejn,[183] who was also appointed on behalf of the Bund, started working there in January 1946 and was replaced by Gershon Fogel[184] in 1948.

As a newspaper of the CKŻP, *Dos naye lebn* was supposed to represent different political views and report on the activities of various political factions, but this ideal did not always work in reality.[185] When browsing through the newspaper's issues, it is rare to find an article describing the activities of the Bund in Poland. The communists, in a tactical alliance with the Zionists, played a dominant role in editing the weekly newspaper, according to the principle that the media and propaganda are of fundamental importance in shaping public opinion.

Bund readers of *Dos naye lebn*, criticised the newspaper for bias and for concealing facts, such as during the May Day parade in 1946, when the newspaper (1946, no. 13) included only a general mention of the Bund's participation, marching in the ranks together with representatives of the local PPS branch. One reader criticised the fact that the number of Bund members in the entire procession was not mentioned and that only two of the five Bund cooperatives in Łódź that took part were mentioned. The Bund militia was also not mentioned. The author ended his letter with the following words:

> In my opinion – and I do believe that other readers share my thoughts on this – *Dos naye lebn* should offer a frank and objective depiction of Jewish life, and if the newspaper is unwilling or unable to do so, it would be better if it did not give reports of this kind at all, because such reports as the newspaper had so far given only concealed the work and development of Jewish life in new Poland.[186]

Since the newspaper distorted the image of the May Day parade, we can only assume how skewed the portrayal of other, more controversial events and issues could have been. During the Presidium meetings, *Dos naye lebn* was criticised by representatives of all parties, including the Bund. Furthermore, the newspaper

183 AŻIH, Archives of the Presidium and Secretariat, ref. 303/I/11, Protocol no. 4, from 24 January 1946, f. 18.

184 J. Nalewajko-Kulikov, „'Syjonistyczna z lekkim zabarwieniem PPR-owskim'. *Dos Naje Lebn* (1945–1950) – gazeta Centralnego Komitetu Żydów w Polsce," in: *Żydzi a lewica. Zbiór studiów historycznych*, ed. A. Grabski, Warsaw 2007, pp. 257–278.

185 L. Olejnik, „Prasa żydowska w Łodzi w latach 1945–1949," *Acta Judaica Lodziensia* 2011, no. 1, pp. 99–104.

186 A lezer, „Ofener briv tsu der redaktsye *Dos naye lebn*," *Folkstsaytung* 1946, nos 2–3, p. 2.

was considered to be in competition with other Yiddish newspapers. Bund representative, S. Fiszgrund, characterised it as follows:

> Currently, when *Dos naye lebn* is published once a week, other publications do not have the opportunity to print. It is beyond any doubt that a newspaper is needed, but frankly, not of this nature. It does not appeal to us – it is Zionist with a slight tint towards PPR. This weekly does not express the public opinion or the Central Committee's opinion. It does not print submitted notes or publishes them in an arbitrary summary form.[187]

Salo Fiszgrund's view was supported by lawyer Fishel Hercberg[188] who claimed that *Dos naye lebn* was a "[…] one-sided, biased" newspaper,[189] "[…] and this is due to the fact that editors belong to the same political group." The author of the critique had in mind the representatives of the PPR.

Bundists frequently criticised the content published in the paper and expressed their opinions on the matter during the Presidium meetings of the CKŻP.[190] The Bund faction demanded that the newspaper be reformed so that it would once again be the opinion-forming organ of the Committee, a Jewish newspaper for all Jews, and not the press organ of a single party the PPR faction.[191] Salo Fiszgrund repeatedly called for the appointment of a new editorial board. He emphasised that the current one did not allow everyone to contribute, such as the Bundist Leo Finkelstein.[192] He stressed that *Dos naye lebn* was the press organ of the PPR faction within the CKZP, not of the Zionist movement or the Bundist movement.[193]

Bulletin of the Jewish Press Agency, which was published from 13 November 1944 to 1950, was also the subject of dispute and criticism from various parties, including representatives of the Bund. Initially it was published in Lublin, and from 1945 in Łódź under the direction of editor Ozjasz Szlajen, first in typescript form and then in duplicated typescript. The editorial board was subordinate to the Department of Culture and Propaganda of the CKŻP. Like *Dos naye lebn*, it was supposed to represent the views of all political factions by publishing

187 AŻIH, Archives of the Presidium and Secretariat, ref. 303/I/12, Protocol no. 80, from 8 October 1946, f. 171.

188 Fishel Hercberg – barrister, journalist affiliated with Poale Zion Right.

189 Mistake in the original: "not biased."

190 Ibid., ref. 303/I/21, Protocol no. 50, from 28 May 1947, f. 56.

191 Ibid., ref. 303/I/21, Protocol no. 64, from 10 July 1947, f. 157.

192 Ibid., ref. 303/I/21, Protocol no. 69, from 29 July 1947, f. 196.

193 Ibid., ref. 303/I/30, Protocol no. 72, from 12 October 1948, f.16.

articles or reprints of articles concerning the activities of all parties. The task of the *Bulletin* was

> to inform about all manifestations and events in Jewish life in the country, and to provide news to authorities and periodical publications both domestically and abroad.[194]

In this case, even the communist Szymon Zachariasz considered it to be a distinctly Zionist newspaper,[195] mainly containing information about the activities of Zionist organisations in Poland and abroad, which intensified at the beginning of 1946.[196]

The Bund was completely dissatisfied with its involvement in editing *Dos naye lebn*, considering it a platform for competing factions – the Communist and the Zionist. According to those involved, the small number of articles about the Bund's activities on the 'Jewish Street' may have had an impact on the limitation of the dissemination of its ideology and programme and the recruitment of new members.

194 „Biuro Statystyczne," *Biuletyn Żydowskiej Agencji Prasowej* 1945, nos. 39/49, f. 2.

195 A. Grabski, *Działalność komunistów wśród Żydów w Polsce (1944–1949)*, Warsaw 2004, pp. 114–115.

196 See: *Biuletyn Żydowskiej Agencji Prasowej*, 1944–1949.

Chapter Three
The Bund on the 'Polish (political) Street'

The Bund's attitude towards the politics of 'Lublin Poland'

The Bund members who envisioned their future in Poland supported the new regime from the very beginning of the establishment of the government of the so-called People's Republic of Poland in Lublin, led by the Polish Committee of National Liberation (PKWN), believing that the success of the new government and good relations with it were crucial for the future of the Bund in Poland. The Bund Committee in Lublin[197] was one of the first organisations to write to the PKWN, immediately after the organisation was founded in September 1944. It was a declaration in which the Bund representatives stated: "[…] we stand on the platform of the PKWN's 'July Manifesto'. We hereby declare our participation in the work of the PKWN as the government for the construction of a Democratic Poland."[198]

Shlomo Herszenhorn and Michał Szuldenfrei were employed within the PKWN structures, the former of whom took on the role as a consultant for the assistance of the Jewish population at the PKWN Presidium.[199]

Representatives of the Bund's Central Committee repeatedly declared their support for all resolutions passed by the State National Council (KRN) and subsequently by the Legislative Sejm elected in 1947.

In June 1946, before the referendum, Jewish political groups, including the Bund, issued a statement to the Jewish community calling for participation in the referendum and voting '3xYes'. They also actively engaged in the organisation

197 The 'Lublin' period of the Bund ended on 25 February 1945, when the members of the Bund's Central Committee moved to Łódź and Warsaw. According to Szuldenfrei, the so-called 'Warsaw period' of the Bund began at that time. It was also the beginning of the organisational work and the establishment of Bund branches in towns and cities where Bund committees had existed before the war (YIVO Archives, ref. RG 1478 Supplement 2 – Scherer Collection, File 70).

198 AAN, PKWN, ref. I/47, f. 25a, letter to the Chairman of the PKWN, Edward Osóbka-Morawski, dated 24 September 1944, signed by Szudelnfrei, Herszenhorn and Jaszuński.

199 AAN, PKWN, ref. I/47, f. 29.

of meetings preceding the referendum.[200] The agitation for mass participation in the referendum and voting in accordance with the political directive of the 'democratic bloc' was carried out not only during meetings but also in the party press.[201] At the turn of 1946/1947, Bundists participated in yet another campaign preceding the elections to the Legislative Sejm.

Throughout the existence of the Bund after the end of World War II, the party leadership sought to ensure that its political stance was identical to that of the authorities of People's Poland. This is evident in aspects that we would nowadays call 'historical policy', defining the attitude and interpretation of recent events – constantly present in the period of post-war political struggle between the satellite government of the PRL and the legal (PSL) and the illegal armed underground opposition.

Many Bundists who had survived the war in exile in the depths of the USSR had to a certain extent 'erased' this period from their lives, and did not share their harrowing experiences with the public. The topic of the living conditions and experiences of the Bundists in the USSR (and members of other organisations affiliated with the party) did not officially exist, even though the majority of the Bund members who were active in People's Poland had survived the war in the 'inhuman land', experiencing exile, starvation, poverty, and even imprisonment and hard labour.

This attitude could have been related to the belief that, despite this, or perhaps because of it, they survived the war and avoided death in German Nazi extermination camps, as many recounted in conversations years later.[202] Comparing their own tragic experiences in the USSR with the fate of their compatriots under German occupation (often the death of spouses and families in ghettos and camps) was a harrowing juxtaposition of greater and lesser evil, leading more often to silence than to remembrance.

All this meant that the Bund milieu was just as willing to get involved in political life, much like the PPR faction within the Central Committee of Jews in Poland. Most likely, some Bund activists realised that only acceptance of and

200 „Stronnictwa żydowskie wobec referendum ludowego," *Biuletyn Żydowskiej Agencji Prasowej* 1946, no. 65/175, f. 2; „Wiec żydowskich partyj politycznych w Łodzi," ibid., no. 67/177, f. 3.

201 „Di yidishe arbeter un folks-mentshn hobn geshtimt dray mol 'yo'," *Folktsaytung* 1946, no. 5, p. 2.

202 Interview with Dina Schein (née Hiziger-Tajtelbaum) and her husband Mendel Schein, who had been in the USSR since 1939, where they had fled from Nowy Sącz, conducted by M. Rusiniak-Karwat, in May 2008 in Rishon Letsiyon (Israel).

participation in the new order would allow the party to exist in People's Poland. This unequivocal political stance was the reason for the uncompromising attitude toward the 'London government', public criticism of General Władysław Anders and, above all, their critical view of the National Armed Forces (NSZ) due to its ties with the nationalist camp. The political groups behind them were accused – according to PPR propaganda – of anti-Semitic actions in Poland before the war, as well as of complicity in the Holocaust during the war.[203]

At the same time, as a counterpoint to the 'Polish reactionary', the suicide of Shmul Zygielbojm in May 1943 was included among the new Bund heroes. The party press, on the other hand, remained silent about the circumstances surrounding the deaths of two other prominent pre-war Bund leaders – Henryk Erlich and Victor Alter – who lost their lives in unexplained circumstances in NKVD prisons in the USSR.

In the first years after the end of the war, the Bundists also expressed their equal recognition and admiration for both the Warsaw Ghetto Uprising and the Warsaw Uprising, in which some of them took part. On the first anniversary of the outbreak of the Uprising in August 1945, Fiszgrund, one of the participants (as a member of the Jewish Combat Organisation), gave a lecture where he described the origins and course of the uprising, emphasising the heroic participation of civilians, including Jews, in the fighting, while criticising, in line with the narratives of contemporary propaganda, the "irresponsible actions of reactionary Home Army (AK) leaders." He concluded his speech by mentioning many Bundists who "[…] fell in combat, convinced that they were giving their lives for the just cause of Free and Democratic Poland."[204]

From the moment of its revival, the Bund aligned its political and historical discourse with the propaganda of the so-called democratic bloc. It saw the bloc as a guarantee of equal rights in political life for the Jewish community, a national minority. This led to a selective presentation of elements of its own tradition and organisational identity, and thus to a kind of hypocrisy in relation to the tactics adopted.

---

203 Bundists were critical of the Polish Government in London, General Anders and NSZ in the party press, including, e.g. on the occasion of the May Day celebrations, on front-page party proclamations supporting the policy of the 'democratic bloc' (see, e.g.: "Święto klasy robotniczej," *Głos Bundu* 1948, no. 4 (17), p. 2).

204 „Ciekawy odczyt o powstaniu w Warszawie i o udziale Żydów w powstaniu," *Biuletyn Żydowskiej Agencji Prasowej* 1945, no. 58/68, f. 3.

The Bund's representation in the State National Council (KRN) and in municipal councils

For the Bund, having a representative in the KRN, a kind of parliament, and representatives in municipal councils was an important factor demonstrating the party's status. This enabled the party not only to make its presence felt in Polish political life at the time but also to present the point of view of the Jewish community in the national and local government forums, a point of view different from that of the Zionists and concerning the future of Polish Jews after the war.

The first Bund representative in the KRN was Szuldenfrei. During sessions, he always considered the interests of not only the Bund, but also the entire Jewish community in Poland. In his speeches, which as he emphasised – he gave as a socialist on behalf of the Bund, he addressed issues concerning not only Jews but he also commented on Polish topics, including:

> [...] the five-month period of Polish Committee for National Liberation (PKWN) rule [...] has fulfilled the fundamental demands outlined in the July Manifesto. This fact provides the Bund with a basis to fully and unreservedly join the demands of all democratic Polish parties for the establishment of a Provisional Government.[205]

His speeches during KRN sessions were printed in the Bund press and in the press organs of the CKŻP – in *Biuletyn Żydowskiej Agencji Prasowej*[206] and *Dos naye lebn*.[207] In his remarks, he often criticised the views of the Zionist Emil Sommerstein. He drew attention to the perennial problem of anti-Semitism, not only in Poland.[208] He emphasised the concept of living and acting according to *doykayt* (Yiddish for 'local-ness') and the necessity of rebuilding the Jewish *yishuv* in Poland (*nusekh poyln*). He criticised Sommerstein's statements regarding the necessity of calls of Polish Jews to emigrate to Palestine.[209] Szuldenfrei

205 *Sprawozdania stenograficzne z posiedzeń Krajowej Rady Narodowej*, Warsaw 1946 (quoted from: Szaynok, *Bund i komuniści żydowscy w Polsce po 1945 r.*, p. 309).

206 See, e.g. "Przemówienie posła dr. M. Szuldenfreia na VIII sesji Krajowej Rady Narodowej," *Biuletyn Żydowskiej Agencji Prasowej* 1945, no. 53/63, f. 1–2.

207 See, e.g. "Redes fun di yidishe deputatn oyf der VII sesye funem landishn natsyonal rat," *Dos naye lebn* 1945, no. 5, pp. 2–3.

208 "Rede fun dr m. shuldenfrey oyfn LNR," *Folkstsaytung* 1946, no. 1, pp. 7–8.

209 One of the responses to Emil Sommerstein's statement: "I feel obliged to respond to the speech by Deputy Sommerstein. I would not like to give the impression that Deputy Sommerstein's position reflects the opinion of the entire Jewish community. In fact, it reflects the opinion of only a part of the Jewish community. The Jewish worker and the Jewish intellectual worker do not have their eyes fixed on the emigration paths, wherever they may lead – to America or to Palestine. The Jewish

emphasised that the emigration plan had never been the position of the majority of Polish Jews.

He often expressed his support for the Polish authorities, which – in his opinion – were striving to strengthen democracy in Poland.[210] He supported a Polish-Soviet alliance, to prevent the revival of Nazism in Germany. He also highlighted the need for unity in the Polish labour movement, to promote the country's development, industrialisation, modernisation, and prosperity.[211] Additionally, Szuldenfrei also spoke out about Jews connected with 'Anders' order centres' which supported the initiative for emigration to Palestine.

As a representative of the Bund in the State National Council, he stated that before the Kielce pogrom, i.e. before July 1946, representatives of Polish Jewry had warned of the existing danger and manifestations of anti-Semitism among the Polish population. He highlighted:

> This concern was not alleviated in any way by the establishment of the institution of the Commissioner for the Productivisation of Jews. This appointment occurred without consultation with Jewish social organisations and raised doubts within the Jewish community about the necessity and the true goals of this institution. In these current tragic, decisive moments, we stand against the moods of despair among the Jewish population. We call on the Jewish community to resist these moods, to fight against the remnants of fascism and any manifestations of nationalism, and to rebuild their living and social positions here – in this place. But we expect the Polish government and society to fulfil our demands in the fight against all forms of anti-Semitism. We do so with the belief that the working Jewish population will find their liberation from the particular terror of anti-Semitism only in close connection with the general struggle of the working masses of Poland for freedom and democracy.[212]

The anti-emigration (effectively anti-Zionist) declaration of the Bund, which stemmed from the party's traditional programme, integrated it into the post war process of political transformation and structurally into the so-called democratic bloc. Support for the unity of the 'democratic bloc', both during the elections

worker and the Jewish intellectual only see one goal ahead of them – to engage in creative work here in Poland based on solidarity with the Polish working class." („Przemówienie posła dr. M. Szuldenfreia na VIII sesji Krajowej Rady Narodowej," *Biuletyn Żydowskiej Agencji Prasowej* 1945, no. 53/63, f. 2)

210 „Mowa dr. M. Szuldenfreia na KRN z 2 I 1945 r.," ibid., 1945, no. 2/12, f. 4.

211 *** (*Przemówienie posła dr. Michała Szuldenfreia, członka ogólnożydowskiego Związku Robotniczego „Bund" na VII sesji Krajowej Rady Narodowej*), ibid., no. 31/41, f. 3–4.

212 „'Ten głos ma swój sens moralny i sens polityczny'. Przemówienie tow. posła d-ra M. Szuldenfreia w Sejmie, wygłoszone 21.06.1947," *Głos Bundu* 1947, no. 7 (11), p. 2.

to the Legislative Sejm and after it was convened, was expressed by Szuldenfrei in the Assembly on 21 April 1947, stressing the traditional ties between the Bund and the PPS:

> "Our voice in the Sejm is a single voice, but it is not lonely – it is combined with the voices of the entire camp of Polish democracy. Our socialist voice – the voice of the Bund – unites with the voices of the Polish Socialist Party. And in this unity, too, lies its strength."[213]

Szuldenfrei's attitude was met with opposition from the PPR faction at the CKŻP, which disagreed with the idea that the position of the Bund, as expressed by its representative, should be identified with the position of the entire Jewish community in Poland.[214] This could have been a harbinger of rivalry between Jewish communists and Jewish socialists associated with the Bund which would affect the party's future.

In addition to parliamentary representation, the Bund also strived to have its own representation in local government, in the municipal councils in cities and towns where Bund committees existed, as it had before the war. In Tarnów, where Bundists were an influential group in the Jewish community, they were represented by their council member in the Municipal National Council (MRN), Aharon Szporn, and had their own representative in Social Services.[215] In Lower Silesia, where repatriates from Eastern Borderlands and re-emigrants from the USSR were settled, the Bund member, Mayer Trajber, sat on the Wałbrzych MRN,[216] while in Duszniki-Zdrój in 1946, the Bund even had two representatives on the Municipal Council.[217] Additionally, the Bund member Moses Lisiak[218] sat on the Presidium of the MRN in the city of Włocławek. These few representatives of the Bund in the KRN, the Sejm, and local authorities were members of a party that was already small in number compared to its pre-war prominence within the Polish Jewish community.

---

213 Ibid.

214 Szaynok, *Bund i komuniści żydowscy*, p. 310.

215 „Życie społeczne i partyjne. Tarnów," *Głos Bundu* 1946, no. 4, p. 8; „Fun partaj-lebn. Tarnow," *Folkstsaytung* 1946, no. 4, p. 4.

216 P-N., "Fun partey-lebn. A grus fun valbzhikh," *Folkstsaytung* 1946, no. 4, p. 6.

217 „Życie społeczne i partyjne. Duszniki-Zdrój," *Głos Bundu* 1947, no. 1 (5), p. 8.

218 AŻIH, the Bund, files n., Letter from the Presidium of the Municipal National Council of the City of Włocławek to the Włocławek Bund Committee. October 1947.

The Bund's collaboration with the PPS

While on the 'Jewish Street', Bund members often collaborated with the PPR faction within the CKŻP (as opposition to the Zionist group), on the 'Polish Street' they strengthened their ties with the PPS. Bund members ran on the PPS list in elections to the State National Council (KRN) and, in 1947, to the Legislative Sejm.

The Bund's relationship and attitude toward active Polish parties after the war in the PRL, and its cooperation with them, were a continuation of the inter-party alliances established before the war, particularly with the PPS. This was solidified by the Bund's accession to the Labour and Socialist International in 1930.[219] The Bund and the PPS maintained contacts during the German occupation in the General Government – it was one of the important channels for passing information about the Holocaust, also serving to rescue individuals.[220] As the Bund members underlined: "In this half-century, the Bund, fought for freedom and socialism in solidarity with the PPS."[221] Therefore, after the war, the Bund considered itself the party most closely associated with the PPS, as the oldest and largest organisation of the socialist movement in the country in which they both operated in and which, as declared, were guided by the same ideals.[222] It should be mentioned that in the post-war Bund, there was a faction that even supported the continued existence of the party as a separate section within the PPS.

It is worth understanding that, as with the shape and attitude of the Bund in post-war Poland, the revival and continued activity of the PPS in Poland was significantly influenced by a group of members who survived World War II in

219 M. Trębacz, „Bund – Międzynarodówka – PPS. Historia współzależności," *Biuletyn Instytutu Pamięci Narodowej* 2011, no. 7 (128), pp. 29–36.

220 Evidence of close cooperation between these political groups can be seen, for example, in the reprints of press articles in the underground press of the Bund in the Warsaw Ghetto, such as in the youth publication *Yugnt shtime* (e.g. information about the death of Mieczysław Niedziałkowski, with details from: AAN, The Collection of the Underground and Insurgent Press, ref. 356/1-3 – *Yugnt shtime* 1941–1942, a number of issues). Many socialists were also part of the central and local structures of the Government Delegation for Poland and the "Żegota" Council to Aid Jews, which, as its name suggests, provided assistance to the Jewish population, including saving their lives (for more on this, see: T. Prekerowa, *Konspiracyjna Rada Pomocy Żydom w Warszawie 1942–1945*, Warsaw 1982).

221 „Braterstwo broni i celów," *Głos Bundu* 1947, no. 7 (11), p. 2.

222 *Dr. Michał Szuldenfrei. Przewodniczący CK Bundu w Polsce, poseł na Sejm, 50 lat Bundu (1897–1947)*, ibid., nos 8–9 (12–13), p. 1.

the Soviet Union, some of whom joined the activities of the Union of Polish Patriots,[223] which was formed in the Soviet Union. This shared experience brought the Bund closer to the PPS than to the PPR.

In the pre-election campaign and during the election on 19 January 1947, the Bund participated with the PPS in the so-called democratic bloc. This was probably influenced by their ideologies dating back to pre-war times (ideological community) as well as wartime cooperation in Poland, and experiences from the Soviet Union. The Bund had candidates on the national lists for the Sejm, including Michał Szuldenfrei and Grisha Jaszuński. Bund representatives also ran for office in local elections and were on joint electoral lists with the PPS in cities such as Szczecin, Łódź, and the region of Lower Silesia.[224] The Bund's Warsaw Committee, elected a national election committee, consisting of Ignacy Falk, Shaya Szechatow, Shmuel Rychter, Abraham Zilbersztejn, Krum, Fayner, Rutka, Krishe, and Gecl.[225]

Cooperation with the PPS extended to local party committees. Also among the journalists of the PPS press organ, *Robotnik*, was the Bund member Grisha Jaszuński. The Bund's Central Committee, emphasising its ideological alliance with the PPS and its declared collaboration, joined in the fundraising for a monument dedicated to Mieczysław Niedziałkowski,[226] a Polish socialist and activist who was executed by the Germans in June 1940 in Palmiry near Warsaw.[227]

Beyond the political sphere, collaboration was pursued in the cultural realm with organisations affiliated with the PPS. An example of this is the Warsaw Bund Committee, which in October 1946 decided to strengthen its cooperation

---

223 On the PPS, see: J. Holzer (Wacław Pański), *Agonia PPS. Socjaliści polscy w sojuszu z PPR 1944–1948*, Warsaw 1981, pp. 5–6.

224 AŻIH, the Bund, files n., Protocol no. 24 of the meeting of the Warsaw Bund Committee on 9 December 1946; Protocol no. 25 of the meeting of the Warsaw Bund Committee on 18 December 1946.

225 Ibid., Protocol no. 25 of the meeting of the Warsaw Bund Committee on 18 December 1946.

226 „Symboliczne złotówki na pomnik tow. M. Niedziałkowskiego," *Głos Bundu* 1947, nos 5–6 (9–10), p. 12.

227 Mieczysław Niedziałkowski (1893 Vilna – VI 1940 Palmiry near Warsaw), Polish socialist, PPS activist, until 1939 editor-in-chief of the PPS newspaper *Robotnik*. Arrested in December 1939 by the Gestapo, he was shot as part of action AB, which aimed to exterminate the Polish intelligentsia (see, i.a., "Khronik fun di letzte teg. Mietshislav niedzhialkovski," *Yugnt shtime*, November 1940, no. 2, f. 13).

with the PPS on a cultural level.[228] In Częstochowa, weekly discussions and lectures by Bund members were organised in partnership with the PPS.[229] Additionally, the PPS youth group, OM TUR, cooperated with Tsukunft, the Bund's youth organisation, together during May Day parades, inviting each other to meetings and conferences, and summer and winter camps.[230]

A spectacular example of inter-party cooperation in the field was the mutual participation in various types of ceremonies and anniversary commemorations, which were important for propaganda purposes at the time. An example of this is Wrocław, where on the occasion of the 49th anniversary of the Bund, during the ceremony, among the speeches of many representatives of Polish socialists, Stanisław Piaskowski, the Chairman of the Provincial Committee of the PPS and a Voivode, underlines the continuity of good inter-party relations in his speech: spoke warmly of the enduring good relations between the parties.

> In heartfelt words, he recalled [...] the shared struggle, always supported together by Polish workers from the PPS and Jewish workers from the Bund. In conclusion, he stated: "The terrible venom of hatred towards Jews, left as a legacy of Hitler, must be eradicated. This can only be accomplished by workers' parties, and they will achieve this goal through their joint fight against the enemies of progress."[231]

Not only did PPS representatives participate in the ceremonial congresses organised by the Bund, but Bund members were also invited to, for example, the annual PPS congresses in Warsaw. It was indicated that:

> Whenever representatives of the Bund take part in central or regional meetings of the PPS, they do not feel merely like invited guests. Above all, they have a sense of belonging to the same great, noble Polish socialist family. This is the result of a political fact – that the Bund is an integral part of the socialist movement in Poland – and a historical fact 55 years of the PPS operation in Poland, and a little bit less, but still – 50 years of the Bund's life and activity in Poland.[232]

The May Day celebrations provided an opportunity to demonstrate the inter-party alliance between the PPS and the Bund. In most towns and cities where

228 AŻIH, the Bund, files n., Protocol no. 19 from the meeting of the Warsaw Bund Committee 28 October 1946.

229 L. Brener, „Dzieje żydowskiego osiedla po wyzwoleniu," *Głos Bundu* 1946, [no. 1], p. 8

230 I. Luden, „Sotsyalistishe yugnt-republik 50 yor bund," *Yugnt veker* 1947, nos 7–8 (8–9), p. 11, 14; W. Kaczmarek, „Mir marshirn tsuzamen," *Yugnt veker* 1947, no. 1 (2), p. 2; „Zitsung fun der hoyptart fun O.M. „TUR"," ibid., 1947, nos 7–8 (8–9), p. 3.

231 „Życie społeczne i partyjne. Wrocław," *Głos Bundu* 1946, no. 4, p. 8.

232 AŻIH, the Bund, files n., editorial material of *Głos Bundu*.

the Bund branches existed, the party members marched together with the PPS in May Day parades, just as they did in Warsaw, for example.[233]

All this brought the Bund closer to the PPS rather than the PPR. The Bund clearly focused on strengthening the position of the PPS within the 'democratic bloc' and it seems that its activities constitute a delicate element of the Bund's political game at time when the unification of the PPS and the PPR and the practical transition to a 'one-party' system had not yet been decided.

Relations and contact with the PPR

When discussing the contacts between the Bund and the PPR, I also consider the PPR faction in the CKŻP. In their reports on the party's activities and their accounts of various events, the Bundists often referred to the PPR, even when they referred to the faction, treating them – quite rightly – as a single political entity. While the cooperation with the PPS was harmonious and multifaceted, the Bund's contacts with the PPR were full of tensions both on the political 'Polish' and 'Jewish street'.

The main place of controversy and even confrontations between the Bund and the PPR faction were the meetings of the Presidium of the CKŻP, during which the Bundists criticised the activities of the PPR faction. Bund representatives made sure that the PPR representatives did not overreach their importance and did not diminish the contributions of other organisations, such as during fundraising for the electoral fund in 1947, when the PPR faction attempted to take credit for their significant achievements.[234] This also applied to other issues related to the representation of the Jewish community in Poland towards the authorities of the PRL.

The Bund's relationship with the PPR faction caused a lot of controversy on the 'Jewish Street'. Relations were strained, and it was particularly objectionable when it came to the surveillance and censorship of not only publications and statements of Polish Bundists members but also those of Bund representatives who had emigrated from Poland after the war and settled in Western countries. Members of the PPR faction at the CKŻP wrote critical reviews of articles from *Unzer Tsayt*[235] about its attitude towards the political situation in Poland. Bund

233 Ibid., Protocol no. 32 from the meeting of the Warsaw Bund Committee, 23 April 1947.

234 AŻIH, Archives of the Presidium and Secretariat, ref. 303/I/6, Protocol no. 18, from 6 February 1947, f. 101.

235 *Unzer Tsait* (Unzer tsayt)–published monthly in the years 1941–2005 in New York by the representation of the Polish Bund in America. From 1947 – a press organ

members living in the United States were considered by the PPR faction to be the main advocates of the 'anti-Soviet hype' during and after World War II, in which Jewish socialists outside of Poland were reportedly outpacing the American press in their criticism. From articles about the situation in the PRL and its prospects, PPR members selected sentences in which the Western European Bund representatives criticised the new regime, the Polish authorities, and the USSR. One of the authors of a report published by the PPR faction also noted the discrepancy between the Polish Bund and the American Bund on the recognition of the Polish Government-in-Exile, which as he stated with surprise, did not hinder contacts and a visit by Bund representatives from Poland to New York in 1946. Among other things, he wrote, almost as a political denunciation:

> In the early 1946 (20 February – 20 March), a delegation from the Bund's Central Committee in Poland visited New York. The delegation included: Dr. Szuldenfrei, Fiszgrunt,[236] and Jaszuński. Dozens of informational rallies about Poland were held, attended by members of the delegation, which means that the American Bund's representation could not have been unaware of the official political stance of the Polish Bund. And yet, the "American representation" maintained an antagonistic attitude towards the democratic government in Poland and the People's Democracy. Judging by what was published in *Unzer Cajt*,[237] Dr Szuldenfrei and other delegates did not speak about fundamental issues of the People's Democracy and were warmly received by the most reactionary and fierce opponents of the Polish People's Republic among the 'labour leaders', such as [David – author's note] Dubiński, [Adolf – author's note] Held, Fajnberg. It was reported that Szuldenfrei "gave a heartfelt speech about the role of *Unzer Cajt*." Similarly, Fiszgrund mentioned that the receipt of a microfilm of an issue of *Unzer Cajt* by the 'underground Central Committee' was one of the most comforting moments." Jaszuński also emphasised the "connection between the pre-war *Folkstsaytung*, the illegal press in Hitler's Poland, *Unzer Cajt* [!] and the renewed *Folkstsaytung* (from *Unzer Tsayt* nos 3–4, 1946).
>
> I believe he is right, but how can Polish Bundists, who took a stance of solidarity with the democratic government in Poland and opposed the 'London' orientation, feel such a sincere connection with *Unzer Cajt* which, as we can see, aligns itself with the 'London' orientation and opposes the People's Democracy – that shall remain their secret.[238]

---

of the Bund "World" Coordinating Committee. Transliteration of the title in the book taken from the monthly's title page.

236 Should read: Fiszgrund.

237 Proper Polish transliteration of the monthly was used in the text (Eng. *Unzer tsayt*).

238 Quoted from: AŻIH, the Bund, files n., A. Len (Gordin), *Reprezentacja Bundu polskiego w USA* (b.d.).

The Bund group in America was considered by the representatives of the PPR faction in the CKŻP as a tool in the hands of the milieu affiliated with *Forverts*.[239] Furthermore, they believed that the Bund in Poland was unable to expand its activities without financial support from *Forverts*-related sources. From such an opinion, it was only a step away from considering the Bund as a 'hostile agent'.

In 1947, representatives of the PPR faction in the CKŻP were also interested in the Coordinating Committee in America and its executive members, who had been associated with Poland and the 'Polish' Bund before 1939 and had emigrated before or during the war.[240] A report characterised these individuals (Emanuel Nowogródzki, Chaim Wasser,[241] Pinkus Minc (pseudonym Aleksander), Fajwel Szrager, Lucjan Blit), highlighting their hostile attitude towards the political situation in Poland at the time.[242]

The materials prepared by the PPR faction in the CKŻP, were intended to show that the domestic Bund only apparently sided with the 'democratic bloc', as it maintained cordial but politically incorrect contacts with the European and American Bund. The purpose of these materials was to discredit the leaders of the local Bund, and as such they could become part of the political struggles and a reason for the liquidation of the party.

The situation on the ground was even more diverse. Cooperation with different political groups was an individual matter in each town and city, depending on personal connections. In many towns and cities, the Bund maintained friendly

239 *The Forward*, commonly known as *The Jewish Daily Forward* (also known as: *Forverts* and *The Yiddish Forward*), is a Jewish newspaper published in the USA since 1897. Originally published as a daily newspaper in Yiddish, it was very popular among immigrants from Central and Eastern Europe. Currently, the weekly is published in Yiddish and in English.

240 On the Bund's Coordinating Committee, see: chapter VI: "Contacts with the 'Western' Bund".

241 Chaim Meir Wasser (1890 – 9 September 1953 New York) was one of the leaders of the left-wing faction of the Bund during the Second Polish Republic, he was also a member of the party's Central Committee. After the outbreak of World War II, he travelled via Vilna, USSR and Japan to New York with a visa obtained from the Japanese Vice-Consul Chiune Sugihara. There, he continued his work in the milieu of Polish Bundists. In the autumn of 1946, he travelled to Poland to help rebuild the structures of the Bund (information from: "Chaim Wasser," *Unzer Tsayt* 1953, no. 10, pp. 1, 4–5).

242 AŻIH, the Bund, files n., A. Len, *Wszechświatowa konferencja Bundu* (b.d.).

relations with both local PPS and PPR branches.[243] In Jelenia Góra, the Municipal Committee of the Bund cooperated with the PPS and PPR, as highlighted in their reports. This resulted in financial support for a winter camp which was organised by the Tsukunft youth organisation.[244] In Kraków, guests from the PPR attended the opening of a new Bund party premises in 1946, expressing their appreciation for the Bund's activities. A letter from Dr Bolesław Drobner, a member of parliament from the Provincial Committee of the PPS, was also read out, which was intended to underline the parallel nature of contacts with both parties.[245] In Białystok in 1946, during the celebrations of the 49th anniversary of the Bund, the celebrations were attended, as emphasised, by representatives of "both fraternal political parties, the PPS and PPR, as well as trade unions."[246]

This political ritual, which maintained the unity of all parties in the 'democratic bloc', did not conflict with the activities of the PPR's, which aimed to discredit the Bund – first within the framework of the CKŻP and, in the future, on a national level. The criticism of the Bund could be used by the Communists against individual activists as well as against the party as a whole.

243 On the Bund's correct relations with the PPR – speech delivered by Fiszgrund during PPR's first convention in 1945 (information from: „Przedstawienie żydowskich robotników na pierwszym zjeździe PPR," *Biuletyn Żydowskiej Agencji Prasowej* 1945, no. 111/121, f. 3).

244 „Życie społeczne i partyjne. Jelenia Góra," *Głos Bundu* 1947, no. 1 (5), p. 8.

245 „Życie społeczne i partyjne. Kraków," *Głos Bundu* 1947, no. 1 (5), p. 8.

246 „Życie społeczne i partyjne, Białystok," *Głos Bundu* 1946, no. 4, p. 8.

Chapter Four
Forms of the Party's Operation

Local committees

It is documented that there were around 44 municipal committees of the Bund in the PRL between 1944 and 1949. In the available archival documentation, there is no precise information about which of them were registered. In terms of professional structure, the Bund's ranks were predominantly made up of workers, most of whom carried with them the burden of wartime experiences in the USSR. It was these individuals, returning from deportations and labour camps, in the new post-war borders of Poland, and not in their hometowns in the Kresy region (Eastern Borderlands), who rebuilt not only party life but, above all, their own lives. It is difficult to reconstruct the full list of committees. The Central Committee of the Bund also had problems with this. It is also uncertain how many committees existed simultaneously, as these numbers fluctuated due to members relocating and emigrating, which, in turn, also led to the dissolution of committees.

The largest number of committees existed in Lower Silesia (the headquarters were initially in Dzierżoniów and, from 1946, in Wrocław). All of them were subordinate to the Central Committee, which was based in Łódź from 1945 to 1946 and later in Warsaw. There were also provincial committees which operated in places such as Warsaw or Wrocław. Municipal committees were in operation, as well. Not all of these committees had their own premises, but not all needed them, due to their small size and less frequent activities. Committees with more developed structures employed members in party kitchens as cooks and kitchen aides, as officials, chauffeurs, guards, treasurers, and workers in the Bund cooperatives.[247]

The committee structures varied and were mostly very different from the pre-war ones. This was mainly due to the number of members in the local organisation and the financial resources available to the committee. In the post-war period, it sometimes took more effort to establish a small committee than a large one, which was also linked to the number and activity of Jews in the area. In their reports on the activities of the organisation, the representatives of the

247 See.: AŻIH, the Bund, files n., correspondence between the Bund committees in the years 1945–1948.

various committees, members of the Bund, often emphasised that despite the difficult situation of the Jews, they had not lost their spirit and were striving to develop the organisation.[248]

The fluctuation in membership was the reason for the stagnation and poor activity of the committees. On the one hand, repatriates from the USSR were arriving; on the other, existing members were leaving in search of family, work or choosing to emigrate. One example is the Piotrków Committee, whose members dispersed as soon as they resumed their activities in 1945, taking the Committee's seals, membership lists and other items with them. In October 1945, the branch was re-established, building everything from scratch.[249]

One of the main activities of the committees was to care for the youngest – children and young people who had survived the Holocaust. At the beginning of the 1947/1948 school year, the Bund organisation in Szczecin opened the Ruta Berman Children's Home, named after the teacher and Bund activist who had perished during the German occupation. The Home accommodated thirty children.[250] Other orphanages (known as 'Frebel schools') operated in Łódź and Bielawa, each accommodating sixty children, in Wrocław, for thirty children (a total of four 'Frebel schools' with 200 children). Semi-boarding schools were also established in Szczecin and Legnica, for sixty children.[251]

One of the most active and largest committees was the Łódź Bund Committee.[252] It had the most developed party structure, similar to the pre-1939 era. This was because Łódź had the largest concentration of the Jewish population after the war and thus, the strongest Bund organisation.[253] At least until early 1947, the headquarters of most Jewish institutions operating in People's Poland after

248 „Z życia partii", *Głos Bundu* 1946, nos 2–3, p. 10.

249 AŻIH, the Bund, files n., Report from the Piotrków Bund Committee from 15 February 1946.

250 Ibid., letter from 4 October 1947 from Ignacy Falk to Leybtschke Berman – widower of Ruta Berman.

251 AŻIH, American Jewish Joint Distribution Committee. 1945–1949, ref. 350/2372, quantity in June 1948.

252 According to the data presented by Andrzej Rykała („Łódź na mapie skupisk żydowskich Polski (po 1945 r.)," in: *Społeczność żydowska i niemiecka w Łodzi po 1945 roku*, eds. A. Lech, K. Radziszewska, A. Rykała, Łódź 2010, p. 298), the committee had not been formally registered.

253 In terms of numbers, the Jewish community in Łódź in the years 1945–1950 constituted only a dozen or so percent of the pre-war community of over 200,000 and after the war, a portion of this population consisted of new settlers (information from: L. Olejnik, "Społeczność żydowska. Struktury życia społeczno-politycznego

1944 were located there.[254] At the same time, in the early days of the Bund's, the editorial offices of newspapers published by the party and its youth organisation, Tsukunft, were also based in Łódź.[255]

The Łódź Bund Committee, which was elected in the spring of 1946, consisted of: Gershon Fogel (chairman), Bono Winer,[256] Shmuel Hurwicz[257] (secretary), Leyb Pudłowski, Marek Edelman,[258] Pinkus Wołkowicz, Avreml Kahan,[259] Hersh Fajgenbaum, and Yudl Kersz.[260]

In the spring of 1946, the Łódź Bund Committee was one of the largest, with 250 members. The structure resembled the Bund organisation from before 1939. The party opened and ran the Israel Lichtenstein Children's Home (for Jewish working-class children aged 4–7),[261] the Morgnshtern[262] sports club, an orchestra, a communal kitchen and a drama club. The organisation included the Repatriation Council, the Kultur Lige (Yid. for 'Culture League', organiser of literary and artistic events), a cultural commission (which at the beginning of 1946, consisted of around forty Bundists), and a speakers' circle set up to train activists and deepen Marxist knowledge (twenty-five members). The Committee also ran labour cooperatives.[263]

łódzkich Żydów w latach 1945–1950," in: *Społeczność żydowska i niemiecka w Łodzi po 1945 roku*, eds. A. Lech, K. Radziszewska, A. Rykała, Łódź 2010, pp. 139–140).

254 L. Olejnik, „Prasa żydowska w Łodzi w latach 1945–1949," *Acta Judaica Lodziensia* 2011, no. 1, pp. 99–111.

255 Throughout the post-war period, the headquarters of the Tsukunft Central Committee were located in Łódź.

256 See: Biography.

257 See: Biography.

258 See: Biography.

259 See: Biography.

260 „Fun partay-lebn. In proletarishn lodzh," *Folkstsaytung* 1946, no. 4, p. 6; „Życie społeczne i partyjne. Łódź," *Głos Bundu* 1946, no. 4, p. 8. Among the leading activists in the Łódź Bund Committee we can also mention Moses Lederman.

261 Israel Lichtensztejn Children's Home was established on the initiative of the Łódź Bund and Kultur Lige. In the autumn of 1946, fifty children were staying in the Home (information from: "Z życia partii. Łódź," *Głos Bundu*, October 1946, nos 2–3, p. 10).

262 Morgnshtern (Yid.: for 'morning star') – sport organisation. For more information on Morgnshtern, see: R. Gechtman, "Socialist Mass Politics Through Sport: The Bund's Morgnshtern in Poland, 1926–1939," *Journal of Sport History* 1999, no. 2, vol. XXVI, pp. 326–352.

263 „Z życia partii. Łódź," *Głos Bundu* 1946, nos 2–3, p. 10; „Życie społeczne i partyjne. Łódź," *Głos Bundu* 1947, no. 1 (5), p. 8.

Meetings for members and supporters were held regularly at the branch headquarters on Jaracza Street, mainly on Fridays. During these meetings, lectures were given not only by people associated with the Bund but also by invited guests from the PPS, who sympathised with the Bund. The meetings were conducted in accordance with Bundist ideology, addressing political topics and promoting the Yiddish language and Jewish culture. Some of the meetings were, therefore, academies dedicated to Jewish writers who were considered the fathers of Yiddish literature, such as Mendele Moykher Sforim (whose life was presented to an audience by Bono Winer and Yudl Kersz).[264] During the meetings, lectures were also given on life in other countries, for example, on 15 December 1945, David Klin gave a lecture titled "Paris – London" during which he presented his reflections after a trip to France and the United Kingdom.

The Łódź Committee organised campaigns to combat anti-Semitism. The film *Mir kumen on* (Yid. for: *We Are Coming*; Polish title: *The Way of Youth*), about the activities of the Medem Sanatorium for Jewish Children in Miedzeszyn near Warsaw, which had been banned in Poland before the war, was shown at film screenings. New Year's Eve balls were also held at the Committee's premises. The anniversaries of the founding of the Bund and the Warsaw Ghetto Uprising were also commemorated. The local activist and predecessor of the Łódź Bund, Israel Lichtenstein,[265] was not forgotten, and on the anniversary of his death, Jewish socialists gathered at his grave in the Jewish cemetery in Łódź to honour his memory.[266]

The Council for Repatriates of the Łódź Bund fought for improvement in the living conditions of people arriving in Poland from the USSR. Gershon Fogel

---

264 „Z życia partii. Łódź," *Głos Bundu* 1946, nos 2–3, p. 10; „Życie społeczne i partyjne. Łódź," *Głos Bundu* 1947, no. 1 (5), p. 8.

265 Israel Mordechai Lichtenstein „Gutman" (1883–1933 New York), teacher and educationalist. From 1910 he lived in Łódź, where he was a member of the Jewish council. He was also an activist of TSYSHO (Tsentrale yidishe shul-organizatsye, Central Jewish School Organisation) and a member of the Bund's Central Committee. He combined his political activities with the fight for the development of the Yiddish language and promoted education in this language (information from: M. Trębacz, "Bund – Międzynarodówka – PPS. Historia współzależności", *Biuletyn Instytutu Pamięci Narodowej* 2011, no. 7 (128), p. 35).

266 Bono [Winer], „Fun partay-lebn. Lodzh," *Folkstsaytung* 1946, no. 1, p. 7; "Di arbet in der lodzher bundisher organizatsye," *Folkstsaytung* 1946, nos 2–3, p. 8; „Fun partay-lebn. In proletarishn lodzh," *Folkstsaytung* 1946, no. 4, p. 6; "*** Łódź (ŻAP)," *Biuletyn Żydowskiej Agencji Prasowej* 1945, nos 33/43, f. 3; *Akademia Bundu w Łodzi*, ibid., 1945, nos 85/95, f. 3.

and Bono Winer tried to obtain secure housing for them, frequently intervening on their behalf several times with the mayor of Łódź in the summer of 1946.[267]

The Bund Committee rented a building from the Provincial Jewish Committee in Łódź, it was located in the Jewish theatre. Among other things, the Bund carpentry cooperative was located there. Inside, party slogans and a portrait of Israel Lichtenstein were hung on the walls. At the turn of 1946 and early 1947, a dispute arose between the Bund Committee and the Provincial Jewish Committee over the premises because the Bundists refused to relinquish the rented premises where Jewish organisations affiliated with the CKŻP planned to reopen the theatre. They argued that it would be too expensive to adapt another building for the carpentry cooperative.[268] This state of affairs persisted until the Bund was dissolved in January 1949, along with the Łódź Committee in January 1949.

There were few Bund members in Lower Silesia. Committees were established in towns where pre-war Bundists had settled.[269] The first committee in this part of Poland was formed as early as October 1945 in then Rychbach (now Dzierżoniów). This was also where the main Bund centre was initially located, as well as the Provincial Committee until 1946. The second major centre was located in Wrocław. According to the 1946 census, there were 118 Bund activists in Dzierżoniów (205 individuals, including their family members). The chairman was Jakub Belek, and the secretary was David Tendlarz. The Bundists in Dzierżoniów focused primarily on rebuilding the Jewish community and promoting culture. In order to provide employment for the Bundists (and others outside the party), cooperatives were set up under the Dzierżoniów Committee, such as 'Dziewiarz', as well as a kitchen, a hostel, and a party library.[270]

There were two Bund committees in Wrocław: the Provincial Committee, which was chaired by Israel Perelsztejn from 1946, and the Municipal Committee,

267 "Vegn recht far repatriantn tsu bakumen a voynung. Intervents fun lodzher komitet fun 'bund' baym lodzher shtot-prezident," *Folkstsaytung* 1946, no. 6, p. 1.

268 AŻIH, Archives of the Presidium and Secretariat, ref. 303/I/6, Protocol no. 1, from 3 October 1947, f. 3.

269 For more on the Bund committees in Lower Silesia, see: A. Grużlewska, „Ogólnożydowski Związek Robotniczy 'Bund' na terenie powiatu dzierżoniowskiego," *Bibliotheca Bielaviana 2015*, 2016, online https://www.academia.edu/108869609/Og%C3%B3lno%C5%BCydowski_Zwi%C4%85zek_Robotniczy_Bund_na_terenie_powiatu_dzier%C5%BConiowskiego [access: 31 January 2023].

270 AŻIH, the Bund, files n., correspondence between the Bund Committee in Rychbach and the Central Committee in Warsaw from the years 1946–1948.

which was chaired by Abram Goldberg.[271] Between 1945 and 1948, 220 people declared their intention to join the party through the Municipal Committee.[272] At the end of 1947, when the Wrocław Municipal Committee was at its peak, there were 118 members.[273] One of the challenges faced by the Provincial Committee after July 1946, following the Kielce pogrom, was addressing the fear among the Bundists, including their desire to emigrate. In many cases, attempts were even made to prevent party members from legally leaving the country. One of the measures to prevent people from leaving was to provide childcare. In October 1946, the Wrocław Bundists opened the Vladimir Medem Children's Home, which accommodated the children of Jewish workers, including tailors, shoemakers, and bakers. It was decided to teach them Yiddish, through play, for example, by preparing and staging performances in this language with them during organised events. The organisers stressed: "[…] we are currently the only children's home in Wrocław where we attract children to their mother tongue."[274] This committee worked together with the PPS on the 'Polish Street' and actively participated in ceremonies and commemorations organised by Polish socialists.

The Bund organisation was founded in Legnica at the end of May 1946. Initially, it consisted of 8 members. After a wave of repatriation in the summer of 1946, its membership grew to 105 people. Throughout the entire existence of the Legnica Committee, 160 people submitted membership declarations.[275] Aron Besser[276] was the chairman, and Mendel Ceder[277] the secretary. From the beginning, the Committee underlined the importance of political campaigns to recruit new

271 AIPN, Wr 032/403, vol. 1, pp. 9–10.

272 AAN, the Bund, ref. 30/IV/13, vol. III, Membership declarations, Wrocław.

273 AŻIH, the Bund, files n., Register of party members in Wrocław from 27 December 1947.

274 Ibid., Report on the activities of the Wrocław Bund Committee for the period 1 January – 30 June 1947.

275 AAN, the Bund, ref. 30/IV/13, vol. I: Membership declarations (Legnica); AŻIH, the Bund, files n., Registers of the Bund members: 1 June 1946 – 33; 14 October 1946 – 34; 10 December 1946 – 117.

276 Aron Besser (b. 1913 Kłobuck – ?) in 1939, he lived in Kalisz. He survived the war in the USSR, and then returned to Legnica where he was active in the local Bund. In the files of survivors, he stated the place of employment as the Bund Committee in Legnica (information from: AŻIH, ref. 303/V/425/B 6815).

277 Icchak Mendel Ceder (b. 1912 Warsaw – ?) before the war he lived in Warsaw, where he worked in a soap shop. During the war he was in the USSR. After the war he returned to Legnica, where he served as a secretary of the Bund Committee (information from: AŻIH, ref. 303/V/425/C bn 100, Ceder Icchak).

party members among Jewish workers in Legnica's factories. Two cooperatives (tailoring and shoemaking) were organised to increase the productivity of the Jewish population, and the creation of a workers' library was planned.[278] In the press, the Bundists from Legnica emphasised their own achievements:

> Our organisation engages in many political and cultural activities. The library and workers' theatre are continuously developing. There are three cooperatives which operate both rationally and purposefully.[279]

Wałbrzych was the third-largest city in Lower Silesia in terms of Jewish populations.[280] The Bund also found fertile ground for development there. The founders of the Bundist group were Mayer Trajber and Yosl Frid.[281] Recruitment campaigns at the end of 1946 brought 25 new members into the Bund in Wałbrzych.[282] In total, between 1945 and 1947, 189 membership declarations were submitted, most of them during the first half of 1946.[283] Party members reported in the press:

> The Committee systematically organises meetings, lectures, and political discussions. The 'Tsukunft' youth organisation is also very active. There are numerous Bundist party units among Jewish miners employed in the coal industry. Bundist press publications – *Głos Bundu*, *Folkstsaytung*, and *Yugnt-veker*[284] – are widely distributed in large quantities.[285]

278 „Z życia partii. Dolny Śląsk. Lignica" [original spelling], *Głos Bundu* 1946, nos 2–3, p. 10.

279 „Życie społeczne i organizacyjne. Nasi korespondenci piszą: Lignica" [original spelling], *Głos Bundu* 1947, no. 4 (8), p. 8.

280 P. Wieczorek, „Żydzi wałbrzyscy po II wojnie światowej," *Kwartalnik Historii Żydów* 2004, no. 3, p. 380.

281 P-N., "Fun partay-lebn. A grus fun valbzhikh," *Folkstsaytung* 1946, no. 4, p. 6. More information on the Wałbrzych Bund Committee: P. Wieczorek, *Żydzi w Wałbrzychu i powiecie wałbrzyskim 1945–1968*, Wrocław–Warsaw 2017, *passim*.

282 „Życie społeczne i partyjne. Wałbrzych," *Głos Bundu* 1947, no. 1 (5), p. 8.

283 AŻIH, the Bund, files n., Membership declarations – Wałbrzych.

284 *Yugnt veker* – magazine published by Tsukunft from October 1946 until April 1948. For more information on the press published by Tsukunft, see: M. Rusiniak-Karwat, "*Tsukunft* publishing operations in Poland after 1945," *pl.it / rassegna italiana di argomenti polacchi* 2022, no. 13, p. 52–64.

285 "Życie społeczne i organizacyjne. Nasi korespondenci piszą: Wałbrzych," *Głos Bundu* 1947, no. 4 (8), p. 8.

In Szczecin, where the Bund did not exist before 1939, one of the most active and well-organised Bund Committees was established after the war, to which the smaller committee in Golęcino, a city district, was subordinate. In total, they had 157 members in the second half of 1946 (including 36 people in Golęcino). Abram Sobol was the chairman, with Israel Fruchtman as the vice-chairman. The Committee had good premises in the city centre (initially at 29 Lutniana Street, and from December 1947 at 4 Krasińskiego Street), which was important for organising party meetings.[286]

> In the city centre, there is a three-story party building that houses the following institutions: the Workers' Tavern which provides nutritious and inexpensive meals for the members and supporters, two cooperatives: a tailors' and shoemakers' ones, a party club with a reading room and a large meeting hall, as well as a boarding house for the youth.
>
> Also in Gołęcin [!], the organisation has a party office, the Workers' Kitchen, and a shoemakers' workshop.[287] It was emphasized that – regardless of the atmosphere of panic and fear fostered by the Zionists – we shall continue our efforts for the benefit of Jewish workers.[288]

The Committee in Tarnów was a committee with a long tradition and continued to operate during the German occupation (there was an Underground Bund Committee in the Tarnów Ghetto). It was re-established in May 1946, with Usher Bleiweiss[289] as chairman. At the time, the Tarnów Bund organisation had 85 members out of a total of around 500 Jews in the city. In 1948, it had only 42 members, which accounted for 5% of the party members in Poland. Throughout the entire post-war existence of the Bund, nearly 200 membership cards were issued to the Tarnów Committee. Having their own premises from the very beginning made their work much easier. The Bund maintained a strong influence

---

286 AIPN Szczecin, ref. IPN Sz, ref. 009/622, vol. II, f. 15; AŻIH, the Bund, files n., correspondence from the years 1946 1948 between Szczecin Committee and other Bund committees; M. Semczyszyn, "Szczecin – 'najmłodsze żydowskie osiedle w powojennej Polsce'. Miejsca związane z działalnością Żydów w mieście w latach 1945–1950," in: *Szczecin i jego miejsca. Trzecia Konferencja Edukacyjna, 10 XII 2010 r.*, ed. K. Rembacka, Szczecin 2010, p. 259.

287 „Z życia partyjnego. Szczecin," *Głos Bundu* 1946, no. 1, p. 8.

288 „Z życia partii. Szczecin," *Głos Bundu* 1946, nos 2–3, p. 10.

289 Usher Bleiweiss (1907, Tarnów – 1985), member of the Bund. He spent the Second World War in the Tarnów Ghetto, Szebnia, and then in hiding. He represented the so-called right-wing direction of the Bund (information from: AŻIH, CKŻP, WEiS, ref. 303/V/425/B b 9559, Bleiweis Uszer; AIPN Kraków, ref. IPN Kr, 075/214, vol. III, f. 29).

in the city throughout its existence. The focus was on cultural and educational work, and meetings and gatherings were organised on ideological and anniversary topics. They ran a library containing over 800 volumes and a reading room for periodicals. The Committee also helped find housing for six Jewish families.[290]

Another major committee operating from 1945 was the Municipal Committee in Częstochowa, established and led by Częstochowa Bund members who during World War II were active in the Underground Bund Committee, initially in the Częstochowa Ghetto and, after the arrest of its members, in the Hasag Labour camp (also in Częstochowa). The members included Liber Brener and Motl Kusznir,[291] the chairman – Moses Lederman,[292] and the secretary – Józef (Yosl) Krauze (Kroyze). In Częstochowa, the number of members did not exceed thirty to thirty-six people. The Committee's headquarters, which also housed the party library, was also the venue for Saturday meetings and cultural events co-organised with the PPR faction.[293]

One of the first committees to be established in Poland was the relatively small Committee in Białystok (13 members on 5 November 1945, 20 members on 10 June 1946, and up to 29 in 1947). Its leadership included Pesach Bursztejn[294] as chairman, Chana Robinzon as secretary, and Abraham Borkowicz. It should be

290 A.B., „Fun partay lebn. Tarnow," *Folkstsaytung* 1946, no. 1, p. 7; J. Kwiek, „Dzieje ludności żydowskiej w Tarnowie po II wojnie światowej," *Kwartalnik Historii Żydów* 2005, no. 3, pp. 362–363. On the subject of the Jewish community in Tarnów after the war, as well as the activities of the Bund, see e.g.: A. Wierzcholska, *Nur Erinnerungen und Steine sind geblieben. Leben und Sterben einer polnisch-jüdischen Stadt: Tarnów 1918–1945*, Paderborn 2022, pp. 577–612 (Polish edition: *Wspomnienia i kamienie. Życie i śmierć polsko-żydowskiego miasta. Tarnów 1918–1956*, tr. J. Górny, Kraków–Budapest–Syrakuzy 2023, pp. 585–610).

291 See: Biography.

292 See: Biography.

293 AŻIH, the Bund, files n., Correspondence between Częstochowa Committee and the Central Committee of the Bund from the years 1945–1948, among others regarding books sent to the Bund Library in Częstochowa (last letter from 19 June 1948); Programme of the event on 29 September 1945 at the Kameralny Theatre in Częstochowa opened with a lecture delivered by Szuldenfrei; Membership declaration of the Częstochowa Committee; M. Frajdeles, "Fun partay lebn. Tschestochov," *Folkstsaytung* 1946, no. 1, p. 7; R. Federman, "Der 'Bund' in Tschenstochov in di yorn nokh der tsveyter velt-milkhome," in: *Tschenstochov. Nayer tsugob materyal tsum bukh 'Tschenstochover yidn' / Tschenstochov. A New Supplement to the Book 'Tschenstochover yidn'*, ed. S. D. Singer, New York 1958, pp. 86–96.

294 Pesach Bursztejn (1909–?) in 1939 he lived in Białystok, during the war imprisoned at KL Auschwitz. After the war, he returned to Białystok, where he helped rebuild

noted that in their documentation, they referred to themselves as an organisation or a group, never as a party. The first meeting of the Committee took place on 15 July 1945. As in other committees, the members primarily focused on helping children, conducting cultural work, and developing Jewish schools with Yiddish-language lessons. They organised weekly meetings in their own premises to discuss political and local issues, as well as anniversary events to celebrate the founding of the Bund.[295]

In Duszniki-Zdrój, there was a very small Bund community of twelve people in 1946. Its activities were related to the operation of the 'Eldorado' Holiday Home, which had a library with books in Yiddish.[296]

Although the Bund began its activities in Lublin after the war, a small committee (of about 17 people) was formed there in early 1948, led by Aleksander Goldszmid, after the central office was moved to Łódź in mid-1945, and then to Warsaw. In 1946, on the first anniversary of Leon Feiner's death, the Committee organised a memorial service together with the Provincial Jewish Committee in his honour.[297]

From early 1946 until 1948, a committee of twenty to twenty-five members was active in Piotrków Trybunalski. The chairman was Aron Horowicz, and the secretary was Różka (Ruchla) Lasman-Goldblum.[298] The main objective of the committee was to prepare housing for repatriates from the USSR and to organise means of subsistence for them.[299]

The Municipal Committee in Świdnica existed from the summer of 1946 until the spring of 1948. It had around fifty members and was headed by Shmul Top. Small committees of a few to over a dozen members existed in Jar (the 'Chrobry' sanatorium), where less than five people belonged to the Bund, in Jelenia Góra, Kalisz (probably existing only in 1946), in Kamienna Góra and in Lubawka, with

---

the Jewish community, including the Jewish Committee and the Bund (see. AŻIH, WEiS, ref. 303/V/425/B 18264, Bursztejn Pejsach).

295 AŻIH, the Bund, files n., Report from the celebration of the 49th anniversary of establishing the Bund in Białystok on 18 October 1946; Report on the activities of the group in Białystok in the period 15 July 1945 – 11 June 1946.

296 AŻIH, the Bund, files n., correspondence from the 'Eldorado' Holiday Home from the period from 1946 to 1948 [mainly to the Bund Central Committee in Warsaw – author's note].

297 "Fun partay-lebn. Lublin," *Folkstsaytung* 1946, no. 4, p. 6.

298 AŻIH, the Bund, files n., reports on the activities of the Committee in Piotrków Trybunalski in the years 1946–1948.

299 A. [?], "Pietrkov," *Folkstsaytung* 1946, no. 1, p. 8.

a total of twenty-three people. In all likelihood, small committees existed from January 1946 to May 1948 in Kłodzko (9–15 people)[300] and Ludwików (20–25 people). We know little about the activities of the committees in Międzyrzec Podlaski, Gdańsk, Zabrze, or Nidzica, except that they existed. At the turn of 1946/47, the committee in Niemcza in Lower Silesia had around ten members, as did the committees in Złotoryja, Ząbkowice and in Zagórze, there were between ten and sixteen members.

In Nowa Ruda, the committee existed at least from the summer of 1946, when the repatriates from the USSR arrived, until mid-1948. Beniamin Wajn was the secretary, and Calel Kruk was the chairman. The committee had between fifteen to twenty-three members.[301] In 1948, the Bielawa Committee had a branch of the workers' tavern on what was then Bieruta Street (today Piastowska), which provided food for the Bund members and their families. Small organisations also operated in Bielsko, Boża Góra (Lower Silesia), Bystrzyca and Bytom, subordinate to the Provincial Committee in Katowice (which also supervised committees in Sosnowiec, Bielsko, and Gliwice)[302] and in Przemyśl.[303]

Little information is available about the activities of the Kraków Committee, where the Bund's traditions date back to the early 20th century. A Bund group, consisting of ten people, also existed in Krośniewice in 1946, though little is known about its activities. Leon Radzicki was the secretary. The preserved correspondence mainly concerns issues related to the distribution of *Folkstsaytung* and the assistance provided by the Central Committee.[304] In Ziębice, "the Party devoted a lot of energy to combating panic among the Jewish population."[305] The committee most likely existed from 1946 to 1948 and had its own canteen and a

300 AŻIH, Ibid., correspondence sent by the committee in Kłodzko in the period between 25 January 1946 and 28 May 1948.

301 Ibid., List of members of the Bund in Nowa Ruda from 8 June 1946 – 15 people; List of members of the Bund from 20 December 1946 – 23 people.

302 See, i.a. AŻIH, the Bund, files n., correspondence between local Bund committees and the Bund Central Committee in Warsaw.

303 Ibid., Invitation to a Jubilee, 9 November 1947.

304 Ibid., file on the Bund Committee in Krośniewice, List of members from 22 November 1946: (10) Fasenfest Mordcha, Radzicki Leon, Kaszub Szyja, Ajzyk Sala, Radzicki Bernard, Radzicka Róża, Radzicki Abram, Radzicka Hela, Appel Abram, Lubraniecki Hersh Lejb; there are 13 members on yet another list – Fasenfest Mordcha, Radzicki David, Lubraniecki Hersh Lejb, Kaszub Fiszel, Kaszub Szyja, Radzicka Hela, Radzicki Abram, Radzicki Lejb, Kozak Lipman, Strykowski Lejzor, Hofman Chaskiel, Hofman Abram Jehuda, Strykowski Jakub.

305 „Z życia partii. Dolny Śląsk. Ziembica," *Głos Bundu* 1946, nos 2–3, p. 10.

common room.[306] The chairman of the Ziębice Committee was Abram Witkies, the secretary was David Prezman, and Wolf Tejtelbaum was the treasurer. In Żary, on the other hand, the children's organisation, Skif, founded by the local branch of Tsukunft, was very active in addition to the Bund from 1946.[307]

In Strzegom, as in most towns and cities, the committee existed from November 1946 to November 1948. Jakub Manusiewicz was the secretary. In December 1946, it had nineteen members, including the artist Symcha Szumacher. By the end of its existence, it had twenty-two Bund members. They had their own party premises, which officially opened on 23 March 1947. Representatives of the Bund from Dzierżoniów and Legnica, as well as local representatives of the PPS and the PPR, attended the opening. It was proudly noted that a portrait of one of the founders of the Bund, Bejnisz Michalewicz, and the party's banner were on display.[308]

The Bund Committee in Włocławek was a small committee with around thirty members that were active after the war with a long-standing tradition. It was led by Chaim Tabacznik-Goszczyński. The Committee organised the anniversary celebrations of the founding of the party. It was one of the few that was not dissolved until January 1949, when the party was also dissolved.[309]

There was a Bund member in Płock, who was probably not affiliated with any Bund committee despite declaring that he had joined the organisation and was in contact with it by post.[310]

The existence and size of the committees did not always influence the quality of the members' activities for the party. This depended largely on the charisma of the people associated with the committee, and on the finances and – in most cases – on whether it was established in a town or a city where the Bund had been active before World War II. The committees in the so-called Recovered Territories faced a more daunting task, as everything had to be built from scratch, and there was a high level of migration. Only the Szczecin Committee is an example

---

306 AŻIH, the Bund, files n., Correspondence of the Bund Committee in Ziębice.

307 "Fun lebn, arbet un kamf," *Yugnt veker* 1946, no. 1, p. 15; "Fun gezelshaftlekhn un partay-lebn. Fartsvaygte partay-lebn in zhari. Skif – organizatsye," *Folkstsaytung* 1948, no. 5 (33) p. 7.

308 AŻIH, the Bund, files n., Correspondence of the Bund Committee in Strzegom in the period from 8 November 1946 until 14 November 1948.

309 Ibid., Protocols of the Committee in Włocławek for the period: 1947 – January 1949.

310 AŻIH, the Bund, files n., correspondence of Prusak from Płock with the Bund's Central Committee, March 1948.

of a well-organised unit in the new territories, which influenced its development as well as the number of party members.

In many cases, committees provided employment opportunities and served as a surrogate family for those who had lost their families during the war. However, the size of the committees, their membership numbers, and the lack of regular communication between them partly caused their operation to fail.

Warsaw Bund Committee

The Warsaw Bund Committee was established in the summer of 1945 by a group of seven Jewish socialists, less than a year after the Bund was re-established in PRL. On 12 August 1945, the new party headquarters at 2 Skaryszewska Street (near the Eastern Railway Station in the Praga district) was officially opened. The event was attended by the Bund members as well as representatives of the PPS and the PPR.[311] By May 1946, the number of members had risen to seventy.[312] The party's headquarters, similar to the headquarters of the Central Committee of Jews in Poland, as well as many government offices, were located on the right bank of the Vistula River.

In less than a year, fifty-four membership cards were issued, fifteen committee meetings were held, as well as seven party assemblies and a jubilee rally marking the 48th anniversary of the Bund. Four notice boards were mounted on the wall at the party's headquarters, which included history of the party and the rebuilding of party life in the destroyed Warsaw.[313] Regarding numbers, the committee was not one of the largest. According to data presented during the First National Conference of the Bund in Łódź on 16–17 June 1945, there were 30 members in Warsaw, while at the same time, for example, in Łódź there were 106 members, Częstochowa had 41, and Tarnów had 30. In total, approximately by that time, 320 people had joined the party nationwide.[314] The party newspapers, *Folkstsaytung* and *Głos Bundu*, often emphasised that the small number of Bund members active in the Warsaw Committee was due to the difficult housing conditions in the ruined capital, which meant that many lived outside Warsaw.

311 „Uroczyste otwarcie lokalu warszawskiej organizacji 'Bund'," *Biuletyn Żydowskiej Agencji Prasowej* 1945, no. 64/74, f. 3.

312 AŻIH, the Bund, files n., Circulars of the Warsaw Bund Committee of 1946.

313 „Fun partay-lebn. Varshe," *Folkstsaytung* 1946, nos 2–3, p. 6.

314 AŻIH, the Bund, files n., Report on the 1st National Bund Conference in Łódź on 16–17 June 1945.

In mid-1946, the Warsaw Bund Committee was composed of the following members: Chairman Salo Fiszgrund, Vice-Chairman Sioma Temczyn (representing Tsukunft), Secretary Shaya Szechatow,[315] Ignacy Falk, Shmuel Rychter, Abraham Zilbersztejn, Rutka[316] and Izrael Czyżyk.[317] During this time, the headquarters were relocated to 40 Targowa Street.[318] In April 1947, another election for the Warsaw Committee took place, in which the following people were on the list of candidates and were subsequently elected: Ignacy Falk (40 votes), Shmuel Rychter (39), Matwiej Bernstein[319] (39), Rutka (39), Abraham Zilbersztejn (35), Nejman (31), Sioma Temczyn (29), Shaya Szechatow (28), and Krum (28). Among the non-elected were: Eksztejn (8 votes), Nisnbojm (8), and Sztern[320] (21).

The structure of the Warsaw Bund Committee, as well as other local committees, was similar to the structure of local Jewish committees in Poland. The following committees existed in the Warsaw Committee: Repatriation Department (chairwoman: Rutka; secretary: Abraham Zilbersztejn), Productivity Department, Economic Department (chairman: Shmuel Rychter), Cultural Department and Finance Commission. Additionally, the Committee hosted the Bund's Historical Commission.[321] The Committee also oversaw the activities of Tsukunft and Skif, which hoped to preserve the party's ideology among the younger generation and to expand the party's ranks with new members in the future.[322]

The most important goal of the Warsaw Bund Committee was to assist repatriates in rebuilding their lives. They tried to secure housing for them. In the first

315 After Shaya Szechatow left Poland, his place was taken by M. Gut in 1948 (information from: AŻIH, the Bund, files n., documents referring to the Warsaw Bund Committee).

316 Probably referring to Rutka (Ruta) Kirszenblat-Grynszpan (1914 Warsaw - 1994 Holon), a Bund activist; after the war she worked as a clerk for the CKŻP. In the 1950s, she and her husband Abraham Grynszpan emigrated to Israel (information from: AŻIH, CKŻP WEiS, ref. 303/V/425/K bn 3204/130831).

317 „Fun der varshaver partay-organizatsye," *Folkstsaytung* 1946, no. 4, p. 5.

318 In 1946, a dispute arose between the Warsaw Bund Committee and the Joint over the premises at no. 22 11 Listopada Street, where the Joint's warehouses were located. The Bundists were strongly urged to give up the premises at this address (information from: AŻIH, the Bund, files n., Protocol of meetings of the Warsaw Bund Committee from 1946).

319 See: Biography.

320 AŻIH, the Bund, files n., Protocol no. 33 of the general meeting of the Warsaw Bund Committee 23 April 1947.

321 Ibid., Protocol no. 2 of the meeting of the Warsaw Bund Committee 27 May 1946.

322 Ibid., Protocol no. 1 of the meeting of the Warsaw Bund Committee 24 May 1946.

moments after arriving in Warsaw, they could find shelter at the party hostel at 2 Skaryszewska Street, which initially housed the party's headquarters. Attempts were also made to run a soup kitchen in this branch. The Bund's activities in this area were often limited due to a lack of sufficient material resources. As in other towns and cities, the Bund in Warsaw also sought to establish production cooperatives in order to create jobs for the Jewish community, including party comrades.[323]

The work of the WBC did not differ from the activities of other branches. A reading room with newspapers and books was organised, and efforts were made to acquire books for the library on the history of the Bund and the entire Jewish community, in both Yiddish and Polish, as well as foreign literature in English. As part of the weekly meetings, cultural and educational activities were carried out in addition to organisational and strictly political matters. As in other towns, presentations were posted on notice boards, and lectures were organised by party members (for example, Grzegorz Jaszuński gave a lecture on socialist conferences in London and Paris, Michał Szuldentrei addressed 'Current Issues in Domestic Politics', Shlomo Herszenchorn shared impressions from his visit to the USA, and Ignacy Samsonowicz discussed the electoral situation). Guest speakers from abroad included Yaakov Pat, Chaim Wasser, Charles Zimmerman from New York, and comrades from the PPS. The meetings discussed current political and economic issues in the country. The Cultural Department was responsible for these types of activities. Mourning ceremonies were organised in honour of deceased Bund leaders, like comrades Portnoy and Vladimir Kosovsky. Such events were held among others, in venues such as theatres ('Praska Rewia' and 'Roma').[324]

The Committee members endeavoured to commemorate the heroic deaths of Bund members during the Warsaw Ghetto Uprising and in the extermination camps. Warsaw Bund members and party representatives from across the country attended memorial gatherings and party anniversaries. It is worth noting that all major party conventions were held in Łódź and Wrocław. Only the main celebration of the 50th anniversary of the Bund, to which party representatives from outside Poland and socialists from various parts of the world were invited, took place in Warsaw at the Roma Theatre in November 1947.[325]

323 „Z zycia partii. Warszawa," *Głos Bundu*, 1946, nos 2–3, p. 10.

324 AŻIH, the Bund, files n., Protocol of the meeting of the Warsaw Bund Organisation on 22 May 1946; Protocol no. 3 of the meeting of the Warsaw Bund Committee on 3 June 1946; Protocol no. 2 of the meeting of the Warsaw Bund Committee 17 June 1946.

325 For more on the subject, see: Chapter Four, sub-chapter: 'May Day celebrations and anniversaries'.

During its almost four years of operation, the Warsaw Committee attempted to develop the party's activities at the highest level, trying to establish cooperation with other Jewish institutions and have its representatives in the Warsaw Jewish Committee. Compared to other committees, such as those in Łódź, Wrocław, and Szczecin, the structure of the Warsaw Committee was less developed. In this case, the committee's activities were influenced by the fact that it was based in the capital city and the memory of the Warsaw Ghetto significantly affected the Committee's activities.

May Day celebrations and anniversaries

The leaders of the Bund tried to strengthen the social and emotional ties of the party members with its ideology, programme and leadership, as well as with its individual organisational units. This was achieved through intra-party events organised for members and anniversary celebrations for a broader audience. These activities served as one of the most important methods for integrating party members and supporters, as well as a way of promoting the principles of its ideology.

For working-class communities, including Jewish socialists, one of the most important dates on the calendar was the May Day celebrations. As in previous years, this was accompanied by a traditional ceremony after the war. Preparations for the celebrations were meticulous. On the eve of the holiday – since pre-war times – committees organised galas and formal gatherings, to which representatives of allied organisations were invited. The whole setting was intended to mobilise all committee members to take action. Artistic performances were staged during the assemblies, which were organised by party members as well as by youth and children's organisations. The committee leadership took advantage of the high attendance at these gatherings to present a summary report on their annual activities.

The May Day events were also organised according to the same ritual after the war. From 1946 onwards, Bund members organised assemblies on the eve of the holiday, 30 April. They were held in all existing Bundist communities, and in Wałbrzych they were held jointly with the local PPS and PPR committees.[326] In the same year around 1,000 people mainly from the local Jewish community, attended a rally in Łódź, at the Bund's headquarters in the H. L. Poznański Culture Centre (formerly Czary Cinema), with the Bund's May Day Committee

326 P-N.[?], "A grus fun valbzhikh," *Folkstsaytung* 1946, no. 4, p. 6.

(comprised of, among others, M. Bornsztejn, Gershon Fogel, and Fishke Nejman). Representatives of the Bund who spoke included Gershon Fogel, Grisha Jaszuński, Bono Winer (on behalf of Tsukunft), David Klin, and PPS representative Artur Karaczewski (editor of *Kurier Poznański*). The ceremony, like other Bund meetings or assemblies, ended with the singing of the Bund anthem *Di shvue* (Yiddish for 'The Oath')[327] and the PPS anthem titled *Czerwony sztandar* (Red Banner).[328]

The anthem was a regular feature of all party ceremonies. Lyrics of *Di shvue* took on a new meaning in the reality of the Second World War, especially the words of the last verse:

> We swear our boundless loyalty to the Bund,
> Only the Bund can free the slaves now.
> Our red flag flies high and broad.
> We swear our loyalty of life and death![329]

The anthem's profound meaning retained its relevance even after the war.

During the May Day parades, the Bund, as a party, was able to demonstrate not only the continuity of its existence but also, through its banners express its stance on the political reality and support for the government and its policies at the time.[330] In 1946 Jewish workers in Łódź marched with banners displaying the current slogans of the 'democratic bloc': "Fight against anti-Semitism, against the NSZ gangs, against fascism and reaction, for a new democratic Poland, for reconstruction, for socialism."[331] The marches also reflected the actual political alliances with other parties and organisations. In 1946, Bundists marched alongside members of Trade Unions in Lublin.[332] In Tarnów, on the other hand, around 300 people participated in a 'united front' march, with members of the Bund, PPR, PPS, and Trade Unions marching together. In Warsaw, the Bund and

327 *Di shvue* (Yid. for 'oath'), anthem of the Bund, lyrics written in 1902 by Sh. An-sky [?].

328 „Yidishe arbeter unter di royte fener fun ‚bund'. Varshe. Tarnow. In tschenstochov. In pietrkov. Impozante may-fayerung in lodzh," *Folkstsaytung* 1946, nos 2–3, p. 8.

329 Quoted from: *In Love and in Struggle. The Musical Legacy of the Jewish Labor Bund* (CD released by the Workmen's Circle/Arbeter Ring, New York).

330 P. Sowiński (*Komunistyczne* święto. *Obchody 1 maja w latach 1948–1954*, Warsaw 2000) describes it as being complicit in the system and making your presence felt by taking part in a directed parade – a demonstration.

331 "Yidishe arbeter unter di royte fener fun ‚bund'. Impozante may-fayerung in lodzh," *Folkstsaytung* 1946, nos 2–3, p. 8.

332 "Fun partay-lebn. Lublin," *Folkstsaytung* 1946, no. 4, p. 6.

Tsukunft marched under their own red banners with Yiddish inscriptions, but together with the PPS. In Częstochowa, Bund members also began the march under their own banner, marching alongside the PPS and PPR members. Around 800 people participated in the march in Łódź, and among 20 banners that were flying in the wind, there were ones of the Bund, Tsukunft, and Skif, as well as co-operatives such as 'Przyszłość' (Future), 'Wygoda' (Comfort), 'Igła' (Needle), and 'Malarz' (Painter). The Bund militia, than existed in the city, marched in their own uniforms.[333]

One of the most important events for the Bund committees, and in post-war Poland, were the main events, the anniversaries of the founding of the party.[334] While the 'round' anniversaries were celebrated in a special way before the war, after the war, each of them, except for the 51st anniversary in 1948, when the process of the party's liquidation was underway, was celebrated with great pomp and ceremony. They were attended by a large audience, including people from outside the party. In Łódź in 1945, on the 48th anniversary of the party's founding, the celebrations were attended not only by members of the Bund, but also by representatives of the PPS (editor Artur Karaczewski) and the PPR (Władysław Młotecki).[335]

In 1946, during the celebrations of the 49th anniversary of the Bund in Dzierżoniów –

> ...about 1,000 people gathered in the largest city hall. Welcoming speeches were delivered by Comrade L[eon] Erlich on behalf of the Bund and by the town's Mayor and representatives of the PPS, PPR, Poale Zion Left, Tsukunft, Skif. A paper on the 49th anniversary of the Bund was delivered by Com.[rade] Ferdman.[336]

The aim of the celebrations was, among other things, to highlight the connections between the Bund and other organisations, to emphasise the splendour of the party's traditions and, above all to highlight the long-standing history of the movement and to introduce the founders and individuals who had a significant impact on the development of the party before 1939. After the war, new heroes

---

333 „Yidishe arbeter unter di royte fener fun ‚bund'. Varshe. Tarnow. In tschenstochov. In pietrkov. Impozante may-fayerung in lodzh," *Folkstsaytung* 1946, nos 2–3, p. 8.

334 Before the war, 'round' anniversaries of the party's existence were celebrated with great pomp and ceremony, i.e. the years: 1927, 1932, 1937 (information from: G. Pickhan, "Uwagi o Bundzie," *Kwartalnik Historii Żydów* 2003, no. 1 (205), p. 55).

335 „Akademia Bundu w Łodzi," *Biuletyn Żydowskiej Agencji Prasowej* 1945, no. 85/95, f. 3.

336 „Życie społeczne i partyjne. Dzierżoniów (Rychbach)," *Głos Bundu* 1947, no. 1 (5), p. 8.

joined the canon of founders – people who died in the ghettos and German concentration camps, especially the fighters of the Warsaw Ghetto.

The anniversary celebrations were also used to highlight the development of the Yiddish language and culture at the time.[337]

As mentioned in the Introduction, the year 1947 was mainly characterised by the solemn celebration of the 50th anniversary of the Bund, which was – "a great manifestation of the love and attachment of the Jewish proletariat to its party."[338] All local committees organised celebrations in the autumn of 1947.[339] These consisted of an official part, during which a speaker presented the achievements and key events from the 50-year history of the Bund. There were also speeches by invited representatives of the PPS and PPR, as well as local institutions and organisations. This was followed by an artistic programme with performances by well-known Jewish artists and theatre groups run by Tsukunft and Skif. The speakers at these events were usually representatives of the Central Committee – e.g. in Kraków, Michał Szuldenfrei, who was associated with the Bund in the city before the war, in Legnica- Grisha Jaszuński, in Wałbrzych- Salo Fiszgrund, and in Ziębice- Ignacy Falk. In Włocławek, where one of the slogans of the event was the fight for socialism, the anniversary was celebrated by the entire Jewish community. Among the guests were the city mayor Ignacy Kubecki (PPS), Antoni Milewski (PPS), Popek[340] from OM TUR, representatives of the Jewish Committee and Motl Kusznir, as the speaker.[341]

All the celebrations were arranged according to a set plan. The longest preparations were made for the main celebration, which took place on 15 November in Warsaw at the Roma Theatre (where, e.g. a commemoration of the 5th anniversary of the outbreak of the Warsaw Ghetto Uprising was held in 1948). The

---

337 AŻIH, the Bund, files n., letter from the Bund Central Committee, signed by its secretary – Salo Fiszgrund, addressed to all party comrades [undated].

338 „Centralna akademia w Łodzi," *Głos Bundu* 1948, no. 1 (14), p. 5.

339 The Warsaw Bund Committee also organised, independently of the central celebrations, a separate anniversary academy on 31 October 1947 at the headquarters of the Provincial Jewish Committee at 28 Jagiellońska Street, during which, among other things, Salo Fiszgrund solemnly handed over the new party banner (information from: AŻIH, CKŻP. Culture and Propaganda Dept. 1944–1950, ref. 303/XIII/83, broadcasts from November 1947; "Akademia w Warszawie," *Głos Bundu* 1948, no.1 (14), p. 5).

340 First name unknown.

341 AŻIH, the Bund, files n., Protocols of the Włocławek Committee for the period: 1947 – January 1949; „Uroczystości jubileuszowe w Krakowie," *Głos Bundu* 1948, no. 1 (14), p. 7; „Akademie i uroczystości w kraju," ibid., p. 16.

programme for the convention and the list of delegates who were to come from all over Poland to celebrate the party's half-century together were drawn up well in advance. The Central Committee sent out questionnaires to all Bund committees to determine the number of delegates from the Bund, Tsukunft, Skif, as well as party veterans, who would be attending and to find out which committees had party banners. About 1,500 delegates[342] and guests from fifty Polish towns and cities took part in the convention, as well as a representative of Orbach,[343] the Bund organisation from Italy (representatives of other Bundist groups from outside Poland declined to attend, citing the organisation of their own celebrations). Organising such a large event involved obtaining numerous permits (e.g. the consent of the Main Office for Press, Publications, and Public Performances at the Presidium of the Council of Ministers for the increased volume of Bund newspapers) and raising funds to cover, for example travel expenses of Bund delegates, and their accommodation.[344]

The Bund also ensured that the event was well publicised – those who could not attend the convention in person could listen to a live radio broadcast in Yiddish. The broadcast was aired on a nationwide programme, which was also available outside of Poland.[345]

---

342 For example, 31 people arrived for the convention from Częstochowa (information from: AŻIH, ibid. List of delegates and guests arriving for the Bund convention in Warsaw, to be held in October 1947: (delegates: Sztajnic Helena, Glik David, Erenfrid Alter, Kifer Pola, Wajchman Berek, Lederman Mojżesz, Brener Liber, Kusznir Motek, Sztajnic Eliasz, Krauze Józef, Prozer Hersh, Kowalski Fajwel, Kusznir Rivka, Edelist Genia; guests: Lederman Sara, Rozental Chaim, Dimant Salomon, Pieczysty Ruwen, Lewkowicz Mordka, Wajsberg Zygmunt, Kurcbard Mania, Erenfrid Chana, Miodownik Izrael, Kowalska Liba, Kon Adam, Monat Dora, Wajcman Jakub, Kazimierczak Józef MP, Gronkiewicz Jan MP, Dimant Bela).

343 First name unknown.

344 AAN, the Bund, ref. 30/IV/4, vol. II, f. 313, 365, Letter from the Main Office of Press, Publications and Public Performances at the Presidium of the Council of Ministers in Warsaw to the Central Committee of the Bund, 24 October 1947; Letter to the Security Office in Warsaw, 5 November 1947, to issue permission for the gathering of guests at Grzybowski Square on 16 November 1947, in order to proceed to the Jewish cemetery on Okopowa Street in Warsaw; AŻIH, the Bund, files n., Circular no. 18 from the Central Committee of the Bund to all Bund organisations, Warsaw 17 October 1947, containing guidelines related to the organisation of the celebrations, travel, programme and accommodation.

345 AŻIH, CKŻP. Culture and Propaganda Department. 1944–1950, ref. 303/XIII/83, broadcast from November 1947.

The convention was not only an important opportunity to demonstrate the continuity of the party and its ideological programme (Szuldenfrei delivered a speech on the 50th anniversary of the Bund and Bielicka-Blum presented on the history of the Tsukunft; and Edelman spoke about the Bund during the German occupation). The large number of guests, including Polish workers and ideological allies from other organisations and parties, was to show the (albeit increasingly illusory) power and resilience of the Bund.

During the ceremony, Yiddish and Polish were spoken due to the presence of individuals not associated with the Jewish community. The following were present at the Roma Theatre: government representatives (Minister Tadeusz Dietrich gave a speech), a delegation from the Central Committee of the PPR (Colonel Franciszek Blinowski made a speech), the Provincial Central Committee of the PPS (Deputy Marshal Stanisław Szwalbe made a speech on behalf of the PPS), the Central Commission of Trade Unions, and the Central Committee of the Democratic Party (MP Marek Ferdynand Arczyński made a speech). The events ended the following day with the funeral of Leon Feiner ('Mikołaj'), who had died in 1945. His remains were brought from Lublin to Warsaw. The funeral was concluded by the laying of wreaths at the graves of Bundists who fought during the Warsaw Ghetto Uprising.[346]

The anniversary celebrations and May Day parades were not only intended to integrate party members, as well as present their programme and stance on current events. The most important goal for the Bund leaders was to emphasise the continuity of the party's existence and to show that the Bund still existed on both the 'Jewish Street' and the 'Polish (political) Street'. It was also possible to show which groups it was forming local alliances with, within each town or city. The Bund marched under its own banner, and their youth and children's organisations, also wore uniforms. This was intended to show that the party still had a chance of surviving. Artistic performances by children and young people in Yiddish during anniversaries and assemblies, showed that the language is still alive among the youngest, ensuring its potential to develop and survive on the 'Jewish Street'.

A certain novelty, not only during anniversary celebrations but above all during the May Day celebrations, was marching together with the communists – something the Bundists strongly opposed before 1939. It was also a sign of change and a spectacular symbol of acceptance of the PPR, which was becoming the leading party. The Bund's opportunism toward the PPR, despite maintaining

346 „Uroczystości jubileuszowe 50-lecia Bundu w Polsce. Nadzwyczajny Zjazd Partyjny w Warszawie. 1500 delegatów w sali 'Roma'," *Głos Bundu* 1948, no. 1 (14), pp. 4–5.

close contacts with the PPS (through many local Bundist organisations), was probably dictated by the hope of maintaining proper contacts with the party exercising real power in the state.

Disputes over the 'Jewish language' (Yiddish)

Among the leaders of the Jewish community, political parties, and various organisations, there was a dispute over the national language they should use among themselves. They also debated among each other about the language in which they should educate their children, the future of the nation. This conflict was the continuation of a dispute that had been ongoing since the late 19th century. Before the Holocaust, Yiddish – often referred to simply as the 'Jewish language' – was the everyday language in the shtetls, while Hebrew was mainly the language for studying the Holy Scriptures. According to the 1931 census, about 80% of people of Mosaic faith declared Yiddish as their mother tongue. During World War II, the language used on a daily base was re-evaluated. In many cases, knowledge of only Yiddish was a death sentence, as it hindered their ability to survive the war using so-called 'Aryan' papers. In other words, only a good command of Polish offered them a chance to blend into Polish society and survive. During the war, even the youngest children hidden among Poles underwent a natural process of linguistic and cultural Polonization. On the other hand, children who survived the war in the USSR were often Russified and spoke Russian after returning to Poland.[347]

Despite the partial shift from the 'Jewish language', most newspapers published by the Jewish community after the war were printed in Yiddish. Most of the documentation for Jewish organisations and parties was also kept in this language. No research has survived (and probably was not conducted) on the popularity of newspapers in both languages: Yiddish and Polish, among the Jewish community, so it is difficult to determine which of them had more readers.[348] The Bund decided to publish newspapers in Polish and Yiddish, while its affiliated organisations, Tsukunft and Skif, opted to publish their newspapers in Yiddish.[349]

347 For more on the subject, see: A. Grabski, M. Rusiniak, „Język żydowski jako przedmiot sporów politycznych wśród polskich Żydów (1944–1949)," in: *Jidyszland – polskie przestrzenie*, eds. E. Geller, M. Polit, Warsaw 2008, pp. 263–264.

348 J. Korzeniowski, „Bibliografia czasopism żydowskich wychodzących w PRL, 1944–1950," *Biuletyn Żydowskiego Instytutu Historycznego* 1986, nos 3–4, pp. 148–149.

349 Tsukunft published the aforementioned *Yugnt veker* (1946–1948). In Lower Silesia it also published a 4-page brochure titled *Unzer tsukunft* in March 1947. Meanwhile, Skif published *Khavershaft* (1947–1948). In August 1946, a brochure in

This debate had been a cornerstone of the Bundist ideology since the party's foundation. After the war, heated discussions on the superiority of Yiddish over Hebrew took place within the CKŻP and Jewish committees, as well as during meetings and conferences organised by the CKŻP's Education Department, which was responsible for the education of the youngest generation.[350] The Bund's unwavering stance on the Yiddish language was demonstrated not only by the constant struggles and disputes over its superiority, but above all by the reprinting of an article by Shlomo Mendelsohn titled "Yiddish or Hebrew" in *Głos Bundu*. The article, was originally published in 1930 in the journal *Nasza Walka*, proved the continuity of the Bund's position:

> The circumstances have aligned so that the fight for the Yiddish language – the living vernacular of the people – is primarily waged by the working class. The bourgeoisie either strives for assimilation or seeks an aristocratic Hebrew culture. The petty bourgeoisie is culturally and politically sterile. The only active force that has raised the banner of mass culture, that has proclaimed its goals and is leading the struggle to rehabilitate the common people, their language, talents, and capacity for creation, is the Jewish proletariat.
>
> Over several decades, Yiddish literature has grown, either directly or indirectly influenced by this movement. […] A vast network of Yiddish theatres has been established, secular Jewish education flourishes, and extensive cultural work is being carried out, elevating the Jewish worker spiritually and bringing them closer to the achievements of European culture at large.
>
> The struggle between Yiddish and Hebrew thus represents a clash of two cultures: the culture of the aristocrats and the culture of the workers.[351]

Polish titled *Wolna Młodzież* came out – a two-page supplement to *Głos Bundu* (AŻIH, the Bund, files n., Circular no. 12 Central Committee of Tsukunft from 13 October 1946). For more on the press published by Tsukunft and Skif, see: M. Rusiniak-Karwat, „Dzieci przyszłością partii. Skif w powojennej Polsce," *Kwartalnik Historii Żydów* 2018, no. 4 (268), pp. 842–844; idam, "*Tsukunft* publishing operations in Poland after 1945," *pl.it / rassegna italiana di argomenti polacchi* 2022, no. 13, pp. 52–64.

350 S. Bergman, „Przyczynki do historii Bundu," *Biuletyn Żydowskiego Instytutu Historycznego* 1992, nos 2–3 (162–163), pp. 123–124; A. Grabski, M. Rusiniak, „Żydowscy komuniści po Holokauście wobec języków polskiego żydostwa," in: *Nusech Pojln. Studia z dziejów kultury jidysz w powojennej Polsce*, ed. M. Ruta, Kraków Budapest 2008, pp. 58–64.

351 Sz. Mendelsohn, „Język żydowski czy hebrajski?," *Głos Bundu* 1948, nos 2–3 (15–16), p. 8.

On one hand, the Bund representatives advocated for the development and preservation of the Yiddish language, and on the other hand, they realised that in order to reach new potential members of the organisation and to have a greater impact in post-war Poland, they had to speak Polish. This led to the increasing use of the Polish language, as evidenced by the purchase of Polish-language books for party libraries.[352] Treating Polish as an equal language while opposing Hebrew opened up a new area of conflict with Zionist circles, which believed that in Palestine, the nation should return to the roots of the Hebrew language and culture.

The development and preservation of the Yiddish language was postulated not only during meetings and gatherings within the Bund and affiliated organisations but also during the sessions of the Presidium of the CKŻP. The Bund activists argued:

> Fiszgrund: "In our Committees, both Central and Provincial, officials consistently use the Polish language. In fact, upon entering a Jewish Committee, one gets the impression of being in a Polish institution. This absurd practice must come to an end. It is essential to remind the Committees that the official language in our institutions is Yiddish."[353]

Even Bund activists were inconsistent in their demands. During another session of the CKŻP Presidium, Fiszgrund advocated for publishing *Oyfgang*, the Youth Department's bulletin, also in Polish. It was to be addressed to "the Polish public and to Jewish students who do not know the Yiddish language."[354] In this case, promoting the party's ideology and programme was secondary to the language issue.

During the First Teachers' Congress, on 1–3 November 1946 in Łódź, in order to establish new curriculum guidelines that had been adapted to the realities of the time, the Bundists,[355] in discussions about the curriculum in Jewish schools emphasised the need to continue the existence of the Bund-affiliated pre-war school organisation,[356] where the language of education was to be Yiddish.

---

352 AŻIH, the Bund, files n., Protocol no. 29 from a meeting of the Warsaw Bund Committee on 9 July 1947.

353 AŻIH, Archives of the Presidium and Secretariat, ref. 303/I/5, Protocol no. 4, from 13–14 July 1946, f. 63.

354 Ibid., ref. 303/I/8, Protocol no. 100, from 4 December 1947, f. 182.

355 The Bundists participating in the Congress: Ignacy Falk (as a Chair of the School Commission at the CKŻP), Shlomo Hershenhorn, Salo Fiszgrund, Leo Finkelsztejn and Ludwik Łozowski. Among the Bundists-teachers were–Alman, Ferdman, Tencer and Luba Bielicka-Blum (information from: "Życie społeczne i partyjne. Zjazd Nauczycielski," *Głos Bundu* 1946, no. 4, p. 8).

356 TSYSHO (Yid.: Tsentrale yidishe shul-organizatsye, Central Jewish School Organisation), secular educational organisation in Poland, where Yiddish was the

Another controversial issue was the proposal to introduce Hebrew into the curriculum from the second year of primary school, which was strongly opposed by Fiszgrund.[357] However, in the resolution that concluded the Congress, it was decided, contrary to the position of the Bund, that "the principle of using Yiddish as a language of instruction should be fully implemented, with a broad consideration of teaching Hebrew according to the programme of the Central Committee of Jews in Poland."[358]

The issue of the language that children would use also arose during the organisation of the Child Welfare Commission under the CKŻP and in the establishment of ideological and educational guidelines for orphanages, boarding schools, and schooling. Bundist Shlomo Herszenhorn, who was in charge of the Commission, advocated for Yiddish to be the everyday language, which was met with opposition from Zionists. The matter was referred to an inter-party commission, which approved Yiddish as the language to be used by children in orphanages.[359]

The controversies surrounding the Jewish languages was an ideological dispute and a consequence of the rivalry between Zionists and non-Zionists (communists and Jewish socialists – the Bund) and the debate over the status of Yiddish in the newly emerging Jewish state. In this context, Jewish parties and organisations, as well as individual members of the community, had to make decisions regarding their place of residence and future path in life. For those who planned to stay in Poland, it was difficult to argue for the superiority of Yiddish over Polish or Hebrew. On the contrary, it was Polish, when Jewish towns and districts had disappeared, that dominated over Yiddish, as it became the natural language of communication for practical reasons. It is hard to imagine how one could live in Poland at that time, where Jews could no longer function in the closed enclaves like the shtetls had been before the war, using only one of the 'Jewish' languages. Moreover, these same Bundists who advocated for the use of Yiddish amongst Jews realised that the future of the Jewish community depended on younger

language of education. It was in operation in the years 1921–1939. See more: *Lerer-yiskor-bukh. Di umgekumene lerer fun tsysho shul in poyln*, ed. Kh. Sh. Kazdan, Nyu york 1952–1954.

357 *Życie społeczne i partyjne. Zjazd Nauczycielski*, p. 8.

358 Quoted from: H. Datner-Śpiewak, „Instytucje opieki nad dzieckiem i szkoły powszechne Centralnego Komitetu Żydów Polskich w latach 1945–1946," *Biuletyn Żydowskiego Instytutu Historycznego* 1981, no. 3 (119), p. 50.

359 On the subject of Yiddish and Jewish children, see: H. Datner, „Szkoły Centralnego Komitetu Żydów w Polsce w latach 1944–1949," *Biuletyn Żydowskiego Instytutu Historycznego* 1994, nos 1–3 (169–171), pp. 103–119; Datner-Śpiewak, *Instytucje opieki*, pp. 37–51.

generations, who either did not know the languages of their ancestors or treated them as secondary languages. Bund members themselves no longer taught children *mame-loshn* (Yid.: mother tongue), because then they could have discussions in front of the youngest children about things they did not want them to know.

Cooperative movement – the idea of productiveness

One of the main issues on the 'Jewish Street' in post-war People's Poland was the productivisation of Jewish society. Many Jews arriving from the USSR or those emerging from hiding had to settle in new locations, take up new jobs, and pursue new professions. Representatives of the CKŻP sought to prevent Jews from returning to their previous places of residence (in areas that became part of People's Poland) or to their former professions and occupations. This position was mainly held by members of the Polish Workers' Party (PPR) faction, who sought a fundamental reconstruction of the Jewish community in post-war Poland, including, above all, the 're-specialisation' and retraining of Jews. According to the doctrinal principles of communism, the working class was to become the leading force of the state while a trader or shopkeeper was not a profession worthy of a socialist at that time. In addition, there was a clear intention to change the pre-war situation in which Jews were identified with trade, mediation, speculation, and small-scale craftsmanship.

During many meetings of the Bund, it was argued that the productivisation and centralisation of the Jewish population in one place (e.g. in the Recovered Territories, in Szczecin, or in larger urban centres in Lower Silesia) would improve the perception of Jews and become a preventive measure against anti-Semitism. Integrating Jews into the reconstruction of the country, in this case the economy, was seen as a way to gain favour within Polish society. At the end of July 1946, the government administration in Warsaw established the Government Commission for Productivisation of the Jewish Population, which granted long-term loans to newly established Jewish cooperatives. Within the framework of the CKŻP, the Productivisation Department was established in 1945, and in 1946, the ORT was registered, whose tasks included spreading professional knowledge, as well as the creation of workshops, and cooperatives.[360]

360 M. Grynberg, „Problemy zatrudnienia ludności żydowskiej w Polsce w pierwszych latach po II wojnie światowej," *Biuletyn Żydowskiego Instytutu Historycznego* 1986, nos 1–2 (137–138), pp. 97–114; P. Kendziorek, *Program i praktyka produktywizacji Żydów polskich w działalności CKŻP*, Warsaw 2016; A. Skibińska, „Powroty ocalałych," in: *Prowincja noc. Życie i zagłada Żydów w Dystrykcie Warszawskim*, eds.

Jewish workshops and cooperatives were established at the same time as Polish cooperatives, and grew out of the desire for self-sufficiency and the need for work. The cooperative movement had existed in the Jewish community since the end of the 19th century. Various cooperatives and workshops emerged before 1939, but in most cases, they did not bring positive experiences or results.[361] After 1945, the assumption was that it would be different, or at least that it was the prevailing political doctrine. The government's favourable attitude towards the initiatives, encouraged the dynamic development of the cooperatives. The Bank for the Productivisation of the Jewish Population in Poland, was established in 1945 in Lublin as part of the Commission, it provided assistance in the creation of various types of facilities. In total, at the beginning of 1949, there were about 200 cooperatives within the headquarters of the 'Solidarity' Central Union of Productive Cooperatives, created on the initiative of the CKŻP in February 1946, employing approximately 16,500 workers, more than half of whom were Jewish.

For the Bund, the creation of cooperatives was one of the ways of implementing the party's ideological programme, promoting these types of economic activities and at the same time, demonstrating the party's resilience and its contribution to the reconstruction of Jewish community life. In addition to providing jobs for the Bundists, the cooperatives were also intended to recruit new party members from among the employees. In line with the Bund's ideology, which advocated for the reconstruction of the Jewish settlements in Poland, the cooperatives were a very good way of implementing this idea. Work could provide a livelihood and, above all, prevent emigration from Poland. The cooperatives that were established by the Bund, competed to some extent with the kibbutzim established by the Zionists, which aimed to prepare potential emigrants for building an economy in the land of Israel. However, the Bund opposed merging its cooperatives with other Jewish initiatives of a similar type, let alone Polish ones. In the latter case, this was in line with the ideology of national and cultural autonomy, which

B. Engelking, J. Leociak, D. Libionka, Warsaw 2007, pp. 554 561; E. Waszkiewicz, „Powstanie, rozwój i zanik skupiska Żydów na Dolnym Śląsku (1945–1968)," in: *Współcześni Żydzi – Polska i diaspora. Wybrane zagadnienia*, ed. E. Waszkiewicz, Wrocław 2007, p. 19.

361 M. Grynberg, *Żydowska spółdzielczość pracy w Polsce w latach 1945–1949*, Warsaw 1986, pp. 27–51; M. Bialkower, „Tsum 25-tn internatsyonaln kooperativn tog," *Folkstsaytung* 1947, no. 3 (22), p. 5.

the Bundists strived for even in the post-war reality.[362] However, this led to the continuity of the phenomenon of alienation and detachment from Polish society.

The establishment of cooperatives had an additional ideological motivation. Thanks to the existence of cooperatives, the majority of the Bund members, who according to the occupational structure, made them members of the 'leading' working class.[363] In this respect, the Bund cooperated more closely with the 'democratic bloc' parties than with Jewish organisations. According to August Grabski, only the PPR faction at the CKŻP sought to create new cooperatives and workers' circles. However, this thesis is untenable in the light of new research.[364] Each political group attempted to emphasise its own contributions in rebuilding the Jewish community and none was objective in its assessments. Moreover, the development of all the cooperatives was financed by the CKŻP. The establishment of cooperatives by 'competing' political groups reduced the credit available to cooperatives in other centres. Furthermore, as faction representatives noted, in party-affiliated cooperatives, jobs were generally given to members of the founding party. They also emphasised that the maintenance costs of these cooperatives (funded, as mentioned above, by bank loans) were disproportionate to the profits. However, it is difficult to confirm this today, as complete financial records have not been preserved.[365]

Bundists stressed in the press and during party meetings, their contributions to the development and existence of cooperatives in towns and cities, places

362 A. Rykała, „Łódź na mapie skupisk żydowskich Polski (po 1945 r.)," in: *Społeczność żydowska i niemiecka w Łodzi po 1945 roku*, eds. A. Lech, K. Radziszewska, A. Rykała, Łódź 2010, p. 298.

363 In the declarations filled out by people who, after the war, expressed their willingness to join the party or organisations affiliated with it, the majority of them were manual labourers in Jewish cooperatives, such as: shoemakers, bootmakers, tailors and seamstresses, milliners, linen workers, corset makers, hosiery workers, spinners, embroiderers, glove makers, hatters, cap makers, pressers, textile workers, cooks, bakers, confectioners, cobblers, weavers, locksmiths, carpenters, printers, typesetters, varnishers, hairdressers, furriers, chauffeurs, painters, bristle workers, turners, upholsterers, boilermakers, butchers, guards, bookkeepers, coopers, welders, tinsmiths, saddlers, tanners, watchmakers, warehouse assistants, cleaners, sales clerks, manicurists, housewives, as well as individuals without a profession (information from: AŻIH, the Bund, files n., Membership declarations from the years 1945–1948 filled in with the intention of joining the Bund).

364 See: Grabski, *Działalność komunistów wśród Żydów*, p. 175.

365 AAN, PPR KC Secretariat, ref. 295/VII-149, f. 36.

where they were active. For example, in Tarnów in 1946, there was a Tailors' Labour Cooperative which stated:

> Thanks to our comrades, the only important workers' institution in Tarnów continues to operate, despite several attempts by certain Jewish elements to shut it down or at least transfer it to the 'Allied side'.[366]

Various Bund-affiliated cooperatives were active in Lower Silesia,[367] Łódź, and Szczecin, among other places.[368] These were mostly tailors' cooperatives, such as 'Igła' ('Needle') in Wałbrzych and Legnica, as well as transport cooperatives. In order to highlight their contribution to productivity, the Bundists in Kraków established a transport cooperative they named 'Przewóz' ('Transport') in 1948.[369]

Party reports sometimes gave incorrect information regarding the affiliation of specific cooperatives – as in the case of Szczecin, where the Bundists initiated the cooperatives but in fact were created within the framework of the 'Solidarność' (Solidarity) Central Association of Manufacturing Cooperatives [CSW] [370] Similarly, data about cooperatives that were members of CSW 'Solidarność' (as of October 1947) also contradict the reports on the activities of the Bund-affiliated cooperatives, as the lists of cooperatives overlapped, with the exception of a

366 „Życie społeczne i partyjne. Tarnów," *Głos Bundu* 1946, no. 4, p. 8.

367 In 1946, tailors' cooperatives were established in Zagórze and in Legnica. There was also a transport cooperative in Wrocław (information from: "Fun partay-lebn. Nider-shlezye. Zagórze, Lignice, Wrocław," *Folkstsaytung* 1946, no. 4, p. 6)

368 In Szczecin, where one of the largest and most active Bund committees existed after the war, its members, under the leadership of Bundist Yankl Rajs, managed to establish – with great effort – several cooperatives in 1946. These included the shoemaking cooperative 'Frayhayt' (Yid.: 'Freedom'), the tailors' cooperative 'Eynikeyt' (Yid.: 'Unity'), and the construction cooperative with the Polish name 'Budowa' (Construction). It is likely that not all these cooperatives were owned by the party and instead operated within the framework of CSW 'Solidarność' (Solidarity) (information from: "In nayem yidishn-yishev – Shtchecin. Unzere kooperativn," *Folkstsaytung* 1947, no. 8 (17), p. 7; "Z życia partii. Szczecin," *Głos Bundu* 1946, nos 2–3, p. 10).

369 AAN, the Bund, ref. 30/IV/5 vol. II, f. 261 – from 17 February 1948 (Salo Fiszgrund's certificate concerning the establishment of the 'Przewóz' Bund cooperative).

370 CSW 'Solidarity' was established in February 1946. Its main task was to look after and coordinate the work of the existing inter-party cooperatives and to stimulate the formation of new ones (information from: M. Grynberg, "Problemy zatrudnienia ludności żydowskiej w Polsce w pierwszych latach po II wojnie światowej," *Biuletyn Żydowskiego Instytutu Historycznego* 1986, nos 1–2 (137–138), p. 104).

bakery cooperative, which was only listed among the Bund cooperatives.[371] From the preserved records, we know that the 'Igła' (Needle) cooperative network, belonged to the Bund, and the Bund Central Committee repeatedly sought loans from the Bank for the Productivisation of the Jewish Population to support their development.[372]

Each of the cooperatives, whether Bundist or cross-party, operated in a small space and employed between a few to over a dozen or so workers.[373] In order to be hired or given a position, many people participated in training courses organised by the Bund committees, often with assistance from ORT staff.[374]

The development of cooperative movements not only guaranteed new jobs, but most importantly, it influenced the integration of the Bundist community and the recruitment of new members. Furthermore, it was meant to demonstrate that the Bund, as a party, still existed on the 'Jewish Street' where it also had an impact on improving the living conditions of society. The cooperatives funded by state banks also had doctrinal tasks, to increase the number of the working class, regardless of efficiency and profitability.

Social aid for the party members and its supporters

The material problems of the Bund members were among the most common problems the Committees faced in their everyday work in the early post-war years. People were returning from exile in the USSR, from German forced

371 In reports on the inter-party cooperatives in Łódź – members of the CSW 'Solidarity' – there were, i.a. 'Igła 1', 'Igła 2' (clothing), 'Zgoda' (footwear and leather), 'Przyszłość' (carpentry), 'Jedność' (clothing), room painters, 'Osnowa' (weaving), which also appeared in the Bund documents as belonging to it (information from: M. Grynberg, *Żydowska spółdzielczość pracy w Polsce w latach 1945–1949*, Warsaw 1986, p. 169; I. Lipski, "Lodzher bundishe kooperativn," *Folkstsaytung* 1947, no. 13 (22), pp. 5, 7).

372 Among other things, correspondence has been preserved regarding the application for a loan for the development of the 'Igła' cooperative in Dzierżoniów, Wałbrzych and Legnica as well as reports on the activity of the 'Dziewiarz' cooperative from the years 1946–1947. AŻIH, the Bund, files n., correspondence with the Bund Central Committee regarding application for a bank loan to develop the cooperative from the years 1946–1948.

373 Ibid., correspondence between the Bund Central Committee with the local committees from the years 1946–1947.

374 J. Grynblat, „Kopniak życia," in: *Losy żydowskie. Świadectwo żywych*, vol. III, ed. M. Turski, Warsaw 1996, p. 118.

labour camps, from transit camps in Germany and other countries (including DP camps), or were coming out of hiding where they had been during the German occupation. Most were left without any means of livelihood. The central authorities were constantly concerned with providing material assistance to the Bund members and their families, as well as financing the activities of the committees of the re-emerging party. Financial and material resources came from several sources – initially, from benefits granted by the authorities of the PRL, then from donations and contributions collected from the Bund members who had joined the party, and finally from foreign aid obtained from organisations outside Poland with ideological ties to Jewish socialists.[375] In 1946, the Jewish Labor Committee[376] provided assistance to left-wing Jewish parties, sending 89,000 dollars to be distributed among the Bund, Poale Zion Left, and Hashomer Hatsair.[377] The high exchange rate of the dollar in Poland meant that these were significant amounts, though still disproportionate to the scale of the needs. Additionally, gifts in the form of books and children's clothes were arriving from America.[378] Material aid was also constituted a drop in the ocean of needs.

One of the main charities that supported Jewish communities in the People's Republic of Poland after the war was the Joint.[379] Between 1946 and 1948, the financial and material aid it sent was directed to the Bund, among others. Through the CKŻP, monthly financial subsidies and vouchers for food, household chemicals, and winter clothing were received and distributed to local committees for their members. The party leadership had to submit monthly reports to the Joint representatives in Poland including a breakdown of the financial and material

---

375 The author has not encountered any information about the use by the Bundists or the Jewish public in general of the aid Poland received from the United Nations Relief and Rehabilitation Administration (UNRRA).

376 Jewish Labor Committee (JLC) was established on 25 February 1934 in New York, as a response to Hitler's rise to power. The Bundist emigrants were among its founders. The JLC brought together non-communist circles of Jewish workers whose common goal was to fight fascism, Nazism, and anti-Semitism. One of the leading JLC activists was Yaakov Pat (for more information on the subject, see: C.P. de Bollardière, "The Jewish Labor Committee's Bundist Relief Network in France, 1945–1948," *Kwartalnik Historii Żydów* 2013, no. 2 (246), pp. 293–301).

377 Grabski, *Działalność komunistów wśród Żydów*, p. 130.

378 AŻIH, the Bund, files n., correspondence of the Bund Central Committee in Warsaw addressed to Tsukunft and the Representation of the Polish Bund in New York.

379 On the Joint activity in Poland in the years 1945–1949, see: A. Sommer-Schneider, *Sze'erit hapleta. Ocaleni z Zagłady. Działalność American Jewish Joint Distribution Committee w Polsce w latach 1945–1989*, Kraków 2014, pp. 90–167.

resources distributed. In the Bund Central Committee, these matters were handled by Shaya Szechatow and Ignacy Falk.

The expenses of the Central Committee included:

- Individual assistance – benefits (89–111 people in January 1947; 75 people in June 1948);
- Maintenance of 23 soup kitchens which served 2,130 meals per day in June 1948;
- Maintenance of dormitories (hostels) with 70 beds in 1947, 20 beds in 1948;
- Maintenance of the 'Eldorado' Holiday Home in Duszniki-Zdrój;[380]
- Support for summer and winter camps for youth from Tsukunft and Skif;
- Maintenance of four orphanages (Froebel's homes) for 180 children;
- Support for full-day schools;
- Support for education: clubs, community centres, evening courses, sports activities, choirs, and drama circles;
- Administration (administrative expenses, maintenance fees for the premises, and 20 staff members in 1947; 26–28 employees working in the Bund committees in 1948).[381] The Joint emphasised that the funds received from them should not be allocated for the financing of holiday homes or summer and winter camps. The Bund was frequently prompted to send budget reports, which it failed to do.[382] Each month, the Bund received between 250,000 and 600,000 Polish zlotys from the Joint, which made up part of its total income. For example, in January 1947, the Bund received 600,000 zlotys from the

380 The Workers' Holiday Home in Duszniki-Zdrój, known as 'Eldorado', was a retreat where Bund members went to recuperate and regain their health. Yitzhak (Ignacy) Feldman was a member of staff there. He survived WW2 in the USSR. Post-war he returned to Lower Silesia (information acquired during an interview the author conducted with his son, Marian Feldman, in Warsaw in 2012). There was a library and a reading room in the 'Eldorado' Holiday Home, as well as a Bund Committee, to which all the Bundists staying in Duszniki belonged to (see: "Otwarcie sezonu letniego w Robotniczym Domu Wypoczynkowym w Dusznikach-Zdroju," *Głos Bundu* 1948, nos 2–3 (15–16), p. 16; I. El-ski, "Bundishe opru-kolonyes in dushniki un baym yam," *Folkstsaytung* 1947, no. 15 (24), p. 5).

381 Information on the figures and statements of assistance provided in this chapter are taken from: AŻIH, American Jewish Joint Distribution Committee. 1945–1949, ref. 350/2372, no page number, quantity in June 1948; AAN, the Bund, ref. 30/IV/9, 30/IV/10, 30/IV/11.

382 AŻIH, American Jewish Joint, ref. 350/2372, letters from the Joint Secretary General – J. Gitler-Barski to the Bund Central Committee in Poland.

Joint and 2.4 million zlotys from other institutions, which accounted for 20% of the all income.[383]

The maintenance of the 'Eldorado' Holiday Home in Duszniki-Zdrój posed a problem, as it consumed a significant portion of the financial resources. The Home was established on the initiative of the Bund and was considered by other political groups as belonging to the Bund, although in reality, it was used by employees and members of many other Jewish organisations, including the CKŻP and provincial Jewish committees. For this reason, the Bund repeatedly proposed at the meetings of the CKŻP Presidium for the Home to also be maintained with the Committee funds.[384]

The Bund's press and other publications

The Bund began publishing its own newspaper almost immediately after the party was re-established. This is how the party intended to make its presence felt on the 'Jewish Street'. Their other aim was to reach surviving Bund members and those who had been affiliated with the Bund before the war through organisations linked to the party and its supporters. The newspapers primarily served as a source of information about the party's current activities. Its role was to report on important events in the party's life: conventions, conferences, and establishment of party committees in cities and towns, wherever there were concentrations of Jewish residents after the war.

Through the press, the Bund clearly outlined its tasks and political programme in the new reality of the PRL, while also engaging in debates with other political movements. The press also had the task of upholding the tradition of the Bund's long-standing activities and underlining the continuity of the Bund as part of the workers' movement and the importance of Jewish socialists in its functioning. The press, while promoting the party in the Jewish community, also had the task of attracting new members to the party and to organisations affiliated to the Bund, as well as showing the existence of these organisations, their activity, openness and resilience.

It should be mentioned that since the founding of the party in 1897, Jewish socialists had been publishing press materials under the names of the central and local committees, as well as producing numerous brochures and leaflets, e.g. on the occasion of the May Day celebrations or the birthday of the Jewish writer Mendele

383 Ibid., no page number, cash report for the month of January 1947.

384 AŻIH, ref. 303/I/7b, Protocol no. 71 from 1 August 1947, f. 211.

Moykher Sforim.[385] The Jewish socialists did not stop their publishing activities even in the ghettos during the German occupation. In the Warsaw Ghetto, the Bund and Tsukunft published a total of eleven press titles using the method of duplication.[386] It is also likely that in the Łódź Ghetto, several issues of the *Byuletin* (Bulletin) were also published, but they have not survived to the present day.[387]

After the fall of the Warsaw Ghetto Uprising in 1943, when the Germans liquidated the Jewish district, the Bundists who were engaged in underground activities on the 'Aryan' side began publishing the *Biuletyn W[ewnętrznego] B[undu]* from February 1944. The last available and known issue, number 4, was published on 1 May 1944 (it is believed that six issues were released).[388] The editors of the publication were Leon Feiner ('Mikołaj'), Ignacy Samsonowicz, and Stanisław Liwszyc.[389] It is difficult to determine how long the publication continued. During the Bund conference in Lublin in November 1944, this newspaper title was not mentioned. This was most likely due to the composition of the conference participants, many of whom had survived the war outside the General Government, – in the USSR or, like Grzegorz Jaszuński, in the Vilna Ghetto. As previously mentioned, back then – and until January 1945 – the 'Lublin Bund' was organised by these Bundists. The two Bund groups did not meet and merge until January 1945 in Lublin during a party meeting.[390]

---

385 See, e.g.: M. Fuks, „Prasa żydowska w Polsce XIX i pierwszej połowy XX wieku (do końca II wojny światowej)," *Rocznik Historii Czasopiśmiennictwa Polskiego* 1977, vol. XII, n. 1, pp. 27–55; *Biblyografye fun oysgabes aroysgebn durkh di arbeter-parteyen in poyln in di yorn 1918–1939*, ed. I. Szajn, Warsaw 1963, pp. 30–56.

386 *'Itonut ha-mahteret ha-yehudit be-varsha* (*The Jewish Underground Press in Warsaw*), ed. intr. and annot., Y. Kermish, vol. I, Jerusalem 1979–1980 *passim*; *En Direct du Ghetto. La presse clandestine juive dans le ghetto de Varsovie*, ed. D. Blatman, Paris 2005 *passim*; R. Sakowska, *Ludzie z dzielnicy zamkniętej*, Warsaw 1993, pp. 165–174. *Archiwum Ringelbluma. Konspiracyjne Archiwum Getta Warszawy*, vol. XVI: *Prasa getta warszawskiego: Bund i Cukunft*; part I: *Bund*, intr. and ed. M. Rusiniak-Karwat, part II: *Cukunft*, A. Jarkowska-Natkaniec, Warsaw 2016. Part I contains all available issues of the press titles published in the Warsaw Ghetto by the Bund.

387 L. Dobroszycki, „Zaginiona prasa konspiracyjna z lat 1939–1945," *Najnowsze Dzieje Polski 1939–1945*, 1963, vol. VII, p. 176, item no. 13; *Biuletyn*, the Bund; Łódź, ghetto [1940–1941], manuscript.

388 AAN, The Collection of the Underground and Insurgent Press, ref. 117, *Biuletyn W.B.*

389 *Itonut ha-mahteret ha-yehudit*, *passim*.

390 „Zebranie 'Bundu' w Lublinie," *Biuletyn Bundu*, April 1945, [no number], pp. 14–15.

In April 1945, *Biuletyn Bundu. Wydawnictwo Centralnego Komitetu Bundu w Polsce* [The Bund's Bulletin. Publication of the Bund Central Committee in Poland] was published. Its graphic design and format were similar to issue number 4 of *Biuletyn W.B.* which was printed earlier, although there was no mention of any connection between these two publications. The first page of *Biuletyn Bundu* read:

> We are coming back after five years. Five years marked by a great tragedy for the nation and the Jewish working class. [...] We return after five years, carrying the heroism of our illegal press, published on the barricades of combat. We refer to the old, 47-year tradition of the 'Bund' and its press.[391]

Biuletyn Bundu, just like other Jewish publications released immediately after the war, was printed in Łódź, where there were printing presses that had not been destroyed by the Germans. The editorial office was located on one of the Bund Committee's premises, at 17 Cegielniana Street, apartment no. 5 (now Jaracza Street). The magazine was edited and published by an editorial board whose members are not named. Three issues of *Biuletyn* were published in Polish, in April, July, and November, each issue had 16 pages.[392] Moreover, three issues of *Biuletyn* in Yiddish were published between August and October 1945, titled *Byuletin fun bund. Oysgabe fun tsentral komitet fun bund in poyln* (Yid.: The Bund's Bulletin. Publication of the Bund Central Committee in Poland), which was longer than the Polish edition. For example, the third issue of the Polish-language *Biuletyn* contained only part of the material translated from the Yiddish-language *Byuletin* from October. Both publications contained articles and reports about the Bund's current programme and its stance on the political situation in the People's Republic of Poland. There is no information available regarding the number of copies printed or its distribution, and it is also difficult to determine the editors.

The magazine mainly featured reports on the first meetings and resolutions adopted during the party congresses in Lublin. The texts were most likely written

391 „Wracamy," *Biuletyn Bundu*, April 1945, [no number], p. 1.

392 According to Józef Korzeniowski, 7 issues of *Biuletyn* were published in the period between February 1944 and October 1945 (see: J. Korzeniowski, „Bibliografia czasopism żydowskich wychodzących w PRL (1944–1950)," *Biuletyn Żydowskiego Instytutu Historycznego* 1986, nos 3–4 (139–140), p. 148). During archival research, the author was unable to locate any other issues. The Bundists themselves, when launching the publication of *Folkstsaytung*, mentioned three issues of *Biuletyn* in Polish. The number seven and the publication end dates refer to both *Biuletyn W.B.* (4) and *Biuletyn Bundu* (3), which may have been regarded by Korzeniowski as one and the same Bund press title.

by people involved in rebuilding the Bund, members of the party's Central Committee who also worked as journalists, such as Ignacy Samsonowicz or Grzegorz Jaszuński. The reports from the local committees probably came from Liber Brener (Częstochowa) and Leyb Pudłowski (Łódź). Both men actively participated in the process of party's reconstruction.

From November 1945 to February 1946, there was a pause in the Bund's press publications. The Central Committee justified it as follows:

> After the publication of three issues of *Biuletyn Bundu* in Yiddish and Polish, there was a longer break due to technical reasons in further activities of the Central Committee.
>
> We would now like to inform you that despite all the technical difficulties, we have decided to resume publishing a periodic party press organ under the old title *Folkstsaytung*. The first issue is ready for print and will be published soon.[393]

In post-war Poland, the main magazine published by the Central Committee of the Bund was titled *Folkstsaytung* (Yid.: People's Newspaper). The same title was used for the most important press organ from 1918 until September 1939 (from 1931 under the title *Di naye folkstsaytung*). The post-war paper was intended as a continuation of the pre-war Bund daily, not only because of the reference to the old title but also due to its identical graphic design, format, and internal layout. The publishers expected the magazine to be as successful among the Jewish working class as the pre-war *Di naye folkstsaytung*.[394] However, the year of publication was not consistently stated, which would have emphasised the continuity of the title even more. By giving the publication the name most associated with the Bund, the party underlined its long-standing publishing tradition, its continuous existence, and its unchanging ideological and political programme.

The editorial board also included journalists who had worked for *Di naye folkstsaytung* before the war, even using the same pseudonyms as before, such as: Sonye Blond (Dina), Mordechai Bernstein (Matwiej, M. Zeldin, M. Byteński), Abraham Wolf Yasni (Jasny, A. Wolf, A.W.),[395] Grisha (Grzegorz) Jaszuński (G.J.),

393 AŻIH, the Bund, files n., Circular no. 3/46 from 16 February 1946, by the Bund Central Committee, addressed to all party organisations in the country.

394 J. Sh. Hertz, „*Folkstsaytung* 1918–1939," in: *Di yidishe prese vos iz geven*, eds. D. Plinker, M. Canin, Sz. Rozenfeld, Tel Aviv 1979, pp. 151–169; P. Szwarz, *Folkstsaytung*, in: *Fun noentn oyver*, vol. II: *Yidishe prese in varshe*, Nyu york 1956, pp. 303–439; R. Gechtman, „The Rise as Reflected in the *Naye Folkstsaytung* 1935–1936," *Gal-Ed* 2000, vol. XVII, pp. 29–55; A. Brumberg, „On Reading the Bundist Press," *East European Jewish Affairs* 2003, vol. XXXIII, no. 1, pp. 100–117.

395 Wolf Yasni (Jasny), real name Abraham Wolf Cyperman (1894 Żelechów – 1968 Tel Aviv), journalist. Before the war, he was the editor of *Di naye folkstsaytung*.

and Ignacy Samsonowicz (I. Samson).[396] From August 1946 onwards, Matwiej Bernstein was mainly involved in the newspaper and was responsible for all editorial and administrative matters, most likely until the editorial office was moved to Warsaw in the spring of 1947. Until then, all correspondence (including planning content for future issues) from the editorial office of *Folkstsaytung* was signed with his name.[397]

The editorial board focused on several key topics and programme issues. These were primarily issues concerning the situation of Jews in Poland and the rebuilding of their lives in the country. Already in the first issue in February 1946, the so-called 'Polish option' was frequently pointed out. Secondly, the activities of Zionist organisations in Poland and worldwide were harshly criticised. The Zionists were accused of inciting fear and for calling for emigration.[398] Thirdly, articles were published supporting the new political system and the Bund's participation in the reconstruction of the People's Republic of Poland. A great deal of space was devoted to rebuilding the local branches of the organisation.

Each issue contained circulars from the party's Central Committee. A regular column was also introduced: "Fun partay-lebn" (Yid.: 'from the life of the party'), dedicated to information from across the country (obtained from correspondence). The publication also featured many articles about the Bund in the past, aiming to help members learn and deepen their knowledge of their party's founders and key activists who had contributed to its development. To highlight the heroism and fighting spirit of the Bundists, Tsukunft members, or Skifists, articles were published describing the struggle against the German occupier in the ghettos and the role of Jewish socialists in the Warsaw Ghetto Uprising. There was no mention, however, of the Bund members who had been deported to the Soviet Union and their often tragic fate.

To highlight the tradition of the Jewish socialist movement, articles about the party's origins and its predecessors were published frequently. Articles on the history of the movement appeared in Bundist newspapers as early as the interwar

---

He spent the war in the USSR. From 1946, he was a regular contributor to *Folkstsaytung*. He also worked for *Dos naye lebn* and for the Central Historical Jewish Commission. In 1949, he legally emigrated to Israel together with his wife Chava and two children. He obtained an emigration visa on 31 March 1949 (information from: Yad Vashem Archives, Wolf Yasni Collection, ref. P-5/1).

396 P. Szwarz, *Folkstsaytung*, in: *Fun noentn oyver*, pp. 425–428.

397 See: AAN, the Bund, ref. 30/IV/23, vol. I–II.

398 For more on the subject, see: Chapter V: "The Bund versus Zionism".

period, as well as in the underground press in the Warsaw Ghetto.[399] The first pages were dedicated to the Bund's ideological and programme matters, while the last, contained reports on the activities of municipal party committees and addressed the development of Jewish literature and culture. Often, the last page was filled with information about the press fund and its donors. The publication also reprinted statements by party leaders promoting the Bundist ideology before 1939, emphasising its relevance.[400] The articles were written by professional journalists, party members, and people associated with the socialist movement. Some of the articles were not signed.

In the first issue was published in February 1946, first featured texts that described the position of the Bund in the new political situation (p. 1, L. Hodes, *Tsvishn angstn un hofenung* [Yid.: "Between anxiety and hope"), a platform for cooperation with the CKŻP. The anti-Zionist stance, opposition to the White Paper, emigration, and anti-Semitism were emphasised (p. 2, *Tsu der yidisher bafelkerung in poyln*, [Yid.: "To the Jewish society in Poland"]). Gershon Fogel described the Bundist faction within the CKŻP in his article *Af bundishe vegn* (Yid.: "On a Bundist path").[401]

The magazine was initially intended to be published as a monthly. The second double issue was printed in May 1946.[402] Four issues were published regularly, followed by a break. The first issues of the magazine were published in Łódź, where the largest Jewish population in central Poland was concentrated. At the end of October 1947, the Bund opened its own cooperative and Ringen printing house (Yid. for 'link', Polish name was 'Ogniwo') in Warsaw, where it printed other newspapers for the Bund and its affiliated organisations.[403]

In April 1947, the following notice appeared in *Folkstsaytung*:

> The central organ of the Bund in the Yiddish language, *Folkstsaytung*, which had previously been published in Łódź as a monthly, will now be printed in its own printing

---

399 See: e.g. *En Direct du Ghetto. La presse clandestine juive dans le ghetto de Varsovie*, ed. D. Blatman, Paris 2005, *passim*.

400 E.g. M. Zeldin, "Di ershte may-fayerungen," *Folkstsaytung* 1947, no. 5 (14), p. 10 (on the history of the movement); "Prese-keyt," ibid., 1947, no. 6 (15), p. 8 (press fund); Dr M. Szuldenfrei, "Zol lebn unzer alt-nayer „Bund"!," ibid. 1947, no. 16–17 (25–26), p. 1 (on the Bund's politics at the time); "Yidishe karbones fun hitler-merder konen nisht zayn ka bagloybte eydes kegn zeyere tlinim," ibid. 1948, no. 6 (34), p. 2 (on the fate of Bundists under the Nazi occupation).

401 *Folkstsaytung* 1946, no. 1.

402 *Folkstsaytung* 1946, nos 2–3.

403 AAN, the Bund, ref. 30/IV/4, vol. I, f. *passim*.

> house in Warsaw starting from 1 April. It will be published bi-weekly, on the 1st and 15th day of each month.
>
> The address of its editorial office and administration is: *Folkstsaytung* – Warsaw-Praga, 44 Targowa St, apt. 8.[404]

The publishers wanted the magazine to become a weekly as soon as possible, but there was no mention of turning it into a newspaper.[405] The decision to turn *Folkstsaytung* into a weekly was made during the 8th Bund Congress in Wrocław in March 1947, but one of the obstacles to implementing this plan was the lack of authors.[406]

The circulation of the magazine was approximately 10,000. Given the small number of Bund members, the magazine was intended for a broader Jewish community and for readers outside of Poland. It was published until January 1949, until when the Bund was dissolved. A total of forty-nine issues were published, including eight double issues.[407] After the publication of the first issue of *Folkstsaytung*, its presence in the publishing market was noticed and acknowledged outside of Poland. A summary of the entire issue and reprints of selected articles appeared in *Unzer tsayt* in New York.[408] It read:

> [...] its publication [of *Folkstsaytung* – author's note] is a response and a challenge to the dark forces that believed Jewish life in Poland had been completely erased. Its publication testifies to the continuity, a further step in life, and a new affirmation that the golden 'time' goes on.[409]

Lucjan Blit from London, among others, sent his acknowledgements:

---

404 „Życie społeczne i organizacyjne. 'Folkscajtung' – dwutygodnikiem," *Głos Bundu* 1947, no. 4 (8), p. 8.

405 AŻIH, the Bund, files n., letter to Leo Finkelsztejn from the Bund Central Committee in Poland from March 1947.

406 AAN, the Bund, ref. 30/IV/23, vol. I, letter from 25 March 1947 to I. Trunk, f. 117.

407 In the list of press published by the Bund, Józef Korzeniowski mentioned the youth supplement – *Yugnt shtime* from issue 3 (12) of 1 April 1947. After archival and library queries, the author was unable to find either the supplement, or any post-war magazine with this title. The title was not mentioned in other scholarly publications or in primary sources, nor was there any information on it in the documentation on the Bund (J. Korzeniowski, "Bibliografia czasopism żydowskich wychodzących w PRL (1944–1950)," *Biuletyn Żydowskiego Instytutu Historycznego* 1986, nos 3–4 (139–140), p. 149).

408 "Banayt di *Folkstsaytung* in varshe," *Unzer tsayt* 1946, nos 3–4, p. 12–13.

409 Ibid., p. 12.

> I am writing to you from a distant city, so that you, comrades, know that the name you have given to the Bundist newspaper in Poland has great significance in the lives of each of us who, at some point in our lives, were affiliated with the former *Folkstsaytung.*
>
> So that you know, comrades – editors and publishers – that in the new *Folkstsaytung* lies a spiritual strength and moral courage drawn from the great tradition of this newspaper. For Jewish socialists, for Bundists, it has become a focal point for their faith and their life's struggle.[410]

In July 1946, the Central Committee of the Bund decided to publish *Głos Bundu* in Polish, which was largely the equivalent of *Folkstsaytung.* It was an opinion-forming press organ intended not only for people (including Bundists) who understood Yiddish but also for assimilated Jews unfamiliar with the language, members of Polish political movements with similar ideologies, and their youth organisations. Ignacy Samsonowicz was appointed the editor of the magazine. The title *Głos Bundu* also drew from historical Bundist publications under the same name, issued between 1904 and 1905, as well as *Głos Bundu. Tygodnik Socjalno-Demokratyczny* (The Voice of the Bund. Social Democratic Weekly), published in Warsaw from March 1919 to March 1920 (26 issues in total). The latter was edited by Henryk Erlich, a prominent pre-war leader of the Bundist movement.[411]

Due to the lack of preface, it is difficult to determine whether *Głos Bundu* was planned as a bi-monthly, monthly, or quarterly publication. It was only with issue 7 (11) dated 15 August 1947 that the masthead stated that it was a monthly publication. Before the first issue of the magazine, which was supposed to be published in August 1946, the Central Committee sent a letter to the Central Office of the Paper Industry in Warsaw requesting for paper for 20,000 copies of the *Głos Bundu* single issue.[412] However, the masthead of the newspaper did not include numbering, but it was also not marked that it was a daily issue. Probably, the continuation depended on the sales and readers' opinions. Perhaps it was planned to be published regularly, as evidenced by the correspondence between the Central Committee and local committees in June and July 1946.[413] Probably

---

410 L. Blit, „Di traditsyes fun der *Folkstsaytung,*" *Folkstsaytung* 1946, nos 2–3, p. 1 (a letter dated to April 1946 from London).

411 *Bibliografye fun oysgabes*, p. 53; M. Fuks, „Prasa żydowska w Polsce XIX i pierwszej połowy XX wieku (do końca II wojny światowej)," *Rocznik Historii Czasopiśmiennictwa Polskiego* 1977, vol. XII, n. 1, p. 32.

412 AAN, the Bund, ref. 30/IV/6, vol. I, letter from 12 August 1946 from the Secretary of the Bund Central Committee Salo Fiszgrund to the Central Office of Paper Industry in Warsaw, f. 58.

413 See: ibid., ref. 30/IV/23, vol. I–II, *passim.*

around 10,000 copies of the magazine were published and unlike *Folkstsaytung,* it was published in Warsaw from the very beginning.

Głos Bundu covered a similar range of topics as *Folkstsaytung.* The first issue began with an article in a similar tone to an article in *Folkstsaytung.* On page 1, there was an anonymous text titled *Jakie jest wyjście?* (What is the solution?) which reflected on the possibility of Jews living in post-war People's Poland after all the pogroms, specifically referencing the Kielce pogrom of 4 July 1946, and other anti-Jewish incidents. The article concluded that "the only solution to the current situation can only be our socialist, Bundist approach."[414] The front page featured an article by Zbigniew Mitzner, editor-in-chief of the PPS press organ *Robotnik* [Labourer], titled *Socjalizm mądrych* [Socialism of the wise], stressing the necessity of collaboration with Polish socialists. Other contributors included Grzegorz Jaszuński, Henryk Jabłoński (Secretary of the Central Executive Committee of the Polish Socialist Party and chair of TUR), Ignacy Falk, and Liber Brener, among others. Part of the magazine was an appendix for the Tsukunft youth organisation, titled *Wolna Młodzież* [Free Youth], considered by many researchers to be a separate magazine.[415]

In total, 17 issues of *Głos Bundu* were published, including four double issues, from August 1946 to May 1948.

In 1948, *Głos Bundu* was published as a monthly, while *Folkstsaytung* was published as a weekly. These details were reported to the Polish Film Directorate by Ignacy Samsonowicz, editor-in-chief of *Głos Bundu.*[416]

Although the last issue of *Głos Bundu* was published in May 1948, its publication officially ended with the dissolution of the Bund. Formally, however, it was not until 19 January 1949, that the Central Committee, on behalf of the editorial board, sent a letter to the Department of Social Affairs of the Main Office for Press, Publications, and Performances regarding the discontinuation of the magazine.[417] As late as June 1948, the editorial board responded to a letter from Wanda Kragen, a translator and writer from Kraków:

---

414 „Jakie jest wyjście," *Głos Bundu* 1946, [no. 1], p. 1.

415 See, e.g. E. Koźmińska-Frejlak, „Powojenna prasa żydowska w języku polskim (1944–1950)," in: *Studia z dziejów trójjęzycznej prasy żydowskiej na ziemiach polskich (XIX–XX w.),* ed. J. Nalewajko-Kulikov, Warsaw 2012, p. 214, annotation no. 14.

416 AAN, the Bund, ref. 30/IV/22, vol. I, letter from the editorial office of *Głos Bundu* to the Polish Film Directorate from 28 April 1948, k. 20.

417 AAN, the Bund, ref. 30/IV/22, vol. I, k. 32.

> The editorial board of *Głos Bundu* politely informs that it is unable to determine when your review will be published in *Głos Bundu*, as the publication has been temporarily halted. [...] We apologise for the delay (caused by the editor's illness).[418]

The last correspondence signed by the editor dates back to April 1948.[419] Therefore, the lack of paper allocation could have caused the closure of the publication long before the formal dissolution of the party. Considering that the Bund's press was one of the main means of promoting the party's programme and ideas, and provided information about its internal life and the activities of its members, the discontinuation of *Głos Bundu* could lead to the weakening of party structures and to the inactivity of its members.

As the number of publications issued by the Bund increased, party members tried to promote the newspapers in order to reach as many Jewish communities and Bund committees as possible, while also increasing sales and income. On behalf of the Central Committee, the organisation of the press distribution within the Bund's Press Department was managed in 1946 by Samek [Shmuel] Rychter, and later by Shaya Szechatow.[420]

Since the publication of *Głos Bundu*, and *Folkstsaytung* resulted in two Bund newspapers, Matwiej Bernstein[421] suggested that the party committees should set up press committees tasked with selling as many copies of each issue as possible. In places where no such committee had been set up, a press commissioner should be appointed.[422] The Editorial Board called for propaganda campaigns to be organised by local committees. Current lists of Bund committees were compiled so that they could be sent the latest press publications.[423] Special recruitment campaigns were carried out[424] and local Bund committees received a

---

418 Ibid., ref. 30/IV/22, vol. I, letter from 16 June 1948 to Wanda Kragen, on behalf of the editorial office, f. 30.

419 See: ibid., ref. 30/IV/22, vol. I, f. *passim*.

420 AŻIH, the Bund, files n., Protocol no. 5 from a meeting of the Warsaw Bund Committee from 17 June 1946.

421 Matwiej Bernstein began working in the editorial office in 1946, after his return to Poland from the USSR.

422 Ibid. [undated], letter from Matwiej Bernstein addressed to all party committees (most likely July–August 1946).

423 AAN, the Bund, ref. 30/IV/23, vol. I, letter from 8 June 1946 from Izaak Szmulewicz (employee at the *Folkstsaytung* administration) addressed to Ignacy Falk with a request for a list of Bundist organisations, in order to be able to send the party press to them, f. 14.

424 Similar campaigns, in which publishers sought out readers and encouraged them to buy their magazines, as well as recruit new subscribers, were carried out in

set number of copies to sell. This was considered a party task. According to the correspondence and financial reports, it was not always successful.[425] The only significant success was likely connected with the publication of the expanded 'jubilee' 10th issue of *Folkstsaytung* in January 1947.

Following the pre-war tradition of 'press days', the editorial board of *Folkstsaytung* released a special 16-page issue on 1 February 1947, with an illustrated supplement. The content consisted of the articles: *"Zwycięstwo Bloku Demokratycznego (po kampanii wyborczej)"* (Victory of the Democratic Bloc, following the electoral campaign), *"Rok 1946 w międzynarodowej polityce"* (The Year 1946 in International Politics, by Grisha Jaszuński), *"Moje pierwsze wrażenia z Polski"* (My First Impressions of Poland, by Chaim Wasser), *"Po Kongresie Syjonistycznym"* (After the Zionist Congress, by S. H-c [Hurwicz]), *"Twórczość poety proletariackiego Abrahama Rejzyna"* (The Work of the Proletarian Poet Abraham Rejzin, by Shlomo Mendelsohn), *"Nowela"* (Short Story, by Lejb Olicki). It also included reviews: by Wiktor Szulman[426] on the book *Pionyern un boyer. Memuarn* by John Mill (New York 1946), and by Wolf Jasni on the book *Tragedye w ghettach i obozach* (Tragedies in the Ghettos and Camps)[427] by Dr Yosef Kermisz. The issue also featured numerous other informative articles about the Jewish labour movement.[428]

The issue included an insert with photographs from the history of the Bund up to 1939, covers of Bund press, and current activities of various local committees and organisations affiliated with the Bund. In January 1947, the Warsaw Bund Committee committed to distributing 1,000 copies of the 10th issue of *Folkstsaytung*.[429] The committee in Strzegom also requested 100 more copies of the magazine.[430]

---

post-war Poland by Zionist organisations. *Mosty* (Bridges) created a press network. *Opinia* (Opinion), on the other hand, appealed not for the addresses of organisations but for the addresses of individual people, in order to reach the recipients directly. It was also emphasised that the sale of publications should improve the publisher's finances and enable further publication (information from: Koźmińska-Frejlak, *op. cit.*, pp. 224–227).

425 AAN, the Bund, 30/IV/23, vol. II – letter to Matwiej Bernstein (editor of *Folkstsaytung*) from the Bund Committee in Piotrków from 6 September 1946, f. 71.

426 A. Grabski, „Wiktor Szulman," *Polski Słownik Biograficzny*, no. 201 (vol. 49/2), 2013.

427 The author did not manage to get hold of the title.

428 „Specjalny numer *Folkscajtung*", *Głos Bundu* 1947, no. 2 (6), p. 7.

429 AŻIH, the Bund, files n., Protocol no. 28 from a meeting of the Warsaw Bund Committee from 7 January 1947.

430 State Archives in Wrocław (hereafter: AP Wrocław), All-Jewish Union Bund in Poland, Provincial Committee in Wrocław (hereafter: Bund), ref. 79/4, letter from

For example, the committees in Ziębice and Zagórze organised a campaign to sell the magazine under the slogan: "No Jewish worker without *Folkstsaytung*." The Łódź Tsukunft decided to sell 1,000 copies on the streets, along with subscription coupons for the magazine. Zagórze sold 250 copies as part of the campaign.[431]

The problem of distributing the entire print run of *Głos Bundu* and *Folkstsaytung* stemmed from the fact that the number of copies of each issue far exceeded the number of Bund members. Based on the number of distributed magazines, it is difficult to estimate both the number of Bund members and readers. The fact that getting a refund (from the Central Committee of the Bund) for copies sold shows that only some of the newspapers were sold. We have the figures for *Głos Bundu* up to issue 7 (from August 1947). Larger committees (i.e. those with a higher number of members) received about 200–250 copies of each issue to distribute.

The list of towns and cities to which *Głos Bundu* was sent provides important information about where Bund committees existed between August 1946 and August 1947.

The newspaper was sent to the following towns and cities:

> Białystok, Bielawa, Bystrzyca, Częstochowa, Duszniki-Zdrój, Gęszcze Puste, Jawor (only the issue from August 1946 – 10 copies), Jelenia Góra, Kamienna Góra (Lubawa), Katowice, Kłodzko, Kraków, Kruszniewica[?], Legnica, Lublin, Łódź (here 2,000 copies of the issues nos 1–6, number 7 – 1200)[432], Niemcza, Nowa Ruda, Piotrków Trybunalski, Pietrolesie (Pieszyce), Przemyśl, Rychbach (Dzierżoniów), Szczecin, Strzegom, Świdnica, Tarnów, Wałbrzych (300 copies each), Warszawa, Włocławek, Wrocław, Zagórze, Ząbkowice, Żary and Ziębice. In total, 5,220 copies of the issue from August 1946 were sent out; 6,785 copies of the issue nos 2–3; 6,760 copies of the issue no. 4, and 5,879 copies of issue no. 7.[433]

In the case of *Folkstsaytung,* issue nos 2–3 (from May 1946), 7,581 copies were distributed, including 50 free copies in Łódź, 310 copies sent abroad, and 50 copies sent to Jewish committees in towns where the Bund did not have its own organisation (7,941 copies in total). As far as issue 4 (from June 1946) is concerned, 8,759 copies were distributed, with 400 sent abroad, bringing the total to 9,159 copies.[434]

---

the Bund Committee in Strzegom to the editor's office of *Folkstsaytung* regarding sending more copies, f. 38.

431 AAN, the Bund, ref. 30/IV/23, vol. I, f. 57.

432 Ibid., ref. 30/IV/22, vol. II, f. 17.

433 Ibid., vol. II, c. 35.

434 Ibid., ref. 30/IV/23, vol. I–II.

Readers of the Bundist press in Poland came from various towns and cities in Poland and abroad. Members of the pre-war Bund living abroad, showed great interest in the press published in Poland. Requests for further issues were sent to the Central Committee of the Bund from countries such as Chile, Australia, Canada, the USA, and Palestine.

The *Folkstsaytung* was distributed in Poland and abroad, not only to Jewish organisations but also to individual readers. One reader, who ended up in the United Kingdom after the war, suggested that *Folkstsaytung* be transformed into a daily newspaper, as he considered it an important tool in the struggle against the challenges of post-war Poland. He contributed one pound to the press fund and urged others to contribute to the paper's development, as well.[435]

By publishing the press in both Polish and Yiddish, they gained access to a potentially broader audience. The Polish-language *Głos Bundu* was an opinion-forming magazine, aimed not only at Jewish socialists, but also to other assimilated Jewish groups and to Poles. The Yiddish language press was aimed at people who could read in that language. Publications in Yiddish were directed at the Jewish community, whose members had the opportunity to rediscover their native language after the war, when most of them had no contact with it. Meanwhile, young people and children were given the opportunity to learn the language of their ancestors the language of the Jews from East-Central Europe. Requests for *Głos Bundu* also came from public libraries and the KRN (National Remembrance Committee) library.[436]

It is difficult to reconstruct the editorial work of both publications, as *Folkstsaytung* was published in Łódź and *Głos Bundu* in Warsaw. It is very likely that the content of each issue was strongly influenced by the Presidium of the Bund Central Committee as well as by the editors of the respective publications. In addition, the content of the individual issues published at the same time often complemented each other. In the summer of 1946, readers and field correspondents were asked to send information and reports on activities intended for publication in both magazines to the editorial and administrative office of *Folkstsaytung* at 17 Jaracza Street, apt. 5 in Łódź.[437] Editorial meetings were held in private homes – for example, in April 1947 one was held at Grzegorz Jaszuński's residence.[438]

---

435 AŻIH, the Bund, files n., letter to the Bund Central Committee in Poland from Liber Gotlob (Gottlob) from Brandon in Great Britain from 28 May 1947.

436 AAN, the Bund, ref. 30/IV/22, vol. I, correspondence arriving at the *Głos Bundu* editorial office from various organisations with requests for free issues, *passim*.

437 AŻIH, the Bund, files n., Letter penned by Matwiej Bernstein addressed to all party committees [undated; most likely July-August 1946].

438 AAN, the Bund, ref. 30/IV/23, vol. I, letter from 26 April 1947, f. 87.

The editors commissioned or requested articles from pre-war Bund members who were currently living abroad, particularly on topics related to the history of Jewish socialism. They sought contributions from participants, organisers, and witnesses of the fight and resistance of the Warsaw Ghetto Uprising.[439]

In their efforts to reach the widest audience possible, the editors also invited people associated to Bund members to collaborate with them, such as Irena Krzywicka (a writer, journalist, and literary translator). She was offered to collaborate on a commemorative article about one of the founders of the Bund, Noyekh (Józef Portnoy), who was also her stepfather.[440]

The editors of *Głos Bundu* paid fees for commissioned articles. For example, Jerzy Kirchmayer, a military historian, writer, and publicist, received 3,250 zlotys for an article on the Warsaw Ghetto Uprising.[441]

The exact number of permanent staff members in the editorial teams is difficult to determine. Sometimes the same people contributed articles to both *Głos Bundu* and *Folkstsaytung*. In March 1948, three people worked for both editorial teams, as indicated by the correspondence regarding the issue of discount cards by the Warsaw Municipal Transport Company in 1948.[442]

The magazine earned money not only through the sale of individual issues, but also from paid advertisements and notices.[443]

Every press agency in Poland was facing major obstacles, and distribution was not the only problem that they had to overcome. They also had a shortage of authors, financial resources and the state's strict control over the publishing industry. From 1944 onwards, the Polish Government established a series of administrative bodies that regulated the press, granting concessions for printing and, most importantly, controlling the allocation of paper. Every issue of a periodical had to be submitted to the Central Office for Press and Publishing

---

439 AAN, ibid., ref. 30/IV.22, vol. I, Letter from the *Głos Bundu* editorial office to Rachela Auerbach (Łódź), Maurycy Anhalt (Kraków), Nachman Blumental (Warsaw), Wanda Kragen (Kraków) from March 1948 with a request for an article for the anniversary of the outbreak of the Warsaw Ghetto Uprising, f. 3–5, 7.

440 Ibid., Letter from the *Głos Bundu* editorial office to Irena Krzywicka from 9 March 1948 in Warsaw, f. 6.

441 Ibid., letter from the *Głos Bundu* editorial office to Jerzy Kirchamayer to Warsaw from 21 April 1948, f. 18.

442 Ibid., letter from the editorial office to the Warsaw Municipal Transport Company from 10 March 1948, f. 12.

443 Ibid., ref. 30/IV/23, vol. I, letter from the administration of *Folkstsaytung* to all Bund committees and press commissions from 1947, f. 5.

Control in Warsaw for approval prior to printing.[444] Similarly, when there was a plan to expand the publication's volume, the Bund had to request permission from the same body.[445] Perhaps these restrictions, as well as the lack of opportunities to criticise the Polish authorities at the time, had an impact on the infrequent publication of the magazine in Polish.

In addition to the press, occasional prints were also published to mark important anniversaries. In April 1946, the Bund published a brochure titled *Za Waszą i Naszą Wolność* ('For Your Freedom and Ours') marking the third anniversary of the Warsaw Ghetto Uprising. It contained articles about the Warsaw Ghetto, the Uprising, and the Bund members who fought in it. In the introduction, the author stressed:

> It is no coincidence that the brochure published by the Central Committee of the Bund, dedicated to the anniversary of the Warsaw Ghetto Uprising, bears the title "For Your Freedom and Ours!" Throughout the entire German occupation, until the liquidation of the Warsaw Ghetto, "For Your Freedom and Ours" was published monthly. The 'Bund' spoke to the thousands of Jewish and Polish workers on several thin sheets of paper, hand-printed on a duplicator. In addition to radio news, which at that time was quite a sensation, our publication provided a sober assessment of the political situation at that time and the much-needed words of encouragement.[446]

Also included were political declarations:

> Today [...] we live in an independent Poland, in Poland for which we fought relentlessly on both sides of the wall, amidst the fires and ruins of the ghettos [!] in the forests of Lublin, Białystok, in Belarus and Volhynia, in the Warsaw August Uprising, in the ranks of the Polish Army.
>
> We remain faithful to our banners and our idea! We now have new tasks, and different work lies ahead of us. But our spirit is the same. We fought and will always fight for Freedom, Equality, and Socialism, for Your Freedom and Ours![447]

The Bund, through its Historical Commission, published *Byuletin fun der historisher komisye baym tsentral komitet fun bund in poyln* (Yid. for 'Bulletin of

---

444 Ibid, ref. 30/IV/6, vol. I, letter from the *Głos Bundu* editorial office to the Central Office for Press, and Publishing Control in Warsaw from 15 October 1946, requesting permission to publish the second issue of *Głos Bundu*, f. 65.

445 Ibid., ref. 30/IV/4, vol. II, letter from the Central Office for Press, Publishing and Performances Control at the Presidium of the Council of Ministers to the Bund Central Committee in Warsaw from 24 October 1947, f. 313.

446 ***, „Za Waszą i Naszą Wolność" from April 1946, a brochure, p. 1.

447 Ibid., p. 8.

the Historical Commission at the Bund Central Committee in Poland') from October 1946 to February 1947.[448]

The words of the Bund members from Poland could also be found in the Magazines published by organisations affiliated with the Bund, such as Tsukunft (*Yugnt veker, Unzer tsukunft*) and Skif (*Khavershaft*)[449], as well as in *Dos naye lebn* and the PPS newspaper titled *Robotnik* (Grzegorz Jaszuński). Additionally, the Bund's influence was visible abroad, in publications such as the New York *Unzer tsayt* and the Paris-based *Unzer shtime*. Oftentimes, these were reprints of articles originally published in the press in Poland.

The press was the most important means of social communication at the time and undoubtedly played a significant role in the lives of the surviving Jews, including party members. The decision to continue publishing titles from before 1939 was driven primarily by the desire to mark their presence on the then 'Jewish Street'. The aim of the publications in Yiddish aimed to preserve the Yiddish language and Jewish culture (*yidish un yidishkeyt*). The magazines in Polish were intended to reach new readers outside of the Yiddish-speaking community.

Historical Commission at the Bund Central Committee and the Bundists' involvement in shaping the image of anti-Nazi resistance

Bund members who survived World War II and decided to rebuild the party in the new post-war reality considered it an important task to preserve the organisation's history, including the underground activities of the party and its affiliated organisations during the German occupation. In particular, they aimed to document the Holocaust and the Warsaw Ghetto Uprising. To this end, they proposed a special unit within the Bund as early as the autumn of 1944. The

448 See: in Chapter Four sub-chapter titled: „The Historical Commission at the Bund Central Committee and the Bundists' involvement in shaping the image of anti-nazi resistance."

449 Contributors to *Yugnt veker* included, i.a. Mordechai Bernstein (using the pen-name M. Zeldin) on the youth movement in the Warsaw Ghetto; Moshe Kligsberg (see, e.g.: M. Zeldin, *Di ‚tsukunft'- prese in geto, Yugnt veker* 1946, no. 1, pp. 2–3; Idem, *„Tsukunft"- arbet in geto (materyaln un dokumentn)*, ibid., 1947, no. 1 (2), p. 12; M. Kligsberg, *Miriam shifman – a simbol fun dor*, ibid., no. 9 (10), pp. 4–6). It should be noted that the two last issues of *Khavershaft* were published as a supplement to *Folkstsaytung* (no. 10 (38) from 19 April and nos 12–13 (40–41) from 1 June 1948).

last war and the Holocaust drastically reduced the population of Polish Jews. As a result of the war, most of the documents pre-1939 were lost, and archives and libraries of the Bund and its affiliated organisations (Tsukunft, Skif, Morgnshtern) were also lost. Most of the library and archival resources were either destroyed or scattered.

The members of the Central Committee sought to reconstruct events from the earliest period of the Bund's activity. They often emphasised the necessity of such an endeavour while the last witnesses of the past era were still alive and could provide testimonies or share preserved documents and photographs. They also intended to commemorate the Bundists as well as Tsukunft and Skif members who had lost their lives during the German occupation, as well as to reconstruct the underground activities of the Bund and its affiliated organisations. However, this effort to preserve the organisation's history was selective and completely ignored the issue of commemorating the fate of Jewish socialists (as already mentioned above) who found themselves in the USSR during the war, including those who had perished there, such as pre-war Bund leaders Victor Alter and Henryk Erlich, or the Bund's pioneer Anna Rozental.

On 16–17 June 1945, on the second day of the First National Conference of the Bund in Łódź, among many proposals concerning the reconstruction of party organisations, David Klin put forward a motion to establish a commission for these activities: "The Central Committee of the Bund should establish a Commission to compile materials concerning our role and work in the ghetto and on the 'Aryan' side."[450] During the discussion, conference participants pointed out that without the knowledge of history, it would be impossible to rebuild Jewish life or properly fulfil their duties.[451] In the summer of 1945, the Bund branch in Białystok received instructions from the Central Committee regarding activities to reconstruct the party's archives.[452] A few months later, on 16 December 1945, at one of the first meetings of the Bund's Central Committee in Łódź, the attendees decided to establish the Department for Historical Work at the Central Committee of the Bund in Poland (Yid.: *Referat far historishe arbetn baym ts.k. fun bund in poyln*). Its tasks included, above all, collecting materials

450 AZIH, the Bund, files n., Report from the First National Conference of the Bund in a Reborn, Democratic Poland.

451 *Byuletin fun der historisher komisye baym ts. k. fun bund in poyln* (Yid.: Bulletin of the Historical Commission at the Bund Central Committee in Poland) February 1947, no. 3, p. 2.

452 AŻIH, the Bund, files n., Protocol no. 3 from 8 August 1945 on the activity of the Bund Committee in Białystok.

on the Bund's activities during World War II to honour the fallen Bundists and to preserve the party's achievements during the occupation.[453]

The department was established primarily due to the passion of the members of the post-war Bund's first central authorities. Most likely, the new unit for historical and archival tasks was modelled on the Central Jewish Historical Commission (Yid.: 'Tsentrale yidishe historishe komisye', CŻKH), established in August 1944 and operating under the CKŻP,[454] as well as on the Jewish Scientific Institute (Yid.: *Yidisher visnshaftlekher institut*, hereafter: YIVO),[455] founded in 1925 with its main headquarters in Vilna.

At the end of 1945, a circular was issued to inform Bund members about the establishment of the Department for Historical Works under the Central Committee of the Bund. It was sent to local Bund committees and published in *Folkstsaytung*. The circular recommended that each committee appoint a delegate responsible for overseeing historical and archival work and be responsible for

453 AP Wrocław, the Bund, ref. 79/7, Circular of the Department for Historical Work under the Central Committee of the Bund in Poland, signed by Gershon Fogel, undated, f. 40; see also: "Cirkulyar," *Folkstsaytung* 1946, no. 1, p. 3.

454 Central Jewish Historical Commission was founded in August 1944 in Lublin. Its organisational structure was based on the Central Commission based in Warsaw and on Provincial Branches. In the autumn of 1947, in accordance with the 1944 statute of the Commission, it was transformed into the Jewish Historical Institute. Its main tasks included commemorating the Holocaust during the German occupation, collecting sources from this period in the form of archival documents, publications, press, and leaflets, recording the testimonies and witnesses' accounts, and publishing historical and popular works. Information from: AŻIH, Central Jewish Historical Commission at the Central Committee of Jews in Poland (hereafter: CŻKH), ref. 303/XX/3, Statute CŻKH, ff. 1–5; M. Horn, „Działalność Żydowskiego Instytutu Historycznego w Polsce w latach 1944–1979," in: *Trzydzieści pięć lat działalności Żydowskiego Instytutu Historycznego w Polsce Ludowej (Dzieje Instytutu i jego zbiory)*, Warsaw 1980, pp. 5–14.

455 Yidisher visnshaftlekher institut (Yid.: Jewish Scientific Institute) was founded in Berlin in 1925, but the founders chose Vilna as its headquarters. The Institute's staff began sociological, ethnographic and demographic research, as well as analysing the economic situation of Jews in Poland and other countries in Central and Eastern Europe, and conducting systematic research into Jewish language and literature, within the framework of four sections: philological, historical, economic and statistical, pedagogical and psychological (see, i.a.: *Żydowski Instytut Naukowy, jego cele i badania*, Vilna 1930; A. Cała, *Ostatnie pokolenie. Autobiografie polskiej młodzieży żydowskiej okresu międzywojennego ze zbiorów YIVO Institute for Jewish Research w Nowym Jorku*, Warsaw 2003, p. 9).

cooperating with the head of the department at the central level. The department was initially headed by Gershon Fogel. For the headquarters, the Bund chose the office of the Łódź branch of the Bund and the Central Committee of Tsukunft, which was located at 17 Cegielniana Street, apartment no. 5 (now Jaracza Street).[456]

In the available files concerning the Bund in Poland after 1944, as well as in the files in institutions collaborating with the party, there is no information on the work of the department until the summer of 1946. Therefore, it is impossible to determine whether the appeal to submit files and to delegate a person to cooperate had the intended effect.[457] The activities of the department, which was transformed into the Historical Commission under the Central Committee of the Bund, were better documented when Matwiej Bernstein took charge after returning to Poland from the USSR in the summer of 1946.[458]

The main objectives and tasks of the Historical Commission were outlined by the Bund Central Committee members in a circular dated 21 August 1946:

1. To collect materials regarding the participation of the Bund, Tsukunft, and Skif in underground activities from 1939 until the liberation of Poland.
2. To rebuild and gather materials about the movement prior to the year 1939.[459]

The Commission planned to create a list of party members (including biographical notes and photographs, if possible) who perished during the German occupation. They also aimed to collect photographs (if they had been preserved) and memoirs of surviving comrades about their personal experiences during the war. The intention was to reconstruct the party archives, collecting as many documents, accounts, and photographs as possible, showing the entire history of the party's activities to date. It was assumed that copies of the photographs would be made and the originals would be returned to their owners. The Bund

456 AP Wrocław, the Bund, ref. 79/7, Circular of the Department for Historical Work under the Central Committee of the Bund in Poland, signed by Gershon Fogel, undated, f. 40; see also: "Cirkulyar," *Folkstsaytung* 1946, no. 1, p. 3. From the beginning of 1946, the editorial office of *Folkstsaytung* was located there, too.

457 Also in the report on the functioning of the CŻKH at that time, the circular was not mentioned in the chapter: "Współpraca z pokrewnymi instytucjami w kraju i zagranicą," in: N. Grüss, D. Grünbaum, *Rok pracy Centralnej Żydowskiej Komisji Historycznej*, Łódź 1946, pp. 20–24.

458 AAN, the Bund, ref. 30/IV/23, vol. I, wire from M. Bernstein to I. Falk from July 1946 in which Bernstein informs about his arrival in Poland; AŻIH, the Bund, files n., Circular no. 14 of the Bund Central Committee from 27 August 1946, f. 11.

459 AŻIH, the Bund, files n., Circular no. 13, issued by the Bund Central Committee, 21 August 1946 in Warsaw.

authorities promised to publish information about the documents sent, including a list of 'donors' of the archival materials in the *Folkstsaytung*.[460]

As mentioned when creating the structures of the Historical Commission, the Bund Central Committee was able to draw on the experience of institutions of a similar nature, whose employees or associates were Bund members, such as Liber Brener and Motl (Motek) Kusznir (research staff of the Central Jewish Historical Commission – field reporters in Częstochowa). After the Historical Commission was established, they actively worked in their hometown to expand the party archive collection and documented their recollections of the Częstochowa Ghetto and the camps.[461] In the course of their work, they had to familiarise themselves with the instructions issued by the Central Jewish Historical Commission on how to collect and describe memoirs and how to conduct interviews.

The goal of both institutions (the Central Jewish Historical Commission and the Historical Commission of the Bund Central Committee) was to archive documents from the war and the German occupation. In addition, the Bund extended the time frame of its research to include the earlier period of the party's existence. Both commissions based their organisational structure on local branches. In the case of the Central Jewish Historical Commission, these were Provincial Commissions. The Historical Commission of the Bund Central Committee, as mentioned above, initially proposed appointing one person to cooperate with each party committee. Subsequently, the plan was to create local branches of the Commission.[462] In the Central Jewish Historical Commission, different employees were responsible for specific tasks at the central office. In the case of the Bund's Historical Commission, most of the work was handled primarily by Matwiej Bernstein. He was the recipient of the correspondence addressed to the Commission.

Matwiej's involvement in the Commission's work was no coincidence. In the 1920s, he met Max Weinreich, a teacher at the Vilna Jewish Teachers' Seminary and the director of YIVO. Under his leadership, the Commission drew from the traditions of YIVO, with which he was associated with until his arrest on 29 August

460 Ibid.

461 List of the Central Jewish Historical Commission, pp. 54–55. N. Grüss, *Rok pracy Centralnej* Żydowskiej *Komisji Historycznej*, Łódź 1946; AAN, the Bund, ref. 30/IV/16 – Matwiej's correspondence with Motl Kusznir and Moses Lederman from 1946, f. 13, 20, 25–27; ibid., ref. 30/IV/18 – correspondence between M. Bernstein and M. Kusznir, *passim*.

462 To compare the main ideas behind the functioning of the commissions, see: AŻIH, CŻKH, ref. 303/XX/3, CŻKH's statute, f. 1–5; ibid., the Bund, files n., Circular no. 13.

1940. His professional experience, knowledge, and pre-1939 party activity were assets in archival and research work. Thanks to his earlier involvement, he enjoyed the trust of the Jewish community. Many Bund members knew him personally and considered him as a trustworthy person and friend. He was an authority for younger party members as a pre-war teacher at the Warsaw School of Legal Officers.[463]

From the very beginning, the Commission focused on the organisation of collection campaigns (Yid.: *zaml-aktsyes*) aimed at gathering as much information and materials as possible about the Bund and its members during the German occupation. The Historical Commission intended to publish a monograph on the history of the party during the war. It also reached out to Polish communities for help in providing information:

> Since the majority of our nation's heroes perished in the unequal struggle against the occupying force and few witnesses – Jews, who participated in the underground struggle for freedom – remain alive, we appeal to you, Poles, to gather all materials, anything you know about the activities of the Bund or individual Bund members during the period of resistance and uprisings under the German occupation, and bring them either in person or submit them in writing to the address provided below.[464]

The aim was to show the underground activities of the party, the fate of the Bund members in ghettos, camps, and on the 'Aryan' side, their heroic struggle against the Germans, and to honour the memory of those who fell and were murdered during World War II, especially those who perished in the camps, ghettos, during uprisings and rebellions, especially during the Warsaw Ghetto Uprising.[465]

In November 1945, the Central Committee of the Bund published a book by Marek Edelman titled *Getto walczy (Udział Bundu w obronie getta warszawskiego)*[466] [The Ghetto Fights. The Bund's Role in the Defense of the Warsaw Ghetto], which was partly a memoir by a participant and hero of these events, and part historical work, containing information gathered from fellow conspirators and fighters. Articles were also published in the Bundist press, containing

463 AAN, the Bund, ref. 30/IV/18, letter from 16 September 1946 from Częstochowa to Comrade Matwicj, f. 1.

464 „Odezwa Komisji Historycznej Bundu," *Tygodnik Informacyjny. Organ Wojewódzkiego Komitetu Żydów Polskich w Szczecinie* 30 October 1946, nos 7–8, p. 2.

465 No author [?], „Odezwa Komisji Historycznej Bundu," *Tygodnik Informacyjny* 30 October 1946, nos 7–8, p. 2.

466 Warsaw 1945. First edition in English translation titled *The Ghetto Fights* (New York 1946) was published by the American Representation of the General Jewish Workers' Union of Poland.

memories from the war, including testimonies of children saved from the Holocaust. All these accounts, statements, and studies, revealed the brutality and depravity of German Nazism, incomparable to anything the Jewish people had experienced throughout history.[467]

The Bund members sought to create a list of deceased party members and obtain information about them, which could later be used to write biographical notes.[468]

By collecting materials on the activities of the party and affiliated organisations prior to 1939, the Historical Commission aimed to at least partially reconstruct the Bund's archives, which had been destroyed during the war. To inspire local committees to work hard, Matwiej sent out letters asking people to send photographs of himself and other Bund members from that time, as well as photos of the party's activities, including youth camps, with instructions on how to describe the photographs (e.g. information about the people in the photos and their fate).[469]

Due to the large volume of materials sent, and the need to process and organise them, the Commission was divided into five sections in the autumn of 1946: the archive, biographical index, photo album, library, and bibliographic section.[470] Since then, the Commission's organisational structure was similar to YIVO and the Central Jewish Historical Commission. The work of the Historical Commission at the Bund Central Committee corresponded with the Historical Section of YIVO. The bibliographic index was equivalent to the Central Bibliographic Office at YIVO. The archive and library collections were built thanks to the generosity of many people. The Historical Commission at the Bund Central Committee, like the two previous institutions, had its own publishing plans. There were plans to publish a monograph of the Bund for individual towns and cities.[471]

---

467 See, e.g. *Głos Bundu* 1948, nos 2–3 (15–16), entire devoted to the 5th anniversary of the Warsaw Ghetto Uprising. It included texts on the experiences in the ghettos, the organisation of armed uprising, but also memoirs and documents describing experiences in the camps, e.g. R. Grynbaum-Sznurbachowa, *Byłam w komorze gazowej... (autentyczna opowieść więźniarki z Oświęcimia)*, p. 2.

468 AŻIH, the Bund, files n., Committee in Tarnów, Committee's correspondence with the Historical Commission in 1946.

469 AAN, the Bund, ref. 303/IV/16 – Matwiej Bernstein's correspondence addressed to specific individuals and various institutions from 1946.

470 „Dergreykhere rezultatn," *Byuletin fun der historisher komisye baym ts. k. fun bund in poyln*, October 1946, no. 1, pp. 6–7.

471 On the structure and activities of YIVO, see: *Żydowski Instytut Naukowy, jego cele i badania*, Vilna 1930.

The original documents created during the German occupation were a very valuable part of the Bund's archive. They came from the so-called underground archive of the Bund in the Warsaw Ghetto, part of which was found in 1946. The party press wrote about this event with delight.

> [...] Recently, a tin can was retrieved, at the time of danger carefully stored on the 'Aryan' side where part of the Central Committee of the Bund's archive was hidden. It is now being studied and processed by the Party Historical Commission. The can contained newspapers, brochures, notes, diaries, and other authentic records that constituted the chronicle of the Tsukunft youth organisation, affiliated with the Bund in Warsaw from the beginning of 1941 until June 1942. The book of Tsukunft protocols from the same period was preserved, too.[472]

Among the documents found in the can were written accounts of experiences of people living in the ghetto, protocols, reports, underground press published by the Bund and Tsukunft, as well as two publications issued by the *Sotsyalistishe yugnt biblyotek* (SIB, Yid. for 'Socialist Youth Library'), the Tsukunft publishing house: *Lider* and a work edited by Abrasha Blum – *Parizer komune – 1871–1941. Zamlbukh*, Warsaw 1941. Among the documents prepared underground included, *Dziennik Warszawskiego Komitetu Cukunftu z okresu od 1 stycznia 1941 roku do 23 kwietnia 1942 roku* (The Diary of the Warsaw Tsukunft Committee from 1 January 1941 until 23 April 1942) as well as a book with Protocols from Tsukunft meetings in the Warsaw Ghetto, among others.[473] The Commission set itself the goal of locating the entire underground Bund archives from the Warsaw and Łódź Ghettos.[474] Bernstein, writing under the pen-name M. Zeldin in *Yugnt-veker* (the press organ of Tsukunft) emphasised in his historical articles that the Bundists had only recovered a small part of the archive after the war. The remaining materials and documents, hidden in various places, still lie beneath the rubble of the ghetto. The documentation that was found became a

472 M. Byteński, „Prasa podziemna," *Głos Bundu* 1946, nos 2–3, p. 8.

473 AAN, the Bund, ref. 30/IV/17, lists of the Bund newspapers in the recovered underground Bund archive, f. 17–18; *Byuletin fun der historisher komisye baym ts. k. fun bund in poyln*, October 1946, no. 1, pp. 7–10.

474 During the war, many organisations hid their archives from the enemy. Among these was the underground archive of the Jewish Combat Organisation, also recognized as the archive of Dror (Jewish youth organisation with a socialist-Zionist character, affiliated with Poale Zion Right). In October 1946, the Presidium of the CKŻP planned to grant a subsidy for its retrieval (information from: AŻIH, Archives of the Presidium and Secretariat, ref. 303/I/3, Protocol no. 80 from 8 October 1946, k. 166).

source for articles published in post-war press about the activities of the party in the Warsaw Ghetto.[475]

Bono Winer, one of the Tsukunft activists in the Łódź Ghetto, decided to return to Łódź after the war, and to search for the youth organisation's hidden archive, which documented its underground activities during the German occupation. He found one of the two boxes of documents. Upon emigrating from Poland, he took the rescued documents abroad.[476]

In addition to the documents from the Bund and its affiliated organisations, the underground and later post-war archive, included press from other political groups published in the Warsaw Ghetto,[477] and the underground press of Polish socialists outside the ghetto.

By the autumn of 1946, the archival collection had been expanded to include other newspaper titles published by the Bund and Tsukunft before the outbreak of the war in 1939.[478]

As part of their work on a biographical index, by October 1946, the Bundists had collected over 1,000 names of party members who perished during the German occupation. A file was created from the names, which was supplemented with more detailed personal data. This was achieved for about 120 individuals of the deceased and murdered. Photographs of some of them were also obtained.

An important achievement of the Commission was the collection of a large number of photographs and the creation of an album. The album was divided into three sections:

475 See, i.a.: M. Zeldin, „Literatur un kultur. Mendele, i.l. perets, sholem-aleykhem, a. rayzen un andere yidishe shrayber tsugast bay der bundisher yugnt in varshever geto (oyfn samekh fun materyaln fun bundishn geto-arkhiv)," *Folkstsaytung* 1946, no. 8, p. 4; Idem, „Di ,tsukunft'-prese in geto," *Yugnt veker* 1946, no. 1, pp. 2–3; Idem, „Materyaln un dokumentn (fun arkhiv baym ts. k. fun ,bund')," *Yugnt veker* 1947, no. 3 (4), pp. 20–21.

476 Ch. Rosenfarb, *An Oak Has Fallen*, in: *Bono Wiener Remembered / Dos bono viner gedenkbukh*, Montreal 1997, pp. 30, 32. Documents submitted to the Bund Archives in New York, currently at YIVO (ref. RG 1452 – Bono Wiener Collection). Among the documents there are, i.a., telegrams from the Łódź Ghetto and Winer's diary from the ghetto.

477 AAN, the Bund, ref. 30/IV/17, letter from 17 January 1947 from the editorial office of *Mosty* – published by the Zionist party Hashomer Hatsair, regarding transfer of the Hashomer Hatsair publication recovered in the underground archive of the Bund, f. 16.

478 AAN, the Bund, ref. 30/IV/17, lists of the Bund press found in the recovered underground Bund archive, ff. 17–18; *Byuletin fun der historisher komisye baym ts. k. fun bund in poyln*, October 1946, no. 1, ff. 7–10.

1. Up to 1939;
2. The underground;
3. The reborn movement.

The first section, consisting of two albums, included approximately 500 photographs documenting events in the life of the party and the organisations and institutions affiliated with it, such as Tsukunft, Skif, Morgnshtern, the Vladimir Medem Sanatorium in Miedzeszyn, Kultur Lige, and others.[479]

Inside the albums the photographs were organised thematically, and each photograph was assigned a serial number (an Arabic numeral), which also served as its reference number. By 30 August 1946, a portion of these photographs had been sorted, described, and catalogued by Matwiej.[480] On the front of each photograph, there is a reference number and a stamp with the inscription in Yiddish: *Arkhiv baym tsentral komitet fun bund* (Yid. for 'Archive at the Central Committee of Bund'). The archival work was facilitated by the fact that some of the photographs were accompanied by descriptions, in accordance with the Commission's guidelines. From the war period and occupation, it was possible to collect a set of photographs of fighters from the Warsaw Ghetto, photographs of the Bund's underground committee in the Łódź Ghetto and Tsukunft in the Tarnów Ghetto, as well as other localities. Photographs of Jewish partisans were also collected. [481]

The majority of the collection consist of photographs taken after 1945, documenting the activities of Bundist organisations in the post-war period. Some of these photographs, taken before 1946, were described and compiled in an album titled *Bund in banaytn poyln* (Yid. for *The Bund in Reborn Poland*). They were published in the press from 1946 to 1948 – in *Yugnt veker, Głos Bundu*, and *Folkstsaytung*, as an appendix to articles about the revival of Jewish socialist life. [482]

In the library and bibliographic section, efforts were focused on collecting books and articles primarily related to the history of the Bund. The library's collection included works published both prior to 1939 and after the war. Donations

479 *Byuletin fun...*, October 1946, no. 1, pp. 11–12; ibid., November 1946, no. 2, pp. 21–22. Albums are kept in the Documentation Department of the Jewish Historical Institute.

480 AAN, the Bund, ref. 30/IV/23, vol. I, Matwiej's letter to Abram Stolar in Warsaw, ff. 22–23.

481 Information from, i.a. *Byuletin fun...*, November 1946, no. 2, p. 23.

482 On the newspapers published after the war, see: Chapter Four, sub-chapter: "Bund's press and other publications."

came from individuals and institutions in Poland and abroad. This section also collected local newspapers containing information on the party's activities.[483]

Initially, information about the activities of the Historical Commission were distributed by the Secretariat of the Bund Central Committee in the form of circulars sent to the Bund and Tsukunft committees or published in *Głos Bundu*, *Folkstsaytung*, and the children's publication *Khavershaft*. As the Commission's work expanded, the first issue of a journal titled *Byuletin fun der historisher komisye baym ts. k. fun bund in poyln* ('Bulletin of the Historical Commission of the Bund Central Committee in Poland') was published in October 1946. It was an information and propaganda magazine about the achievements and plans of the Commission.[484] The Bulletin was addressed to readers both in Poland and abroad.

Between October 1946 and February 1947, three issues of the magazine were published. Each issue consisted of over twenty pages of duplicated typescript, containing reports on the Commission's activities, programmes and plans for the future, as well as guidelines for archival and research work. It also published responses to correspondence from committees and individuals. The value of the publication was highlighted in *Głos Bundu*. It was a visible testimony to the activities of the Historical Commission in the field of collecting and systematically processing materials documenting Jewish life and the history of the socialist movement in Poland.[485] Today, the *Byuletin fun...* remains the only source for studying the scope and methodology of the Commission's work.

In the third issue of *Byuletin fun...*, the Commission presented a new research project and included further instructions on how to collect and sort documents. The issue included:

> [...] a wealth of informative material concerning the Commission's work, as well as a survey project regarding the biographies of deceased or murdered [by the Nazis] teachers from prewar secular Jewish schools in Poland.[486]

The content of the February 1947 periodical did not suggest that the publishing work would be discontinued.

---

483 *Byuletin fun...*, November 1946, no. 2, pp. 26–35; ibid., February 1947, no. 3, pp. 13–22.

484 In this case, it was also modelled on YIVO, whose news organ was a bulletin with similar content to the Bund's *Byuletin*.

485 „Biuletyn Nr 2 Komisji Historycznej," *Głos Bundu* 1946, no. 4, p. 8.

486 „Życie społeczne i organizacyjne. Nr 3 Biuletynu Komisji Historycznej przy C.K. Bundu," *Głos Bundu* 1947, no. 4 (8), p. 8.

The Historical Commission operated alongside a majority of the Bund and Tsukunft committees and, in accordance with the assumptions contained in the aforementioned circular of August 1946, had local representatives in most of the Bund committees. Their tasks included encouraging party members to provide documents of historical value (for the time it takes to make copies) or to hand them over to the Commission, as well as collecting documents. Similarly, the leadership of Tsukunft, also decided to support the Commission's work at the first (seventh)[487] post-war conference, held on 9–10 June 1946 in Łódź, and following the example of the Bund, decided to delegate one member from each Tsukunft committee to assist with the Commission's work.[488]

Members of the Bund, Tsukunft, and Skif sent photographs, books about the Bund and the history of the Jewish community in the town or city where they had lived before the war, including those Jewish settlements that were located beyond the Polish borders after the war. This was necessary to write the Bund monograph.[489]

The committees in Szczecin, Częstochowa, Tarnów, Włocławek and Wrocław were among the most active committees working for the Commission.[490]

The Szczecin Committee had a Historical Commission, which in the autumn of 1946, consisted of about thirty associates collecting materials. News about their activities and the results of their work were published in *Tygodnik Informacyjny,* the organ of the Provincial Committee of Polish Jews in Szczecin and broadcast on the Szczecin radio.[491]

The Bund Committee in Częstochowa created a special commission to collect materials on the history of the Bund among its residents, who were mainly displaced persons from the Eastern Borderlands. Motl Kusznir was assigned to work with Matwiej. His memoirs were included in the CŻKH archives and in 1946 they were published in New York in a collective volume dedicated to the Bund

487 Tsukunft members used double numbering of conferences, recording the number of the conference since the organisation was founded in brackets to show continuity of activity.

488 *Byuletin fun...*, November 1946, no. 2, p. 23.

489 M. Bernstein's correspondence with the Committee in Włocławek in 1946, aiming to collect documents for the memorial book titled *Bund we Włocławku*, AAN, the Bund, ref. 30/IV/16, *passim.*

490 Ibid., *passim.*

491 *Byuletin fun...*, November 1946, no. 2, p. 24; „Z życia społeczno-politycznego Szczecina. Z działalności Bundu," *Tygodnik Informacyjny* 1946, nos 5–6, p. 6.

underground in the ghettos.[492] Liber Brener, chairman of the Częstochowa Bund Committee and the CŻKH representative from Częstochowa, sent materials to the Commission. His life story and experiences were similar to Kusznir's. He also wrote his memoirs and shared them with other institutions.[493] Thanks to them, memoirs of the Bundists from the period of the German occupation were sent from Częstochowa to the Central Office. In accordance with the instructions received, an attempt was made to include as many Bundists' names and emissaries from other ghettos as possible.[494]

Representatives of the Włocławek Committee, wanting to commemorate the history of the Bund in their city, established a special commission to work on producing a monograph of the Włocławek Bund. The commission consisted of: Chaim Tabacznik-Goszczyński, Pinkus Wołkowicz, Jakub Slucki, Itsche Sztern, Leyb Lejster and Moshe Alman.[495] In the autumn 1946, work was underway on the monographs of: Sosnowiec (written by Liber Brener), Piotrków (written by Ignacy Samsonowicz), Łódź (compiled by Tabaksblat[496]), and Vilna (edited by Grisha Jaszuński).[497]

Initially, comrade Reuven[498] was appointed to work in the Tarnów Committee. Together with the local Bund chairman, Usher Bleiwess, he provided information regarding the Bund's activities in the Tarnów Ghetto, biographical details of the party members, photographs from before 1939, and documents testifying

---

492 M. Kusznir, "Di tetikeyt fun 'bund' in der tsayt fun der hitleristisher okupatsye in tschenstochov," pp. 306–315, in: *In di yorn fun yidishn khurvn. Di shtim fun untererdishn bund*, Nyu york 1948.

493 L. Brener, "Tschenstochover geto," in: *In di yorn fun yidishn khurvn. Di shtim fun untererdishn bund*, Nyu york 1948, pp. 295–306. Memoirs of M. Kusznir and L. Brener from the time of German occupation were included in one of the Memorial Books dedicated to the Jews of Częstochowa in the section: *Khurbn tschenstochov*, ed. R. Mahler, *Tschenstochover yidn*, Nyu york 1947.

494 AAN, the Bund, ref. 30/IV/18, letter from Częstochowa from 16 September 1946 to Matwej, ff. 1–3.

495 Ibid., ref. 30/IV/16, *passim*; ibid., ref. 30/IV/17, *passim*; *Byuletin fun...*, November 1946, no. 2, p. 17.

496 First name remains unknown.

497 AAN, the Bund, ref. 30/IV/16, Matwiej's letter to Moses Lederman from Częstochowa from 11 October 1946, f. 27.

498 The author was unable to establish his surname.

to the activities after 1945.[499] In the autumn of 1946, Moshe Brukner, a printer by profession, was selected to work in the Commission.[500]

It is important to highlight the activities of the committees in Legnica and Wrocław, which also sent documents and photographs related to the activities of Bundists before the war in the places where they used to live (mainly in Eastern Galicia), as well as their post-war activities in Lower Silesia.[501]

A separate unit for historical work was also set up in the Warsaw Bund Committee, to which Shaya Szechatow, Abraham Zilbersztejn, and Izrael Czyżyk were elected in 1946.[502]

As part of the cooperations and in connection with the exchange of documents, the Commission maintained contacts in Poland with the CŻKH and, outside of Poland, mainly with YIVO in New York. It also collaborated with the Bund and Tsukunft committees in other countries. Thanks to this cooperation, it was able to acquire materials and exchange information on the history of the organisations and the fate of individual Bundists.[503]

The founding members of the Commission, wanted to involve members of Tsukunft and Skif in the work from the very beginning. The Bundists assumed that the young people would help by collecting materials about the fallen members of their respective organisations during the war and the German occupation. Skif members were asked by the Bundists to send photographs and documents related to the work of the children's organisation in the ghettos. The Commission's staff also requested that those who survived the war in the camps and ghettos should describe their experiences and send them through the local Skif committee to the editorial office of *Folkstsaytung*.[504] The members of Tsukunft were asked to send information about the fallen fighters from the Warsaw, Łódź,

499 AŻIH, the Bund, files n., outgoing correspondence of Tarnów Committee; AAN, the Bund, ref. 30/IV/17, letter from the Bund Committee in Tarnów to Matwiej from 23 November 1946, f. 53.

500 AŻIH, the Bund, files n. (information from the post-war party declaration of Moshe Brukner).

501 AAN, the Bund, ref. 30/IV/16, outgoing correspondence from the chairman of the Historical Commission at the Bund Central Committee, Matwiej Bernstein, to various individuals and institutions, f. 13–27, 43, 89–94; ibid., ref. 30/IV/17, incoming correspondence addressed to Matwiej, f. 21, 53, 63.

502 AŻIH, the Bund, files n., Protocol from a meeting of the Warsaw Bund Committee from 30 September 1946.

503 AAN, ref. 30/IV/17, Correspondence with Szajkowski, *passim*; AŻIH, the Bund, files n., correspondence with YIVO, the Bund and Tsukunft in New York.

504 *Byuletin fun*... October 1946, no. 1, p. 6.

Białystok, and Piotrków Trybunalski Ghettos, as well as the partisans, in order to compile their biographies.[505]

Another way of engaging young people (similar to pre-war competitions for children and youth organised by YIVO[506]) was the announcement in March 1947 of a youth competition titled "Under Nazi Occupation in Poland." The organisers were the Central Committee of Tsukunft and the Historical Commission of the Bund Central Committee. The rules of the competition were similar to those before the war. Just like the works sent in to YIVO, they could be written in Polish or Yiddish and signed with their real names or pseudonyms. The competition was aimed at young people from Poland and abroad, representing different political views as well as non-partisans, who were willing to write down their memoirs and send them to the Central Committee of Tsukunft in Łódź. The competition targeted those "who lived in Poland at the outbreak of the war and later found themselves in ghettos [!], camps, or partisan units."[507]

The deadline for submissions from those living in Poland was 15 June 1947, and for those from abroad it was 1 July 1947. Cash prizes were offered as an incentive to take part in the competition: 10,000 zlotys for first place and three prizes of 5,000 zlotys each for the following places. The award-winning works planned to be published in book form. The Central Committee of Tsukunft appealed to all local branches to appoint one of the youth organisation's members to be responsible for the competition and to spread the information as widely as possible. In order to spread the word about the competition, members of the Historical Commission and the Bund Central Committee planned to post up posters in various Jewish institutions and place announcements in Polish newspapers.

A secondary success of the competition was to create a list, including the current addresses, of Tsukunft members who had survived the war in ghettos, camps, or in partisan units in Poland. The memoirs were to be submitted, similar to the YIVO competitions, in the form of a diary, a short story, or an excerpt from a longer piece of work, no shorter than 10,000 words. It was requested that participants were asked to include as many names and dates as possible in their accounts. The aim was also to honour and commemorate those who had perished.

505 „Akhtung, khaverim!," *Yugnt veker* 1946, no. 1, p. 3.

506 For more information on the subject, see: A. Cała, *Ostatnie pokolenie. Autobiografie polskiej młodzieży żydowskiej okresu międzywojennego ze zbiorów YIVO Institute for Jewish Research w Nowym Jorku*, Warsaw 2003.

507 „Życie społeczne i organizacyjne. 'Pod okupacją hitlerowską w Polsce' (Konkurs na pracę młodzieżową)," *Głos Bundu* 1947, no. 4 (8), p. 8.

The competition jury consisted of representatives of various institutions: Leo Finkelsztejn[508] – chairman of the Jewish Writers and Journalists Union, Major Dr Yosef Kermisz – Secretary General of the CŻKH, Luba Bielicka-Blum – chairwoman of the Tsukunft Central Committee, Marek Edelman[509] – former commander of the Jewish Combat Organisation in the Warsaw Ghetto, and Matwiej Bernstein – representative of the Party Archive and Historical Commission at the Bund Central Committee. After the competition ended, copies of the winning entries were to be sent to scientific institutions engaged in similar topics, including the CŻKH in Warsaw and YIVO in New York.[510]

It is difficult to determine whether any entries were ever submitted, as there is no information on this available in the Bund and Tsukunft archives, nor are there any surviving memoirs from Tsukunft or Skif members submitted for the competition.[511]

A small exhibition was organised in December 1946 at the Municipal Bund Committee in Wrocław, modelled on the YIVO, which organised an exhibition of the Jewish press in Vilna in 1928, to showcase previous achievements and promote the successes achieved. This was also an attempt to encourage people to work in the Historical Commission and to highlight the Bund's presence on the 'Jewish Street'. The exhibition displayed part of the Historical Commission's collection. Archival materials and photographs related to the Bund's activities prior to 1939 and during the occupation were displayed in four rooms.[512] The press commented on the exhibition as follows:

> In another room – "The Epic of the Warsaw Ghetto." Illegal underground publications, bulletins, and Bund newspapers in Yiddish and Polish. The bulletin, *Glok* (The Bell), *Shturem* (Storm), *Za Naszą i Waszą Wolność* (For Our Freedom and Yours), *Nowa Młodzież* (The New Youth), and many others. Next to them proclamations and bulletins from the Łódź Ghetto as well as illegal publications by Polish socialists: *Barykada* (The Barricade), *Robotnik* (The Worker), *Gwardia* (The Guard), *Wolność*

508 Leo Finkelsztejn was also a member of the Bund.

509 Marek Edelman was a member of the Tsukunft Central Committee.

510 For information on the competition, see: "Komunikat," *Yugnt veker* 1947, no. 3 (4), p. 24; AŻIH, the Bund, files n., Circular no. 20, issued by the Tsukunft Central Committee in Łódź, 5 March 1947; Circular no. 21, issued by the Tsukunft Central Committee in Łódź, 12 March 1947.

511 A similar competition was announced by the New York branch of Tsukunft in February 1946 on the pages of *Di Tsukunft/The Future* (Feb. 1946, no. 2, p. 3): *Di „Tsukunft" anonsirt. Di konkurs af eseyen.*

512 „Wystawa Komisji Historycznej Bund we Wrocławiu," *Nowe Życie. Trybuna Wojewódzkiego Komitetu Żydów (WKŻ) na Dolnym Śląsku* 1947, no. 1 (10), p. 4.

(Freedom) and two issues of *Trybuna Wolności* (Tribune of Freedom) by the Polish Workers' Party (PPR).[513]

To highlight the collaboration with the Central Jewish Historical Commission, the Bundists also set up a stand at the exhibition with publications and albums published by the Commission, focusing on the Holocaust in various towns. The last room was dedicated to Skif and Tsukunft. The exhibition highlighted the history of the Bund, its long-standing cooperation with the PPS, and the Bund's activities in reborn Poland. The importance of the Commission's work was emphasised by the fact that it was used in the educational process by teachers at the People's University, which operated under the Jewish Provincial Committee in Wrocław. It was also a significant achievement, as the newspaper *Naprzód Dolnośląski*, wrote "many of those who visited the exhibition found either themselves, their relatives or acquaintances among the photos."

The exhibition was well received by not only by the Bundists and the Lower Silesian Jewish community but also by the Lower Silesian PPS.[514]

The propaganda surrounding the success of the exhibition, in connection with the creation of the Archive, was intended to be an incentive for further work but also an attempt to show the Bund as a political organisation with a future that is thriving in the new post-war reality.

I have presented here the activities of the Commission until the spring of 1947 – the time when its headquarters and Archive, along with the editorial office of *Folkstsaytung* were moved to Warsaw. So far, we have documentation on the activities of the Historical Commission.[515] In the documents available to researchers, the last information about the Commission dates back to March and April of 1947 and is related to the organisation of the aforementioned youth competition. It cannot be clearly determined when the Historical Commission was dissolved – whether in the autumn of 1948, before the self-dissolution of the Bund, along with other institutions under the party's Central Committee, or perhaps earlier, before Matwiej Bernstein's departure from Poland in the summer of 1948. In the last third issue of *Byuletin fun...* from February 1947, there are no signs of its activities coming to an end. The content of the next forthcoming issue

513 „Wystawa ocalałych dokumentów archiwum CK Bundu w Polsce," *Naprzód Dolnośląski (Dziennik WK Polskiej Partii Socjalistycznej Dolnego Śląska)* 1946, no. 260 (286), p. 6.

514 Ibid.

515 AŻIH, the Bund, files n., Circular no. 3/47 of the Bund Central Committee from March 1947, signed by Salo Fiszgrund – secretary of the Bund Central Committee and chair of the party's Warsaw branch.

was announced in the magazine. The work on the next project, the creation of a 'memory album' (Yid.: *yizkor-album*) about the history of TSYSHO and teachers working in secular educational institutions was also presented.

The Commission's collection would probably be more comprehensive if it had expanded its research to include the fate of the Bund members under Soviet occupation and in the remote parts of the USSR, where most of the post-war members of the party and affiliated organisations survived the war. However, due to the attitude of the authorities of the People's Poland and the Bund itself toward their eastern neighbour, there was no option of mentioning Soviet repressions or the situation during the war in the Eastern Borderlands and the USSR.

The frequent changes of the Committee's address may have hindered the flow of information and the timely receipt of correspondence.

After the party dissolved itself, the authorities of the Polish United Workers' Party (PZPR) took over most of the archives of the Central Committee. The Jewish Historical Institute mainly received documents sent from local branches. The albums with photographs and undated images, which were the result of the Committee's work, were handed over. Books from the Bund's library were to be transferred to the library of the Society for the Promotion of Culture and Art.[516]

During the Commission's activities and after the liquidation of the Bund in Poland, the destruction of the Warsaw and Łódź Ghettos was shown on the basis of documents collected by the Commission. They described events, including biographies of Warsaw Ghetto fighters, and were supplemented with photographs from the Commission's collection. Thanks to cooperation with Western institutions, some of the archival materials, including photocopies of documents recovered in part of the Bund's underground archive, were transferred to the YIVO Archives in New York, i.e. to the Hersh Wasser collection. The materials collected in Poland formed the source base for monographs and studies published in the USA, Argentina, and Israel after 1950, including memorial volumes of various towns and cities.

Thanks to Bernstein, Winer, and others who, when emigrating from Poland, took with them fragments of archival documents, written memoirs, photographs, and posters belonging to the Commission, saved some of the materials from being destroyed. They were added to the archive collections of the Bund Coordination Committee in New York, among others so that they could be made available to the general Jewish public and used as sources when writing academic

516 AŻIH, the Bund, files n., Letter „Do Kongresu Zjednoczeniowego Partii Robotniczych w Polsce w Warszawie" (undated).

works on the history of Jews in Poland. It was also possible to continue work started within the Commission outside of Poland, including monographs, e.g. the history of the Bund in Łódź by Jacob Sholem Hertz[517] which used materials also concerning party activity after 1945. In another publication,[518] Hertz presented the history of the Bund in photographs, including those taken after 1944 in Poland, thanks to photographs obtained by the Commission.

Moreover, copies of the book *Historisher zamlbukh. Materyaln un dokumentn tsushteyer tsu der geshikhte fun algemeynem yidishn arbeter-bund*, published in Warsaw in 1948 for the 50th anniversary of the party, has been preserved outside of Poland. According to the information inside the book, it was supposed to be an insert in *Folkstsaytung,* issue no. 18 (46) from 15 August 1948, but there is no information about its distribution or sales in the press or in the Bund's documents. It was probably not distributed or sold. The surviving copies come from the collections of Wolf Yasni (a *Folkstsaytung* staff member) and Matwiej Bernstein, who worked on the book. Presumably, they took copies of the book when they left, and the fate of the remaining copies is unknown.

Many Bundists who left Poland after the war, were editors of publications on the history of the Bund thanks to the experience gained while working for the Commission, as exemplified by the books by Yasni and Bernstein.

For the Bundists, it was just as important to commemorate the anniversaries of the Warsaw Ghetto Uprising, as it was documenting the history of the Bund. The Holocaust was one of the most important topics in political life on the 'Jewish Street', alongside the reconstruction of the state of Israel.[519] Information about the underground struggle and the participation of representative of the Bund organisations in it was passed down especially to the youngest members, the 'Skifists' (e.g. during summer and winter camps). These younger members were to grow up in a culture of heroism, dedication and sacrifice, honouring the memory of their older comrades.

The main ceremonies that were a point of contention between different political and social groups within the Jewish community were not the May Day

---

517 J. Sh. Hertz, *Di geshikhte fun bund in lodzh*, Nyu york 1958.

518 Idem, *Der bund in bilder. 1897–1957 / The Jewish Labour Bund. A pictorial history. 1897–1957*, Nyu york 1958.

519 Bundists also remembered their leaders who perished in the USSR during World War II: Henryk Erlich and Victor Alter. However, the decision to commemorate them was made only by representatives of some Bundist committees (information from: AŻIH, the Bund, files n., Protocol no. 25 from a meeting of the Warsaw Bund Committee, 18 December 1946).

parades (which were limited to socialists) but the anniversaries of the Warsaw Ghetto Uprising. Bundists participated in these commemorations from the moment they resumed their activities in the People's Republic of Poland. They also organised fundraisers for the construction of the Monument to the Ghetto Heroes. They argued with representatives of other parties about the order of events and the content of speeches published in the media. These controversies were reported during the meetings of the Presidium of the Bund Central Committee:

> Citizen Fiszgrund reports that the press release on the ceremonies included speeches, that Dr Sommerstein's speech was broadcast, and when citizen Edelman was supposed to speak, citizen Zelicki indicated that his speech should not be broadcast.[520]

In 1948, on the fifth anniversary of the Warsaw Ghetto Uprising, a monument to the Ghetto Heroes was unveiled in Warsaw. Guests from Poland and other countries attended the unveiling ceremony. The organisation of the commemorations and programme of events raised objections from both the Bund and the CŻKH. This was related to the emerging historical narrative surrounding the Uprising and the then policy of the PRL.[521] Jewish communists affiliated with the PPR sought to attribute the Uprising primarily to the communists, which is why Hersh Smolar strongly protested against the speeches of Marek Edelman and Yitzchak 'Antek' Cukierman (a representative of Dror[522]) during the main ceremony, due to their 'political opposition' to the communists at the time.

Ultimately, the organisers (representatives of the CKŻP) decided that both Edelman and Cukierman would speak at the ceremony. The Bund faction within

---

520 AŻIH, CKŻP. Protocol from the Presidium meetings, ref. 303/I/2, Protocol no. 32 from 2 May 1946, p. 107.

521 The erection of a monument in honour of the victims of the Warsaw Ghetto Uprising caused mixed reactions among the Polish population, while the Warsaw Uprising and its participants were the subject of political persecution, criticism, and even repression by the authorities of the PRL. The Polish society perceived the Jewish community not only as enjoying special favours from the communist authorities but even as a political base for that regime, unaware of the nuances and internal controversies within the Jewish community between communists, socialists, and Zionists. Poles' beliefs regarding the situation of Jews in post-war Poland were confirmed, for example, by the participation of the authorities of the PRL in the commemorations of the anniversary of the Warsaw Ghetto Uprising as well as their consent to the erection of a Monument to the Ghetto Heroes.

522 Dror (Heb.: 'freedom'), youth organisation affiliated with Poale Zion Right. Liquidated in Poland in 1949. Its activities included preparing young people for emigration to Israel.

the CKŻP was of the opinion that the ceremony should not have a Zionist character. In addition to the Bund, representatives of the PPR faction, including Hersh Smolar,[523] also protested against this. After the ceremony, Fiszgrund (who was on the 'Aryan side' during the Uprising) concluded that neither the Bund nor the PPR were not adequately represented. In his opinion, the Zionist element prevailed.[524]

At the beginning of 1949, in the final weeks of the existence of the Bund, Fiszgrund called for the Polish press to publish information about the sixth anniversary of the Warsaw Ghetto Uprising so that more people would learn about the atrocities committed by the Nazis.[525] This proposal and the intention to inform the Polish society about German crimes seems absurd – as if the Polish nation had not directly experienced the tragedy of the German occupation, as if the crimes and atrocities only affected the Jewish community.

Bund members in other towns and cities, also sought to preserve and commemorate the memory of Jewish people who perished at the hands of the German Nazis. In Łódź, Shmuel Hurwicz (the Bund representative in the City Council) proposed naming one of the main streets after the Ghetto Fighters.[526] In Piotrków, the Bund members commemorated the Holocaust by erecting gravestones (the report they sent, they did not specify how many there were, only referring to 'them' in the plural) for the fallen Bund members at the local Jewish cemetery, as well as organising mourning ceremonies in their memory.[527] The Bund emphasised at every turn that those who survived the war (out of all who had lived under the Nazi occupation) miraculously escaped the crematoria of the death camps of Majdanek and Treblinka – camps which claimed not only adults but "our children."[528]

The politics of history initiated by the Bund regarding the participation of its members in the Uprising has led to it being identified mainly with Marek Edelman (a member of the Jewish Combat Organisation, ŻOB command) and with other, mostly nameless, members of the Bund affiliated organisations. For years, the Uprising was primarily associated with Edelman, "the guardian of Jewish graves" who appeared almost every year at the Monument to the Ghetto Heroes

523 AŻIH, CKŻP, Archives of the Presidium and Secretariat, ref. 303/I/10, Protocol no. 31, from 15 April 1948, ff. 10–15.

524 Ibid., Protocol no. 41 from 13 May 1948, f.119.

525 Ibid., ref. 303/I/15, Protocol no. 2 from 13 January 1949, f. 11.

526 „Mimochodem," *Głos Bundu* 1947, nos 5–6 (9–10), p. 7.

527 "Fun partay-lebn. Pietrkov," *Folkstsaytung* 1946, no. 4, p. 6.

528 I. K. [?], "A por verter vegn der yidisher shul," *Folkstsaytung* 1946, nos 2–3, p. 5.

to honour the fallen.[529] He was also one of the few surviving insurgents, including those living in Poland, who shaped the narrative on the Uprising through his memories and statements. Only in recent years has information about the participation of the Jewish Military Union (ŻZW) in the uprising, which was marginalised for years, appeared in journalism and scientific literature. This may have been influenced by Marek Edelman's negative opinion of the Union[530] or even the silence surrounding the existence of such an organisation in the ghetto.

529 For more information, see: M. Rusiniak-Karwat, „Marek Edelman – socjalista i strażnik pamięci. Narodziny legendy (1944–1949)," *Studia Polityczne* 2013, no. 32, pp. 281–298.

530 See, e.g. A. Grabski, M. Wójcicki, *Żydowski Związek Wojskowy – historia przywrócona*, Warsaw 2008.

Chapter Five
The Bund versus Zionism

Anti-Zionism

In contrast to groups combining Marxism and Zionism, the Bund's ideological principles strongly deny the existence of a single Jewish nation in the world. Therefore, the Bund opposed the creation of a programme for the reconstruction of the Jewish state.[531] Consequently, it regarded Zionist organisations (both right- and left-wing, even ideologically related) whose primary goal was emigration to Palestine and the creation of a Jewish state to be its main political opponents. Only after nearly half a century of the party's existence did representatives of the Bund committees from various countries revise their definition of the Jewish nation during the First World Conference of the Jewish Labour Bund in Brussels in 1947. The change in the Bund's position was not solely linked to the creation of the foundations of the Jewish state and its ultimate creation in 1948.[532] It seems that this shift was driven by the dispersal of Bund members and affiliated organisations following the end of World War II. The war forced another diaspora, causing Bundist organisations to be formed where several to a dozen Bund members who had left Poland settled. Such committees emerged, for instance, in Mexico, South Africa and, during World War II, in Shanghai, China.[533]

After the end of the war, from the very onset of rebuilding the party in Poland, its activists continued to be supporters of *nusekh poyln* [Yid.: 'rebuilding Jewish life in Poland'] while denying the legitimacy of building a *yishuv* in Palestine. They aimed to restore all forms of social activity of the Jewish population in Poland and opposed the emigration of repatriates from the USSR (mostly residents of the eastern provinces of the Second Polish Republic), from Poland. They often stated: "Poland is our country. We feel connected to Polish democracy."[534]

---

531 A. Grabski, *Lewica przeciwko Izraelowi. Studia o żydowskim lewicowym antysyjonizmie*, Warsaw 2008, p. 93.

532 For more on this subject, see: Chapter Six: "Contacts with the 'Western' Bund."

533 For information on the Bund organisations in the post-1945 world, see: *Jewish Labor Bund. 1897–1957. Published by the International Jewish Labor Bund*, New York 1958; M. Rusiniak-Karwat, "The Road to Freedom. Jewish Socialists in Shanghai," *Hemispheres. Studies on Cultures and Societies* 2017, no. 4 (32), pp. 84–91; D. Slucki, *The International Jewish Labor Bund after 1945. Toward a Global History*, New Brunswick–New Jersey–London 2012, *passim*.

534 Fiszgrund's words, uttered during the CKŻP Presidium meeting (AŻIH, Archives of the Presidium and Secretariat, ref. 303/I/20, Protocol no. 6, from 7 January 1947,

During the inauguration of various organisations and associations of the Jewish community, as well as during other ceremonies, such as the opening of soup kitchens, cooperatives and orphanages, representatives of the Bund committees, speaking on behalf of all party members, often emphasised their negative attitude towards Zionists and their efforts to establish a Jewish state in Palestine.[535] The Bundists' fight against Zionism in post-war Poland was also a fight for the 'hearts and minds' on the 'Jewish Street' decimated by the Holocaust, where the Bund lost its pre-war dominance, which it was unable to come to terms with. The party went from being dominant to being marginalised, both in terms of its size and the attractiveness of its programme, giving way primarily to Zionist parties.

The Bund members' view on this issue is well illustrated by the words of Michał Szuldenfrei:

> Within the Jewish community, the Bund represents the direction that ties the fate of the Jewish working masses to the fate and development of the country in which these masses reside. [...] One of the documents of the Bund's underground movement expressed this political stance in a succinct sentence: "Poland is our homeland. Our future lies in Poland."[536]

In addition to old socialist slogans and the programme of national-cultural autonomy, it was precisely pre-war anti-Zionism that became one of the main pillars of the Bund's ideology post-World War II.[537]

However, in the face of the disappearance of pre-war Jewish proletariat from the Polish landscape, as well as the closed enclaves of shtetls and Jewish districts,[538] the Bund lost its power and appeal. Particularly in the face of mass emigration of Jews from Poland after the Holocaust, the Bund's programme caused the party to be in a state of radical political conflict with Zionist organisations. In addition, the Bund's anti-Zionism[539] differed from the criticism of the Zionist

---

f. 34).

535 AŻIH, the Bund, files n., reports on the activities of local committees.

536 „Z przemówienia towarzysza Dr Szuldenfreia na Kongresie PPS we Wrocławiu," *Głos Bundu* 1948, no. 1 (14), p. 7.

537 N. Weinstock, *Zionism: False Messiah*, London 1979, pp. 32–35.

538 I am referring to the Jewish community, which did not assimilate with Polish society and functioned exclusively within Jewish quarters in cities and towns, the so-called shtetls, communicating only in Yiddish. During the Second Republic of Poland, it was precisely from this section of the Jewish population that the majority of supporters of the Bund's programme originated from.

539 The research on the Bund's hostile attitude towards Zionism over a broad time span was conducted by Yosef Gorny (*Converging Alternatives. The Bund and the Zionist*

project by three other Jewish parties: the Jewish PPR Faction within the CKŻP, the Jewish Democratic Party[540] and the Agudah.[541]

It is important to note one key element of Zionism, namely Jewish nationalism which strives for the creation of an independent Jewish state, as it was this aspect that was primarily criticised by members of the Bund.[542] The other two elements, namely Messianism and socialism (represented by Poale Zion), were criticised to a lesser extent by Bundists.[543]

Labor Movement, 1897–1985, New York 2006). In Poland, the subject has already been studied by Bożena Szaynok (see, i.a.: B. Szaynok, „Sprawa Arie Lernera – nieznany fragment 'walki z syjonizmem' w Polsce w pierwszej połowie lat 50-ych," in: *Polska w podzielonym świecie po II wojnie światowej*, ed. M. Wojciechowski, Toruń 2002, pp. 261–278) and August Grabski (important works, albeit mainly containing information on the theory of anti-Zionism: A. Grabski, *Lewica przeciwko Izraelowi. Studia o żydowskim lewicowym antysyjonizmie*, Warsaw 2008; *Rebels Against Zion. Studies on the Jewish Left Anti-Zionism*, ed. A. Grabski, Warsaw 2011). Still lacking, however, is a presentation of the attitude of Bundists towards Zionism, including towards the World Jewish Congress and the emigration of Jews from Poland.

540 The Jewish Democratic Party, known before the war as Folks partey, or the Folkists, a party with a secular, bourgeois character and supporting Yiddish culture. After the war, it resumed its activities in 1945. It operated illegally, as it was not registered with the Ministry of Public Administration. The party opposed the CKŻP. It aimed to establish secular Jewish communities (information from: Grabski, *Centralny Komitet Żydów w Polsce*).

541 Agudah, was illegal after the war because the Ministry of Public Administration refused to register it. It operated within the Jewish Religious Congregation. It denied the existence of the CKŻP and opposed the Jewish Religious Congregations joining Jewish committees (information from: Adelson, *op. cit.*, pp. 433–447).

542 Members of the Bund also considered themselves to be part of the Jewish nation, but unlike the Zionists, they claimed that they could live as a nation in their country of birth, which did not necessarily have to be a Jewish state. The Bund's nationalism was based on one of the pillars of its programme – *doykayt* (Yid.: 'hereness').

543 In the post-war period, since the establishment of the State of Israel (Hebrew name – *Medinat Israel*, proclamation of independence on 14 May 1948), we witness a struggle against Zionism or Zionists and anti-Zionist campaigns directed not at the ideology, but rather at the State itself. On the topic of anti-Zionism combined with anti-Semitism in the USSR after Stalin's death, see: T. H. Friedgut, *Soviet Anti-Zionism: Origins, Forms and Development*, Jerusalem 1984; *Anti-Zionism and Antisemitism in the Contemporary World*, ed. R. S. Wistrich, London 1990; R. S. Wistrich, *Soviet Anti-Zionism and Anti-Semitism. Another Cycle*, Jerusalem 1984; J. Frankel, *The Soviet Regime and Anti-Zionism: An Analysis*, Jerusalem 1984. On anti-Zionism in Poland post-1950, see, i.a.: B. Szaynok, „Walka z syjonizmem

The Bund's anti-Zionist stance was widely reflected in the party's press, among other things. In almost every issue of *Biuletyn Bundu*, *Folkstsaytung*, *Głos Bundu*, or the youth publication *Yugnt veker*, the Bundists published front-page articles containing critical opinions about Zionists and their policies. They engaged in polemics with Zionist activists, whose statements were published in the Zionist press in Poland and abroad.[544] In addition to the press and publications, party's documents serve as a valuable source of information on the Bund's attitude toward Zionism. Their attitude towards Zionism was expressed during meetings and congresses, therefore we can find information on this topic in party resolutions and circulars, the contents of which were reprinted in newspapers and sent to the committee offices in order to be shared with the general Jewish public.

Thanks to occasional publications, the views of the Bundists reached a wide audience in various parts of the country, including those who could read both Yiddish and Polish. The conflict between the Zionists and the Bund was a constant source of controversy, visible in the forum of the CKŻP and in the regional Jewish committees, during meetings of the Presidium of the CKŻP, as well as in municipal Jewish committees.

Attitude towards Zionists

In the first months and years after the war, Bundists in Poland and their representatives in occupied Germany had to confront Zionist slogans regarding the emigration of Jews from Poland and from Displaced Persons (DP) camps, integrating Polish Jewry into the World Jewish Congress (WJC), Palestine and the establishment of a Jewish state, as well as issues concerning the life of Jews in post-war Poland. Domestically, the occasion was the anniversary of the Warsaw Ghetto Uprising (April 1945) and the issue of Jewish education. The Bundists put a strong emphasis on the need to rebuild Jewish life in Poland while simultaneously voicing opposition to Zionists. Even in their critique of *Dos naye lebn* – a periodical that was addressed to all Jews, published by the CKŻP – the Bundists accused the editorial board of being "[…] Zionist with a slight PPR (Polish Workers' Party) bias. The weekly is not an expression of the general public opinion nor of the Central Committee."[545] They noted with concern that the publication

w Polsce (1948–1953)", in: *Komunizm. Ideologia, system, ludzie*, ed. T. Szarota, Warsaw 2001, pp. 252–271.

544 "Głosy i 'Odgłosy'," *Głos Bundu* 1947, no. 7 (11), p. 8.

545 Political views were shown in the pages of the magazine, e.g. on the attitude towards the State of Israel or the USSR. For more information on the subject, see, i.a.:

ignored the Bund's position: "It does not print submitted notes or print them in arbitrarily abridged form."[546]

The Bundists criticised the Zionists for lacking in faith in the possibility of rebuilding Jewish life in countries outside of Palestine. They emphasised that the Zionists propagated the slogan of 'escape' from Poland, thus abandoning the struggle to continue life in Poland in favour of Palestine. They stated in their speeches: "Wherever Jews are and have the right to full and unrestricted development, that's where they should live."[547] They criticised the Zionists for their pro-emigration slogans and 'emigration work', which they viewed as "[...] a result of the division of not yet extinct [Polish – author's note] anti-Semitic-fascist reactionary centres." The Bundists considered the Zionist subordination of Jewish life to the idea of Palestine as proof of infantile political thinking. In their press, they formulated it as follows:

> Without malice, we note the strange convergence of the idea of the exodus of Jews from Europe with the Nazi dreams of "liberating" Europe from Jewish influence. Following this line of thinking, it must be acknowledged that Hitlerism prevailed, after all...[548]

In addition to ideological arguments, the Bundists used realistic arguments drawn from life. Among other things, they claimed that by calling for Jews from Europe to settle in Palestine, the Zionists were promoting something impossible, even utopian. They believed that the state was not prepared to accommodate such a large number of new residents, nor to provide them with adequate living conditions, housing, employment, food, protection and so forth.

Particularly after the Kielce pogrom, in the pages of *Głos Bundu* and *Folkstsaytung* in August 1946, the Bund members accused the Zionists of exploiting the dire situation of Jews in Poland to propagate Zionist slogans, thus contributing to the panic among the intimidated Jewish population and using this event to promote the idea of emigration.[549]

J. Nalewajko-Kulikov, „'Syjonistyczna z lekkim zabarwieniem PPR-owskim'. 'Dos naje lebn' (1945–1959) – gazeta Centralnego Komitetu Żydów w Polsce," in: ed. A. Grabski, *Żydzi a lewica*, Warsaw 2007, pp. 257–278.

546 AŻIH, Archives of the Presidium and Secretariat, ref. 303/I/12, Protocol no. 80 from 8 October 1946, f. 171.

547 „Po konferencji w Brukseli," *Głos Bundu* 1947, nos 5–6 (9–10), p. 1.

548 Quoted from: A.R. [?], „Naród żydowski a 'państwo żydowskie'," *Głos Bundu* 1946, [no. 1], p. 3.

549 See, e.g. *Głos Bundu* 1946, [no. 1]: „Jakie jest wyjście?" p. 1; „Naród żydowski a 'państwo żydowskie'," p. 3.

Also, during a meeting of the Presidium of the Central Committee of Jews in Poland on 6 August 1946, Fiszgrund accused the Zionists of spreading panic and fear, and of maintaining such an atmosphere for a long time after the pogrom. He emphasised the cynical exploitation of the situation by the Zionists to promote their emigration policy, hiding from those interested in leaving that not everyone would go to Palestine. He also accused them of turning a gathering, during which a declaration intended to calm the mood was to be read, into a pro-Palestinian rally.[550]

In their confrontation with the Zionists, Bundists did not shy away from harsh criticism of the Zionists' exploitation of the situation of Jews who had lost their loved ones and all their possessions during the war, and therefore believed that the establishment of a Jewish state was the best solution for them – the greatest 'fortune'. Bund journalists wrote in the press that the Zionists were willing to do anything to gain those 'few pioneers' to go to Palestine.

According to Bund activists, not only the press and meetings of Jewish committees and organisations were the right place to fight the Zionist agenda, but every opportunity was suitable for this purpose. The Bundists also quarrelled with the Zionists during the commemorations of the anniversaries of the Warsaw Ghetto Uprising. They also criticised the Zionists during the May Day celebrations. They commented on the events of 1 May 1947 as follows:

> Although the **Zionists** here and there attempted to impose **Palestinian** slogans on the demonstrators, the decisive stance of the 'Bund' in defense of the **international** and **proletarian** nature of May Day resulted in the dominance of slogans advocating international working-class unity and solidarity among the working world in the parades.[551]

One element of the Bund's fight against the Zionists was criticism not only of the very idea of emigration to Palestine, but also of people who were associated with Zionist parties. The practice of establishing kibbutzim, which significantly differed from the pre-war ones, was also presented in a negative light at the CKŻP forum.

> If, before the war, the kibbutz was home to idealists, today we encounter people brought there by pure accident. Therefore, the attitude toward present-day kibbutzim must be different. I, for one, believe that supporting these organizations is unacceptable.[552]

---

550 AŻIH, Archives of the Presidium and Secretariat, ref. 303/I/17, Protocol no. 64 from 6 August 1946, f. 68–69.

551 „Warszawa," *Głos Bundu* 1947, nos 5–6 (9–10), p. 12 (bold in the original).

552 Fiszgrund's statement (AŻIH, Archives of the Presidium and Secretariat, ref. 303/I/5, Protocol no. 4, from 13–14 July 1946, f. 63).

Representatives of the Bund Central Committee also criticized Zionist ideology during meetings of local party committees. For example, Grzegorz Jaszuński, in his speech in Wrocław, "[…] presented the post-war Jewish issues with special emphasis on the critical situation of the Zionist movement."[553]

The Bund's criticism of Zionism, manifested in the preaching of anti-Zionist opinions wherever possible, did not go unanswered by Zionist parties, who in their defence, did not shy away from any arguments in a fierce polemic:

> […] The anti-Zionist campaign of the Bund is, of course, not accidental. It is the desire of a bankrupt party, deprived of any influence within the Jewish community in Poland, to create an artificial noise around itself in order to give the impression that it has a stance on Jewish issues.[554]

These words, published by the United Poale Zion, despite their uncompromising nature, largely reflected the post-war reality and the opinion about the Bund on the 'Jewish (political) Street', where Zionism, after the Holocaust and amidst the ruins of the Jewish community, represented hope for the creation of a new better life. The attitudes of the Bund children who became ardent supporters of Zionism after the war and emigrated from Poland, confirmed the validity of these words.[555]

The Bund versus emigration and emigrationism[556]

After the end of World War II, members of the Bund believed that Jews had the individual right to decide to emigrate. They claimed that: "emigration was a fact, and it will remain one. I have nothing against ideological emigration."[557]

553 „Życie społeczne i organizacyjne. Nasi korespondencji piszą: Wrocław," *Głos Bundu* 1947, no. 4 (8), p. 8.

554 ł.h.h.s. [?], „Na czym buduje „Bund"?," *Nasze Słowo. Organ zjednoczonej żydowskiej partii syjonistycznej Poalej Syjon* 1947, no. 3 (15), p. 3.

555 For instance, Wiktoria (Aviva) Blum, daughter of Abrasha Blum and Luba Bielicka-Blum, was a proponent of Zionism. She joined Hashomer Hatsair and emigrated in January 1950 to Israel (information from: W. Blum, in: Yad Vashem [online] http://www.yadvashem.org/yv/en/exhibitions/otwock/histories_blum.asp [access: 20 August 2013] and [online] https://www.yadvashem.org/education/testimony-films/aviva-blum.html [access: 15 September 2024]).

556 For a broader perspective on the Bund's stance on Zionism after WWII, see: M. Rusiniak-Karwat, "Bundists and the issue of emigration from Poland after the Second World War," *European Spatial Research and Policy* 2021, vol. 28, no. 1, pp. 149–159.

557 Fiszgrund's speech (AŻIH, Archives of the Presidium and Secretariat, ref. 303/I/20, Protocol no. 31 from 24 March 1947, f. 156).

The issue of Jews leaving Poland was discussed, among other occasions, during the Bund's National Conference in Łódź on 16–17 June 1945. Participants of the Conference advocated for free emigration and immigration, namely for the right to choose a place of settlement, regardless of the context (be it political or economic reasons). They explained this in the spirit of their doctrine as follows:

> The emigration of a portion of the Jewish population from Poland would not, by any means, change its fundamental goal and ideal. Whether the working Jewish masses find themselves in America, Palestine, France, or Belgium, their task will be – just like that of the Jewish population remaining in Poland – to fight for socialism alongside the proletariat of any given country.[558] Furthermore, the Bund taught the Jewish worker to feel and think not in terms of alienation, but in terms of being a citizen of their country. It taught them to tie their fate to the fate of their country.[559]

After the Kielce pogrom, despite criticism of the Zionists for stirring up emigration sentiments, most Bundists also changed their attitude towards emigration, to a more favourable one, as some of them also left Poland after July 1946. Representatives of the Bund even advocated for the provision of financial assistance to emigrants, but only in exceptional cases, as part of social welfare.[560] In this case, internal conflicts within the Bund emerged, highlighting the clashes between the two factions that had existed within the party even before the outbreak of the war in 1939. The left wing was decidedly more anti-Zionist and some of its members (e.g. Jaszuński) were in favour of close cooperation with the PPR. Another group (e.g. Szuldenfrei) favoured an alliance with the PPS as a separate section within the Polish party. The third group, on the other hand, advocated for the independent existence of the Bund on the political scene (e.g. Fiszgrund), rejecting other options, including emigration.

The Bundists (e.g. Ignacy Falk, Abraham Zilbersztejn – secretary of Tsukunft in Warsaw) belonged to the right wing of the party and doubted the possibility of rebuilding the *yishuv* in post-war Poland. They even advocated for the dissolution of the party and emigration.[561] It was mainly these Bundists and Tsukunft members who were the first to leave Poland, unwilling to accept the self-dissolution of their organisations.

While Bundists were willing to tolerate individual emigration, they criticised the policy of emigrationism, which they blamed on the Zionists. They considered emigrationism to be an ideology that saw emigration as the only solution to the

558 „Jakie jest wyjście?," *Głos Bundu* 1946, [no. 1], p. 1.
559 Michał Szuldenfrei, „50 lat Bundu," *Głos Bundu* 1947, nos 8–9, p. 1.
560 AŻIH, ibid., ref. 303/I/19, Protocol no. 97 from 25 November 1946, f. 26.
561 AAN, Zachariasz, ref. 476/28, f. 155.

situation of the Jewish population in Poland at the time as – protection against anti-Semitic incidents and as a chance for a new life for the entire Jewish community. Jaszuński wrote in *Biuletyn Bundu*:

> We discard emigrationism in favour of the struggle here, alongside the Polish working class, to create conditions of life that would ensure freedom and prosperity for all citizens, regardless of nationality or religion.[562]

He considered the idea of mass emigration to Palestine to be a nationalist utopia hindering the development of Jewish life in the country they inhabited and distracting them from the fight for their rightful national and social rights in their countries of residence – a utopia isolating them from the rest of society.[563]

The issue of emigration, including the emigration of other party members, was discussed at the Bund committee meetings. Participants proposed an increased crusade in favour of staying in the country and appealed for visas not to be issued.[564] Bundists repeatedly emphasised that the borders of all countries,[565] including the United States, should be open to Jews from both Poland and other countries. They emphasised that "the Bund is in favour of abolishing the White Paper and of free emigration of Jews to all countries, including Palestine."

At the same time, during meetings of the Presidium of the CKŻP, the Bund criticised illegal Jewish emigration[566] (Heb.: *brichah*, meaning 'escape').[567] The Bund also criticised the 'Memorandum of the CKŻP for the Anglo-American

---

562 G. Jaszuński, „Emigracja i emigracjonizm," *Biuletyn Bundu* 1945, no. 3, p. 12.

563 "Bundizm un di medinas yisroel," *Unzer tsayt* 1957, nos 11–12; quoted from: *Yid, mensh, sotsyalist. I. Artuski ondenk-bukh*, Tel Aviv 1976, p. 253.

564 AŻIH, the Bund, files n., Minutes from a meeting of the Warsaw Bund Committee, 21 January 1947.

565 AŻIH, Archives of the Presidium and Secretariat, ref. 303/I/10, Protocol no. 39 from 4 October 1945.

566 Ibid., ref. 303/I/9, Protocol no. 33, from 31 August 1945, f. 133; Fiszgrund's statement during a meeting of the Presidium 13–14 July 1946: "[…] we allow and tolerate legal emigration but, as a public-legal institution [CKŻP – author's note], we cannot support illegal emigration" (ibid., ref. 303/I/16, Protocol no. 4 from 8 October 1946, f. 63).

567 On illegal emigration of Jews from Poland, see, i.a.: N. Aleksiun-Mądrzak, "Nielegalna emigracja Żydów z Polski w latach 1945–1947 (część I, II and III)," *Biuletyn Żydowskiego Instytutu Historycznego* 1995, nos 2–3 (175–176); ibid., 1996, no. 3 (179); ibid., no. 4 (180); Y. Bauer, *Flight and Rescue. Brichah, The Organised Escape of Jewish Survivors of Eastern Europe, 1944–1948*, New York 1970; M. Semczyszyn, „Nielegalna emigracja Żydów z Polski 1944–1947 – kontekst międzynarodowy," *Dzieje Najnowsze* 2018, no. 1, pp. 95–121.

Commission', which was prepared on behalf of all Polish Jews in February 1946. This document referred only to free emigration of Jews to Palestine after World War II and the abolition of the White Paper. The Bund, on the other hand, repeatedly claimed that

> …it is a crime to adapt the entire issue of Jewish emigration solely to Palestine.[568] The Bundists argued: "[…] we consider the idea of the exodus from Europe, as well as the desire to subordinate all Jewish life to the Palestinian idea, to be a proof of infantile political thinking."[569]

When the signing of the 'Memorandum' was to take place during the meeting of the Presidium of the CKŻP on 20 February 1946, the representatives of the Bund (Falk, Herszenhorn, and Finkelsztejn) strongly opposed it. Although the draft was signed by Herszenhorn, after which the Bundists withdrew from further work on the document. However, they opposed its content before the final document was signed.[570]

In order to stem the rising tide of emigration, Bundists at the Presidium of CKŻP advocated for a reduction in aid for emigrants. They believed this could have an impact on reducing it:

> […] [Fiszgrund – author's note] aid for emigration was really necessary when the poor were fleeing, those who had nothing. People who are provided with passports and visas can arrange the rest themselves. They are abusing the trust. Remove the entry for emigration allowances. Provide them only in exceptional cases.[571]

To summarise the issue of emigration, one can quote the opinion of Emanuel Scherer, a Bundist living in the USA after the war, published in 1946 in Poland in *Głos Bundu*. He pointed out that while the right of Jews to emigrate should be acknowledged, one should not talk about emigration as the only solution, and

---

568 AŻIH, ibid., ref. 303/I/11, Protocol no. 5 from 29 January 1946, k. 26. In 1947, Finkelsztein went to New York with the Bund's delegation and he never came back: "The Bund is for free emigration to all countries, not only to Palestine. The Bund won't sign the 'Memorandum' as long as it doesn't mention emigration to all countries," ibid., ref. 303/I/11, Protocol no. 11 from 20 II 1946, f. 39.

569 A. R.[?], „Naród żydowski a 'państwo żydowskie'," *Głos Bundu* 1946, [no. 1], p. 3 (bold in the original).

570 Szaynok, *Bund i komuniści żydowscy*, pp. 311–312.

571 AŻIH, ibid., ref. 303/I/13, Protocol no. 92 from 15 November 1946, f. 20.

not about emigration exclusively to the Jewish state.[572] This detailed and reasoned statement is worth quoting in full:

> Are the Zionists, fervently urging Jews to leave their homes in Europe, convinced that Palestine has the necessary conditions for the mass colonisation by European refugees? [...] Let us not prejudge the issue and assume that the Zionists will manage to overcome all the difficulties that, in our view, are insurmountable. Let us assume that they even manage to create a Jewish state without a Jewish majority. So what? Does that mean that the so-called 'diaspora' will cease to exist? Will Jews stop living among other nations?
>
> We are deeply convinced that, regardless of the success or failure of the Palestinian colonisation, the majority of Jews will remain outside of Palestine. After all, even in the past, when an independent Jewish state existed, there were still large Jewish communities in the so-called diaspora, with their own distinct national character. At times, their spiritual influence outweighed that of the metropolis.[573]

Mordechai Canin,[574] a member of the Bund who spent World War II in Palestine, had a different perspective. In 1946, he published an open letter to the members of the Bund in the newspaper *Davar* (the then press organ of Histadrut, the labour union in Palestine, now the General Federation of Workers in the Land of Israel). In the letter, he criticised their post-war attitude towards emigration and their traditionalism, which he felt failed to take into account the situation of the Jewish population in Poland and the prospects of building a Jewish state in Palestine:

---

572 E. Scherer devoted a brochure titled *The Future of Jews* (London 1947) to the subject matter.

573 A.R. [?], „Naród żydowski a 'państwo żydowskie'," *Głos Bundu* 1946, [no. 1], p. 3. Scherer wrote about the future of Jews in Poland also in a brochure: E. Scherer, *The Future of Jews*, London 1947.

574 Mordechai Canin (Tsanin), born Mordechai Yeshaya Cukerman (1906–2009), was a journalist who wrote for *Naye folkstsaytung* in the inter-war period and lived in Palestine from 1942. Founder and editor of the daily newspaper *Letste nayes*, published in Israel from 1948. He wrote about his wartime experiences, including escaping from Europe via Japan to Palestine, in: *Grenetsn biz tsum himl*, Tel Aviv 1969. After the war, in 1945, he came to Poland for a year as a correspondent for *Forverts*. He described his impressions from his travels across the country as well as the Holocaust and the destruction of shtetls, including his hometown of Sokołów Podlaski, in: *Iber shteyn un shtok. A rayze iber hundert khoyrev-gevorene kehiles in poyln* (Tel Aviv 1952). Polish edition of the book: *Przez ruiny i zgliszcza. Podróż po stu zgładzonych gminach żydowskich w Polsce*, tr. M. Adamczyk-Garbowska, Warsaw 2018.

> [...] Instead of boldly facing the reality, we, the builders, adopted a tactic of waiting for the further development of the situation, while calming ourselves down with the adoption of resolutions. But the Jews, who fought for their lives for five years, do not want resolutions; they demand a short, clear answer to their torment. We ought to give them this answer, now or never. The remnants of the salvaged Jewish people are facing an alternative – emigration from the countries where living has become impossible. You have erased Palestine, the only country that is wholeheartedly interested in Jewish immigration, from the map of the world, guided by prejudices and motives that have long lost their meaning. Meanwhile, we all know that other countries, which could accept Jewish immigrants, are closing their doors to them. You, comrades, have stopped the clock's hands and forgotten completely what times we live in. You cling to the views that expired with the first victims of the first gas chambers the Germans set up in Poland, and instead of facing the truth, you hide behind a screen of outdated theories.[575]

Canin's words can hardly be considered a representative opinion of a Jewish socialist, a Bund member. His experience led to an evolution of views and a pro-Palestinian stance, closer to the Zionists.

When Finkelsztejn travelled to the USA with Falk, in a delegation to the Polish Bund Representation in America at the beginning of 1947, he remained there due to health reasons. Representatives of the Central Committee of the Bund in Poland pressured him to return to the country as soon as possible. His unfortunate absence (due to health issues) was treated as an ideological reason for not returning home. He was sent letters with comments not to extend his stay because his stay abroad was seen as incompatible with Bundist ideology and was perceived by the community as a form of betrayal and ultimately a realisation of Zionist slogans.[576] This gave the impression that one of the leading Bund representatives in post-war Poland had taken advantage of the opportunity to leave the country and escape. It could easily have been used by the Zionists against the Bundists in ideological disputes. The actions of one of the most important Bund activists could have been interpreted as the party's consent to emigration, something the left-wing representatives were determined to avoid at all costs in order not to become unreliable, because then the Bund's further activities in this respect would have been untenable.

---

575 M. Canin, „Do towarzyszy z 'Bundu'," *Nasze Słowo (Organ zjednoczonej żydowskiej partii syjonistycznej Poalej Syjon)* 1946, nos 2–3.

576 AŻIH, the Bund, files n., correspondence from March 1947 between Finkelsztejn and the Central Committee of the Bund in Poland, correspondence from April 1947 from Stolar to the Central Committee of the Bund in Poland.

In retrospect, and in view of the liquidation of all Jewish parties in the People's Republic of Poland, it can be said that the Bundists' belief in the continued existence of the Bund in Poland and the halting of Jewish emigration was an illusion. After leaving Poland, most Bund members, tied their fate to the Bund committee in their new country of residence, which became a substitute for a family, it was more than just a Jewish party – *a bundishe mishpokhe* (Yid.: Bundist family).[577] Probably many Bundists who entered the party leadership could not imagine a future in any country other than Poland. Here, they were leaders; in the new countries of residence the organisations had their own leaders, and they would have become ordinary members. Age also played a role in decision-making (most were born before 1900). Not everyone could or wanted to retrain in their old age, learn a new profession, or learn a new language. Many of the leaders worked as clerks or officials in Poland and were fully aware that in the new countries they would become manual labourers.[578]

Therefore, the attitude of the Bund leaders towards emigration and emigrationism was affected by various factors, each playing a vital role. This was due to the traditional ideology of the party, which was considered to be the advocate of the Jewish proletariat in ensuring its proper national and cultural autonomy, disbelief in the possibility of implementing the Zionist programme, but also personal, professional, and life considerations of many activists of the older generation. Demographic changes within the Jewish community (in which mainly young people survived the Holocaust) and the hope for a 'better tomorrow' in their own state built in Palestine meant that in this respect the Bund's programme failed to meet the expectations and aspirations of the community, including their own party and affiliated organisations.

Displaced Persons camps

While opposing Zionist ideas, the Bund members also criticised the Displaced Persons camps,[579] known as DP camps, for Polish and Jewish refugees in post-war

---

577 F. Wolff, "The Collateral Prisoner. A Bundist Holocaust Survivor between Nazi Perpetrators, Anti-Communism and British World Politics," *The International of Communist Studies* 2011, no. 24, p. 79.

578 For example, Szechatow was an accountant in Poland. Having settled in Sweden, he worked in a radio-technical factory (information from: J. Perlsztejn, *Araynfir*, in: Sh. Szechatow, *Yorn fun kamf un gerangl*, Ramat-Gan 1973, p. 10).

579 For more information on DP camps, see.: K. Person, „'I am a Jewish DP. A Jew from the Eternal Nowhere'. Jews from Poland in Displaced Persons Camps in

Germany, Austria, and Italy, where thousands of Jews, former concentration and labour camp inmates, were gathered. Without the help of the United Nations, DPs were unable to return to their previous places of residence or choose a new place to settle.[580] In the press, the Bund members described living conditions in DP camps in a distorted way. Bund members also suggested during the meetings of the Presidium of the CKŻP, that the Zionists, by preventing the return of refugees to their former homes and organising emigration to Palestine, exposed the Jews in the camps to homelessness, misery and demoralisation. They described the poor sanitary conditions in the camps and the health of their inhabitants, as well as the lack of interest from the Zionists in closing these camps. They appealed to the state authorities (the State Repatriation Office) to put a halt on keeping Jews in the camps and to allow them to return to their countries of origin, e.g. to Poland. They called for the "assistance in creating the conditions for (re)settling in the country."[581]

When writing about DP camps, the Bund members drew attention to the lies and illusions of the Zionists regarding emigration to Palestine. They noted that the Zionists were aware that the new homeland was not be able to accept such a large number of people and that not all of the DP camp population would reach Palestine. Some of them would leave for other countries, not necessarily

the Occupation Zones of West Germany: Encounters with Poles and Memories of Poland, 1945–1946," *Kwartalnik Historii Żydów* 2013, no. 2 (246); T. Lewinsky, "Polish-Jewish Displaced Persons in Occupied Germany," in: *Jewish Presence in Absence. The Aftermath of the Holocaust in Poland, 1944–2010,* edited by F. Tych and M. Adamczyk-Garbowska, translated by G. Dąbkowski, J. Taylor-Kucia, Jerusalem 2014, pp. 95–124.

580 DP camps as an instrument in the hands of political party leaders have been described by, i.a., Tom Segev (*The Seventh Million: The Israelis and the Holocaust*, tr. H. Watzman, New York 2000) who criticised not only the camps but also the establishment of the State of Israel. He highlighted not only the positive but, above all, the negative aspects of Zionist organisations and parties, including their passivity and lack of assistance to Jews being murdered during the war, even though by the autumn of 1942, Jews in Palestine were already aware of the truth about the German policy of exterminating the Jewish people. He also revealed the truth about the 'selections' and the decision-making in rescue efforts, showing that preference was given to children who could most easily be indoctrinated and raised as true 'kibbutzniks'. The critical attitude toward the policies of Jews in Palestine, and later in Israel, regarding the Jewish language, was consistent with the stance of the Bund which criticised Zionists for rejecting Yiddish, regarded by them merely as a language of sentiment.

581 AŻIH, Archives of the Presidium and Secretariat, ref. 303/I/20, Protocol no. 8 from 13 January 1947, f. 104.

according to their will, and become a new labour force.[582] While discussing the issue of the camps during a meeting of the Presidium of the CKŻP, Fiszgrund stressed that "the camps are a political instrument of the Zionists."[583] The American Representation of the Bund in Poland and the World Coordinating Committee of the Bund, founded in 1947, held similar views on DP camps. The issue of opening borders for people from the camps was raised, among others, at the International Socialist Conference in Zurich in 1947.[584]

The policy towards DP camps and the people living in them was one of the Bund's next spectacular failures in Poland. Despite the party's efforts, agitation and official activities, Polish Jews left for Palestine more often than for Poland.

Jewish children

In relation to the problem of emigration and Zionist policy in this regard, the representatives of the Bund also addressed the issue of the future of Jewish children, mainly orphans who according to the party, were the future of the Jewish *yishuv* in Poland and the hope for its reconstruction. They considered their emigration to be "undermining the Jewish *yishuv* in Poland."[585] The Bund expressed concern about the legitimacy of the ideology in which these children would be raised outside Poland.[586] Therefore it strongly opposed the emigration of children.

During a meeting of the Presidium of the CKŻP on 31 July 1946, Fiszgrund addressed this issue as follows:

582 "Tsyonistishe politik in lagern," *Folkstsaytung* 1947, no. 12 (21), p. 7.

583 AŻIH, Archives of the Presidium and Secretariat, ref. 303/I/20, Protocol no. 35 from 14 April 1947, f. 181. I. Perelsztejn wrote critically about the camps as tools for spreading "Zionist nonsense" regarding emigration to Palestine and exploiting the stagnation and confusion of the camp residents: "Znamienna odezwa (Sprawa Żydów w obozach dla uchodźców)," *Głos Bundu* 1947, nos 5–6 (9–10), p. 8.

584 AŻIH, the Bund, files n., Correspondence from the European Secretariat in Paris to the Bund organisations in Europe from June 1947; ibid., Minutes from a meeting of the European Secretariat of the World Coordinating Committee of the Bund Organizations and Groups, from 2 December 1947 in Brussels.

585 AŻIH, CKŻP. Archives of the Presidium and Secretariat, ref. 303/I/19, Protocol no. 98 from 27 November 1946, f. 62 (Fiszgrund's statement in which he agrees to sending Jewish children to South Africa).

586 See: ibid., ref. 303/I/15, Protocol no. 37 from 21 May 1946, f. 125 (Fiszgrund's statement in which he fiercely opposed sending 1,000 Jewish orphans to Sweden).

> "[...] Until there is a decision from the Central Committee on the liquidation of the Jewish community (*yishuv*) in Poland, we cannot send children who are well settled here. We may still consider proposals from philanthropic institutions (Mexico, Uruguay), but the Jewish Agency is a political institution, it is Zionist. Can we therefore entrust our children to them?"[587] On another occasion, he pointed out that "**To remove children from a Jewish settlement means to liquidate this settlement.** We firmly oppose to that. Sending children to relatives, orphaned children, is only acceptable under condition that they will not wander through the camps, but will go directly to their destination. We will even approve a certificate to Palestine, but they must go directly there."[588]

The Bundists feared that children sent outside of Poland would be indoctrinated by Zionist organisations and deprived of contact with the Yiddish language in favour of Hebrew, making the Bund's principles foreign to them. By losing the children, the Bund was not only losing potential party members but also the very foundation of its existence in the future.

Criticism of the 22nd Zionist Congress

From 9–24 December 1946, the 22nd Zionist Congress, the first after the war, took place in Basel, during which the prospects of Jewish emigration to Palestine in the context of the Holocaust and the right to settle there was debated. The Congress approved a plan to create a Jewish state in Palestine. The Bund criticised the proceedings and the resolutions of the Congress in the press, stating that the Zionist organisations that participated in it, including the League for a Free Palestine and the Palestinian Salvation Committee, had usurped the right to speak on behalf of the entire Jewish nation regarding emigration and Palestine.

The Bund press, on the one hand, downplayed the importance of the Congress' pointing out that its lack of representatives of the Jewish community, but on the other hand, it could not avoid referring to its resolutions. The resolutions of the Congress were described as half hearted and ineffective.

> **The Congress mainly dealt with political and organisational issues. It was meant to determine the path**[589] that Zionism should follow in the current post-war period, especially whether negotiations with Great Britain should continue and on what terms, and whether concessions should be made. If the Zionist policy was to change, compromises would have to be made, and decisions would need to be made regarding which leaders should take charge of the movement and who should be entrusted with

---

587 Ibid., ref. 303/I/12, Protocol no. 62 from 31 July 1946, f. 60.
588 Ibid., ref. 303/I/12, Protocol no. 73 from 17 July 1946, f. 130 (bold in the original).
589 Bold in the original.

> the leadership of the executive and the Zionist organisation. **In this regard**, the Congress, like no other political assembly – however strange it may seem – did not make any practical decisions. It stepped down from the old path but did not take a new one. [...] **It ended by leaving the Zionist movement in a dead-end street.**[590]

However, the Bund realised that the decisions of the Congress were a real threat to their party's ideology and called its very existence into question, especially since the party's competitors were active in the Polish socialist-Zionists community.

Attitude towards the World Jewish Congress

The position of the Bund towards the World Jewish Congress[591] (WJC) in New York had remained unchanged since its foundation in 1936.[592] After World War II, the World Jewish Congress was widely regarded as an organ of exclusively Zionist policy, and it was accused of focusing only on the issues of Palestine. Bund representatives emphasised at the CKŻP that the Congress was not authorised to represent the interests of the entire global Jewish community.[593] They opposed the participation of Polish Jews in their conferences. The Bundists accused the WJC of being a one-sided partisan body, acting under the influence of the Zionist Congress[594] and promoting a pro-Palestinian agenda, despite the appearance of representing national interests. The Bund in Poland, therefore, viewed it as a threat not only to the existence of the party in Poland but also to the non-partisan character of the CKŻP.[595] Salo Fiszgrund and Ignacy Falk

590 „Po 22. Syjonistycznym Kongresie," *Głos Bundu* 1947, no. 2 (6), p. 2.

591 World Jewish Congress (WJC) was established in Geneva in 1936. It is a Zionist organisation that supports the State of Israel. Currently, its main headquarters are in New York, with a research institute in Jerusalem. It has international offices in many countries. One of the WJC's primary goals has always been to strengthen ties and foster dialogue between Jewish communities in different countries as part of its membership framework.

592 AŻIH, Archives of the Presidium and Secretariat, ref. 303/I/20, Protocol no. 8 from 13 January 1947, f. 37.

593 Ibid., ref. 303/I/12, Protocol no. 67 from 14 August 1946, f. 83, see also: G. Berendt, „Starania organizacji działających w Polsce o przystąpienie do Światowego Kongresu Żydowskiego (1945–1961)," in: G. Berendt, A. Grabski, A. Stankowski, *Studia z historii Żydów w Polsce po 1945 roku*, Warsaw 2000, pp. 12, 17.

594 AŻIH, Archives of the Presidium and Secretariat, ref. 303/I/1, Protocol no. 39 from 4 October 1945.

595 Ibid., ref. 303/I/12, Protocol no. 63 from September 1946, f. 12 (Fiszgrund's speech); ibid., ref. 303/I/13, Protocol no. 90 from 8 November 1946, f. 12.

rightly underlined the Congress's passive attitude towards the Jewish Holocaust under the Nazi German occupation.[596]

During one of the meetings of the Presidium of the CKŻP, Falk stated that the Congress was essentially a Zionist hub. The Bund faction in the CKŻP accused the Zionist representatives in the Committee's Presidium of passing resolutions from both Congresses that were similar or identical, and deliberately not participating because

> [...] he predicted that the World Jewish Congress would be an extension of the Zionist Congress. Szuldenfrei echoed him, stating that "the Bund" has not forgotten that its members are socialists. The World Jewish Congress is a Zionist institution, with representatives of the Jewish bourgeoisie in its ranks. He is not at all surprised that "the Bund" is isolated in this matter. He warns against the illusion that one must participate in every Jewish conference and believes that this principle is unhealthy. Congresses are political, and their direction is also political. He is against participating in the Congress in Paris, stating that the delegation chosen at today's Plenary meeting cannot and will not represent "the Bund."[597]

Members of the Bund were generally opposed to joining the WJC. They justified their position as follows:

> [...] interests of the Jewish community in Poland do not require joining the Congress. The Polish Workers' Party (PPR) must remember that the Zionists will sacrifice the interests of the Jewish community, and the Congress, instead of becoming a centre for mass work, will become a centre for Zionist work.

A year later (in 1948), the position on the Congress remained unchanged:

> We should not be a section of the World Jewish Congress as long as the Polish *yishuv* [settlement] exists. The Central Committee's authority must not be diminished. I oppose joining the World Jewish Congress.[598]

Fiszgrund repeatedly stated that "By deciding to join the WJC, we are turning the CKŻP into a section of the Congress and voluntarily renouncing our sovereignty, and this will be detrimental to the interests of the Jewish population in Poland."[599] During a meeting of the CKŻP's Presidium in December 1947, Falk stated that the Bund would oppose the WJC as long as the Congress remained a Zionist institution.[600]

---

596 Ibid., ref. 303/I/20, Protocol no. 37 from 17 April 1947, f. 192.

597 Ibid., ref. 303/I/8, Protocol no. 11 from 7 May 1945, f. 101.

598 Fiszgrund's speech during a meeting of the CKŻP Presidium in July 1946 (see: ibid., ref. 303/I/12, Protocol no. 63 from July 1946, f. 63).

599 Ibid., ref. 303/I/14, Protocol no. 36 from 16 April 1947, f. 186.

600 Ibid., ref. 303/I/22, Protocol no. 101 from 9 December 1947, f. 207.

The Polish Bund only changed its negative attitude toward the WJC in June 1948, when the authorities of the People's Republic of Poland were clearly moving towards a "one-party" model, and the Bund faced the prospect of self-liquidation and integration into the Polish Workers' Party (PPR). At the CKŻP's Presidium meeting on 16 June 1948, Gershon Fogel, a representative of the Bund faction in the CKŻP, declared his support for the merger of the CKŻP with the WJC, which had taken place five months earlier.[601]

The Bund, which considered itself the heir to the tradition of the oldest and largest party, was opposed to any mergers or coalitions with other groups. The party's activists believed that doing so would result in the loss of their individuality, ideological heritage, and programme. This applied not only, but primarily, to the Congress as a Zionist institution. Therefore, the change in its attitude towards the WJC at the end of the party's existence is a testament to significant re-evaluations, which were undoubtedly influenced by the changing conditions of operation in the People's Republic of Poland.

Attitude towards Palestine – "The Palestinian *yishuv* is no stranger to us"[602]

The Bund considered Palestine to be one of many Jewish communities in the world, but not the only one. In *Głos Bundu*, it presented its attitude towards the Jewish community in the land of their forefathers as follows:

> Every individual Jewish community, including Palestine, constitutes a part of Jewish reality, only a part, and not the entirety of Jewish reality, i.e., it is not the entirety of Jewish existence.[603] As for the attitude toward the Jewish settlement in Palestine, it is – of course – as positive as it is toward settlements in other countries.[604]

In 1945 and 1946, the Bundists believed that even if a Jewish state were to be established, Jews would continue to live among other nations in Palestine, as

601 G. Berendt, „Starania organizacji, działających w Polsce o przystąpienie do Światowego Kongresu Żydowskiego (1945–1961)," in: G. Berendt, A. Grabski, A. Stankowski, *Studia z historii Żydów w Polsce po 1945 roku*, Warsaw 2000, pp. 19–20.

602 Fiszgrund's words (quoted from: AŻIH, Archives of the Presidium and Secretariat, ref. 303/I/21, Protocol no. 43 from 8 May 1947, f. 192).

603 Sz. Dawidowicz, „Einikeit" (quoted from: A. R. [?], „Naród żydowski a 'państwo żydowskie'," *Głos Bundu* 1946, [no. 1], p. 3).

604 A. R. [?], *Naród żydowski*, p. 3.

Palestine does not provide a solution to the Jewish question.[605] A year later, this opinion remained unchanged:

> The majority of Jews will remain in the countries of dispersion regardless of whether there is a Jewish state in Palestine or not, and this majority will be tied to the fate of the peoples living in the countries where they reside.[606]

Repeatedly emphasising that Palestine was not the optimal solution to the Jewish question and that the country would not protect Jews against catastrophes and threats, the Bundists cited cases of Jews returning from Palestine to Poland as evidence, even though the returnees had no close relatives to come back to.[607] The Bundists considered the establishment of a Jewish state and emigration to it to be exaggerated nationalism, with utopian ideals. For this reason, they vehemently opposed the creation of a Jewish state in Palestine. They were, however, very interested in the situation in Palestine and the relations between Jews and Arabs, publishing articles on the topic in the party press.[608] The Bundists participated in various campaigns for Palestine, but – as they themselves stressed – they acted as socialists, not Zionists. The Bund faction in the CKŻP agreed to participate in aid campaigns for Palestine, provided they did not turn into Zionist campaigns.[609] "We are connected with the *yishuv* in Palestine just as we are with other Jewish communities, within the entire Jewish nation."[610]

The Bundists advocated for the abolition of the British martial law in Palestine, which they blamed on political Zionism, and criticised the terrorist acts

605 Dr E. Szerer, „Problemy żydowskiej przyszłości. Żydzi w Europie," *Głos Bundu* 1946, nos 2–3, p. 6.

606 Dr G. Oleg, „Sprawa syjonizmu na trzeźwo," *Głos Bundu* 1947, nos 8–9 (12–13), p. 14.

607 AŻIH, Archives of the Presidium and Secretariat, ref. 303/I/22, Protocol no. 71 from 1 August 1947, f. 204.

608 See, i.a.: A. Ejdelman, „Listy z Palestyny," *Głos Bundu* 1948, no. 1 (14), p. 12; L. Korn, „Na międzynarodowej widowni; 3. Stan wojenny w Palestynie," *Głos Bundu* 1947, no. 3 (7), p. 4. In *Folkstsaytung,* i.a.: „Di situatsye in palestine. A shmues mitn kh[aver] I. Zajd" (1947, nos 10–11 (19–20), p. 2); "Vos hert zikh in palestine" (1947, no. 12 (21), p. 2); "Yidish fodert rekht ba yidn (a briv fun palestine)" (1947, nos 18–19 (27–28), p. 11); "Vos vayter? (di lage in un arum palestine)" (1948, nos 1–2 (29–30), p. 1); A. Fajner, "Unzere korespondentn shraybn. Britishe 'naytralitet' (a briv fun palestine). Spetsyel far der folsktsaytung" (1948, no. 4 (32), p. 3).

609 AŻIH, Archives of the Presidium and Secretariat, ref. 303/I/26, Protocol no. 9 from 29 January 1948, f. 75.

610 Ibid., ref. 303/I/26, Protocol no. 3 from 19 January 1948, f. 86.

committed by Jewish armed organisations.[611] They expressed their opinion on the events in the Middle East in the following fashion:

> After several further acts of terror in Palestine, the British government decided to impose a state of emergency in this unfortunate country. All British civilians were evacuated, and little Palestine was turned into a theatre of war.
>
> Our stance on the matter of Palestine is well-known. However, our attitude toward the Zionist movement does not blind us to the tragic reality of Palestine. We believe that Britain's policy, the policy of *divide et impera*, is not in concordance with socialist principles and can only lead to further bloodshed in Palestine. The imposition of martial law is not a solution to the situation – it is merely an aggravation of already extremely tense relations. Unfortunately, the Labour Party government has failed to make a proper attempt at a constructive resolution to the Palestinian question, creating a situation where increasingly desperate acts of terror are born.
>
> Our criticism of the British policy in Palestine, particularly our condemnation of recent measures such as the imposition of martial law, in no way diminishes our outrage at the activities of Jewish terrorists associated with the Irgun or Stern groups. Terrorists lack any political perspective, and their 'war' with Britain can only deepen the suffering of innocent Jewish civilians in Palestine.
>
> The Zionist movement now faces an alternative – either continue to insist on the unachievable slogan of a Jewish state in Palestine, a source of conflict with the English and Arabs, or find forms of agreement with the Arab population, thereby enabling a peaceful development of the country and, in turn, the Jewish settlement in Palestine [...].
>
> We demand – first and foremost – the immediate abolition of martial law in Palestine![612]

At the beginning of 1947 the Bund blamed not only the British but also the Jews living in Palestine, and especially the Zionist movement, for the spiral of terror and the real possibility of a civil war in Palestine.[613] When on 21 January 1948, a meeting of the Presidium of the CKŻP, voted in favour the Central Committee in the WJC joining the CKŻP, the resolution to ratify the agreement was passed by all the members of the Presidium members, with four members of the Bund faction in the CKŻP voting against.[614]

---

611 Ibid., ref. 303/I/26, Protocol no. 9 from 29 January 1948, f. 83.

612 L. Korn, „Na międzynarodowej widowni; 3. Stan wojenny w Palestynie," *Głos Bundu* 1947, no. 3 (7), p. 4.

613 AŻIH, Archives of the Presidium and Secretariat, ref. 303/I/20, Protocol no. 26 from 3 March 1947, f. 137; see also: Statement of the Bund faction in connection with the Palestinian resolution, included in AŻIH, CKŻP (Archives of the Presidium and Secretariat, ref. 303/I/26, f. 50).

614 Ibid., ref. 303/I/26, Protocol no. 5, from 21 January 1948, f. 64.

The result of the vote shows not only the criticism of Zionism but above all the different position of the Bund's from that of the other parties affiliated with the CKŻP. It was an example of another emphasis on its presence and distinctiveness on the 'Jewish (political) Street', maintaining the party's ideological continuity since its inception. It was also a consequence of the ambitions of the Bundists who – although they had lost their dominant position in the Jewish community, held on to their old and opposed all initiatives that were not their own political undertaking.

The Bund and the establishment of the State of Israel

The establishment of the Jewish state was contrary to the ideology of the Bundists. They never considered Israel (even till the end of their lives, like Icchak Luden)[615] as the only just solution to the Jewish question worldwide.[616] The Bund in Poland and in Western countries opposed the UN's decision on the partition of Palestine, upholding the concept of a binational state.[617] However, after the proclamation of the State of Israel, the Bund in the People's Republic of Poland supported the creation of a new state (unlike the American Bund – as evidenced by the Second Bund Conference in New York in October 1948 – where it was argued that the newly established state endangered the safety of Jews living in Palestine).

In connection with the creation of the State of Israel, the Bund issued a declaration on 14 May 1948 in which it expressed the hope that the new state would pursue a policy of cooperation with the Arab working masses, combat chauvinism both external and internal, and fight imperialism to realise the ideals of socialism. The Polish Bund's shift toward Israel was not dictated by a sudden change of views. It was a consequence of the resolutions of the National Council of the Bund in Wrocław in April 1948, where the first initial discussions of

---

615 We know of Edelman's critical view on Israel from many sources (see, e.g. film by R. Zaretzky, Y. Kipper-Zaretzky titled *The Last Fighters*, Israel 2006).

616 See, e.g.: N. Chomsky, *Hegemony or Survival. America's Quest for Global Dominance*, Metropolitan Books, 2003 (especially Chapter VII: 'Cauldron of Animosities', pp. 129–152); N. G. Finkelstein, *Beyond Hutzpah. On the Misuse of Anti-Semitism and the Abuse of History*, Verso Books 2008; interview with Icchak Luden conducted by the author in July 2006 in Tel Aviv, during which Luden, who had resided in Israel since 1948, said that it was wrong to build a state by the means of power and permanent combat. He was not of the opinion that the establishment of the State of Israel was the sole and right solution to the Jewish question.

617 Sz. Hurwicz, „Syjonizm na forum międzynarodowym," *Głos Bundu* 1947, no. 7 (11), p. 3.

unification with the PPR – effectively an incorporation – were made. In line with its pro-Soviet political policy, the Bund supported the USSR's position on Israel, the newly established state. The proclamation of Israel was seen as a blow to British interests in the Middle East, and the USSR recognised it as an opportunity to advance its political influence.

The Bundists themselves claimed that their negative attitude toward Zionism and the establishment of the State of Israel had been modified compared to pre-war propaganda. Icchak Luden (editor of *Lebns-fragn*, the last Bundist magazine published in Israel) described the Bund's policy toward the Zionists after 1944 in Poland as not anti-Zionism, but non-Zionism, in contrast to the period prior to 1939.[618] In his opinion, the struggle against Zionism in post-war Poland was a fight for survival on the political scene, on the 'Jewish Street'. The Bundists – regardless of doctrinal conditions, regardless of their entire political legacy – were aware that when the Jewish state was created, their main ideological assumptions regarding national and cultural autonomy would no longer be relevant, and the organisation would transform from a political entity into a socio-cultural one, tasked with cultivating the Yiddish language and culture (*yidish un yidishkeyt*) among the Jewish community in Poland and around the world. In their post-war activities, their strategy was mixed with current tactics. Both were doomed to failure in the face of the already existing, but still captivating, vision of building a Jewish state in Israel. In this regard, the Bund lost the ideological rivalry with the Zionists, including competitors from Poale Zion.

618 Interview with Icchak Luden conducted by the author in July 2006 in Tel Aviv.

Chapter Six
Contacts with the 'Western' Bund

'Collaboration' with the Bund institutions beyond Poland

During World War II, many of the Bund's pre-war activists and leaders, who had been the core of the party in the Second Republic of Poland, found themselves in the United States (New York, Chicago, and Miami). They were: John Mill, Franz Kursky, Chaim Wasser, Emanuel Nowogródzki and Shlomo Mendelsohn. Another large group of Bundists remained in France and the United Kingdom during the war (e.g. Lucjan Blit and Emanuel Scherer, who were also associated with the Polish Government-in-Exile after 1945). Bundists who had survived the war under German occupation also ended up in America (e.g. Bernard Goldstein[619]) and emigrated from the People's Republic of Poland after the war. In every country where Bundists ended up, they tried to continue their work by establishing Bundist organisations. Bund committees were created during World War II in Shanghai (China)[620] and Johannesburg (Union of South Africa), among others. Bundists from Poland contributed to the development and growth of the Bund committee in Stockholm (Sweden).[621]

The newly established centres, created by activists arriving from Poland, tried to maintain contact after the war with their comrades who remained in the country and took steps to rebuild the Bund in Poland. Almost from the first months of peace, the emigrants began searching for family members and party comrades and were interested in the situation of the Jewish community in Poland, in their "[…] distant, beloved homeland."[622]

---

619 Bernard Goldstein travelled to New York at the beginning of 1946 at the invitation of the JLC. Information about his departure was published in the Polish press. Bund leaders in Poland realised that the departure of a well-known Bundist would not go unnoticed, so when they decided to release the information themselves, they somewhat explained the departure, cutting off all speculation ("Kh. Bernard gekumen in nyu-york," *Folkstsaytung* 1946, nos 2–3, p. 2).

620 Sh. Gros, "Bundistn in shankhay," *Unzer tsayt* 1957, nos 11–12 (193–194), pp. 91–93.

621 *Jewish Labor Bund. 1897–1957. Published by the International Jewish Labor Bund*, New York 1958; H. Blomqvist, *Socialism in Yiddish. The Jewish Labor Bund in Sweden*, Södertörn 2022.

622 P. Szwarc, "Mir apelirn," *Unzer tsayt* 1945, nos 9–10, p. 5.

One of the main Bundist organisations for emigrants was founded in 1941 in New York under the name 'American Representation of the Polish Bund'.[623] This is how it was described in the Polish party press after the war:

> After the end of the war, the Bundist group realised that the prospects for the Jewish workers' movement in Poland were very modest. Among the Polish Bundists in America, the idea matured to begin **political activity in the territory of the United States,**[624] where approximately five million Jews lived and where such powerful trade union and cultural self-help organisations of Jewish workers existed.[625]

The Bund's representation in the USA began publishing the monthly journal *Unzer tsayt*.[626] Another information and opinion-shaping medium, published in the form of a mimeographed typescript, was the New York-based *Buletin. Yediyes vegn algemeynem yidishn arbeter bund ('bund') in poyln,* which reported on the activities of the Bund in Poland. Publishing news from Poland served an informative and propagandistic function and maintained connections. However, in the later years, the contacts between Polish and American Jews aroused the suspicion of the authorities of the PPR.[627] The articles published in the press and the correspondence between the Polish Bund committee and the 'Western' Bund have been used here to describe the connections between the Bund centres operating in Western countries and the re-established Bund in Poland. They are a previously unused source for the history of the Bund in post-war Poland, but also for its pre-war and wartime history.

From the first issues, in articles expressing opinions on the situation of Jews in Poland during the occupation and after the war, occupied a lot of space in the *Unzer tsayt*. Not only published texts about the fate of the Bund in post-war

---

623 The name was used interchangeably with: American Representation of the Bund in Poland in America.

624 Bold in the original.

625 „Bundowcy polscy w Ameryce (wywiad z tow. A. Stolarem)," *Głos Bundu* 1946, no. 4, p. 5.

626 For more on the history of the American Representation of the Polish Bund, see, e.g.: "Bundowcy polscy." *Unzer tsayt* came out in the years 1941–2005. In 1948, it became a Yiddish-language press organ of the Bund's Coordinating Committee. Its role was to bring together the Bundist community scattered all over the globe. It presented to the Yiddish-speaking community the analysis of political problems including matters related to socialism and workers' rights from the perspective of the Bund ideology. D. Slucki, *The International Jewish Labor Bund after 1945. Toward a Global History*, New Brunswick–New Jersey–London 2012, pp. 32–33.

627 AŻIH, the Bund, files n.

Poland, but they also critically described the activities of the Zionists. Bundists in America expressed their views on the prospects for rebuilding the Jewish settlement (*yishuv*) in Poland. They raised many questions about the future of the Jewish community in the new post-war realities of Poland.[628] They were interested in the political direction of the new Polish authorities,[629] and economic issues (with a view to making People's Poland resemble the Soviet model), as well as the fate of the entire Jewish community and individuals.

There was a regular column in the newspaper *Yediyes fun poyln*[630] (Yid.: News from Poland). In articles about the political situation in PRL at the time, critical views were expressed about the new political order, subordination to Moscow, and Poland's new borders (significant Bundist communities were active in Vilna and Lvov before the war). The future of Poland as an independent state was seen realistically, albeit rather in black and white. However, as late as 1945, it was written: "We will not put on black glasses or rose-coloured ones. We want to keep our eyes open"[631] on what is going to happen in Poland. In the publications of American Bundists, they openly wrote about what some Bundists in Poland probably thought and unofficially shared the opinions of their comrades from across the western border. At the same time, like the Bundists in Poland, the emigrants criticised the Polish Government-in-Exile in London. They assumed that the only path to peace and a better future was friendship with the USSR.[632]

628 Dr E. Scherer, "Yidn in poyln nokh der milkhome," *Unzer tsayt* 1944, no. 11, pp. 8–11; M. Kligsberg, "Vegn dem tsurikufboy fun yidishn virtshaftlekhn lebn in poyln," ibid., pp. 19–23; Ch. Rafalowicz, "An ander meynung," ibid. 1945, no. 3, pp. 34–35; L. H. [?], "Pogromen in poyln," ibid. 1945, nos 9–10 (56–57), pp. 3–5.

629 Rafałowicz, ibid., pp. 34–35; YIVO Archives, ref. RG 1458 – Roman Blit Collection, Folder 5, Roman Blit's letter from 29 July 1945.

630 "Yediyes fun poyln," *Unzer tsayt* 1945, no. 5, pp. 42–43; "Yediyes fun poyln," ibid. 1945, no. 7, pp. 45–46.

631 „Di naye poylishe regirung," ibid. 1945, no. 8 (55), p. 4.

632 Ibid., pp. 3–5. It is expressed well in Roman Blit's letter from 29 July 1945: "[…] it was decided [to publish – author's note] in the issue of *Unzer tsayt* an article describing our ideological rupture with London and acknowledging the existence of the Government in Warsaw. There's also yet another article by Rafał[owicz] ('An ander maynung'). Even Emanuel [Scherer – author's note] 'broke away' from London already. But on my visit at his place yesterday, prior to the meeting, it was also decided to send a welcome telegram to Warsaw, addressed to Szuld[enfrei] to greet all the surviving Bund[ists] who found the strength and energy to build a new organisation in these circumstances. You will find the text of this telegram in the

A large part of the articles on the situation in post-war Poland consisted of reprints of articles published by Bundists in the local press, and reprints of resolutions with programme guidelines regarding the continued existence of the Bund in Poland, with which the Bundists in New York debated.[633] Numerous articles by Emanuel Nowogródzki, who no longer believed in the success of the Bund's reconstruction in Poland after the Holocaust, are an example of scepticism about the Bund's future in Poland.

From 1946 onwards, most articles about Poland described the efforts to re-establish the Bund on the 'Jewish Street'. Among the reprints of Bund newspaper articles published in Poland, the *Unzer tsayt* underlined passages listing the committees organised in various towns and cities. It also highlighted the reconstruction and continuation of Bundist traditions in Poland from before 1939.[634]

Based on official documents, it can be concluded that in the first years after the war, the Bund did not devote much attention to establishing a common political platform between Poland and abroad. The American Representatives of the Bund in Poland emphasised that they "would do everything they could to help in the great work of revival."[635] The period from 1945 to early 1947 was a time of building connections aimed at creating a unified Bundist organisation that transcended beyond the borders of the countries in which the individual national party organisations operated, which was to be something new in the Bund's activities to date.

When Shlomo Mendelsohn, one of the most important pre-war leaders of the Bund in the Second Republic of Poland, passed away in New York on 11 February 1948, his memory was honoured in Poland through obituaries and commemorative articles published in newspapers. It was decided to name the newly built Skif homes in Łódź, Legnica, Szczecin, and Wrocław after him.[636]

July issue of *U.[nzer] tsayt*," (quoted from: YIVO Archives, ref. RG 1458 – Roman Blit Collection, Folder 5, Roman Blit's letter from 29 July 1945).

633 G. Jaszunski, "Iberbrukh," *Unzer tsayt* 1945, no. 8 (55), pp. 12–13; "Dokumentn un materialn," ibid., 1945, nos 9–10, pp. 9–17; Dr M. Szuldenfrei, "Der nayer etap in der geshikhte fun 'bund' in poyln," ibid., 1945, no. 11, pp. 7–11.

634 "Byuletin fun 'bund' numer dray", ibid. 1946, no. 1, pp. 14–16.

635 AŻIH, the Bund, files n., letter of the Representation of the Polish Bund in America to the Central Committee of the Bund in Poland, addressed to Michał Szuldenfrei [undated].

636 Ibid., letter from 13 February 1948 to the Central Committee of the Bund in Poland to the Coordinating Committee Bureau in New York.

American activists were aware of the challenges involved in rebuilding the Bund in post-war Poland, realistically assessing the difficulties faced by their comrades in the country: "Few Jews in Poland escaped from the Nazi knives. Jewish life in Poland was turned into a blood-soaked cemetery."[637] Similar statements were often made by Jews living in Western Europe as well as in post-war Poland – not necessarily by Zionists. All of them, unable to see the possibility of living in a country where not only their loved ones but also the majority of the nation and its culture, created over hundreds of years, had been destroyed, provided justification for the Zionist arguments. This perspective undoubtedly influenced the attitude of the 'Western' Bund's toward the revival of Bundist life in post-war Poland. It is worth emphasising that the evolution of the official position of the Bund in the USA toward the emerging apparatus of power in post-war Poland, including the 'Lublin Government' is also visible and influenced the above position. Despite their favourable stance toward the USSR, Bundists in New York were concerned about the revival of Polish authorities subordinate to their eastern neighbour.[638]

As early as 1945, they wrote with concern in *Unzer tsayt* about the new political direction of the Polish state and the criticism – or even fight – against the so-called London Government. When describing the new political order, they used the term 'Lublin regime'. It eliminated parties that disagreed with Poland's pro-Soviet political line and suppressed forces supporting the Polish Government in London.

Bundists in the USA criticised the 'Trial of the Sixteen' which involved the leaders of the Polish Underground and took place in Moscow.[639] Bundist circles in exile were aware of the satellite character of the Lublin authorities and the Bundist leadership in Poland dependence on them in the People's Republic.

The political discord became evident, for instance, after the Kielce pogrom, when the Central Committee of the Bund demanded to participate in the action condemning the Polish reaction abroad, the 'London Government' and General Władysław Anders, who was blamed for anti-Semitic 'provocations' in Poland, including the Kielce pogrom (4 July 1946). The Bund's American representative, realising the propagandistic nature of the actions taken by the authorities of

637 E. Nowogródzki, „Vegn informatsye fun lublin," *Unzer tsayt* 1945, no. 3, p. 33.

638 Ibid.; "Der englishe prese vegn arest fun di 16 poylishe firer," ibid. 1945, no. 3, pp. 44–45.

639 "Der protses fun di 16 poylishe firer in moskve," *Unzer tsayt* 1945, no. 7 (54), pp. 3–4.

the PRL, strongly opposed participating in such an action.[640] Instead, it limited itself to publishing a resolution in *Unzer tsayt* which was issued by the American Representation of the Bund in Poland. The resolution blamed not only on the Catholic Church, "fascist and nationalist" circles in Poland, but also on the former Anders' army, located outside of Poland, for being anti-Semitic.[641] The American Bundists claimed that the wave of anti-Semitism in post-war Poland was a consequence of German policies in Poland and that anti-Semitism had also been present and visible in Poland before 1939.[642]

Every anniversary of the Warsaw Ghetto Uprising, saw articles about the participation of the Bund members and organisations associated with it during the war.[643]

In addition to dealing with domestic issues, in the early years after the war the Polish Bund's Representation in America tried to care for the interests of the Polish Bund and make its presence felt on the international stage, seeking recognition for the continued existence of the party among socialist groups. An example of this was Emanuel Nowogródzki's intervention with the Labour Party in London when the Bund from Poland was denied the right to participate in the international socialist party conference:[644]

> The Jewish labour movement in Poland today is, of course, far from its former strength due to the small number of Jews who escaped the Nazi genocide. However, the 'Bund' still exists in Poland. It was founded and has now resumed its faithful activities under banners soaked in the blood of freedom, democracy, and socialism. Our party, being revived in Poland, is aware of its international connections and feels entitled to its traditional place in international socialist meetings. The bloodshed caused by Hitler's thugs did not destroy our rights.[645]

640 AŻIH, the Bund, files n., correspondence from July 1946 between the Central Committee of the Bund in Poland and the Bund in New York.

641 „Der pogrom in kyelts," *Unzer tsayt* 1946, no. 7 (66), p. 2.

642 Rafalowicz, *Nokhn keltser pogrom*, p. 3.

643 See, i.a.: Sh. Mendelsohn, „Tsum tsveytn yortog fun geto-oyfshtand in varshe," *Unzer tsayt* 1945, no. 5, pp. 10–12.

644 AŻIH, the Bund, files n., correspondence from New York, Nov-Dec 1946. On the same subject, see also: National Archives, Foreign Office, ref. FO 371/34550, FO 371/34591, FO 371/42806, FO 371/42731, FO 371/47611, FO 371/47648, FO 371/77476.

645 AŻIH, the Bund, files n., correspondence from New York, November-December 1946. Emanuel Nowogródzki's letter to the National Executive Committee. Letter to the British Labour Party addressed to the Secretary Morgan Phillips in London, from 9 April 1946, regarding participation in the international conference of

Emanuel Nowogródzki and Emanuel Scherer sent letters with a memorandum to the Labour Party in London, in which they demanded rights for the Bund as a socialist party with a long-standing tradition, including the right to participate in international conferences. In response, they received a letter from the secretary of the International Department of the Labour Party, Denis Healey, stating that it was decided not to invite the Bund to future conferences, but that post-conference materials would be sent to the party in Poland.[646]

Bund activists who found themselves in America, France, the United Kingdom and other countries did not see the possibility of returning to Poland and growing the party there. For example, Roman Blit, who had arrived in the United States in April 1941, thanks to a visa obtained from the Japanese vice-consul Chiune Sugihara, travelled to Warsaw in July 1947 for a short visit, unnoticed by Bund circles. He wanted to see the extent of the destruction in Poland after World War II for himself, to gain some perspective on everything that had happened, and to decide on his future. The consequence of his visit was the irreversible decision to build a life in New York.[647]

Abram Stolar,[648] who spent the war in the USA and came to Poland after the war to assist with the organisation of the Central Committee of the Bund, stated in an interview with the editor of *Głos Bundu*:

socialist parties planned for 1946 in London, *Byuletin* no. 77. *Yediyes vegn algemeynem yidishn arbeter-bund (‚bund') in poyln* [Yid., Bulletin no. 77. News on the All-Jewish Workers' Union „the Bund" in Poland]. Based on the documents sent to the American Representation of the Bund in Poland: from 15 April to 15 May 1946.

646 Ibid., Morgan Phillips' letter from 16 April 1946 from London to Emanuel Nowogródzki in New York; Letter from Emanuel Scherer and Emanuel Nowogródzki to *The National Executive Committee of the Labour Party* in London from 31 October 1946 from New York; Letter from Denis Healey from 15 November 1946 to Emanuel Scherer in New York.

647 YIVO Archives, ref. RG 1476 – Roman Blit Collection, Folder 11; YIVO Archives, ref. RG 1458 – Lucjan Blit Collection, Folder 11, correspondence between Roman and Lucjan Blit.

648 Lejzer (Abram) Stolar (16 April 1892 – 1986) he worked in the Secretariat of the Warsaw Bund Committee from 1922–1939. After the outbreak of the war in 1939, he found himself in Vilna, from where he travelled through the USSR and Japan, arriving in New York in 1940. There, he was active in the Bundists' circles and at the JLC, organising help for the Bundists under the Nazi and Soviet occupation. He took part in the operation to help Bundists escape from the USSR and to leave the country. For many years, he worked in the administration of the New York-based *Unzer tsayt* (information based on: B. Nadel, "Abram Stolar," *Unzer tsayt* 1986, nos 3–4, pp. 33–34).

> After the end of the war, the Bundists realised that the prospects for the Jewish labour movement in Poland were very limited. Among the Polish Bundists in America, **the idea of launching political activity on American soil**[649] matured – after all, around five million Jews lived in America, and powerful labour unions and self-help and cultural organisations for Jewish workers existed there.[650]

Outside of Poland, Jewish socialists had the conditions and prospects to continue working in the ranks of the Bund where, as in New York, there was a Jewish Labor Committee, to which many Bundists belonged.[651]

After establishing closer contacts with the country, the 'Western' Bundists assessed the situation realistically and often emphasised the lack of conditions for the Bund's development in Poland, where only a few pre-war party leaders and a small Jewish proletariat remained, in comparison to the period before 1939. They were aware that only the new leaders, including Dr Michał Szuldenfrei, Salo Fiszgrund, Grisha Jaszuński, Zdzisław Muszkat,[652] Ignacy Falk, and Gershon Fogel, were still alive. They recognised the losses within the party and the loss of the Bund's influence over the so-called 'Jewish Street', but they supported their comrades in their activities. Despite everything, they saw the purpose in continuing.

The opinion of Bundists living abroad about the situation in Poland is illustrated by a letter from Lucjan Blit from London to his brother Roman Blit in New York, dated 26 May 1946:

> Yesterday, Abram [Stolar – author's note] left on the plane via Paris to Warsaw. From my conversations with him I am certain that he will come back to you [i.e. to New York – author's note] no later than a year from now. Perhaps earlier. The situation in Poland is deteriorating. He may have to return earlier. The departure of almost the entire Warsaw administration (aside from the minister from PSZ) does not bid well for Poland's future. A Professor I spoke with yesterday was not optimistic, either.[653]

As early as the autumn of 1944, almost from the very beginning of the Bund's re-establishment in Poland, regular correspondence with Bundists across Poland's western border was initiated. It was from there that Bundists in Poland received material aid necessary for the reconstruction of the party's structures and affiliated organisations, in addition to aid from the Joint. Funds and material

649 Bold in the original.

650 "Bundowcy polscy w Ameryce (wywiad z tow. A[bramem] Stolarem)," *Głos Bundu* 1946, no. 4, p. 5.

651 On the Jewish Labor Committee, see footnote no. 376.

652 See: Biography.

653 YIVO Archives, ref. RG 1476 – Roman Blit Collection, Folder 5.

resources were also distributed among the surviving Bundists who were coming out of hiding or returning from the USSR as part of the repatriation programme. Some of the donations from the Bund in New York included books and magazines published in Yiddish. These enriched the libraries that were being established by the party committees in various towns and cities across Poland.[654]

On the other hand, copies of magazines published after the war and memoirs from the occupation period were sent from the Central Committee of the Bund in Poland to the USA. In their correspondence, the party leaders raised issues related to the prospects for the Bund's future operation in Poland. The fact that how important those outside the country were to the party in Poland can be found in the numerous requests sent between 1947 and 1948 asking for articles on the history of the Bund for the Jubilee Book (*Yubl-almanakh*) marking the party's 50th anniversary and for a special anniversary issue of the *Folkstsaytung* magazine. Unfortunately, some of these requests went unanswered.

In addition to the exchange of opinions between the representatives of the domestic and émigré Bund, individuals approached the Central Committee of the Bund for help or information. One example of this is the correspondence with Liber (Lieber/Lipek) Gotlob concerning the request for material help to enable him to return to Poland. After the war, he found himself in Brandon, United Kingdom, where he felt isolated because there were no Jews at all in the military camp where he was stationed.[655] Moshe Alman also wrote in his letters from Manchester in the UK about his desire to return to Poland.[656] Some of the Bund committees, e.g. the Częstochowa Committee, maintained contact with their fellow Bundists in America who were associated with the Bund Committee in Częstochowa before the war, such as Rafael Federman. They also received help from them so that the Częstochowa Bund could "operate as normal."[657]

654 AŻIH, Bund, files n., a letter from Ignacy Falk to the Jewish Workers' Committee in New York, from 7 February 1948; a letter from 10 February 1948 to Tsukunft in New York from the Bund's Central Committee in Poland.

655 Ibid., correspondence between Liber Gotlob and Salo Fiszgrund from April June 1947; for more information on Gotlob, his eagerness to return to Poland and the activities of the Bund in Tarnów, see: M. Rusiniak-Karwat, "W imię socjalizmu – poszukiwanie miejsca na ziemi. Przypadek Leona (Libera) Gotloba," *Pamięć i Sprawiedliwość* 2022, no. 1 (30), pp. 356–383.

656 AŻIH, the Bund, files n., correspondence between Moshe Alman and Ignacy Samsonowicz from June 1948.

657 M. Frajdeles, "Fun partey-lebn. Tschenstochov," *Folkstsaytung* 1946, no. 1, p. 7.

The contacts between the 'Polish' Bund and the 'Western' émigré Bund were monitored and analysed by people from the PPR faction within the CKŻP, who noted the discrepancies between the domestic resolutions and the Bund organisations in the West. The political reviewers from the PPR judged that the political "correctness" of the Bundists in the country was a kind of tactic, a deliberate and purposeful action aimed at the survival of the organisation, of which the 'Western' Bund were aware. This assessment of the organisation in the PRL (in terms of political camouflage) did not bode well for the party's activities.

> The 'left-wing' nature of the Bund resolutions in Poland does not alienate these ultra-reactionary Jewish 'Labour-leaders' in America, because they do not take it too seriously, as they generously 'understand' that in 'communist-occupied', semi-totalitarian Poland, it cannot be otherwise. Therefore, the World Bund Conference in Brussels most likely adopted a resolution to give free rein in political matters in each country. [...] There is no doubt that the Bund's tactics in Poland will be coordinated with American Bundists even when the 'representation' and *Unzer tsayt* are dissolved.[658]

The nature of conflict between the 'Western' Bund and the 'Polish' Bund

Post-war contacts between the Bund in Poland and the Bund in the USA were based on the exchange of correspondence and mutual visits dedicated to discussing issues related to the Bund's current policies and the creation of the Bund Coordination Committee, which was to coordinate the activities of Bundist organisations worldwide. The reports from these meetings indicate numerous discrepancies resulting from the clash of two vastly different worlds. This was not only related to the conditions in which the party functioned, but – in many cases, the experiences of war, including those related to the German occupation, were of great importance. Examples of this include Yaakov Pat's descriptions of Poland[659] and Grisha Jaszuński's descriptions of America.

658 Quoted from: AŻIH, the Bund, files n., A. Len, Representation of the Polish Bund in the USA [undated].

659 Jacob, Yaakov (Yankev) Pat (1890–1966), journalist, member of the Bund Central Committee and General Secretary of TSYSHO in Poland before 1939. He left Poland for America in December 1938 to organise aid for the Jewish working class in Poland. There he was caught up in the outbreak of World War II and remained in New York. He was active in the JLC, where he served as Secretary General (information based on: "Kh.[aver] Yankev Pat in a shlikhes keyn poyln," *Unzer tsayt* 1946, no. 1, p. 16; M. Polit, "Jankiew Pat. 'Żydowski brat z ziemi amerykańskiej,

Yaakov Pat described his reflections and impressions after his visit to Poland on the pages of *Unzer tsayt*[660] and in the book titled *Ash un fayer. Iber di khurves fun poyln*,[661] which was published shortly after his return from Poland. The book also serves as a kind of report on the material aid provided to the Bundists in Poland by the Jewish Labor Committee (e.g. support for the printing cooperative in Łódź) as well as contributions from the local communities, as in the case of Białystok.

Pat described Poland as a graveyard where he searched for Jews as if they were the last Mohicans. Traveling around Poland, he met only a few survivors and observed the activities of Jewish committees. His descriptions are filled with stories of people carrying the burden of their wartime experiences. He contrasted the lives of Jews who had survived in areas occupied by the Germans with those who had spent the war deep inside the USSR. It is characteristic that he, a Bundist, repeatedly wrote about people who saw their future outside Poland, affirming the Zionists' plans to emigrate to Palestine. He described, among other things, the activities of kibbutzim and Zionists in Poland. He dedicated very little space to the positive aspects of Jewish life in Poland. Reading his descriptions of Holocaust survivors, one gets the impression that there were so few of them left that it was difficult to find them among Poles.[662]

He brought with him unique 'souvenirs' from Poland – evidence of the crimes committed against Jews by the Nazi Germans, a token of thank you from those he had helped on behalf of the Jewish Labor Committee, and letters from Jews in Poland to relatives in the USA, requesting assistance in leaving Poland to start a new and better life – away from the 'cemetery'. Pat presented a ruined world of Jewish towns and villages, with mentally scarred survivors. Only in the context of Dzierżoniów in Lower Silesia and Łódź did he write about "building a normal life." He described Łódź as the centre of Jewish community life, where

który jest też polskim Żydem'," *Zagłada Żydów. Studia i Materiały* 2020, no. 16, pp. 455–456).

660 E.g..: Y. Pat, "Bundistn un bund in poyln," *Unzer tsayt* 1946, no. 5, pp. 14–17.

661 Published in Yiddish: Y. Pat, *Ash un fayer. Iber di khurves fun poyln*, Nyu york 1946; in English: *Ashes and Fire*, transl. L. Steinberg, New York 1947. The book soon came to be regarded as his best work, a monumental volume on the subject of the Holocaust, hence postulates to translate it into other languages (see: E. Pat, *In gerangl. Yakov Pat un zayn dor*, Nyu york 1971, pp. 380–388).

662 A similar description of Poland can be found in a book by yet another Bundist, Mordechai Canin, titled *Iber shteyn un shtok. A rayze iber hundert khorev-gevorene kehiles in poyln* (Tel Aviv, 1952).

all Jewish political parties, cooperatives, and institutions existed, and where the Bund found fertile ground for development:

> Łódź is now a Jewish laboratory. Łódź should provide an answer to the question of whether there will be a Jewish settlement in Poland or not – if there is no Jewish settlement in Łódź, there will be no Jews in Poland at all, including in Silesia.[663]

In Łódź, a meeting under the slogan "Greetings from Jewish Workers in America to Jews in Poland" was organised by young Jewish workers. The author was quite surprised to see a room full of people. Among the attendees were members of the Tsukunft, dressed in blue shirts and red ties, which looked like something out of the pre-war era, the author stated.

In his description of the reconstruction of Jewish life in Łódź, the author did not overlook the manifestations of anti-Semitism. The whole account was complemented by photographs from the occupation era, from the liquidation of Jewish communities and former campsites, as well as images showing the ruins of cities, towns, and Jewish buildings. The overall description of the scale of destruction and anti-Semitic sentiments was permeated with pessimism. The author often asked himself whether the reconstruction of the Jewish *yishuv* would be successful and whether the Jews in Poland themselves would want it, or whether it was, on one hand, a nostalgic stance, and on the other, a dogmatic position of the Polish Bund, expressing the desire of its members. He presented the repatriates from the USSR as people who viewed Poland as a transit country and were dissatisfied with the country's post-war reality. He devoted a lot of space to Jewish children – their wartime experiences, the search for children in Polish families, their financial situation, the issue of missing families, and Jewish schools.

Yaakov Pat came to Poland against the will of Shlomo Mendelsohn and other Bundists living in America.[664] For him, the trip to Poland was an attempt to find his relatives. He often stressed the importance of assistance from American Jews in rebuilding the "poor life" of Jews in Poland. His descriptions of the destruction were interwoven with descriptions of the hardships of rebuilding and creating a new life in the country. He also described the aspirations of Zionists to leave Poland and the belief of many Jews that they would also be able to rebuild their lives, but only in Eretz Israel.

It is somewhat surprising that Pat, as a member of the Bund and having grown up in pre-war Poland, devoted very little space to describing the re-establishment

663 Pat, *Ash un fayer*, p. 32.
664 Ibid., *In gerangl*, p. 374.

of the Bund and his meetings with Bundists in the municipal committees. For instance, using the example of Białystok, he described a meeting with Pesach Bursztejn, a representative of the Białystok Jewish Committee and the head of the local Bund, who informed him about the existence of a very small Bund organisation, with only twenty-three members. Before the war, the party and its organisations had thousands of members, but only twenty-three remained. As mentioned above, Pat also described the life of the party in Dzierżoniów, where he met comrades from pre-war Warsaw. He described Dzierżoniów as a different world, detached from the rest, where people danced and laughed, where there was life, and where he learnt a lot about the summer camps organised by young people and the children's republic,[665] as well as the Jewish schools of Skif and Tsukunft where "wonderful dreams returned, with brotherhood and friendship; your eyes shone again. Longing stirred. It became cosier again."[666] However, even these joyful descriptions were intertwined with memories of the Jews he met and their experiences during the war.

During his sixty-day stay in Poland in the first half of 1946, Pat became convinced that it was impossible to rebuild Jewish life there, including the Bund, and that the only mission left for them was to fight against anti-Semitism and protect young people, a point he repeatedly raised in his book.

In his reports, Pat pointed out that Bundists, like other Jews, encountered numerous obstacles in attempting to rebuild their lives. The biggest of these was the absence of Jews, including Bundists. He bitterly described the current state of affairs of the party and the entire Jewish community:

> Religious Bundists in Poland are now experiencing a strange inner fire. It is a close-knit family, mostly made up of youth, young labourers, and young boys and girls – former Tsukunft and Skif members. They have no families, no homes, no guarantee of

665 *Sotsyalistishe kinder-republik a.n. abrashe blum* (Yid.: Abrashe Blum Socialist Children's Republic) was most likely established by the Central Committee of Tsukunft in Bielawa, in a former palace of a German magnate. Camps for Skif members were to take place there. During summer and winter camps, aside from fun and play, the participants would learn from their older colleagues from Tsukunft what it took to be a socialist in the new reality (for more information, see: AŻIH, the Bund, files n., letter from 22 June 1947 from the camp's head, Lerman, to the Central Committee of the Bund in Poland with a request for financial help for the Skif camp that was already underway and the planned Tsukunft camp. I. L.[?], "Di lagern fun y.b. 'Tsukunft'," *Oyfgang* 1947, no. 2, p. 19; J. Lerman, "Sotsyalistishe kinder-republik a.n. abrashe blum," *Yugnt veker* 1947, nos 7–8 (8–9), pp. 12–13).

666 Pat, *Ash un fayer*, p. 214.

> settling down. The Bund is their family, their home, their environment, and the sense of their existence. [...] This is not a nice situation for the Bund in Poland. A small town turned into a village, three million Jews shrank to a tiny Jewish tribe. The great Bund turned into a small organisation. All that remained from large, bright dreams is longing.[667]

Edelman was of a similar opinion about Polish Jewry, and he often shared his views in numerous interviews. He even claimed that there were no Jews left in post-war Poland because they had been exterminated by the Germans in 1942. These were widespread opinions formulated not only in the Bund movement.

A different picture of Poland was presented in Shmuel Lejb Sznajderman's book, which also take the form of a report on a visit to Poland *Tsvishn shrek un hofenung (a rayze iber dem nayem poyln)* (Between fear and hope. Travels in new Poland).[668] He came to Poland as a foreign journalist in 1946 (after the Kielce pogrom), Sznajderman[669] who had left Poland before the outbreak of World War II, described the country as not only where the tragedy of the Jews had taken place, but also that of the Poles and that the widespread devastation affected everyone. He described the attitude of the new authorities and Poles towards Jews and did not avoid the problem of anti-Semitism. The image of Poland in this book differs from the image presented by Yankev Pat. In addition to the images of destruction and negative attitudes towards Jews, the author was also able to see the positive aspects of life, such as the reconstruction of Jewish communities. He gave examples of Poles' positive attitudes towards Jews. In contrast to Pat, Sznajderman refrained from passing judgment on the situations he described.[670]

Bund delegations from Poland travelled in the other direction, to a world unaffected by the war. Salo Fiszgrund, Michał Szuldenfrei and Grisha Jaszuński,

667 Quoted from: ibid., *Bundistn*, pp. 16–17.

668 Sh. L. Sznajderman, *Tsvishn shrek un hofenung (a rayze iber dem nayem poyln)*, Buenos Aires 1947.

669 Shmuel Lejb Sznajderman (in the USA: Samuel Loeb Shneiderman; born in 1906 in Kazimierz on the Vistula – died in 1999 in the USA), journalist, in the years 1931–1939 he was a correspondent of the Yiddish press in Paris and a war correspondent in Spain. From 1940, he lived in the USA (information from: A. Grabski, "Jews and Political Life in Poland from 1944 to 1949," in: *Jewish Presence in Absence*, p. 168).

670 In a report by a well-known journalist Henry Szoskes (1891–1964) titled *Poyln – 1946 (Ayndrukn fun a rayze)* (Buenos Aires 1946) post-war Poland was presented, too, from early 1946 (Henry Szoskes was a member of the board of the Hitachdut Zionist party in the Second Republic of Poland, from 1940 in the USA).

among others, visited New York between 20 February and 20 March 1946.[671] During their trip, they stopped in London where they met with the Polish Ambassador to the United Kingdom, Henryk Leon Sztrasburger. Over the course of their month-long stay in the United States, 'Western Bundists' organised many meetings with representatives of various organisations at which the guests from Poland shared information about the current political situation in their country and about the state of the Jewish community, as well as the fates of individuals affected by the war.

The meetings were held in a true 'Bundist spirit', honouring the memory of Bundist heroes who had perished during the war. They served as an opportunity for eye-witnesses of the Holocaust, like Salo Fiszgrund, to recount their underground activities and the Bund's resistance efforts. These gatherings were not just reports but were meant as testimonies to those who had suffered. The press coverage in *Unzer tsayt* noted that the delegates also thanked the American Jewish community for their financial assistance during the war. In the official reports published in the 'American' press, there was no mention of whether the delegates from both Bunds discussed ideological matters or deliberated on the future path the Bund should take in the post-war world.[672] The press wrote that this visit was more important:

> [...] much more than just a reunion of friends and comrades – it carried the historical significance of a crucial fact: Jewish life and the Jewish labour movement have been reborn in Poland. The Bund lives on.[673]

According to the 'Polish' Bund, the main purpose of the meeting was to provide information about the reconstruction of the *yishuv* in Poland and to refute the information sent by the Zionists to organise assistance for Jews in Poland and for the Bund, to support its reconstruction. The foundations for cooperation between the two Bunds was laid, along with the development of a common ideology and political path.[674] The question of adopting a unified position between

---

671 AŻIH, the Bund, files n., Circular no. 3/46, from 16 February 1946, from the Bund Central Committee, addressed to all party organisations in the country.

672 "Di delegatsye fun ts.k. fun 'bund' in poyln in nyu-york," *Unzer tsayt* 1946, nos 3–4, pp. 7–9.

673 Information from.: I. B. Salucki-Hardman, „Mir do – un der bund in poyln. Notitsn tsu der gelegnhaynt fun dem amerikaner bazukh fun di shlukhim fun dem bund in poyln," *Unzer tsayt* 1946, nos 3–4, p. 18.

674 "Tsurikgekumen unzer delegatsye fun amerike," *Folkstsaytung* 1946, nos 2–3, s. 6; "Gemeynzamer komunikat. Fun der delegatsye fun ts. k. fun ,bund' un fun der amerikaner reprezentantn fun ,bund' in poyln;" ibid.1946, no. 4, p. 2.

the two centres was raised during semi-official meetings behind the scenes and through correspondence, such as between Scherer and Szuldenfrei.[675]

After returning to Poland, the members of the delegation to the USA went to local party committees to report on their findings. Jaszuński wrote about his impressions of the trip, which concerned not only meetings with Jewish socialists but also about the country itself and the situation of Jewish workers in the USA, in the Bund newspapers. His description, similar to Pat's depiction of Polish reality, was full of criticism and scepticism but in line with the propaganda of the People's Republic of Poland, which portrayed the USA as a country where the poor proletariat (including Jews) were exploited by the bourgeoisie. Jaszuński's text was aimed at discouraging Jews, especially the Bundists, from emigrating from Poland to America. According to Jaszuński, the majority of American Jews were Zionists, while socialists and communists played a marginal role in political life, and cultural Americanisation was opposed to the aspirations of Jewish cultural autonomy in Poland. These theses, which were part of the communist propaganda, were as follows:

> The risk of assimilation. My feelings from what is called the 'Jewish Street' are nevertheless pessimistic. It seems to me that the five-million-strong American Jewish community is rapidly heading down the path of assimilation.
>
> In the United States today, there are no Jewish schools, except for a small number of afternoon Jewish schools. Jewish books have been printed in editions of 1,000 or 2,000 copies, sold in even smaller numbers, and in reality – they have been read by an even smaller number.[676]

Against such a backdrop, the Bund's activities in Poland must have seemed impressive.

Herszenhorn[677] who also met with the American Bundists, then travelled to New York as a representative of the CKŻP. During the visits of Polish representatives to discussions on political issues (including the attitude towards the Zionist movement) the question of material aid for Jews living in Poland who had survived the Holocaust was raised.[678] In the early 1947, Falk and Finkelsz-

675 YIVO Archives, ref. RG 1478 Supplement 2 – Scherer Collection, File 70.

676 G. Jaszuński, „Pesimistishe eyndrukn fun amerike," *Folkstsaytung* 1946, no. 4, p. 3.

677 During his visit in New York, Herszenhorn represented CKŻP, not the Bund. His departure to America stirred a lot of emotions – e.g. Marek Bitter, a CKŻP employee, was very much against it (information from: AŻIH, Archive of the Presidium and Secretariat, ref. 303/I/1, Protocol no. 42 from 16 October 1945, p. 165).

678 "Khaver dr hershenhorn in nyu-york," *Unzer tsayt* 1946, no. 6, pp. 42–43; AŻIH, the Bund, files n., *Byuletin. Yediyes vegn algemeynem yidishn arbeter-bund (»bund«) in*

tein (member of the Bund and president of the Union of Jewish Writers and Journalists in Poland)[679] also travelled to the Congress of the Jewish Workers' Committee in America.

The following people visited Poland: Charles Zimmerman, Abram Stolar,[680] Chaim Wasser,[681] Rafal Ryba[682] and the aforementioned Yankev Pat, who came to Poland not only as a Bundist but also as a representative of the JLC. The main purpose of the visit was to investigate the fate of the Jews and their situation in post-war Poland. Meanwhile, Abram Stolar's trip to Poland, aimed at helping to rebuild the Bund, was met with scepticism by the Bundist community in New York.[683] After his departure, the 'Polish' Bundists appealed to the American Representation of the Bund in Poland in New York to come to Poland at least for a while e.g. for a year. Former party leaders (Leyvik Hodes, Shlomo Mendelsohn, Leon Oler and Josef Gutgold) were to come to help rebuild the Bund in Poland and strengthen the leadership ranks with their presence. According to representatives of the Board of the Bund in Poland, this could have prevented the emigration of Jews from Poland to the West and to Palestine. The response

---

poyln, no. 77. Based on the documents of the American Representation of the Bund in Poland, from 15 April until 15 May 1946; *Byuletin. Yediyes vegn algemeynem yidishn arbeter-bund (»bund«) in poyln*, no. 78, for the period between 15 May and 15 June 1946.

679 „Życie społeczne i organizacyjne. Sprawozdanie z Kongresu Żyd[owskiego] Komitetu Robotniczego," *Głos Bundu* 1947, no. 4 (8), p. 8.

680 "Khaver abram [stolar] in poyln," *Folkstsaytung* 1946, no. 4, p. 5; J. L. Landsber, "Tetikeyt fun der bundisher reprezentants in amerike. Fayerlekher kabal-ponem farn kh.[aver] abram, velkher hot ibergegebn a grus fun goldenem land," ibid. 1946, no. 6, p. 1.

681 On Wasser's visit in Poland, see, e.g.: AŻIH, the Bund, files n., *Byuletin. Yediyes vegn algemeynem yidishn arbeter-bund (»bund«) in poyln*, no. 81 (based on information from letters and reports from the period 15 September – 15 October 1946); *Byuletin. Yediyes vegn algemeynem yidishn arbeter-bund (»bund«) in poyln*, no. 83 (based on information from correspondence from the period 15 November – 15 December 1946); letter to the American Committee of the Bund – Emanuel Nowogródzki to the Central Committee of the Bund in Poland, from 14 November 1946; „Życie społeczne i organizacyjne, Odczyty tow. Was[s]era," *Głos Bundu* 1947, no. 4 (8), p. 8.

682 Rafal Ryba after the war, he was a member of the Bund in Paris, secretary of the European Secretariat of the Coordinating Committee in Paris. He came to Poland in early 1947, invited by the Central Committee of the Bund (information from: AAN, the Bund, ref. 30/IV/3, vol. XI, f. 32–34).

683 "Gezegenung farn kh.[aver] abram," *Unzer tsayt* 1946, no. 6, pp. 42–43.

to this request was delayed and, despite pressure, it was ultimately decided not to send the former leaders of the Bund and Tsukunft to Poland.[684]

In early 1947, Poland was also visited by Jakub Celemeński (1904–1986), the then-secretary of the Paris Bund Organisation. During the German occupation, he was a member of the underground Central Committee of the Bund in the Warsaw Ghetto and a courier on the 'Aryan' side.[685]

Meetings were organised for all visitors to Poland with the Bundists and the Jewish population in various towns and cities, and they were shown evidence of German war crimes and places associated with the suffering and extermination of the Jewish people. In turn, during the meetings with local Bundists, they spoke about the lives of Jews and the activities of Jewish socialists in America. During his meeting with the Łódź Bund Committee, Yaakov Pat promised material aid for the Bund in Poland.[686] After his return to the USA, the CKŻP received parcels of clothing.[687]

After the visits to Poland and the publication of reports by Pat and others, Bundists in the USA debated about the sense of continuing the Bund in Poland. Some believed in the possibility of rebuilding the Bund in Poland, like Emanuel Scherer (a statement made in March 1945 in London). Others, such as John Mill,[688] saw no purpose in continuing the Bund's activities in the new Polish reality. Bundists outside Poland pointed out that there were not enough Bund members in Poland to influence global Bund politics (Emanuel Nowogródzki), as well as its small significance in Polish politics. They believed that Jews in Poland had the right to emigrate, a position they practically shared with the Zionists.[689] They argued that the new Jewish centre was in the USA after the war. They

684 AŻIH, the Bund, files n., letter of the Central Committee of the Bund to New York, 23 March 1947, and the correspondence from New York and to New York, from April 1947; letter of refusal from New York, 14 April 1947.

685 Ibid., Minutes from the meeting of the Warsaw Bund Committee from 21 January 1947.

686 See, ia.: „Kh.[aver] yankev pat tsu gast bay undz"; „Kh[aver] y. pat in lodzh," *Folkstsaytung* 1946, no. 1, p. 6; the issue contains articles on Yankev Pat's visit in Poland and the meetings he attended in the Bund's committees in Łódź and Warsaw, where he also met with the representatives of almost all Bundist organisations that were in operation in Poland at that time.

687 "Kh.[avers] y. pats bazukh in poyln," *Folkstsaytung* 1946, nos 2–3, p. 6.

688 John Mill (1870–1952), also known as Yosef Shloyme Mil. One of the founders of the Bund. From 1915, he resided in the USA.

689 E. Scherer, „Problemen fun der yidisher tsukunft," *Unzer tsayt* 1946, no. 5, pp. 29–32.

justified their decision to stay there and their attitude towards the Bund in Poland during a party meeting on 22 June 1946 in New York as follows:

> Although we remain in America, we must not be neglectful about assisting Poland, the "old home", our movement there. Still, we are living here, here is the centre of world Jewry in terms of size, and it is our duty to help create a general socialist movement in America. There are many Bundists in the United States, several hundred, and they must retain their singularity [...][690].

Another example of the attitude of the 'Western Bund' towards the 'Polish Bund' and disbelief in the rebuilding of the party's life in post-war Poland, was the dispute over the burial place of Shmul (Artur) Zygielbojm's ashes.[691] Bundists from Poland wanted to transport his ashes to Warsaw so that as part of the party's 50th anniversary celebrations, they could be buried in the Jewish cemetery on Okopowa Street in the grave of the ghetto fighters. Despite objections from party comrades in Poland and against the will of the last surviving relatives, this was not done. Instead, the urn with the ashes was transported from London to New York but not until 1961.[692]

When reading the correspondence from New York, one may get the impression that it is full of reminders and orders to comrades in the country to send information about meetings and other organisational and programme-related matters on time. It is full of reproaches for the lack of response to the letters sent to Poland, while in many cases, they themselves did not reply to correspondence containing requests from the Bund in Poland for weeks, such as in the case of requests to submit articles for the anniversary issue of *Folkstsaytung*. After the war, the pre-war party leaders who had emigrated also wanted to maintain

---

690 Quoted from: Blatman, *For Our Freedom and Yours*, p. 193.

691 Initially, his ashes were buried in an urn at the cemetery in Golders Green in London (information from: J. Beluch-Beloński, "Wspomnienie o Arturze Zygielbojmie," *Głos Bundu* 1947, no. 7 (11), p. 3).

692 AŻIH, the Bund, files n., letter from the Secretary of the Central Committee of the Bund in Poland Salo Fiszgrund to the European Secretariat of the Coordinating Committee in Paris from 6 September 1947, regarding permission to transport the ashes of Artur Zygielbojm to Warsaw; minutes from the meeting of the European Secretariat from 2 December 1947 in Brussels, with the participation of: Nowogródzki, Szuldenfrei and Ryba. See also: M. Rusiniak-Karwat, *Zygielbojm Szmul Mordechaj* [online] https://sztetl.org.pl/en/biographies/4542-zygielbojm-szmul-mordechaj [access: 10 September 2024].

influence, – if not control, over what was happening in Poland, even from a distance.[693]

Daniel Blatman rightly noted that in the post-war reality, the Bund in Poland and in America took different paths and were heading in different directions. The Bund in Poland primarily aimed to save and revive Jewish culture in Central and Eastern Europe, and attempted to revive its former activities. However, in the face of the new post-war reality – with the Bund organisations scattered across all continents – Bundists in New York sought to create a worldwide structure of Bund organisations and Jewish socialist organisations with similar ideological orientations. They held disputes and discussions on this subject. Among the opponents was Yankev Pat, chairman of the JLC (until 1963), an institution affiliated with the Bund. In 1946, in an article in the monthly magazine *Unzer tsayt*, he wrote:

> The World Bund is a dream born out of despair. There are no other Bunds in the world, so there cannot be a world Bund or a world conference of Bund organisations. [...] Let us try not to ridicule ourselves.[694]

Reading the correspondence between the Bundists from Poland and America, we see two different worlds meet, which were divided by a wall made up of varying wartime experiences, post-war realities, and the politics of the countries in which they lived and operated. The exchanges primarily consisted of sharing information and press about the current activities of the Bund, mainly in Poland (usually sent via air mail). Reports, circulars, and newsletters were sent from Poland to New York, where they were featured in publications such as *Byuletin. Yediyes vegn algemeynem yidishn arbeter bund ('bund') in poyln*, which reported on the life of the Bund in post-war Poland. It also reprinted articles from Poland, focusing on the Bund's political activities and the rebuilding of the movement.[695] News that was published from Poland functioned as a source of information and propaganda. The letters also contained information on the whereabouts of Bundists, their search for friends and family members, as well

---

693 Ibid. For example, a letter sent on 24 April 1947 from New York to the Central Committee of the Bund in Poland, signed by Nowogródzki (see.: ibid., correspondence from 1947 between the Central Committee of the Bund in Poland and the World Coordinating Committee of the 'Bund' and Affiliated Jewish Socialist Organizations in New York).

694 Y. Pat, "A bisl apikorses vegn velt tsuzamenfor fun 'bund'," *Unzer tsayt* 1946, no. 12, pp. 15–16.

695 M. Szuldenfrei, "Der nayer etap in der geshikhte fun ‚bund' in poyln," *Unzer tsayt* 1945, no. 11, pp. 7–11.

as mutual assistance requests, including petitions to enable people to visit Poland.[696] Additionally, they exchanged news about finding family members of Bundists who did not live in Poland after the war and they tried to help bring them to New York.[697]

Bundists in the USA frequently stated in *Unzer tsayt* (perhaps to raise awareness among others or justify their decision to stay in America) that Jews – including Bund members – had 'disappeared' from Poland.[698] On the other hand, what was happening in Poland (especially the situation of the Jews and the Bund) was carefully recorded in the pages of *Unzer tsayt*, which was often the only source of information about the country for many Jews from Poland.[699]

Contacts with the Bund in France were similar to that of the US. Until the Coordinating Committee was established, these interactions were friendly and focused on the exchange of information about the party's activities, including the distribution of party newspapers.[700] For many Bundists leaving Poland, Paris was a place where they could stay for longer or shorter periods on their way to the USA or Australia. Therefore, contacts between the committees concerned the recommendations of trustworthy individuals who should be accepted into the party and helped with finding employment.[701] The French Bund also acted as an intermediary in obtaining visas for those travelling to the West.

The former Bund leaders' contacts and interests in Poland were, in fact, a form of remote control over their comrades' activities in the country at the time. This patronising attitude of the US Bundists towards their comrades in Poland may

696 AŻIH, the Bund, files n., correspondence from Michał Szuldenfrei from H. Lejwik and Abraham Eliezer Zelmanowicz from 1945; letter from Emanuel Nowogródzki (as a representative of the American Representation of the All-Jewish Workers' Union 'the Bund' in Poland) to the Central Committee of the Bund in Poland from 1 November 1945; letter from Franz Kursky to Salo Fiszgrund from 29 July 1946 with a request for regular forwarding of the press and publications; correspondence from 27 June 1947 from the European Secretariat to Salo Fiszgrund in Warsaw.

697 Ibid., correspondence from New York to Abram Stolar in Warsaw from 20 December 1946, regarding bringing Maria Gliksman from Poland to her father in New York.

698 See, e.g. "Banayt di 'folkstsaytung' in varshe," *Unzer tsayt* 1946, nos 3–4, p. 12.

699 See, e.g. ibid., 1946, nos 3–4, pp. 12–13.

700 AAN, the Bund, ref. 30/IV/3, vol. XI, f. 5–6: e.g. letter to the Bund in Paris from the Central Committee of the Bund from 4 June 1946, f. 9: Registry of Bundist organisations in Poland to which Paris-based *Unzer shtime* was sent.

701 Ibid., f. 31: letter from Salo Fiszgrund to Paris from 15 February 1947, recommending Gina Kon.

suggest that the pre-war leaders living outside Poland still wanted to decide the fate of the Bund they had co-founded in Poland. In this way, they also emphasised that the 'centre' of the Bund – its large community and leadership – had shifted to the USA.

Participation in the Bund World Conference (Brussels 1947) – the beginning of an end of collaboration

The question of convening a worldwide Bund conference was not a matter of indifference to Bundists in Poland. It was discussed in the press and at national congresses and conferences, local committee meetings, and sessions of the Central Committee of the Bund in Poland, starting from 1945.[702]

In a resolution passed at the session of the Central Committee of the Bund on 16 December 1946, it was stated that: "[...] for the Bund, the proper political goal was and is the struggle for a socialist system in the countries where the Jewish population have settled." However, as a result of the new situation and the emergence of many dispersed small Bund centres all over the world:

> The Central Committee of the Bund in Poland considers it advisable and purposeful to unite the efforts of all Bund centres while maintaining the political and organisational independence of the Bund in Poland. It is necessary to strive for the coordination of activities of all Bund organisations – wherever they operate – for the following purposes:
>
> **A.** shaping and expressing a unified political opinion of the Jewish socialist movement on fundamental social and political issues relevant to this movement,
>
> **B.** organising a unified representation of the Jewish socialist movement on the international stage,
>
> **C.** providing mutual organisational, propaganda, and material assistance. The Central Committee of the Bund in Poland resolves to participate in the conference initiated for these purposes by the American Representation of the Bund in Poland and authorizes its delegation to take a position in the spirit of this resolution.[703]

The first world conference of Bundist organisations was held in Brussels from 4 to 11 May 1947. It was attended by representatives of the Bund organisations and

702 AŻIH, the Bund, files n., Protocol no. 6 from the meeting of the Warsaw Bund Committee from 24 June 1946.

703 Ibid., Resolution of the Central Committee of the Bund from 16 December 1946.

groups from all over the world, including delegates from Poland, Johannesburg, Melbourne (Australia) and Palestine.[704]

The conference was the result of many months of discussions. During the conference, the *Velt-koordinir komitet fun 'bund' un kroyvishe yidishe sotsyalistishe organizatsyes* (English: 'Coordinating Committee of Bundist and Jewish Socialist Organisations in Various Countries) was established. Later, the name "World Coordinating Committee of the Bund and Affiliated Jewish Socialist Organizations" was adopted – which the Polish Bund representatives did not agree with. The existence of such coordinating bodies was a new development in Bundist politics. Until then, Zionists had been the only ones to unite into one single organisation.[705]

In accordance with its political doctrine, the Bund had fought "[…] to preserve Jewish national life wherever Jews reside and to link that national struggle with the broader class struggle for social liberation and socialism."[706] During the fifty years of the party's existence, the Bundists redefined the Jewish nation. Previously, the Bund denied the existence of a single global Jewish nation.[707] As Emanuel Scherer stated, the Bund was no longer a party of one country, and under the new circumstances, there was a need to shift their perspective. Hence, the need to create the Coordinating Committee.[708] During the conference, there was a significant change in the programme regarding the definition of Jewish nationality. The 'World Bund' (following the Zionists, but in a different form) assumed recognition of Jewish national interest shared by all Jewish communities and groups. The conference also agreed to strengthen the 'Jewish settlement' in Poland[709] and to unify the political direction of Bund organisations in different countries.[710]

---

704 Ibid., Invitation to the conference from the American Representation of the General Jewish Workers Union of the Bund in Poland from 7 April 1947.

705 Ibid., A. Len, *Wszechświatowa konferencja Bundu* (undated).

706 A. Grabski, *Lewica przeciwko syjonizmowi. Studia o żydowskim lewicowym antysyjonizmie*, Warsaw 2008, p. 95.

707 Ibid., pp. 93–94.

708 E. Scherer, "Bundishe velt-konferents," *Folkstsaytung* 1946, no. 5, p. 3.

709 AŻIH, the Bund, files n., Press release: *Prese-komunikat. Velt-konferents fun bund in brisl* from May 1947.

710 Ibid., letter from the World Coordinating Committee of the Bund and the Affiliated Jewish Socialist Organizations written by Nowogródzki to the Central Committee of the Bund in Poland from 26 July 1947 from New York.

After its creation, Grisha Jaszuński justified the need for the Coordinating Committee in the Bund newspaper, *Głos Bundu*, stating that the Bund in Poland with a politically and demographically altered Jewish population in Poland:

> [...] can no longer play the central and leading role it held in Jewish life during the interwar period. On the other hand, during the war, significant Bundist centres emerged in various countries, e.g. in France, the United States and Belgium, and these centres developed vibrant independent activities. Ideological differences of opinion between Bundists in various countries became apparent. All these factors led to the convening of the first global conference in the history of our party.[711]

The creation of the Coordinating Committee may not only have been a political necessity but also a desire to fulfil the ambitions of the pre-war party leaders who had lived outside of Poland after the war and were scattered across different countries. It was only possible to maintain their pre-war status by merging all the Bund centres that had been established after the war. Moreover, it was also a way of showing the "political world" that the Bund still existed and played an important role in it.[712] In October 1947, the Coordinating Committee started publishing an English-language magazine called *The Jewish Labor Bund Bulletin* to reach English-speaking readers all over the world.[713] *Unzer tsayt* also became the Committee's press organ.

The Coordinating Committee had two offices – the main headquarters in New York and a secondary European Secretariat in Paris. This arrangement aimed to streamline operations and enable representatives from various Bundist organisations in European countries to participate in the Committee's sessions. The New York office consisted of seven Committee members from America and one representative from the Tsukunft youth organisation.[714] The Bund in Poland was tasked with providing both offices with information about its domestic activities. Szuldenfrei represented the Polish Bund in the Committee. Additionally, the

---

711 G. Jaszuński, „Po konferencji w Brukseli," *Głos Bundu* 1947, no. 5–6 (9–10), p. 1.

712 AŻIH, the Bund, files n., Correspondence between the Bund from America and the Central Committee of the Bund in Poland from 1946.

713 "Editor's Note," *The Jewish Labor Bund Bulletin* 1947, no. 1, p. 1. For more information on the periodical, see: K. Propola, "Propaganda and Methods of Persuasion of Postwar Bund Circles on the Example of *The Jewish Labor Bund Bulletin*," *Piotrkowskie Zeszyty Historyczne* 2021, vol. 22, n. 3, pp. 101–120.

714 AŻIH, the Bund, files n., letter from the World-Cooperation of the 'Bund' and Affiliated Jewish Socialist Organizations in New York to the Central Committee of the Bund in Poland from 30 October 1947.

Central Committee of the Bund in Poland was responsible for approving the meeting minutes of the Secretariat and expressing their opinions on them.[715]

The Committee was envisioned as a hub connecting Bundist organisations in different countries, gathering information about their activities, continuing the policies of Jewish socialists and supporting ideologies common to all Bund organisations. From the very beginning, it was declared that Bundist organisations would retain autonomy in the countries in which they operated.[716]

In a report, probably prepared for the PPR faction of the CKŻP, contained prophetic words, predicting that the time would come when the Bund in Poland would be forced to choose between cooperating with Bundists operating outside of Poland and supporting their political stances – particularly their "negative" attitude toward the current system of the People's Republic of Poland – and aligning with the PPR. The report concluded: "The 'golden middle ground' will not withstand yet another test."[717]

After the establishment of the Coordinating Committee, friction between former Bund leaders living in exile and those who were rebuilding the Bund in post-war Poland and became part of the Central Committee of the Bund was apparent from the outset. Bundists from Poland demanded more influence on decisions and the opportunity to participate in the meetings of the Coordinating Committee. There were disputes between the organisations regarding participation in socialist conferences and the right to vote on whether the Bund should act as an organisation or as a Coordinating Committee. There were also disputes over the content of the reports from socialist conferences, during which mistakes were pointed out, and the importance of the Polish post-war Bund was downplayed.

Bundists from Poland also did not want to allow a situation in which they were replaced by a representative of the Coordinating Committee during their absence at conferences. There was also a strong desire to prevent the Coordinating Committee from displacing the Bund in Poland. It was stressed that

---

715 Ibid., letter from March 1947 from the European Secretariat to the Central Committee of the Bund in Warsaw; letter from the Central Committee of the Bund in Poland to the European Secretariat of the Bund's Coordinating Committee in Paris from 11 June 1947; letter from 25 June 1947 from the European Secretariat to Michał Szuldenfrei in Warsaw.

716 Ibid., Joint stance of the Coordinating Committee including agreements on the organisation and operation of the Coordinating Committee.

717 Ibid., A. Len, *Reprezentacja Bundu Polskiego w USA* (undated).

"the Committee is only an organ, and the organism […] is the Bund as such."[718] Differences of opinion also arose regarding the choice of the country for the 'central' celebrations of the Bund's 50th anniversary.[719] Representatives of the Bund from Poland feared the marginalisation of their party and, consequently, their role in the political world. These concerns were evident, for example, during the dispute over the name of the Coordinating Committee, which was still visible even in December 1947, more than six months after the Committee was established. During a meeting of the European Committee, Szuldenfrei indicated that, according to the arrangements made at the founding meeting in Brussels in May, the name was to be 'Coordinating Committee of the Bund and Affiliated Organisations' rather than – as it was used – 'World Coordinating Committee of the Bund and Affiliated Organizations and Groups'.[720]

The Bund in Poland and the émigré Bund also differed in their positions on Palestine. As mentioned in Chapter Five ("The Bund versus Zionism"), the Bund considered Palestine to be as one of many Jewish settlements in the world, but not the only one. The Jews in Poland considered the establishment of a Jewish state and emigration to be exaggerated nationalism. Bundists opposed the methods of building a Jewish state by force. They pursued an anti-Zionist policy both in Poland and abroad. Both Bund activists in Poland and the USA agreed on this issue. Emanuel Scherer emphasised that "Palestine does not provide a solution to the Jewish question,"[721] Gershon Oleg stated:

> Most Jews will remain in the countries of dispersion regardless of whether there is a Jewish state in Palestine or not, and this majority will be connected to the fate of the peoples living in the countries where they reside.[722]

718 Ibid., letter from the Central Committee of the Bund in Poland to the European Secretariat in Paris from 2 July 1947.

719 Ibid., Minutes from the meeting of the European Secretariat of the Coordinating Committee, 9–10 June 1947 in Zurich; letters from the Central Committee of the Bund in Poland to the office of the Coordinating Committee in New York from 26 July 1947 and from 28 July 1947 from Warsaw.

720 Ibid., Minutes from the meeting of the European Secretariat of the World Coordinating Committee of the Bund and Affiliated Organizations and Groups from 2 December 1947 in Brussels; letter from the World Coordinating Committee of the Bund and Affiliated Jewish Socialist Organizations from New York to the Central Committee of the Bund in Poland from 8 August 1947.

721 Scherer, *op. cit.*, p. 5.

722 Oleg, *op. cit.*, p. 14.

The Polish Bundists saw the creation of a Jewish state as a threat to the continued existence of the Jewish community in Poland. Representatives of the World Bund agreed that Palestine was not the only solution to free emigration:

> (d) Free immigration into Palestine, restricted only by the economic possibilities of the country, should be established. In this respect we do not discriminate between Palestine and other countries into which Jews wish to immigrate.
>
> (e) Palestine is far too small to absorb all the Jewish Displaced Persons. The plight of these griefstricken victims of Nazism must ended by allowing free entry into all countries, Palestine included.
>
> (f) All restrictions regarding the use of the Yiddish should enjoy equal rights with any other language[723].

In the statement, there is a clear support for the establishment of a Jewish state that guarantees equality for both Jews and Arabs, as well as territorial and cultural autonomy. To be sure, the authors emphasised that the newly established Jewish state in Palestine was not the only solution to the Jewish question, and that its establishment must not be associated with covert or open warfare against the Arabs in the state or the Arab nation in neighbouring countries.[724]

From the outset of the Coordinating Committee's activities, its representatives, like the Bundists in Poland, addressed the issue of refugees staying in displaced persons (DP) camps. They demanded that they be given the right to choose whether to settle in a new country or return to their homeland. In August 1947, the Committee issued a Memorandum to the UN regarding this matter, in which they demanded that the situation and rights of people be regulated.[725] They repeated their demands in newspapers and during meetings with politicians. In 1948, the Committee pointed out that it was a disgrace that people were still living in camps similar to concentration camps, even though the war had long since ended. All countries should open their borders to DPs and enable them to rebuild their lives.[726]

As with emigration to Palestine, there were only minor differences in opinions between Bundists in Poland and those who had emigrated to the newly founded Jewish state. The Bundists never considered Israel to be the only and rightful

---

723 "Statements on Palestine. Statement on Palestine and Zionism issued by the New York BUND Organization," 1947, *The Jewish Labor Bund Bulletin* 1948 no. 2, p. 6.

724 Ibid., pp. 5–7.

725 "Memorandum to the UN on Displaced Persons," *The Jewish Labor Bund Bulletin* 1947, no. 1, pp. 2–3.

726 "May Day 1948," *The Jewish Labor Bund Bulletin* 1948, no. 5, p. 2.

solution to the Jewish question in the world. They strongly criticised the UN's decision on the partition of Palestine, advocating for a binational state. After the proclamation of the State of Israel, the 'Polish' Bund (due to Soviet political pressure through the PPR) supported the new state.[727] However, the 'Western' Bund, stated at the 2nd Conference of the Coordinating Committee in New York in October 1948, that the newly founded state endangered the safety of Jews living in Palestine.[728] Additionally, the European Secretariat of the All-Jewish Workers' Union of the Bund in Paris also issued a resolution stating that although the state of Israel had been established, the joint struggle against the socialists for the improvement of the workers' conditions, as well as remembering the German camps and the past. The resolution also expressed hope that Jews and Arabs would live together in harmony.[729]

Bundists from both of the above-mentioned circles also had different attitudes toward COMISCO (Committee of International Socialist Conferences), which was preparing for the creation of the Socialist International, composed of representatives of socialist parties in exile. The 'Polish' Bund opposed this (it was dependent on political sponsors moving towards a communist one-party model) unlike the Coordinating Committee in Western Europe and the USA. In December 1948, a representative of the 'world' Bund, Rafal Ryba (Paris), participated in the COMISCO plenary session.[730] This was at a time when the national Bund was already dissolving its organisational structures.

The conference in Brussels and the establishment of the Coordinating Committee divided the Bund's post-World War II international activities into two parts. With the establishment of the Committee, a new Bund centre was officially created in North America, where most of the party's pre-war founders and activists lived. This had an impact on the marginalisation of the 'Polish' Bund, although from the perspective of the party's self-dissolution, it was an insignificant event for the domestic structures.

---

727 See: *The Jewish Labor Bund Bulletin*, 1948, no. 6 (dedicated to the newly established State of Israel and the Bund representatives' attitude towards it).

728 See: *The Jewish Labor Bund Bulletin* 1948, no. 11 (devoted to the proceedings and resolutions of the 2nd World Bund Conference, 1–8 November 1948 in New York).

729 AŻIH, the Bund, files n., Resolution of the All-Jewish Labour Union of the Bund. European Secretariat, "Paris after the establishment of the State of Israel," 1948.

730 "The Jewish Labor BUND at the COMISCO Session," *The Jewish Labor Bund Bulletin* 1949, no. 13, p. 8.

Withdrawal from the World Bund

On 23 March 1948, the Polish Bund sent a letter to the Coordinating Committee's office in New York (a copy was also sent to the European Secretariat), announcing its withdrawal from the Committee.[731] The letter stated: "We hereby inform you that a plenary session of our Central Committee, held on 21 March 1948, has decided to withdraw the participation of the BUND in Poland in the Coordinating Committee of the Bundist and Jewish Socialist Organizations in Various Countries." At the same time, the leadership of the Polish Bund decided to "[…] no longer participate in the International Socialist Conferences and to withdraw from the International Socialist Committee in London."[732] In the letter, Szuldenfrei criticised the Committee's previous policy and the lack of any signs of activity aimed at the development of Jewish culture.

The Bund authorities in the PPR justified this decision by the ideological and political differences between the Polish Bund and the Bund organisations in most countries within the Coordinating Committee. According to the Polish Bundists, these differences included the criticism of communism and the policies of the Soviet Union by representatives of the Bund from other countries, which the Polish comrades could not support even if they wanted to continue to exist. Polish Bundists also criticised U.S. President Harry S. Truman's doctrine regarding the USSR and the Marshall Plan, which Poland rejected on Stalin's orders. All of these actions were in line with the general political line of the PPR.

> The Executive Bureau of the Coordinating Committee, at its meeting held on April 8, 1948, resolved to postpone the framing of a reply to the Polish BUND Central Committee until after the conclusion of the Executive Plenary Session to which the matter will be presented during the next scheduled meeting, on June 10, 1948, in Brussels.
>
> The Executive Bureau also decided to distribute copies of the Polish BUND letter and declaration to all affiliated organizations, and to limit its own comment, to be included in the letter, to the following:
>
> "Without engaging in a political discussion with the BUND in Poland, we wish to point out that the instances cited by the Central Committee of the BUND in Poland do not correspond to the actual facts. On the background of political developments in Poland after March 18, when Premier [Józef] Cyrankiewicz forecast the liquidation of the Socialist Party through a merger with the Communists, it becomes clear that

731 AŻIH, the Bund, files n., letter from the Central Committee of the Bund from 23 March 1948, signed by the Chair Michał Szuldenfrei to the Bureau of the International Coordinating Committee of the Bundist and Affiliated Socialist Organizations in New York and to the European Secretariat in Paris.

732 "From Our Movement. Poland," *The Jewish Labor Bund Bulletin* 1948, no. 4, p. 7.

> the decision of the Polish BUND to withdraw from the Coordinating Committee was made under pressure of force"[733].

The decision of the 'Polish' Bund was not commented on by its members from other countries. They were all well aware that it was forced upon the Bundists by the communist authorities in Poland, who had forbidden them from being members of the World Coordinating Committee of Bundist Organizations and also closely monitored the Jewish socialist community.[734] The severance of ties was preceded by a cooling of relations between the organisations and the practical evasion of responsibilities by the Polish side, which very rarely sent activity reports to the European Secretariat.[735] With the Polish Bund's withdrawal from the Coordination, the official paths of the Bund diverged. This act also marked the beginning of the self-liquidation of the Bund in Poland.

Following the dissolution of the Bund in Poland in January 1949, the leadership of the 'Western' Bund organisations expressed the opinion that with the liquidation of the Bund in Poland, the hope for the reconstruction of Jewish society in Poland had died, and the communist government had made the existence and development of Jewish cultural life impossible. Bund representatives in the 'West' proudly pointed to the fact that the majority of Bund and Tsukunft members had rejected the possibility of joining the PZPR. They stated that the communists had contributed to the liquidation of Jewish life in Poland, the same forces responsible for the murder of two pre-war Bund leaders, Henryk Erlich and Victor Alter, in the Soviet Union.[736] They claimed that:

> For the thousands of former members of the Polish BUND scattered all over the world, for all those who received their political education in the ranks of the BUND and who nursed a deep sentiment for this famous movement under the proud banners of which they fought glorious battles for liberty, democracy, Socialism, and the national and cultural advancement of the persecuted Jewish people, the end of the Polish BUND is also a personal tragedy. The liquidation of the Polish BUND makes their hearts contract with shame and pain[737].

733 "Behind the Iron Curtain (News from Poland)," *The Jewish Labor Bund Bulletin* 1948, no. 5, p. 6.

734 "The Inside Story," *The Jewish Labor Bund Bulletin* 1948, no. 5, p. 7.

735 AŻIH, the Bund, files n., letter from the European Secretariat in Paris to the Central Committee of the Bund in Poland from 4 March 1948.

736 "Liquidation of the 'Bund' in Poland," *The Jewish Labor Bund Bulletin* 1949, no. 14, pp. 2–3; "The Murder of a Movement," ibid. 1949, no. 15, pp. 1–2.

737 "The Murder of a Movement," ibid. 1949, no. 15, p. 1.

In a rather original way, the Bund members from Poland, who participated in the liquidation of the Bund and were later accepted into the PPR and subsequently to the PZPR were 'punished' by their comrades from the West. In the three-volume lexicon containing biographies of Bund members, there are no entries for Salo Fiszgrund or Ignacy Samsonowicz. Instead, one can read about Michał Szuldenfrei or Zdzisław Muszkat, who stepped down from the political stage.[738] Also, the newspaper *Unzer tsayt* did not publish obituaries or memoirs after the death of those who had become members of the PPR and later the PZPR. In the case of those who emigrated from Poland, in the post-war period, they were also omitted from their own biographies or summarised with the words: "they belonged to the Bund in post-war Poland."[739] The Bundists who participated in the reconstruction of the party in communist Poland and opposed the self-liquidation of the party, and then emigrated from Poland, wrote little or nothing in their memoirs about their post-war party activities in Poland.[740]

The post-war policies of the states, in particular communist Poland and the anti-communist Western democracies, had a major impact on the relationship between Bundists living and working in the countries of the two emerging political blocs. The different political views of Bund members in Western countries and in Poland were evident on many levels until 1948. They mainly concerned the Bund's acceptance of the 'Polish' policy of the PRL at the time, including co-operation with the PPR, which the 'Western' Bund criticised, as well as recognition of Poland's new borders and the mandated friendly relations with the USSR.

When describing the contacts between the Bund in different countries since the establishment of the Coordinating Committee, I assumed that the position expressed by its representatives in New York was the same as that of the representatives of the Polish Bund in the USA. Moreover, *Unzer tsayt*, the press organ of the Bund in the USA, became the press organ of the Committee. Thanks to politically correct contacts, it was possible to obtain as many materials from the 'Polish' Bund as possible and smuggle them out of Poland in order to reconstruct

738 See: *Doyres bundistin*, ed. J. Sh. Hertz, vol. 1–3, Nyu york 1956–1968.

739 E.g. A. Lermer, *Israel Falk (1904–1996)*, in: *Un dokh – dem morgnroyt antkegn. Eseyen*, Tel Aviv 1999, pp. 154–156: in a commemorative piece on Ignacy (Izrael) Falk there is no information on his political activity in post-war Poland. Similar, in the commemorative article on Bono Winer (Wiener) (1920–1995) there's barely a mention that he was a member of the Central Committee of Tsukunft in Łódź until 1948 (see: *Bono Wiener Remembered / Dos bono viner gedenkbukh*, publ. Ch. Rosenfarb, Montreal 1997).

740 See: e.g. Sh. Szechatow, *Yorn fun kamf un gerangl*, Ramat-Gan 1973.

the Bund archives and supplement the library collections. A positive outcome (from a historical perspective) of this mutual cooperation, including collaboration with Polish *landsmanshaftn*, was the collection of documents and photographs that were used in monographs describing the history of the Bund in Central and Eastern Europe and in the creation of the Memorial Books (Yid.: *Yizkor bukh*) documenting the history of the Bund in various towns.

Contact between Bundists from different countries brought many benefits, especially for those who were living outside of Poland. They could gather information about the fate of their loved ones, find out where they lived and even establish contact with them and even help them emigrate from Poland to be reunited with their families. Thanks to these contacts, many Bund or Tsukunft members who decided to emigrate could rely on the help of comrades from Western countries during their adaptation in their new country of residence. In terms of political contacts, there was a clash of two worlds, with different and often conflicting interests in the future of the Bund. Even if the Bund in Poland had not dissolved itself, the dispute and the constant marginalisation of the 'Polish' Bund by the 'Western' members of the Coordinating Committee would probably have led to a breakdown in cooperation and the Bund's withdrawal from the organisation in Poland.

Chapter Seven
The process of the liquidation of the Bund

Conferences in Wrocław (April 1948) and in Łódź (October 1948)

After the Bund's 50th anniversary celebrations, numerous ceremonial events and jubilee publications in the Bund press, which seemed to be proof of the party's vitality and its return to both the 'Jewish' and 'Polish (political) Street', there was a crisis followed by the Bund's final phase of activity in Poland. From March 1948, the first signs of change in the Bund's politics began to appear. After the lavish celebrations, the party began following a path leading toward the 'organic unity' of the labour movement, aligning itself with the Soviet one-party model of political life. At the same time, it withdrew from the World Bund's Coordinating Committee, as mentioned in Chapter Six.

Many activists and members considered this to be a sign of the impending self-dissolution of the party in Poland. This position was most likely related to the attitude of the PPS, an ally on the 'Polish (political) Street' – in March 1948, on the PPS' behalf, Józef Cyrankiewicz agreed to begin preparations aimed at uniting the PPS with the PPR. This process ultimately ended with the unification congress in December 1948, but the PPS had already been under pressure for a long time from the communists who wanted to both conform to the Soviet model and eliminate the competitor by purging its ranks of 'elements' representing the party's vision with its half-century-old tradition, referred to those as 'WRN-men'.[741] In this way, the Bund lost its most important ally in the political arena, and this probably had a decisive influence on the Jewish socialists' decision to follow the path of the PPS. Additionally, the representatives of the PPR faction within the CKŻP exerted constant pressure on the Bund.[742]

741 PPS-WRN ('Freedom-Equality-Independence' – the slogan of the PPS which appeared on the cover of *Robotnik*, the underground name of the party during WWII, which formed the so-called 'big four', i.e. the core political force of the Polish Underground State and the Government-in-Exile. J. Holzer (Wacław Pański), *Agonia PPS. Socjaliści polscy w sojuszu z PPR 1944–1948*, Warsaw 1981, pp. 20–21.

742 B. Szaynok, „Komuniści w Polsce (PPR/PZPR) wobec ludności żydowskiej (1945–1953)," *Pamięć i Sprawiedliwość* 2004, no. 2, p. 196.

From March 1948, joint meetings of the PPR and Bund factions were held in Lower Silesia and Warsaw, during which 'organic unity' was discussed. Representatives of the Bund wanted to understand the conditions under which the two parties were to merge. In Lower Silesia, for example, they wanted to know the position of the PPR on the prospects of the continued existence of a Jewish party in Poland. At that time, the PPR members began to formulate their first demands towards the Bundists, pressuring them to exclude individuals with 'right-wing inclinations' from their ranks. The PPR activists justified this by arguing that only then would it be possible to merge. Another tactic aimed at exerting greater influence over the members of the Bund and disciplining them was to express doubts about their willingness to merge because as Jakub Wasersztrum of the PPR stated:

> The future party will be a new-type party, a Marxist party. Social democracy [!] has failed. However, the Bund does not want to criticise its past activities or even admit that there are people within the party ranks with anti-Soviet and WRN-inclined tendencies. They even revere the Bund's former reactionary leaders.[743] It was difficult for us to cooperate in the past. Today, however, the possibilities for collaboration are greater. I believe that the Bund should join the PPR, purified of right-wing elements. Our party does not have to follow in the PPS' footsteps.[744]

When members of the PPR faction noticed that some local Bund committees had begun to seek subordination to the PPR, and some party members were increasingly interested in joining the PPR as the 'leading party of the working class', its activists made further demands. The PPR members maintained that rapprochement would not happen automatically, instead was there would have to be a period during which the Bund would revise its views, and not only remove the 'unreliable' elements but also undertake a critical assessment of the party's 50-year history and activities. Such pressure began immediately after the Bund's 50th-anniversary celebrations and understandably caused discontent among its members.

Therefore the Bund activists argued the necessity of 'organic unity' with their members with the common interest in rebuilding the Jewish community in Poland and the common struggle against Zionists on the 'Jewish Street'. And yet, many were not convinced by these arguments.[745] During inter-party meetings, the representatives of the PPR not only set the conditions that the Bund members

743 This concerns the leaders of the pre-war Bund who were murdered in the USSR during the war, i.e. Victor Alter and Henryk Erlich.

744 AAN, Zachariasz, ref. 476/28, f. 104 – Minutes from the meeting of the PPR faction and the Bund from 25 March 1948, Wrocław.

745 Ibid., f. 105–106.

had to fulfil in order for the two parties to merge, but also, as in Warsaw, for example, they gave guidelines on how and in which direction the planned Bund conference should proceed. The main concern of the PPR was the question of the Bund joining the PPS, which was still being considered at the end of 1947.[746]

On 3–4 April 1948, at the National Conference of the Bund, which was convened in Wrocław, following two month long preparations. It was attended by 57 delegates representing all Bund organisations in Poland. During the proceedings, two main issues were discussed:

1. The Polish Bund's withdrawal from the Coordinating Committee and its resignation from participation in international socialist conferences.
2. The Palestine problem.

The political report on the first point was delivered on 3 April by Szuldenfrei, chairman of the Bund's Central Committee and member of the Presidium of the Party Conference.[747] During his speech, referring to his statements at the conference in Łódź in 1945 and in Wrocław in 1947, he stressed that throughout this period, the Bund had strived for unity in the labour movement. He stated that:

> "The PPR and PPS are cooperating harmoniously, forming the core of the government coalition in the country. They operate based on the same programmatic platform, jointly overcoming political and economic difficulties, working together on the massive task of rebuilding the country and its economy, and collaborating within unified trade unions, educational organisations, youth movements and so forth."[748] He concluded his speech with the words: "It is necessary to take or accept any initiative to begin the march toward the station of unity in action on the 'Jewish Street', i.e. toward the sincere realisation of a unified front between the Bund and the Jewish comrades from the PPR."[749]

This was a position expressing the party's desire to completely merge into the newly forming communist single-party system. According to the information published in the Bundist press, we know that 22 delegates out of 57, discussed the report, and all unanimously agreed that only through unification would

746 Ibid., f. 107–111; AŻIH, the Bund, files n., Circular no. 33 of the Bund's Central Committee from 22 March 1948, with directives addressed to the Bundists who planned to participate in the Conference.

747 *Głos Bundu* 1948, nos 2–3 (15–16), pp. 14–15: *Krajowa Narada Bundu*; *Referat polityczny tow[arzysza] Szuldenfreia*; *Motywy udziału w Koordynacji*; *Problematyka żydowska w Koordynacji*; *Rozbieżności ideowo-polityczne*; *Rozłam w międzynarodowym ruchu socjalistycznym*; *Stanowisko Bundu w Polsce*.

748 *Stanowisko Bundu w Polsce*, p. 15.

749 Ibid.

the further development and existence of the Jewish community in Poland be possible. This decision effectively meant agreeing to the de facto self-dissolution of the party, motivated by the fundamental strategic goal of maintaining the continuity of Jewish communities in Poland, while preserving their rights to cultural and social autonomy.

On the second day of the conference, political reports on Palestine were presented by Samsonowicz and Hurwicz (members of the Conference's Resolution Committee), and a political resolution was approved, allegedly unanimously, concerning the withdrawal of the 'Polish' Bund from the Coordinating Committee and the deepening of cooperation with the PPR.[750]

It is hard to believe that a party so deeply rooted in tradition could so quickly and definitively sever ties with its past. It must be assumed that the information published in the press was subject to censorship restrictions and had a propaganda character. Their task was to persuade all members of the Bund and its affiliated organisations to support the merger with the PPR, as promoted by the PPR faction. In accordance with the chosen political line, criticism of their position or even a dissenting opinion was banned from the press. Furthermore, if the Central Committee had openly contested the imposed unification procedure, it would have been realised through administrative means, independent of the already limited operational capacity of the party leadership. The sheer number of people participating in the discussion casts doubt on the reliability of the report, as the mood during the Conference was far from enthusiastic. In a report from a joint meeting of PPR representatives and the Bund's Central Committee (Fiszgrund, Jaszuński, Hurwicz, Herszenhorn, Falk) on 31 March 1948, Zachariasz highlighted:

> What was striking about the Bundists present at this meeting was a deep sense of gloom. They were reluctant to engage in discussion, silent and insincere. Rather, they listened to our arguments and observed our behaviour. One could sense at this meeting that the departure of the 'Bund' from the political scene of the labour movement was a historical necessity and that the end was indeed very near. (Only Fiszgrund seemed more willing to engage in a conversation.) […] It seemed that the Bundists (not the rank-and-file members) would enter into 'organic unity' with their heads down, in sadness, as if it were a funeral.[751]

Their mood may have affected the other participants of the meeting a few days later.

---

750 *Dyskusja*, p. 15.

751 Quoted from: AAN, Zachariasz, ref. 476/28, f. 110–111.

We know that Edelman strongly disagreed with Fiszgrund during this meeting when he spoke about the liquidation of the Bund. The hero of the Warsaw Ghetto Uprising accused his opponent – the executor of the idea of creating a 'monoparty' – of being a stooge for the PPR.[752] Other members of the Bund told Zachariasz about reactions similar to Edelman's. According to them, during the meeting, different views clashed, and there was a visible conflict between the 'right' and 'left' wings of the party i.e. supporters of independence and those advocating for self-dissolution and unification with the PPR. Winer, for example, was opposed to 'organic unity' but tactically supported a united front with the PPR. Falk, criticised the idea of rebuilding a Jewish state in his speech. On the other hand, when Symcha Szafir spoke in favour of 'organic unity' and criticised some of the Bundists' views, his speech was repeatedly interrupted by participants who reminded him of his former membership in the Communist Party of Poland (KPP). The greatest advocate of 'organic unity' was Fiszgrund (previously a member of the Bund faction that favoured the existence of party's on the 'Jewish Street'). Fiszgrund also criticised the fact that there was no criticism of the Bund's previous activities.[753] This accusation was just a step away from the 'self-flagellation' which involved a public display of 'self-criticism' – only a few months after the party's achievements and accomplishments were celebrated at its anniversary.

In April, those in favour of 'organic unity' (i.e. unification with the PPR) included: Salo Fiszgrund, Ignacy Samsonowicz, Leyb Pudłowski, Moses Lederman, Symcha Szafir, Izrael Perelsztejn, and Gershon Fogel. Opposing 'unity' were: Zdzisław Muszkat, Bono Winer (Tsukunft Central Committee), Marek Edelman, Avreml Żeleznikow[754] (Tsukunft Central Committee), Avreml Kahan, and Sioma Temczyn. As recalled by participants of the meeting, Żeleznikow

> […] reacted most aggressively to the speeches in favour of organic unity, kept making *tsvishn rufn* [Yiddish for 'interrupting' – author's note] during Fiszgrund's speech, accusing him of being ready to join the PPR. In his own statement on unity, he declared: 'We can agree to a united front, but only up to a certain point'.[755]

The imposed administrative merger with the PPR was for these Bund activists, the antithesis of everything they had believed in and everything they had worked

752 M. Edelman, *Prosto się mówi, jak się wie*, texts selected and edited by P. Sawicka, K. Burnetko, Warsaw 2013, p. 250.

753 AAN, Zachariasz, ref. 476/28, f. 112–113.

754 See: Biography.

755 Quoted from: AAN, Zachariasz, ref. 476/28, f. 115.

for after the war. It was especially difficult for the youth activists to accept, as they were more radical in their judgments due to their youthful intransigence.

Ignacy Falk, Shmuel Hurwicz, Abram Sobol (Szczecin), K. Goldberg (Wrocław), and Matwiej Bernstein[756] abstained from voting.

Zachariasz summarised the course of the meeting as follows:

> [...] We managed to influence the decision so that the national conference of the Bund did not adopt a resolution to join the PPS. At this conference, a general political resolution was adopted which, among other things, spoke of organic unity. However, neither the resolution nor Szuldenfrei's report appealed to us. A positive outcome was that the conference passed a resolution to withdraw from the World Coordination of the Bund and decided not to participate in International Socialist Conferences. [...] In our discussions, we demanded that the Bund acknowledge the existence of right-wing groups or elements within its ranks. The Bund's Central Committee was unwilling to admit this. Some members of the Bund's Central Committee were inclined to agree to organic unity on the condition of establishing an autonomous body for Jewish affairs. The Bund also refused to criticise its pre-war and post-war anti-Soviet activities and continued to glorify its 50-year history as a revolutionary Marxist party.[757]

After the meeting, the members of the Bund were left with no doubt that the fate of their party had been decided. All the actions taken by its representatives, including the draft circulars of the Bund's Central Committee were to be and were dictated by members of the PPR faction.[758] The faction, on the other hand, intended to ask the Bund to form a 'united front' and to conclude a written agreement on this matter even before the party's liquidation.[759]

The result of the meeting was the increased control over printed materials produced by the Bundists, enforced through systematic editorial board meetings between the Bund newspapers and the editorial board of the PPR-affiliated *Folks shtime*. This most likely explains why *Yugnt veker* ceased publication, as the majority of the members of the Tsukunft refused to merge with the Union of Youth Struggle (Związek Walki Młodych, ZWM) organisation, choosing self-dissolution rather than unification.[760]

According to the agreements reached by both parties in March 1948 and the conclusions of the meeting, inter-party sessions were held in every town and city

756 Ibid., f. 115–116.

757 Quoted from: ibid., f. 124.

758 Ibid., f. 124–125, Szymon Zachariasz's letter to the Secretariat of the Central Committee of the PPR addressed to Roman Zambrowski, 5 May 1948.

759 Ibid., f. 125.

760 Ibid., f. 136–138.

where the Bund committees and PPR faction cells existed. Each of these sessions was attended by three representatives from each local committee, forming what was known as 'inter-party six' (*szóstki międzypartyjne*).[761]

On 30 May (in Wrocław) and 8 June (in Łódź), inter-party conferences were held, the effect of which was to establish internal order within the Bund, as conflicting positions on the issue of unification with the PPR were still visible within the party.[762] In addition to ideological discussions aimed at reviewing the Bund's ideological views, these meetings attempted – with varying degrees of success – to build mutual trust and strengthen cooperation. The main focus was on the Skif and the Jewish scouting organisations, with plans to merge the children's organisations. The talks also addressed the inventory of Bundist organisations, including the merging of libraries, cooperatives, educational institutions, as well as cultural and educational facilities.[763]

The report on the activities of the PZPR Team at the Provincial Jewish Committee (WKŻ) in Szczecin from the autumn of 1948 shows how slow the process of the transformation and acceptance of the idea of 'unification' was in the ranks of the Bund:

> Cooperation with the Bund has recently been revived. The Bund cooperatives have been merged with ours. The party handed over its brass band and library to the Society for the Promotion of Culture and Art. Changes on the ideological front are happening very slowly. There is a lack of criticism and self-criticism within the Bund, and even some leftists still revere the Bund's 50-year tradition. The process of ideological reconstruction is progressing rather poorly. Joint meetings with the Bund have convinced us that the ground has not yet been properly prepared. To be sure, we could already today select over a dozen Bundists as candidates, and some even as members of the Party.[764]

This report better reflects the mood within the party (provided the ideological context of the assessment is disregarded) than the official speeches and reports published in the press at the time. The attempt at the 'unification' of political parties in Poland faced resistance from both the PPS and the Bund.

---

761 AŻIH, the Bund, files n., Circular of the Bund's Central Committee, no. 37 from 22 May 1948; Circular of the Bund's Central Committee, no. 38, from 5 June 1948.

762 Ibid., Protocol from 8 June 1948 – 1st inter-party meeting of the Bund and the PPR, "Rede fun khaver sh. hurvitch af der konferents fun di voyevodishe aktivn fun bund un pepeer in vroclav," *Folkstsaytung* 1948, nos 14–15 (42–43), p. 5; Szaynok, *Bund i komuniści żydowscy w Polsce po 1945 r.*, p. 320.

763 AAN, Zachariasz, ref. 476/28, f. 145–159; AŻIH, the Bund, files n., Circular of the Bund's Central Committee no. 43 from 15 November 1948.

764 AAN, Zachariasz, ref. 476/26, f. 113.

On 23–24 October 1948, the Central Committee of the Bund organised its last national conference in Łódź as an independent party.[765] 43 representatives from 31 towns and cities and 7 members of the Central Committee took part in the conference.[766] The meeting was led by Fiszgrund, a supporter of 'organic unity'. During the conference, Hurwicz, on behalf of the Bund, did something the party leaders had so far refrained from – he delivered a self-criticism of the 50-year history of the party, stressing that after the war there was a slow, gradual shift to the left, striving for cooperation with the working class. He called for the removal of right-wing and centrist factions from every committee.[767] This was a harbinger of an impending internal 'purge'.

During the conference, an official resolution was passed, stating among other things, that it was necessary to:

> [...] not the organisational separatism, not the federative structure of the workers' party, nor the national-cultural autonomy[768] are the proper guarantees for the development of Jewish culture. The only guarantee is the activity of the Jewish masses in the field of developing Jewish culture, based on the correct national policy of a revolutionary-internationalist workers' party, under conditions where the proletariat holds power in a socialist community. [...] The goal is to deepen the front of unity with comrades from the Polish Workers' Party across all areas of life, to decisively implement sincere and friendly cooperation at every step, rejecting petty prejudices, with a focus on full organic unity within one powerful internationalist revolutionary Party of the Polish working class, and to deepen the ideological achievements of all comrades by adopting the principles of Marxism-Leninism, through an educational campaign to raise awareness among all party members of the significance of the new historical stage in Poland – the stage of transition from People's Democracy to socialism.[769]

---

765 Many historians regard 1948 (not 1949) as the end-date of the Bund's existence (see, e.g. S. Bergman, "Przyczynki do historii Bundu," *Biuletyn Żydowskiego Instytutu Historycznego* 1992, nos 2–3 (162–163), p. 130).

766 AŻIH, the Bund, files n., Delegations from the local party organisations to the extended plenum on 23 October 1948 in Łódź. According to Zachariasz's report, 41 members took part in it (information from: AAN, Zachariasz, ref. 476/28, f. 202).

767 Information on the conference was also published in the Jewish press (see, e.g.: *Yidishe nayes fun poyln. Vekhntlekher informatsye-byuletin* 1948, no. 33, pp. 3–4).

768 Here the Bund abandoned the most important part of its political programme, the aspiration for national and cultural autonomy.

769 AŻIH, the Bund, files n., Declaration of the expanded meeting of the Bund's Central Committee in Poland with the participation of the representatives of all local organisations, which took place on 23–24 October 1948 in Łódź.

The statement that "[…] the activity of Jewish masses in the field of Jewish cultural development" is only possible on the basis of "[…] the correct national policy of a revolutionary-internationalist workers' party" sounded like a chant or a communist newspeak. It symbolised a hope to preserve the last autonomous demands of the Jewish socialist party, even after its physical death.

During the meeting, Liber Gotlob from Tarnów opted for the fastest possible dissolution of the Tsukunft's Central Committee as an organisation which, as he argued, was engaged in destructive activities aimed at halting any cooperation with the Polish Workers' Party (PPR). He pointed out that the Central Committee of the youth wing was "[…] quietly escaping across the green border, taking a few older comrades with them. They are fleeing just like Mikołajczyk,[770] they are fleeing at a time of severe class struggle, at the time of building socialism."[771] These opinions sounded like denunciations and were a testimony to the demoralisation, the breakdown of solidarity within the community, and internal conflict.

According to Zachariasz, while the mood before the opening of the meeting was very depressing, with some delegates even expressing the opinion that "they had come to a funeral," by the end, after the reports by members of the Central Committee had been presented, and the discussions among the attendees had taken place and all doubts and ambiguities had been clarified, the mood significantly improved, filling everyone with hope for the success of unification with the PPR. Admittedly, some were critical of the fact that they had to engage in

770 Stanisław Mikołajczyk (1901–1966), Polish politician, leader of the Polish People's Party. During World War II, he was the Prime Minister of the Polish Government-in-Exile. After the war ended in 1945, he returned to Poland, where he served as a member of the State Council and the Legislative Sejm. On 21 October 1947, with the help of the U.S. Embassy in Warsaw, he secretly left Poland (information from: Stanisław Mikołajczyk [online] https://www.ipsb.nina.gov.pl/a/biografia/stanislaw-mikolajczyk-1901-1966-premier-rp-dzialacz-ludowy [access: 10 September 2024]).

771 AAN, Zachariasz, ref. 476/28, f. 203. Gotlob's behavior is quite interesting, as he spent the first years after the war in Great Britain, from where he wrote letters to Bund members in Poland to ask for help and to return to his people, including the party. Perhaps, he wanted 'redeem' his stay in a Western country and the fact that he was a soldier in General Anders' army during World War II (information on Liber Gotlob from: AŻIH, the Bund, files n., correspondence from Liber Gotlob from Great Britain; AIPN Kraków, ref. IPN Kr 07/1694, vols. I–II: files concerning Liber Gotlob; M. Rusiniak-Karwat, „W imię socjalizmu – poszukiwanie miejsca na ziemi. Przypadek Leona (Libera) Gotloba," *Pamięć i Sprawiedliwość* 2022, no. 1 (30), pp. 356–383).

self-criticism, which was compared to self-flagellation and humiliation, denying everything they had previously believed in and achieved. Between the acts of self-criticism and the reckoning between the municipal committees and the Central Committee, Gotlob proposed the expulsion of Szuldenfrei from the party[772] because of his liberalism and cowardice which he believed weakened the party's activities. On the other hand, Samsonowicz, at the end of the meeting, insisted that the revision of opinions, the criticism and self-criticism, as well as the willingness to join the PPR were voluntary actions by the Bund, and not forced by the communists. These words alone raised doubts and indicated that this was by no means an initiative of the Bundists themselves but on the contrary, that it had been forced upon them.

It was the last meeting at which the 'Polish Bundists' officially sang the party anthem, *Di shvue*.[773] In December 1948, after the Unification Congress of the PPR and PPS, the Central Committee of the Bund accepted this news with a standing ovation at a party meeting, while at the same time engaging in further self-criticism of its previous activities, and sending a letter of congratulations.[774] This marked the actual beginning of the end for the Bund.

Liquidation of the opposition – exclusion of people with a 'right-wing-nationalist inclination' from the party

From the first meetings between the PPR faction and the Bund, Jewish communists emphasised the need for Jewish socialists to rid their ranks of the 'right-wing element' and, above all, to remove them from leadership positions in various Bund committees. In this way, they encouraged a purge and internal warfare as a method of achieving their own goals. They justified this by claiming that the 'right-wing elements' were hindering efforts to prepare and implement 'organic unity'.[775] They used the example of the committee in Szczecin, where the Bundists referred to as 'right-wing' were mainly concentrated. They also saw the possibility

772 During the National Conference, Szuldenfrei resigned from his position as chairman and member of the Presidium of the Bund's Central Committee. Muszkat also resigned from his position as a member of the Bund's Central Committee (information from: AŻIH, the Bund, files n., Circular of the Bund's Central Committee no. 42 from 27 October 1948).

773 AAN, Zachariasz, ref. 476/28, f. 204–207.

774 AŻIH, the Bund, files n., letter from the Bund's Central Committee from 15 December 1948.

775 AAN, Zachariasz, ref. 476/28, f. 161.

of merging with the PPR, but on the basis of autonomy within the party. Otherwise, most of them were willing to join the Zionists and leave Poland. According to Zachariasz's reports on the Bund, their attitude towards the PPR improved in the second half of 1948, although it was not stated what the improvement was.[776]

In other towns and cities, 'right-wing elements' were removed from the lists of the Bund committees before January 1949 as in Strzegom, where seven people were removed for "[...] right-wing inclinations, subversive behaviour, a complete lack of discipline, and collusion with a profiteering element."[777]

In Kraków in November 1948, during purges within the organisation:

> At the request of comrade Goldszmied, it was decided to remove class enemies and ideologically foreign elements, as well as members who showed no activity, disregarded party work, and were considered devoid of ideology.[778]

Also, during the party meeting on 10 December 1948, the attendees decided to remove individuals who had left the country and did not return their party membership cards from the party ranks.[779]

In total, at the turn of 1949, according to membership lists of Bund members in twenty-two committees, the party had only 842 comrades,[780] of whom 128 (in 12 committees) were removed from the membership lists due to 'right-wing inclinations', lack of party discipline, immoral behaviour, being a 'class-alien element', 'nationalist deviation', or – as in the case of Świdnica – they themselves returned their party cards, or – as in Strzegom – were removed after they had left Poland.[781]

776 Ibid., ref. 476/26, f. 83–84.

777 AP Wrocław, Provincial Committee of the PZPR in Wrocław: Provincial Revision Commission Department, ref. 75/V/48, f. 89.

778 AŻIH, the Bund, files n., Report on the operation of the Kraków Committee for the period from 13 November 1948 until 27 November 1948.

779 Ibid., Report on the activities of the Kraków Bund Committee for the period between 27 November and 10 December 1948.

780 Ibid., Lists of the Bund members: Warsaw – 36, Łódź – 161, Częstochowa – 20, Piotrków – 15, Lublin – 13, Włocławek – 32, Kraków – 39, Tarnów – 42, Chrzanów – 1 (there was no Bund organisation there, Bachner Lejzer's request from 16 January 1949 to enter his name on the list of members of the PZPR), Upper Silesia – 22 (Katowice, Sosnowiec, Bytom, Bielsko, Gliwice – members' places of residence), Wrocław – 85, Wałbrzych – 99, Legnica – 58, Bielawa – 54, Świdnica – 23, Dzierżoniów 17, Strzegom – 16, Nowa Ruda – 12, Kłodzko – 9, Ziębice – 26, Żary – 26, Zagórze – 6.

781 Ibid., List of the Bund members who had been expelled from the party: Warsaw – 7, Częstochowa – 15, Włocławek – 3, Kraków – 21, Tarnów – 23, Bielawa – 3, Świdnica – 10 (two were expelled from the party for inappropriate behaviour towards PPR

One of the committees that dissolved itself before January 1949 was the Przemyśl Committee, whose activists had emigrated from Poland.[782]

The party authorities ordered a list of all members of the Bund (including their home addresses and committee positions) in order to verify their membership status and political views. No precise records of party members exist from the period between 1945 and mid-1948, which makes it difficult to determine the number of committees operating simultaneously, as mentioned earlier. Even the members of the Central Committee were unaware of the exact state of the organisation, – the number of both local branches and members was fluid. Only the self-dissolution and self-criticism, with the exclusion of 'elements' that threatened 'organic unity', made it necessary to draw up accurate lists of party memberships. Paradoxically, the liquidation enforced organisational discipline, which had been lacking in the committees until then.

Liquidation of the Bund, 16 January 1949

On 16 January 1949, an extraordinary Bund Congress was held in Wrocław, attended by members of the Central Committee and delegates from existing regional organisations, as well as representatives of the Central Committee of the PZPR – Władysław Matwin and Szymon Zachariasz. The Congress was preceded by a series of events held between 8 and 15 December 1948, during which the upcoming unification of the Bund with the PZPR was celebrated.[783]

During the Congress, Hurwicz delivered a historical report on the Bund in which he presented a comprehensive self-criticism of the party, emphasising that "[…] the only path to socialism is the way of victorious Marxism-Leninism, it is the way of organic unity of the working class."[784] After him, Fiszgrund read out a political resolution on the party's self-dissolution (see the appendix). Matwin spoke on behalf of the PZPR, calling for a review of the Bundists' attitudes before they joined the PZPR so that together they could "[…] move towards the unification of the labour movement on the basis of the teachings of Marxism-Leninism."

members), Dzierżoniów – 10, Kłodzko – 7, Żary – 11, Zagórze – 2, Szczecin – 17, Wrocław – 13, Łódź – 22 persons, Strzegom – 6.

782 Ibid., Fiszgrund's letter to the workers from the 'Jedność' Cooperative in Przemyśl from 18 November 1948.

783 Ibid., Circular of the Bund's Central Committee no. 44 from 25 November 1948.

784 „Nadzwyczajny zjazd Bundu w Polsce," *Biuletyn Żydowskiej Agencji Prasowej* 1949, no. 5/485, f. 2.

At the end of the session, the Bund Liquidation Commission was elected, consisting of Salo Fiszgrund, Shmuel Hurwicz, Ignacy Samsonowicz, Moses Lederman, and Max Brum. The meeting ended with the singing of *The Internationale* instead of the Bund anthem.[785]

The report on the Congress became the topic of a Jewish broadcast on the Polish Radio on 20 January 1949. Thanks to this, information about the self-dissolution of the Bund and the complex self-criticism was heard outside of Poland, which was probably what the leaders of the PZPR had in mind.[786] Perhaps they wanted to show the 'Western' Bund that their comrades had aligned themselves with communism. For the world Bund, this was a betrayal that negated everything they had built together for over half a century.

Liquidation Commission

In the Central Liquidation Commission at 40 Targowa Street, apartment 7 in Warsaw – (the former headquarters of the Bund's Central Committee) Salo Fiszgrund (chairman of the Commission; former secretary of the Bund's Central Committee) and Max Brum (the Commission's secretary) played leading roles. Their tasks included settling the financial matters of all committees and transferring movable assets from the party inventory to the Central Committee of the Polish United Workers' Party (KC PZPR). For both, this was a kind of promotion within the party. Brum was a member of the Bund's Warsaw Committee from 1946 to 1948. When describing his career path within the party, he noted in his biography that until the second half of 1948, he was:

> [...] an ordinary member of the organisation, not elected (!) by the right-wing majority to any authorities. Only during the period of radicalisation, in the second half of 1948, was I elected to the Warsaw Committee, and at the last Congress, to the Central Liquidation Commission.[787]

The Commission also included: Hurwicz (Łódź; previously a member of the Presidium of the Bund's Central Committee), Samsonowicz (Warsaw), and

785 AAN, Zachariasz, ref. 476/28, f. 233–236; „Nadzwyczajny zjazd Bundu w Polsce," *Biuletyn Żydowskiej Agencji Prasowej* 1949, f. 1–4

786 AŻIH, CKŻP, Culture and Propaganda Department. 1944–1950, ref. 303/XIII/99, Jewish broadcast on 20 January 1949 [numbers of pages missing].

787 Quoted from: AAN, Zachariasz, ref. 476/29, questionnaire for party activists, completed by Brum, f. 20.

Lederman (Częstochowa, former member of the Presidium of the Bund's Central Committee).[788]

The tasks of the Liquidation Commission included closing cases related to the activities of local committees and reviewing (in reality, censoring) the views of Bundists who were potential members or candidates for membership in the PZPR. The Commission members evaluated the applications of potential candidates for the PZPR and submitting their opinions to local party authorities. The Central Commission was also tasked with closing down newspapers published by Bund organisations.[789]

In every town and city where the Bund existed until January 1949, Municipal Liquidation Commissions were established, consisting of people who supported the current situation.[790] The local Commissions were also responsible for making inventories of the assets and transferring them to the municipal committees of the PZPR,[791] as well as gathering documentation of the Bund committee, which was to be sent to the Central Liquidation Commission in Warsaw. The process of transferring the archives began as early as November 1948, after the Conference in Wrocław.[792] The entire Bund Archive, which had been restored after the war,

788 Ibid., ref. 476/28, f. 242–244.

789 AŻIH, the Bund, files n., Circular No. 2 of the Bund's Central Liquidation Commission, from 9 February 1949.

790 Ibid.; AAN, Zachariasz, ref. 476/28, f. 246. Statement from the Liquidation Commission in: Łódź – Fogel Gershon, Hurwicz Shmuel, Pudłowski Leyb; Częstochowa – Lederman Moses, Brener Liber, Krauze Józef; Upper Silesia – Kon Izrael, Biber R., Rybak Adam; Lublin – Goldszmid Aleksander, Borg Shmul, Bojm [Baum] Shloma; Włocławek – Liszak Moyshe, Łęczycki Beniamin, Kinel Chaim; Kraków – Rympel Emanuel, Neuger Stefan, Griner Juliusz; Tarnów – Bleiweiss Usher, Gotlob Liber, Zelkowicz Izak; Piotrków – Horowicz Aron, Rener Jakub; Warsaw – Brum Max, Garensztok (Gausztok) Józef, Galant Hersh; Lower Silesia – Szafer Symkha, Solarz Efraim, Swietycki Izak.

791 AŻIH, the Bund, files n., Handover and acceptance protocol from 2 February 1949 from the former Bund organisation and the recipient, Municipal Committee of the PZPR, from the premises located at Piastowa Street in Legnica. It mainly contained an inventory of the furnishings of the Bund Committee's former headquarters in Legnica.

792 Ibid., Inventory of the property of individual committees. Letter from Tarnów dated 12 February 1949 – a list of items already sent to Warsaw: books (403), banners, cashier's notebook, book of protocols, 7 portraits et al (some of which had already been sent on 15 December 1948). Other lists were sent from the following towns: Lublin, Piotrków, Łódź (Office I, II, large hall, canteen, buffet room, theatre), Pilawa (18 January 1949), Zagórze, Strzegom, Włocławek (3 December 1948),

was also to be transferred to the PZPR Central Archive, a task carried out by the Central Liquidation Commission of the Bund. From the protocol, we know that the following items were transferred: the post-war documentation of the Bund's Central Committee (correspondence, protocols), press materials, photo albums, documents from the period of the German occupation (a total of 18 large packages and 3 small packages), Bund banners, 41 stamps, and 3 bags of tokens.[793]

The acquired documentation is now part of the collections of the Archives of Modern Records (AAN) in Warsaw (transferred from the Archives of the Central Committee of PZPR) under the name: "General Jewish Workers' Union 'the Bund' in Poland, 1900–1948," containing 101 archival units, namely 125 cm of current files. These are mainly files concerning the activities of the Bund's Central Committee. However, not all the documents were transferred to the Archives of the PZPR's Central Committee. Some are currently in the Archives of the Jewish Historical Institute in two collections: "The Bund. General Jewish Workers' Union 'the Bund' in Lithuania, Poland, and Russia (1945–1949)"[794] (containing 134 archival units) and "Tsukunft ('Future' Youth Union, 1946–1949)" (containing eight archival units), as well as in the Department of Heritage Documentation. We do not know when and how they got there. For years, they were stored in warehouses, packed in bundles labelled "to be destroyed," which was not done. The materials mainly consist of correspondence and reports from local committees, posters, photo albums, and individual photographs documenting the activities of the Bund between 1920 and 1947.

Sosnowiec, Warsaw, Świdnica (7 December 1948), Katowice (29 December 1948), Kraków (28 January 1949), Sosnowiec (19 December 1948), Bielawa, Wałbrzych, Legnica (20 December 1948 – inventory of the organisation and the canteen), Częstochowa, Kłodzko (committee's seat, II lecture room, kitchen, common room and canteens; signatures: Chairman Beniamin Ber Kałuszyner, secretary – Aron Bokser, common room official Zacharia Szwarc; 1 December 1948), Dzierżoniów (28 November 1948). Circular of the Bund's Central Committee no. 43 of 15 November 1948, containing guidelines for the inventory of the property of the Bund Committees. From the Circular of the Bund's Central Committee nos 1–49 dated 3 January 1949, we know that despite frequent reminders from the Bund's Central Committee, not all organisations responded to the guidelines sent out and did not submit inventories by early January.

793 AAN, Zachariasz, ref. 476/28, f. 307–309.

794 The name is incorrect because these are files of the Bund operating in Poland after World War II and the name was as follows: "All-Poland Workers' Union 'the Bund' in Poland" (Yid.: Algemeyner yidisher arbeter-bund in poyln). Meanwhile, the name in the title refers to the Bund prior to 1939 as it was binding at the time, too.

The Liquidation Commissions were instructed to transfer the Bund canteens to the cooperatives, such as 'Zjednoczenie' Cooperative in Legnica, as well as to settle financial matters from previous activities and ensure that employees continued working there after the handover.[795] They set the deadline for completing this process for the end of May 1949. The intention to quickly close all obligations and liquidate all Bund institutions led to the fact that, from mid-January, the employees of these institutions were not paid, which means they were unhappy and unwilling to cooperate. Therefore, in order to transport items such as books, merge libraries, and transfer them to the 'Yidish bukh' publishing house, or transport printing machines and hand them over to the editorial office of *Dos naye lebn,* the Liquidation Commission had to rely on transportation resources provided by the PZPR.[796]

Former Bundists' view on the situation in Poland

The number of Bundists who expressed a desire to join the PZPR, both before and after the party's dissolution, is difficult to estimate. As a result, each member individually submitted a self-criticism or, as was the case in Legnica, representatives of the Central Committee of the Bund and Tsukunft did so on behalf of the entire local organisation.[797] Joining the communist party was also an individual decision. Starting from late 1948, and particularly after 16 January 1949, Bund members began to submit self-criticism and declare their intention to join the PZPR.

This was a humiliating process, especially for ideological activists of the socialist movement, who were able to see for themselves how the doctrine was implemented in the Soviet way. On the other hand, the declarations of joining the PZPR were sometimes tragi-comic. The decision to have previously belonged to the Bund was justified in various ways by the converts to communism:

> Comrade Światycki – I am a farmer by origin. I hereby state that while I was a member of the Bund, I was a disciplined member, but I have always sided with the communists. My children belonged to the KPP, and I was even proud that my children were

795 AŻIH, the Bund, files n., Protocol written down on 9 February 1949 at the seat of the 'Zjednoczenie' Cold-Cuts Cooperative in Legnica, at 45 Chojnowska Street.

796 Blatman, *For Our Freedom and Yours*, p. 216. In February 1948, the Bund had seven libraries (Warsaw – 200 books, Szczecin – 120, Częstochowa – 25, Włocławek – 25, Żary – 25, Bielawa – 20, Ziębice – 15); information from: AAN, the Bund, ref. 30/IV/5, vol. II, f. 220: Ignacy Falk's letter to the JLC in New York from 7 February 1948.

797 AAN, Zachariasz, ref. 476/28, k. 182.

communists. I hereby declare that it was my only dream to become, at the end of my life (I am ca 70 years old), a member of the United Party. (**He was unanimously accepted**).[798]

Comrade Grynszpan – I am a son of impoverished parents. I had worked to support my family since my childhood, as my father had passed away at a young age. It is well known that it was very difficult to find work in the past. It was precisely at that time that I met comrades who belonged to the Bund and advised me to join the party. They claimed it would help me find work. I did as they'd advised me to do, and from then on, I was a member of the Bund. (**Com[rade] Rozen proposes to accept Com[rade] Grynszpan into the Party. The above motion was unanimously accepted**).[799]

Others justified their resignations from the Bund in this way in their requests to the municipal committees of the PZPR:

I, Benjamin Radziner, member of the '9 May Tailors' Cooperative', having been in Tsukunft and later in the Bund, was always a proponent of the United Front of the Working Class. I have always believed that the liberation of the working class could only happen through a consistent Marxist working-class party. This is what we now observe in our country, in which socialism is being built. When I arrived from the Soviet Union after the war, I joined the workforce to help build a democratic Poland. Due to the inconsistent stance of the Bund's Central Committee with regard to everything we are currently experiencing in our country, I consider it my duty to break away from all of this. I am asking you to accept me into the United Workers' Party, and I assure I will be a disciplined and dedicated member of the Party.[800]

I, Hersh Ubfal, employee of the 'Atelier Mod' Tailors' Cooperative in Kłodzko, hereby address the Party with a following matter – I have been a member of the 'Bund' party in Kłodzko since 1946. Throughout my membership in the Bund, being an honest worker, I was a supporter of close cooperation with the Polish Workers' Party. My efforts in this area were, for reasons unknown to me, constantly postponed and hindered by my superiors. [...] In the recent past, the Bund demonstrated an anti-Soviet attitude and close contacts with foreign Bundist organisations, which were typically socialist-reformist, and other similar sins. At the present moment, with the merge of the two workers' parties, the Bund falls, by force of circumstances, out of the Polish workers' movement. Therefore, I hereby declare that I sever all ties with my former

798 AP Wrocław, Provincial Committee of the PZPR in Wrocław: Provincial Revision Commission Department, ref. 74/V/48, f. 31 (in the sub-chapter titled *Former Bundists' view on the situation in Poland* bold is copied from the original documents).

799 Ibid.

800 AAN, Zachariasz, ref. 476/28, f. 185.

party and sincerely wish to cooperate with the United Party of the Polish Working Class in the task of building a Socialist Poland.[801]

Sometimes, the reasons for joining were presented in a surprisingly self-critical manner:

Winter Jakob – a worker who had long awaited unification, always demonstrated a negative attitude towards the organised Bund. Pro-Soviet. (**Proposal: accept as a member of the party**).

Zand Majloch – a barber who was a Zionist. He joined the Bund in 1947 for a monetary payment. He is a good worker at the State Telephone Factory. (**Proposal: accept as a candidate**).

Igiel Izrael – a janitor at the Shoemakers' Cooperative. He was in the Bund for financial profit, politically uninformed. (**Proposal: accept as a candidate**).[802]

A description of the f[ormer] Bund member [in Dzierżoniów] – Wajcman A., manager of the 'Dziewiarz' Cooperative. According to his account, he had belonged to the KPP before the war and joined the Bund in order to secure employment at that cooperative. Wajcman is sociable, meticulous, and dedicated to his job. He has a positive attitude towards the present-day reality. (**Qualified as a PZPR candidate**).[803]

Kon Lea, wife of Leyb – utterly antisocial, was in the Bund because her husband was a member. (**Proposal: do not accept as a member of the party**).

Lieberman Gecel – he wanted to join the PPR for two years, but remained in the Bund at the request of the PPR. He works at the tailors' cooperative. (**Proposal: accept as a member of the party**).[804]

These are the main reasons for rejecting applications for membership in the PZPR, as formulated by representatives of the Bund's Liquidation Committee:

Bekser Aron – passive attitude towards the PZPR and the USSR (**Do not accept into the PZPR**).

Magier Józef – negative attitude towards the PZPR and the USSR (**Do not accept into the PZPR**).[805]

801 Ibid., f. 189.

802 AP Wrocław, Provincial Committee of the PZPR in Wrocław: Provincial Revision Commission Department, ref. 74/V/48, f. 64.

803 Ibid., f. 78.

804 Ibid., f. 64.

805 Ibid., f. 34.

Goldfarb Hersh – unsuitable for the party due to his immoral past. A troublemaker, clings to the parties from which he expects personal benefits. After the dissolution of the Bund, he is likely to align with Zionists. (**Proposal: do not accept**).[806]

Szmulak Chaim – antisocial type, unsuitable for the party. He is only interested in girls, cafés, clothes, and nothing more. (**Proposal: do not accept**).[807]

A description of the f[ormer] Bund member, Toszer Icchok – employee at the 'Dziewiarz' Cooperative. A kill-joy, a Marshall's Bundist. He does not care for or contribute to the growth of the Cooperative, he even hinders its development and progress. One of those who oppose the introduction of the piece-rate system. (**Qualified: do not accept**).[808]

The following individuals received different evaluations from their fellow comrades selected for the Bund Liquidation Commission and were qualified for admission to the PZPR:

Description: f[ormer] Bund member Aronowicz, employee at the '9 Maja' Tailors' Coop[erative] – a good worker. He contributed greatly to the expansion of our workplace. He has a positive attitude towards the present-day reality. (**Qualified as a PZPR member**).[809]

Description: f[ormer] Bund member Radzyner Benjamin, employee at the '9 Maja' Tailors' Coop[erative] – an honest man. He has a positive approach to work and diligently fulfills all assigned tasks. He has a v[ery] positive attitude towards our Party's resolutions. He parted ways with the Bund already before the Congress, having realised that the party did not represent the interests of the working class. (**Qualified as a PZPR member**).[810]

Description: f[ormer] Bund member Gotlib Shaya, employee at the 'Dziewiarz' Coo[perative] – a conscious and honest proletarian who works socially, also as a secretary of the Society for Polish-Soviet Friendship. He is active within the Cooperative, he's a member of the skilled-workers' Commission. (**Qualified as a PZPR member**).[811]

Description: f[ormer] Bund member Rubinsztejn Hersh, employee at the 'Odrodzenie' Cooperative – a disciplined labourer. He has a positive attitude towards the present-day reality. He supports all the actions we carry out at the workplace, even if he is politically under-informed. (**Qualified as a PZPR candidate**).[812]

806 Ibid., f. 35.
807 Ibid., f. 65.
808 Ibid., f. 81.
809 Ibid., f. 75.
810 Ibid., f. 76.
811 Ibid., f. 80.
812 Ibid., f. 84.

After the dissolution of the Bund, the transition to the PZPR was an individual matter. Very often, the decision to admit a new member depended on their attitude toward the USSR, the PZPR, and the Society for Polish-Soviet Friendship. We do not have complete data on how many people expressed their willingness to join the PZPR or how many were accepted. We do know that the majority of the Bund members in Częstochowa joined the PZPR, in Tarnów, Kraków, Łódź, Legnica (45 people) and other towns in Lower Silesia, it was a minority of former Bund members. Those who did not join the party were often discouraged and mostly withdrew from political life or emigrated to France, as did most of the members of the Central Committee of Tsukunft.[813]

Many former Bund members who did not join the PZPR could not come to terms with the dissolution of the party, such as Jakub Hampel from Łódź, who was suspected of being right-wing in the Bund.[814] Those who remained in Poland, criticised the existing regime and maintained contacts with Bund members in Belgium and France. These activities were meticulously recorded by the County Public Security Offices until the late 1950s, when they were investigating former Bundist circles, mainly in Łódź, Wrocław, Legnica, Szczecin, Katowice, and Tarnów.[815]

---

813 Blatman, *For Our Freedom and Yours*, p. 216; Szaynok, *Ludność żydowska na Dolnym Śląsku*, pp. 174–175.

814 AIPN, Łódź, ref. IPN Ld (Provincial Office for Public Security. Łódź) 668, vol. I, f. 136: History of the Bund 1946–1953: „Hampel Jakub – he belonged to the Bund before the war, is a staunch traditionalist, and cannot accept that the Bund has been dissolved. He is in contact with right-wing Bundists from the USA. Officially, he speaks out against the PZPR and adheres to the policies of Western democracy. He is hostile toward the movement. Workplace competition was considered by him as forced labour. He is hostile towards the present-day reality."

815 E.g. AIPN Warsaw, ref. IPN 00231/205, vol. V; AIPN Warsaw, ref. IPN BU 1572/3529 (author: Ministry of Public Security in Warsaw); AIPN Wrocław, ref. IPN Wr 032/249 (author: Provincial Headquarters of the Citizens' Militia (MO) – Wrocław IV; artefact file of the Kuźnica County); AIPN Kraków, ref. IPN Kr 075/214 (file of the Provincial Headquarters of the Citizens' Militia in Krakow – individuals of Jewish nationality, codename 'Trapez' – 1946–1953. Question of the Bund's milieu in Tarnów); AIPN Łódź, ref. IPN Ld PF10/668, vols. I–IV (History of the Bund 1946–1953, author – Provincial Bureau of Internal Affairs in Łódź – Department X); AIPN Katowice, ref. IPN Ka, D I 5263 (Hensel Regina 1941–1961 Rybnik), ref. D I 6587 (Hildebrand Genowefa, 1963). On the subject of spying on Jewish communities in Poland, including information on former Bund members, see publications such as: M. Grądzka-Rejak, "'Zbierać informacje o akcji przygotowawczej i sytuacji w organizacji…'. Działalność 'referenta do spraw żydowskich'

The dissolution of the Bund, like that of the other Jewish parties, was inevitable. One can only wonder whether the January 1949 Congress, during which a humiliating self-criticism took place, thus destroying the ideals that most of the participants had dedicated themselves to since their youth, was indeed necessary. Perhaps this course of events was influenced by the fact that the activities of the Bund members after the war were not only criticised by Zionist parties from outset, but also observed by representatives of the PPR faction within the CKZP. The files of Zachariasz (a representative of the PPR faction) one can find not only reports on the activities of the 'Polish' Bund, but above all on the Bundists contacts with 'Western' comrades, their participation in foreign conferences or the results of queries in the Bundist press published abroad that discussed Poland's politics. Copies of Bundists' correspondence found in his archives may indicate that there were informers in the PPR faction of the Bund, whose task was not only to monitor the party's internal operation for the communists, but also to interfere with shaping the Bund's political trajectory.[816]

By mid-1949, the Bund had ceased to exist after more than 50 years of activity in Poland. The attempt to revive the party after the war, in the new political conditions, did not fail, but the style in which this end came about, disgraced the activists. The party did not have the courage to openly protest, or even to remain passive. It denied its legacy, and in the following stages of its post-war activities, drifted as a de facto communist satellite, only to be dismantled by them, not only in reality but also in name. The memory of the Bund in post-war Poland was also doomed to oblivion, as expressed in the order to destroy the archives. There was no place for an 'old' type party in the construction of the 'new' communist order.

przy WUPB w Krakowie w latach 1947–1950," *Pamięć i Sprawiedliwość* 2021, no. 2 (38), pp. 540–561; M. Semczyszyn, B. Szaynok, „Kwestia ludności żydowskiej," in: *Aparat bezpieczeństwa wobec mniejszości narodowych w Polsce w latach 1944–1956*, ed. J. Syrnyk, Warsaw 2019, pp. 26–58; A. Sommer, „Działalność służb bezpieczeństwa wobec środowiska żydowskiego na terenie województwa krakowskiego w latach 1949–1954, na przykładzie rozpracowania obiektowego o kryptonimie 'Jordan' i 'Zator'," *Kwartalnik Historii Żydów* 2007, no. 224, pp. 435–451; B. Szaynok, „Tematyka żydowska w działalności MBP/MSW (1945–1989)," in: *Internacjonalizm czy...? Działania organów bezpieczeństwa państw komunistycznych wobec mniejszości narodowych (1944–1989)*, Warsaw–Wrocław 2011, pp. 270–295.

816 AAN, Zachariasz, ref. 476/28.

Epilogue

In the summer of 1944, pre-war members of the Bund who found themselves in the territories of so-called 'Lublin Poland', that had been liberated from the German occupation, attempted to rebuild the party. The initial period of the Bund's revival and activity in the People's Republic of Poland defined the party's main goals in the post-war reality. The activists present at the party's first organisational meetings in Lublin formed a provisional central leadership, which effectively became the de facto statutory authority and played a decisive role in shaping the party's operation until its self-dissolution in 1949.

The post-war period of the Bund's activities in Poland can be characterised primarily by attempts to confront the new reality, which was a consequence of the Holocaust and meant the de facto marginalisation of the party, which in the 1930s, was the most important political force on the 'Jewish Street' (particularly in terms of numbers) operating among Jewish workers. Its ranks were decimated by the war, and the 'Jewish Street' to which – the Bund so readily referred to – had been reduced to ruins, or rather to the debris of the Warsaw Ghetto in post-war Poland.

Beyond its traditional slogans – fighting for socialism, international brotherhood among all proletarians and oppressed labourers, and striving for dominance on the 'Jewish Street' – Bund organisations in Poland (and beyond) decided to commemorate the history of the movement and the events of the recent war, including the Holocaust and the Warsaw Ghetto Uprising. Moreover, the 'Polish' Bund, aligning itself with the political framework of the 'democratic bloc', remained silent on the fate of Bundists who had survived the war in the depths of the USSR or in the ghettos in Poland's Eastern Borderlands, which were incorporated into the Soviet Union. It chose not to speak of the martyrdom of its comrades in the East who had died as a result of Soviet and German repressions, and various groups of collaborators.

The prospects of the party's activities in the People's Republic of Poland and its future were a subject of debates in the post-war period, dividing the Bund into factions, and moreover subject to the influence and pressure from both the communists (the PPR faction within the CKŻP) and the Zionists. The difference of opinions in such a small group as the Bund after the war, had an impact on its operations and ultimate fate in Poland. Two main positions emerged within the party. The first advocated for the necessity of existing in a microscopic 'Jewish Street', itself divided into three smaller groups, each having different opinions regarding future alliances with political parties on the Polish political scene and the possibility of merging with them. The second position favored dissolving the party and encouraging Jews to leave Poland.

The Bund members' different experiences and war experiences influenced the functioning of individual committees, and, above all of the local and central authorities. There was also a clear difference in attitude towards the political situation at the time between those who had survived the war under Nazi German occupation and those who had survived the war in the USSR. The shadow of concentration camps and gas chambers influenced the former groups' decision to leave Poland, as they could not imagine continuing to live in a country that was seeped with their traumatic experiences and that same country which they perceived as a 'graveyard' of Jews. The latter were more inclined to rebuild the Bund in post-war Poland and to align themselves with the new policies of the Polish People's Republic, which they supported almost uncritically.

They did, however, seem to forget that they were still perceived as 'social fascists', and that the Bolsheviks and their representatives in the People's Republic could only see them as 'fellow travellers' (*paputchiki* in Russian), who, as the history of Soviet Russia shows, would be thrown out at a 'certain point in history', i.e. once they were deemed no longer useful, *paputchiki* would be cast away to the 'dustbin of history', as had happened to so many before them.

Regardless of the internal party disputes and disagreements about the future, the Bundists, referring to the social-democratic tradition, unanimously strove to make their presence felt on the 'Jewish Street' and regain their dominant position there. They competed mainly with the communists, but also with the Socialist Zionists. Both the communists (the PPR faction within the CKŻP) and the Bundists wanted to have the greatest possible influence on the shape of the 'Jewish Street' and on the development of the Jewish settlement in Poland, including efforts to curb sentiment towards emigration.

In the latter case, they competed with various other Zionist parties for influence among Jewish workers. This was particularly evident in the work of the Jewish party representatives within the structures of the CKŻP where different visions of rebuilding Jewish life in Poland clashed. One of the key ideological currents was *nusekh poyln* (Yid.: 'the Polish option') which stressed reviving and preserving Jewish culture and Yiddish (*yidish un yidishkeyt*) – the language of Jews from Poland and, more broadly, East-Central Europe.

For the communists, the structures of the CKŻP were a makeshift and temporary form of organising Jewish life, thanks to which they would be able to unite all Jews under the banner of the PPR. The Bundists, on the other hand, believed that the Committee would be a lasting structure, whose role they perceived in accordance with their concept of national-cultural autonomy of Jews in Poland, expressed in slogans such as *doykeyt* (Yid.: 'hereness'), *mishpokhedikeyt* (Yid.: 'familiariness'), and *yidishkeyt* (Yid.: 'Jewishness', encompassing Jewish culture and the Yiddish language). They believed that by being active in the CKŻP, they would not only realise their main programme goals but also gain a dominant influence over the Jewish community in Poland.

The forum of the CKŻP and the Jewish committees, was therefore a space of vibrant democratic debate, where different views and visions for the rebuilding the Jewish *yishuv* in Poland clashed between the three most diverse groups of parties and organisations: Zionists, communists, and Jewish socialists. The Bund's activity within the CKŻP and its conflict with the PPR faction was similar to the political disputes in People's Poland, including the relations between the PPS and PPR. Both substitutes for democratic structures on the 'Jewish street' and on the broader Polish political scene were fundamentally at odds with the Soviet-style, single-party model. Their existence came to an end with their eventual merger – or, more accurately, absorption – into the PPR.

An important factor demonstrating the party's importance was the fact that the Bund made its presence felt on the 'Polish (political) Street', delegating a representative to the State National Council (KRN), the provisional parliament, and by having Bund representatives sit on city councils and in the Legislative Sejm through its alliance with the PPS, with whom it shared a pre-war tradition. This allowed them to present their own vision on the future of the Jewish community in Poland in the state and local government forums, which differed from the Zionists' vision. They were also able to emphasise their attitude towards the policies of People's Poland at the time and express their support for the unity of the 'democratic bloc'.

As before the war, the Bund was ideologically closer to the PPS than the PPR. Cooperation with the PPS was harmonious and multifaceted, whereas relations with the PPR were strained in most towns and cities where the Bund existed, both on the 'Polish' and 'Jewish (political) Street'. The PPR sought to dominate all parties and organisations, imposing its political agenda on them. The communists were particularly keen on winning over the youth, recognising them as the future of any political movement. Meanwhile, Jewish socialists, who repeatedly emphasised the traditional ties between the Bund and the PPS, focused on strengthening the position of Polish socialists within the 'democratic bloc'. To this end, they supported and cooperated with OM TUR, the PPS-affiliated youth organisation. As previously mentioned, it seems that the party's activities in cooperation with the PPS constituted a delicate element of the Bund's political strategy at a time when the unification of the PPS and PPR, and consequently – the transition to a one-party system – was not yet a foregone conclusion.

The Bund's attitude towards emigration and emigrationism was one of the main ideological pillars of the party's programme, which was anti-Zionism. In the post-war reality, the Bundists realised that they were unable to engage in a programme-related debate with Zionist parties, whose ideology of rebuilding a Jewish state was becoming increasingly realistic, additionally conditioned by the Holocaust and the lack of prospects for rebuilding Jewish life in Poland.

The Bundists held onto their vision of restoring Jewish traditions and rebuilding the party with almost dogmatic persistence, even if it was against the odds. Therefore, they did not agree with mass emigration to the Land of Israel (emigrationism), although they agreed with the freedom to choose the country of settlement. They were aware that every Jewish emigrant leaving Poland weakened the chance of a Jewish community existing in Poland and also called into question the meaning of the Bund's existence in a country where there would be no Jewish proletariat.

On the other hand, the Bund's reluctant acceptance of emigration represented a modification of its pre-war programme. Perhaps, the Bundists realised that leaving Poland was inevitable, and that the party would only be able to exist if larger Jewish communities were to be established in the diaspora outside the Land of Israel. Emigration to Palestine undermined would have spelt the end of the Bund, as its anti-Zionist slogans would have become obsolete and incompatible with the policies of the emerging Jewish state. Furthermore, the slogans of national-cultural autonomy (preserving the traditional Yiddish culture), one of the main pillars of the party, would have lost its relevance. The Bund would become social-cultural organisation with the aim of cultivating *yidish un yidishkeyt*, which actually happened after 1948 in the Jewish state.

In addition, many of the older generation of leading activists in Poland did not want to leave the country and start all over again for personal, sentimental and professional reasons. They realised that their position in the party would change outside of Poland, in Palestine/Israel, Western Europe, or the United States – they would become ordinary members. For some, the attempt to revive the 'Polish' Bund may not have been about rebuilding a political movement but rather about reconstructing a lost *family* – not in the biological sense, but as a social and ideological brotherhood forged through shared beliefs and years of party activism. Their opposition to emigration after the war was also part of the political transformation and, structurally forming the 'democratic bloc'.

In retrospect and in view of the dissolution of all Jewish parties in the People's Republic of Poland in 1949–1950, it can be said that the Bundists' belief in the possibility of a party, especially on the left, was a utopia given the absence of a Jewish proletariat. The majority of Jews returning from the USSR, despite their traumatic experiences, were closer to the communists if they were to continue their future in Poland, or to the Zionists for whom Poland was only a transit country on their way to Palestine. When emigrating from Poland, they left nothing behind, as rebuilding a life in the country was not easy, considering the anti-Jewish atmosphere associated with a high number of Jewish communists in the repression apparatus and the number of pogroms and anti-Jewish incidents in the years 1945–1946. The growing sense of alienation and the accompanying fear motivated a large part of the Jewish community to emigrate and embrace Zionist ideas rather than socialism.

As before the war, the Bundists tried to create their own organisations for children and youth, stressing that the future of the nation and the party depended on them. In this case, they feared that the emigration of children from Poland would result in the loss of potential party members and, consequently, the end of party's existence. Moreover, they realised that their education would be in Hebrew, which would eradicate the Yiddish language, culture, and tradition from their lives.

Therefore, the Bund established party-run orphanages, such as in Wrocław, to prevent the children from being indoctrinated by Zionists and, consequently, emigrating to Palestine. The Bundists were determined to instil in the youngest generation a love for everything related to Yiddish and to teach them the language of their ancestors. For this reason, children's newspapers were only published in Yiddish. The Bundists also fought for curricula in Jewish schools, including Yiddish lessons. In this case, too, the lessons of the past war were not learnt: that only assimilated Jews had a chance of survival and development in Polish society, those who knew Polish could blend into society, even when escaping from ghettos and Nazi German camps.

The Bund's policy towards the DP camps and the people in them was one of the party's most spectacular failures in Poland. Despite the Bundists' efforts, agitation, and official campaigns, more Polish Jews from the transit camps emigrated to Palestine more often than they returned to Poland. In this respect, too, the Zionists were spectacularly successful with their programme and the prospect of rebuilding the Jewish state.

As a political party, the Bund was against any form of alliances or coalitions with other organisations, which is why it took a negative view of the World Jewish Congress, especially since it was a Zionist organisation. It was also critical of the alliance between the Polish Jews and the WJC through the representation of the CKŻP. The Bund believed that, in doing so, Polish Jews would lose their own autonomy and the voices of Jews worldwide. This objection was a symbolic act and contributed nothing, as representatives of other political factions held different views on the matter. The Zionists considered the Congress as an expression of their aspirations, while the communists viewed it as a forum for conducting politics aimed at 'imperialist states'. The Bund's criticism of the Congress, as well as its veto in the vote on the Central Committee's membership into the WJC, was yet another assertion of its existence, individuality and separate views among other political groups on the 'Jewish Street', despite losing its position as the largest and most influential party.

The change in attitude towards the WJC in June 1948 and the declaration of support for the establishment of the State of Israel on 14 May 1948 were related to the process of the party's self-liquidation and its integration into the PPR. Both acts were a result of previous inter-party meetings between the Bund and the PPR faction, which had been taking place since March 1948, during which preliminary discussions about unification with (in actual fact incorporation into) the PPR took place. At that time, the PPR – in line with its pro-Soviet policy, supported the USSR's position towards the newly established State of Israel. Unanimity on this issue was to show that the Bund was capable of ideological change and had began to revise its views, even on an issue so fundamental to its programme.

The post-war policies of the states, particularly communist-dominated Poland and the anti-communist Western democracies, had a significant impact on the relations between Bundists living and operating in the two emerging political blocs. The Bund's different political views in Poland and abroad were evident on many levels until 1948. They mainly concerned the question of the Bund's acceptance of the 'Polish' politics of the People's Republic at the time: – cooperation with the PPR, which the 'Western' Bund criticised, recognition of Poland's new borders and declaration of friendly relations with the USSR.

The relationship between the 'Polish' and 'Western' Bunds was characterised by the clash of two civilisations and culture, and there was no understanding and no desire for understanding from the first moments after the war. The 'Polish' Bundists, who saw their future in PRL, could not and did not want to support the policies of the 'Western' Bundists who were criticised by the Jewish communists in Poland, if only because they lived in countries 'corrupt by capitalism' on the western side of Poland's border. Furthermore, representatives of the 'Western' Bund, including those who had been active in Poland before the war, wanted to officially relocate the Bund's 'centre' to the USA. They also wanted to control the activities of their comrades in Poland from a distance and continue to decide on the fate of the Bund, which they had helped found in Poland. They also wanted to export the Bund's documentation from Poland in order to write the history of the party, including its underground activities in camps and ghettos.

To this end, during the conference in Brussels in May 1947, the Coordinating Committee of Bundist and Affiliated Jewish Socialist Organizations in Various Countries was established. It can be said that this event divided the post-war Bund's activities on the international stage into two phases. It also had an impact on the marginalisation of the 'Polish' Bund, as the main leaders of the Coordinating Committee lived in Western countries. The differences in the political systems of the countries in which the Bund organisations were located influenced the relations within them and the difference in views, for example, on the newly established State of Israel, which the 'Western' Bundists did not support.

Bund members in the USA, also tried to commemorate the Jewish fate during World War II in the USSR, including the imprisonment in forced labour camps of the key figures of the pre-war Bund, such as Victor Alter, Henryk Erlich or Leon Oler, which was impossible in Poland due to the state on its Eastern neighbour. As part of the Historical Commission established by the Bund's Central Committee, the 'Polish' Bund members focused on commemorating the fate of Jews under the Nazi German occupation only. The inability to share their experiences of Soviet repression, including their imprisonment in forced labour camps, and the emphasis on commemorating the Holocaust under the Nazi German occupation, may have had a negative impact on relations within the committees and their development. One of the benefits of the contact between the 'Bunds' was the help they provided during the adaptation to the new country of settlement, including assistance in finding work.

The absence of a Jewish proletariat and, consequently, of supporters of Bundist ideology was the reason behind the limited size of the party and consequently, to the success of the local committees, which were far from the model Bundist organisation in terms of their structure. Small committees, with a dozen or so members, could not influence the development of the local Jewish communities or lead a strictly political organisation. This led to a selective combination of elements from their own tradition and organisational identity. The activities of most committees focused on celebrating the party anniversaries, organised with the help of the Bund's Provincial Committees, as well as celebrating Labour Day on 1 May, which involved marching alongside other 'friendly' and 'brotherly' organisations, primarily the PPS.

These celebrations, apart from affirming the sense of their continued existence, were also a form of recruitment campaigns for the Bundist organisations. Participation in the parades was a way to not only highlight their presence but also demonstrate the Jewish socialists' support for the policies of the People's Republic of Poland. The presence of members of the youth organisation (Tsukunft) and the children's (Skif) was to demonstrate the party's potential for further growth and survival. A certain novum, compared to the period before 1939, was marching in processions together with the communists. It was not only a sign of change, but also a form of acceptance by the Bund of the leading role of PPR.

Just like before the war, the Bund sought to look after its members by providing them with material assistance. Perhaps the Central Committee believed that by offering temporary aid and securing jobs either – within the party structures or in newly established labour cooperatives – it could expand the working class, recruit new members, retain existing ones and, thus prevent them from leaving Poland. The Bund was the only party that separately created labour cooperatives on the 'Jewish Street', therefore participating in the so-called productivisation of Polish Jews. The development of party-affiliated cooperatives was primarily intended to demonstrate that the Bund still existed as a political force and had an impact on improving the living conditions of the working class.

The Bundist press in the post-war period was one of the main sources of information about the party's programme and ideology, as well as a platform for expressing views on other political groups from both the 'Jewish' and 'Polish' street. The party retained the titles of its pre-1939 publications after the war to highlight the continuity and long-standing tradition of the party, including its publishing legacy. While the press was primarily addressed to party members, it could also be of interest to readers who were not directly affiliated with the Bund. Circulation numbers were inflated to at least three times the actual number of party members, and the circulation of publications such as *Głos Bundu* far exceeded that of *Folks shtime*, published by the PPR faction. This may have also been a form of propaganda, projecting an image of a 'non-existent success', also on both political 'Streets'.

After the war, the Bund also focused on the development of Skif and Tsukunft. Party activists believed that, with the help of the youth, the party would survive and revive Yiddish as the language of the masses. Summer and winter camps were organised for members of both organisations and served as vehicles for education and, at the same time, indoctrination, as well as a form of social and psychological assistance, so important in the post-war reality. With the help of Tsukunft members, efforts were made to instil in young people the core principles of the socialist vision, which at that stage, aligned with the policies of the People's Republic of Poland. The aim was to present Jewish youth as model workers actively participating in the reconstruction and development of the economy of the country in which they lived and sought to build their future.

However, the control of the youth organisations by older members of the Bund and Tsukunft did not prevent a split between the older and younger 'comrades' when the party and its affiliated organisations were dissolved and merged with those subordinate to the PPR. When the self-liquidation of the Bund was already a foregone conclusion, most of the youth activists criticised the actions of the older 'comrades' and, by the summer of 1948, emigrated from Poland. Unlike the Bundists, they did not surrender – they continued their activities within the ranks of Tsukunft in the West, upheld the ideas of Jewish socialism, and criticised the policies of the 'Polish' Bund's leadership and the People's Republic of Poland.

After the elections to the Legislative Sejm in 1947, and especially in 1948, when discussions between the PPS and the PPR about unifying the two parties began, the Bundists realised that they had to follow the example of their Polish allies and unite with the PPR. Consequently, they expressed their willingness to completely 'merge' the Bund to the newly formed communist 'monoparty'. This was to happen after the elimination of 'right-wing elements' from the ranks of the party ranks which were a threat to 'organic unity'. This meant agreeing to the party's de facto self-dissolution and what was – most difficult of all – to publicly expressing 'self-criticism' and renouncing half a century of the Bund's tradition and achievements, just months after the grand celebrations of the party's 50th anniversary. The Bund leaders, or at least some of them, believed that this would at least maintain the continuity of Jewish communities in Poland and preserve their cultural and social autonomy.

The dissolution of the Bund, as well as other Jewish parties, was predetermined by the communists. In retrospect, one may question whether it was necessary to 'self-flagellate', to abandon ideals and to deny all one's achievements of the post-war years. On the other hand, the Bund's activities in post-war Poland were doomed to failure not only because of the absence of a Jewish proletariat, but also because of the infiltration of Bundist circles by members of the PPR faction and by individuals acting as informants from within the party.

At the beginning of 1948, after withdrawing from the Coordinating Committee and losing their main political ally, the PPS (which had begun talks with the PPR about unification), the Bundists in Poland decided – in an act of desperation, with no political allies left – to follow the path chosen by the PPS. In addition, in the face of inevitable dissolution, they may have realised that 'by stepping out in front', they could protect many comrades employed in the Bund-affiliated organisations and institutions from losing their jobs. Key figures in the liquidation process, such as Fiszgrund and Samsonowicz, joined the PZPR after the party's self-dissolution, thus maintaining significant influence within the Jewish community. Samsonowicz was a journalist for *Folks shtime* and Fiszgrund became a member of the board of the Social-Cultural Association of Jews in Poland (TSKŻ). Established in 1950 to replace the CKŻP, TSKŻ remained aligned with the PZPR until 1989.

Apart from emigration or merging with the PZPR, some members of the Bund ceased all political activity and devoted themselves to family life and private affairs. One of the few people who remained in Poland was Marek Edelman, who remained a staunch critic of the Jewish state and Zionism until the end of his life. He also did not change his social-democratic beliefs, engaging in the struggle for a democratic change in Poland.

Appendices

1. Resolutions passed at the National Conference of the Bund in Łódź on 16–17 June 1945 – (the political platform of the Bund in post-war Poland)

I. Political resolutions

The Second World War resulted in the complete defeat of fascist regimes in almost all countries, and the consolidation of close cooperation between the three dominant democratic powers, the Soviet Union, the United States, and the United Kingdom, which ensured lasting world peace.

The Soviet Union and the Red Army deserve special recognition for their contribution to this achievement, and we extend our sincere and heartfelt friendship to the Soviet Union worldwide, particularly among the international proletariat.

The war has caused a deep shock in all capitalist countries and has led to an intensification of class differences. In all these countries, the working class and peasantry are rising to power and fighting for a change in the social system. The balance of social forces is clearly shifting in favour of the proletariat.

The same social process is also taking place in Poland. Power has been seized by the working class and peasantry through the Provisional Government, which is implementing a minimal socialist programme. The policy of this government, which is based on establishing Poland's foreign relations through a close alliance primarily with the Soviet Union, and its domestic policy on fundamental social reforms and on ensuring the working class's power in the country, is the only realistic and just course.

On the other hand, the policy represented by the so-called London orientation is harmful to the interests of the proletarian, as is anti-Soviet policy, calculated to cause conflicts within the socialist states and it supports extreme reactionary elements in the country.

In accordance with these principles, the Conference confirms the Party's previous policy of supporting the policy of the Provisional Government and opposing the London orientation.

II. Resolution on anti-Semitism

Anti-Semitism is still present in Poland and is even increasing in some circles, poisoning the lives of the remaining Jewish population who survived the Nazi massacre. The Jewish population feels threatened in its existence due to the frequent murders committed against Jews and the expulsion of Jews from smaller towns and villages.

Anti-Semitic slogans and crimes are a political weapon used by the Polish reactionary forces to obscure the true nature of their struggle against Polish democracy for power in the country.

The Conference protests against the hypocritical actions of those Polish reactionary groups in London that, proclaim supposedly democratic slogans and advocate for Jewish equality, while at the same time supporting ant-Semitic gangs at home and using anti-Jewish slogans in their fight for democracy.

The Conference believes that the Jewish labour movement should focus – based on solidarity with the Polish labour movement – with the camp of democracy, closely cooperate with it in cleaning up the atmosphere which has been poisoned by anti-Semitism, and contribute to conducting a constant and systematic repressive and propaganda campaign in this direction.

III. Resolution on emigration

In the wake of the ordeal experienced under the German occupation, as well as the ongoing open or covert anti-Semitism in Poland and the lack of personal security for Jews, a desire to emigrate has arisen among some of the surviving Jewish population as an escape from anti-Semitic excesses at home.

While generally supporting the freedom to emigrate, the Conference considers it necessary to oppose 'emigrationism' as an ideology which presents emigration as the only solution to the current situation of the Jewish population in Poland.

Such an ideology is, in its essence, reactionary, as it dissuades the Jewish population from fighting for the democratisation of the country, it shifts the issue of anti-Semitism from the social and class framework to the nationalist one, and thereby obscures the objective picture of the ongoing social struggle.

The spread of this ideology is harmful to the Jewish population itself, as it prevents them from working creatively in the country, keeping them on standby to emigrate.

The Conference opposes these sentiments and tendencies with the ideology of the proletarian struggle at home – in solidarity with the Polish labour movement – for the victory of democracy and the welfare of the entire working class by integrating the Jewish population into the process of productive labour.

IV. Resolution on the activities of the Jewish committees

The Conference states that the 'Bund's' attitude towards the tasks and activities of the Jewish committees in Poland is and should remain positive.

The Conference calls on all comrades, especially those delegated to Jewish committees, to actively cooperate in these committees.

The Conference believes that the main task of the Jewish committees is to make the Jewish population in Poland productive, and accordingly, calls on comrades to support the efforts of the productivity departments of the Central Committee of Jews in Poland and local committees, whose task is to involve Jews in the work of rebuilding the country.

Source: AŻIH, the Bund, unsorted files

2. Resolution of the Bund's Central Committee passed on 30 July 1946

After considering the political situation and referring to the resolution adopted at the party meeting held in Łódź on 6–7 July 1946, the Central Committee of the 'Bund' in Poland states:

I. Over the past few months, there has been a sharp escalation in the political struggle for power in Poland between the ruling democratic camp and the camp comprising the legal opposition and the underground reactionary movement.

Against the backdrop of this escalation in the general political situation, the situation of the Jewish population has drastically deteriorated, which culminated in the Kielce pogrom, as well as constant murderous attacks on Jews by reactionary gangs and drastic acts of anti-Semitism in various areas of social life- with a simultaneous lack of response to anti-Semitic sentiments, even from some circles of the Polish proletariat.

All these manifestations have a shocking effect on the Jewish population, who begin to doubt the possibility of living in Poland, and therefore is completely understandable that a significant part of the Jewish population seeks to emigrate.

II. In this general political and specifically Jewish situation, the task of the 'Bund' is:

a. To intensify efforts to maintain and strengthen the economic, social and cultural position of the Jewish population remaining in Poland,
b. To strive to ensure that the part of the Jewish population wishing to emigrate from Poland is granted the freedom and facilitation of emigration; to advocate simultaneously for the opening of immigration-receiving countries; and to warn the Jewish population against illusions about existing immigration opportunities and the threat of moral and spiritual stagnation posed by prolonged residence in the camps in Germany;

c. On spreading political awareness that in Poland – as in other countries – the fate of the Jewish population and its possibilities of existence and development depend on breaking the reaction on the consolidation of democracy, and the final victory of socialism.

Source: *Głos Bundu* August 1946, [no. 1], p. 3

3. The Resolution of the Nationwide Bund Conference on the Kielce Pogrom

The Nationwide Conference of the 'Bund' Jewish Socialist Party, which took place in Łódź on 6–7 July 1946, expresses its vehement protest in response to the tragic events that took place in Kielce on 4 July 1946.

Shocked by the new brutal mass murder, a horrific pogrom, provoked, organised, and carried out by armed hooligans and fascist elements against the defenceless Jewish inhabitants of Kielce, during which more than forty Jews and two non-Jews were killed and more than forty Jews were injured, the 'Bund' Conference meeting states: both the scope and the course of the pogrom-like events in Kielce show clearly and undeniably that reactionary-fascist elements had prepared larger-scale anti-Semitic attacks according to old and tried methods, with the aim of murdering and eliminating the entire Jewish population of Kielce and the surrounding area.

The 'Bund' Conference notes with regret and indignation that in a city like Kielce, the fascist murderers and thugs have almost one hundred percent achieved their intended goal. They gained support from a section of the local militia, who disarmed the Kielce Jews and left them at the mercy of the murderers. The bandits rampaged, robbed and murdered defenceless citizens throughout the day until the Polish Army and security forces intervened, they were sent directly by senior government officials. These troops restored order and saved the remaining Kielce Jews from extermination.

The Conference believes that the issue of strengthening the fight against anti-Semitism in all its forms should be raised in full seriousness before the democratic and progressive public opinion of the country. The Conference appeals to the Polish Socialist Party and the Polish Workers' Party, as the two major mass organisations of the Polish working class, as the vanguard of the Polish working population, to take the initiative and organise a large-scale mass campaign against anti-Semitism, aimed at conducting an awareness campaign among the broadest working masses to raise awareness about the harmfulness of anti-Semitism.

The Conference appeals to the responsible government officials to immediately undertake a vigorous and ruthless purge against all direct and indirect perpetrators of the recent anti-Jewish incidents, against all anti-Semitic agitators and instigators. Once and for all, those who poison the atmosphere in the country, who disgrace the good name of Poland, who call for murder and destruction, who continue Nazi atrocities in the new democratic Poland, must be marked with a hot iron.

The National Conference demands, on behalf of the surviving Jewish population of Poland, the ruthless imposition of the death penalty for all anti-Semitic instigators and agitators, as for people calling for mass murders, as traitors of Poland. We demand that the Jews be provided with proper protection and care by the state security authorities. The conference believes that a representative of the Jewish population should be included in the state commission of inquiry into the Kielce pogrom.

The Conference expresses its deep conviction and strong belief that the democratic people's government, enjoying the full trust and support of the Jewish population, will find the proper means and ways to eliminate all manifestations of anti-Semitism and to ensure conditions in which Jews will find work, peace, and security.

The Conference considers it necessary to organise an armed self-defence for the Jewish population in Poland, supported by the security authorities.

The Conference calls on the Jewish public abroad to launch a major campaign against the reactionary emigration circles led by General Anders, which are responsible for and are directing the anti-Semitic campaign in the country.

The Conference calls for the intensification of the struggle for a complete reconstruction of society according to new socialist principles. Only socialism can guarantee a free and happy life for Jews and all of humanity.

Source: AŻIH, the Bund, unsorted files

4. Resolution of the Central Committee of the Bund after the Socialist Conference in Antwerp[817]

After hearing Comrade [Michał] Szuldenfrei's report from the International Socialist Conference in Antwerp, the Central Committee of the Bund in Poland passed the following resolution on 7 December 1947:

---

817 The Socialist Conference in Antwerp took place between 21 November and 1 December 1947. It concluded with the admission of the Social Democratic Party of Germany into the group of delegates, despite opposition from the Polish Socialist

1. The Central Committee of the Bund in Poland approves the report of Comrade Szuldenfrei, recognising that he defended the position of the Bund in Poland in all matters in accordance with the political line of our Party.
2. The resolution of the Conference in Antwerp is to grant the Bund the status of full participant in the International Socialist Conferences and the course of the discussions on this issue demonstrated the recognition of the international socialist movement for the Bund, which was expressed in particular in the speeches of the representatives of the Polish Socialist Party (PPS) and the Belgian and Norwegian socialist parties, as well as in the result of the vote (14 votes in favour, two against – i.e. the British Labour Party and Palestine, 2 abstentions – i.e. the Netherlands and Luxembourg).
3. The Central Committee of the Bund acknowledges that despite the opposition of the other two members of the Bund delegation (from the USA and France), Comrade Szuldenfrei had the right to participate on behalf of the Bund in Poland and rightly took part in a separate meeting held during the Conference in Antwerp, on the initiative of several left-wing delegations (Polish Socialist Party, Italian and Hungarian socialist parties). According to the resolutions of the Bund Conference in Brussels, the Bund in Poland retains complete political independence, and participation in this meeting was an expression of the Bund's affiliation with the left in the socialist camp in Poland.
4. Regarding the resolution on the defence of peace, the delegate of the Bund in Poland demanded to abstain from voting for the resolution put forward by the majority, and instead to vote for the amendment proposed by the socialist left. However, due to the difference between the delegates from Poland and the delegates from the USA and France, the Bund delegation decided to abstain from voting in both cases. Contrary to this understanding, the Bund delegate in France, designated to vote on behalf of the delegation, voted in favour of the majority resolution, which was met with a protest from the Bund delegate in Poland.
5. The Central Committee of the Bund in Poland acknowledges that the Bund's delegation abstaining from voting on the admission of the German Socialist Party (SPD) is a political mistake, that is a consequence of ideological differences within the Bund delegation. Only the Bund in Poland was firm in demanding a vote against the admission of the German Socialists, both

Party, the Czechoslovak Social Democratic Party, the Hungarian Social Democratic Party, the Workers' Party of the Land of Israel, and the Bund. The Conference concluded with the formation of the Committee of the International Socialist Conferences.

for general socialist and political reasons, as well as for specifically Jewish reasons. Bund delegates from the USA and France took a different position, and since it was impossible to agree on a position, they abstained from voting, with a declaration made on this issue by the Bund delegation expressing an internal compromise, necessary due to the Conference's treatment of the Bund delegation as a whole.

6. The Central Committee of the Bund in Poland deems it necessary to consider at the next meeting of the Coordinating Committee of Bund organisations, how to avoid such erroneous outcomes in the future and to ensure that the Bund delegation in Poland can properly express its political line at future international political conferences.

Source: AŻIH, the Bund, unsorted files

5. Declaration of the Bund faction (at the Central Committee of Jews in Poland, CKŻP), submitted to the CKŻP by Comrade [Salo] Fiszgrund regarding joining the WJC (World Jewish Congress).

The main task of the CKŻP is to rebuild and strengthen the Jewish community in the new democratic People's Poland. This task can be accomplished with the loyal cooperation of all progressive forces in Jewish society within the framework of committees.

For these purposes, all parties represented in the CKŻP have joined together in agreement. However, the political parties have not renounced their separate ideologies and programmes. They are free to conduct their own work.

The CKZP, as a representation created by individual political parties, cannot be drawn in or exploited for social actions or organisational mergers that do not align with the common line of cooperation and agreement. Such actions and conduct conflict with the nature of the CKŻP and create an obstacle to fulfilling its tasks.

We consider the Central Committee's decision to join the World Jewish Congress (WJC) as an act of such behaviour.

The attempt to justify the affiliation with the necessity of cooperation among all Jewish communities is incorrect for the following reasons:

The cooperation of all Jewish communities, which is absolutely necessary and justified, must be based on the consolidation of all socially progressive and nation-building trends of individual Jewish centres.

The tasks and objectives of this cooperation should be shared by all Jewish communities:

a) The revival of Jewish life in all communities,
b) The fight against anti-Semitism and racism,
c) Combating chauvinism and nationalism in Jewish life,
d) Equal treatment of all Jewish communities,
e) The shared responsibility in continuing Jewish life, culture and language.

It is understood that it is in the best interest of the Jewish communities everywhere that their consolidation should be part of the broader international camp of progress and democracy, and actively oppose all imperialist and anti-Soviet forces, plans against world peace and attempts to sever Poland's western territories.

We welcome and support such cooperation and consolidation. However, it is false and harmful to present the World Jewish Congress (WJC) as such an organisation.

The WJC is an organisation whose exclusively Zionist character and objectives are beyond doubt. Its activities are reduced to a single task: to mobilise Jews from all communities for the purposes of political Zionism.

During the war, when our nation was suffering the catastrophic destruction and all efforts should have been directed at fighting fascism in an attempt to save Jews from annihilation, the WJC did not play a significant role, and even then, its activities were specifically primarily geared towards mobilising public opinion for the cause of political Zionism.

After the war, during the period of rebuilding the destroyed centres in Europe, the WJC did not offer help in this regard either, but quite the opposite, those who promoted the harmful and deceptive slogan of *Exodus Europae* found a place in the ranks of the WJC and its governing bodies.

It is no coincidence that both in the summary of the talks between the delegation of the CKŻP and the WJC and after the resolution to join, the cardinal issue of Jewish culture and the Jewish language is conspicuously omitted. This is yet another clear piece of evidence that within the framework of the World Jewish Congress, there is no room for the tasks we consider to be the most important foundation for the cooperation between Jewish communities.

We therefore believe that joining the World Jewish Congress, carried out against the fundamental and categorical opposition of one of the political factions within the CKŻP, is in clear contradiction to the forms established within the Jewish committees. It represents a breach of the framework in which the committees were constructed.

This merger has been made without our consent and against our will, and the representatives of the CKŻP to the WJC have no right to act on behalf of the entire Jewish community in this case.

For our part, we will continue to defend our rightful position in the forum of Jewish social life.

Source: AŻIH, CKŻP. Archives of the Presidium and Secretariat, ref. 303/I/9, Protocol no. 3 from 19 January 1948, ff. 25–26

6. Political Resolution (of the Bund in Poland regarding withdrawal from the Bund's Coordinating Committee)

National Conference [21 March 1948] states:

1) The current historical period is characterised by a significant escalation of the international political situation. This tension is the result of an intensified offensive of the capitalist-imperialist camp, which is consolidating under the leadership of the American reaction against the forces of progress, freedom, and socialism.
2) Intensified intervention policy in favour of the reactionary regimes in Greece and China; economic aid plans for countries that, lose economic and political independence as a result; 'consistent' measures to re-build Germany's military-industrial potential and subordinate it to Anglo-Saxon imperialism; the political and military bloc of Western Europe, as well as the fierce anti-Soviet campaign and persecution of communists, left-wing socialists, and people's democratic regimes; open war propaganda and increased armament – these are the stages on the road to an imperialist offensive directed against the positions of the working class and democracy.
3) We have entered a period of decisive events. A political and social struggle has broken out between the forces of reaction and progress, between the forces marching toward socialism and the forces striving to maintain the bankrupt and historically obsolete capitalist system at all costs. In these historical and decisive struggles, the reformist camp in the socialist movement has taken a position contrary to the interests of the working class and socialism, a position that echoes the worst and most regrettable traditions of pre-war reformism and opportunism.

    Supporting American imperialism on the international political and diplomatic stage; retreating from a policy of consistently perusing broad social reforms; the harmful theory and practice of the so-called 'third force' on both an international and national scale; a policy of breaking up the labour movement; an active political and organisational campaign against those parts of the socialist movement which follow the path of cooperation with the communists; the use of the Socialist Conference Bureau as an instrument of struggle against the left-wing socialist faction of the labour movement –

this is the activity characteristic of the development path of the reformist socialists. This is the path of the Labour Party in England, the Socialist Party in France and other socialist parties in Western Europe.

4) The withdrawal of the Polish, Czechoslovak and Hungarian Socialist Parties from the 'Comisco' as well as the strong protest declaration and solidarity of the Italian Socialist Party with the left-wing socialist parties at the last session of the 'Comisco' Bureau in London – this is the response of the left-wing socialist faction of the labour movement to the new right-wing shift of the socialist reformists.

   The Bund in Poland, as a revolutionary-socialist organisation and as a political component of the Polish socialist movement, has deemed it appropriate in this situation to withdraw from the bureau of socialist organisations.

5) The intensified offensive of global imperialism, directed primarily against the Soviet Union and the People's Democracies, creates an objective necessity and pushes for a close consolidation of the ranks of the working class. The deepening of social reforms in the people's democracies, the entry into the phase of direct socialist reconstruction and the ideological rapprochement that has occurred between the socialists and communists on the basis of Marxism as a result of a long-term united front cooperation have accelerated the possibilities for the realisation of political and organisational unity. The recent statement by the General Secretary of the Polish Socialist Party (PPS) and the press declaration of the General Secretary of the Polish Workers' Party (PPR) are proof that in Poland, too, the Marxist workers' camp is moving towards full unity of the working class in the further development of the united work front between the PPR and the PPS.

6) In light of the political situation on both an international and national scale, together with the deepening of ideological differences in the workers' camp regarding extremely serious fundamental political issues, and after the experiences of the Socialist Conference in Antwerp, – which show that the representatives of the Bund in Poland could not find common ground on fundamental political issues with the representatives of the Bund in France and America – the Bund in Poland does not consider it possible to remain in the Coordinating Committee of Bund organisations.

   The National Assembly fully endorses the resolution of the Central Committee's plenary session regarding the withdrawal from the International Coordinating Committee of Bund organisations.

   In light of the extremely important process of deepening the consolidation of the Marxist camp in Poland, the National Assembly of the Bund in Poland declares: It is of great political importance that the Jewish working-class community also sees an improvement in cooperation between the Bund and Jewish comrades from the Polish Workers' Party (PPR) on the basis of the struggle for a constructive and creative Jewish national settlement, on the active participation of the Jewish masses in the process of the political and social reconstruction of the country, and so that the unified front, realised in this way, creates objective conditions for ideological rapprochement with the prospect of organic unity among Jewish workers. The National Assembly expresses the Bund's readiness to continue efforts to achieve these stated goals.

The National Assembly also considers it necessary to stress the importance of loyal cooperation with all democratic groups in the struggle for the national character of the settlement, as well as for strengthening its political, social, economic and cultural position in Poland.

Source: „Rezolucja polityczna," *Głos Bundu*, 19 April 1948, nos 2–3 (15–16), p. 15

7. Letter from the Central Committee of the Bund in Poland to the Unification Congress of Workers' Parties in Poland in Warsaw

Dear Comrades!

At this momentous time, as the great historical act of uniting the working class in Poland is realised, we send you our warmest greetings. We wish the Congress fruitful deliberations in charting the way for the further consolidation of proletarian power and the victorious march toward Socialism.

Comrades!

We are experiencing a period of intensified offensive of the global reactionary and imperialist camp. The international camp of reactionaries and warmongers, in which the so-called 'socialists' under the banner of [Ernest] Bevin and [Léon] Blum play a disgraceful role, by carrying out a vile campaign against the Soviet Union and the forces of progress. They are intensifying the terror against revolutionary forces in capitalist countries and are intervening in colonial and dependent nations to suppress national liberation movements. This camp can only be effectively opposed by a revolutionary international labour movement, consolidating the powerful forces of progress and peace under the banners of the revolutionary unity of the proletariat.

The unity of the working class which is currently underway in Poland means a further strengthening of the international front in the struggle of workers worldwide – based on the powerful Soviet Union, a bastion of peace, progress and Socialism, based on the leading force of the international workers' movement – the All-Union Communist Party (Bolsheviks).

The unification of the Polish working class will be a great inspiration for an intensified struggle to build Socialist Poland – a prosperous home shared by all its working citizens.

Central Committee of the Bund, December 1948
Source: AŻIH, the Bund, unsorted files

8. Protest by Tsukunft (regarding the verdict announced by the Nuremberg War Crimes Tribunal)

Following the announcement of the verdict in the Nuremberg trial, the Central Committee of the Tsukunft Socialist Union of Youth in Poland sent the following telegram to Lord [Geoffrey] Lawrence, Chairman of the International Military Tribunal:

LORD LAWRENCE, CHAIRMAN OF THE INTERNATIONAL MILITARY TRIBUNAL, NUREMBERG.

On behalf of the Jewish working youth in Poland, we protest against the lenient sentence for the war criminals and enemies of humanity.

Six million Jews murdered, millions of murdered citizens of other nationalities, persecution of the workers' movement, concentration camps, gas chambers – this is the balance of their criminal activity. The guilt of the murderers has been proven.

The Socialist Jewish Youth does not demand vengeance, but rather proper justice. In the name of this justice, we demand the death penalty for all the accused without exception, as they are the greatest criminals known to the history of mankind.

We're protesting most strongly against the verdict for Baldur [Benedikt] von Schirach, the founder and leader of the 'Hitler Youth' [*Hitlerjugend*] organisation, for he had raised German youth in the spirit of bloodthirsty fascism.

We mourn the fact that the Tribunal's verdict contradicts the opinion and will of all progressive humanity. The Socialist Youth, regardless of the Tribunal's verdicts, will continue to fight against fascism and racial hatred, for a world of freedom and social justice.

Central Committee of the TSUKUNFT Union of Socialist Youth in Poland.
2 October 1946, Łódź
Source: AŻIH, the Bund, unsorted files

9. Resolution of the Extraordinary Congress of the Bund in Poland, passed on 16 January 1949.

The achievements of the international working class in recent decades.

The achievement of ideological and organisational unity based on Marxism-Leninism by the Polish working class.

The process of deep ideological revaluation and intensive self-criticism that took place in the ranks of the Polish 'Bund', particularly after the conference of the leading party activists held in Łódź on 23 and 24 October 1948.

The removal of right-wing influences and unstable elements in our party. All this has made the current Extraordinary Congress of the 'Bund' in Poland ready to adopt the following resolutions:

I.

Assuming that it is in the interest of the international proletariat, that it is in the interest of all peace- and freedom-loving nations, that it is in the most vital interest of the Jewish masses who are particularly threatened by any form of capitalism, fascism, reaction and imperialism, lies in the acquisition and consolidation of a strong, revolutionary power of the working class with the perspective of struggle and a decisive march forward towards Socialism,

standing on the position that only full political, ideological and organic unity of all creative and revolutionary forces in Poland, based on revolutionary Marxism and internationalism, supported by the hardened and victorious All-Union Communist Party (Bolsheviks), creates the real conditions for a decisive transition from the system of People's Democracy to Socialism,

<u>we solemnly declare that the revolutionary and internationalist Polish United Workers' Party is the sole and exclusive representative of the interests and aspirations of the entire working class in the country.</u>

II.

As a result of a critical analysis and ideological evaluation of the 'Bund's' principles in general and specifically Jewish matters – we hereby conclude:

Historical experience has shown that although the 'Bund' was the first to inspire and mobilise Jewish masses to fight for Socialism and cultural self-activity, the Menshevism of the Russian 'Bund', its organisational and national separatism, and the social democracy of the Polish 'Bund' in the interwar period, caused Jewish workers organised in the Bund to distance themselves from the revolutionary sector of the workers' movement. This was politically wrong and damaged the interests of the socialist struggle.

Referring to the revolutionary currents of the 'Bund', to those directions that gravitated towards and brought Jewish workers into the ranks of the communist sector in the workers' movement,

By eliminating all traces of social democracy, all traces of negative attitude toward the Soviet Union, which were expressed in the politics of right-wing leadership of the Polish 'Bund',

Having drawn all the consequences from the experiences of the international proletariat over the last several decades from the struggles and achievements of the Great Socialist October Revolution,

Driven by the fervent will to actively participate in the struggle for the realisation of socialist ideals – ideals for which generations of workers and revolutionaries, including Jewish ones, gave their lives – we see in the of the Unification Congress of the Polish Workers' Party and the Polish Socialist Party a guidepost for the further struggle on the path leading to Socialist Poland.

III.

We affirm that the Polish United Workers' Party provides the Jewish masses the opportunity to engage in their own national and creative activity, and we express our conviction that the self-criticism carried out and initiated by the left-wing faction, which was particularly expressed at the aforementioned Łódź Conference, that the elimination of the ideological and organisational influence of right-wing elements, that the cooperation with the Polish Workers' Party, and the transition of our party to Marxism-Leninism prepared the ground for the Bundists to join the Polish United Workers' Party!

In the belief that it is the deepest desire of every revolutionary Jewish worker, that it is the realisation of the ideals and the will to fight for Socialism, which has been a driving force for the members of the Polish 'Bund' –

"The Extraordinary Congress of the 'Bund' in Poland resolves to call on its members to join the Polish United Workers' Party in order to participate in its ranks in the struggle for Socialism, which is the highest ideal of all working Humanity, and which is also the ideal of the Jewish working masses!

Long live the Polish United Workers' Party!
Long live Socialist Poland!
Long live the Union of Socialist Soviet Republics!
Long live the international solidarity of the working class!
Long live Socialism!

Extraordinary Congress of the 'Bund' in Poland
Wrocław, 16 January 1949.
Source: AŻIH, the Bund, unsorted files

Biographies

Bernstein (see also: **Bernsztejn, Bernstejn**) **Mordechai Wolf, Comrade Matwiej** (1905 Byteń, Nowogródek Province, today Belarus – 1966 New York), a clerk by profession; activist in Tsukunft and later the Bund. Bernstein worked for the Warsaw branch of YIVO. He came from a Hasidic family and he received a thorough religious education in his father's cheder and then in yeshivot in Baranovichi, Słonim and Białystok. He then decided to break away from his previous life and moved to Vilna, where he attended the Jewish Teachers' Seminary. There, he also joined Tsukunft. After moving to Warsaw in 1926, he worked as a secretary at the Central Committee of the Bund. In the years 1936–1939 he was associated with the Warsaw Bund Committee. He wrote for Bund newspapers, including *Folkstsaytung*, *Unzer tsayt*, *Vokhnshrift far literatur*, *Yidishe shriftn*, and for Tsukunft's *Yugnt veker*. He signed his texts with his surname, his party nickname 'Matwiej' and his penname 'M. Zeldin'. In the 1930s, he served as a bridge between former yeshiva students who had left their community and the Jewish proletariat associated with the Bund.

Following the outbreak of World War II, he fled to Vilna, where he was arrested on 27 August 1940, he was then tried and deported to Vorkuta (USSR) in the spring of 1941. In July 1946, he returned to Poland. He took an active part in the work of the Bund, including serving as one of the lecturers in a course for the Tsukunft instructors in Otwock in December 1947. He led the Historical Commission of the Bund's Central Committee and worked in the editorial office of *Folkstsaytung*. In August 1948, he left Poland illegally together with others who did not agree with the Bund's self-dissolution. In September 1948, he arrived at a DP camp in Feldafing, Germany, where he stayed until 1952. He then lived in Buenos Aires before moving to New York in 1961.

Throughout the entire post-war period, Bernstein dedicated himself to commemorating the history of the Jewish communities in Europe. He collaborated with YIVO in New York and served as the editor or co-editor of numerous memorial books [Yid.: *yizker bikher*] documenting the fate of Jews in towns such as Byteń, Zamość, Prużana, Żyrardów or Puławy. He was also the author of books dedicated to the history of German Jews.[818]

818 AŻIH, WEiS, ref. 303/V/425/Bbn 1365 – Mordechai Berenstejn; „Kurs dla referentów młodzieżowej organizacji Cukunft," *Głos Bundu* 1948, no. 1 (14), p. 16; J. Sh. Hertz, *Di geshikhte fun bund in lodzh*, Nyu york 1958, p. 469; A.C., „Mordekhai

Bielicka-Blum Luba (1905 Vilna, today Lithuania – 1973 Warsaw), a nurse, activist of the Bund organisations in Vilna and Warsaw – Tsukunft, the Bund and the women's organisation YAF (*Yidishe arbeter froy organizatsye*). Wife of Abrasha Blum. In 1925, she graduated from the Nursing School at the Jewish Hospital in Warsaw, which she managed from August 1939. From the spring 1943, she stayed on the 'Aryan' side.

After the war, she was the director of the Children's Home in Otwock. She was a member of the Tsukunft's Central Committee and dedicated herself to helping young socialists return to normal life after their wartime experiences. In 1949, she was yet again appointed the director of the Nursing School No. 3 in Warsaw.[819] She received the highest award in nursing – the Florence Nightingale Medal awarded by the International Red Cross.

Brener Liber (1901[820] Turzysk, Volhynia, today Ukraine – 1986 Israel), a teacher by profession, associated with the Bund Committee in Częstochowa. Brener came from a poor Hasidic family. He taught at the TSYSHO schools in Volhynia, and from 1929 at the Perets School in Częstochowa. He also taught at the Kultur Lige. From 1934 until the outbreak of World War II, he was a manager at TOZ (Society for the Protection of Health) responsible for summer camps for children. During World War II, he was a member of the Bund's Underground Committee in the Częstochowa Ghetto and then in German forced labour camps, including Hasag in Częstochowa. After 1945, he was one of the leading Bund activists in Poland, including the party's committee in Częstochowa. After the Bund was liquidated, he was one of the few former Bundists who continued to actively participate in the life of the Jewish community. He published his memoirs titled *Vidershtand un umkum in tshenstokhover geto* (Warsaw, 1950). In 1952–53, he was the head of the Finance Department at the Main Board of the TSKŻ, and in 1955, he was the chief accountant. In 1957, he emigrated with his family to Israel where he continued to be active in the Bund, including writing for the *Lebns-fragn* magazine.[821]

Velvel Bernshteyn," in: *Doyres bundistn*, vol. III, pp. 301–303; M. Rusiniak-Karwat, "Bundists under Soviet Occupation: the Case of Matwiej Bernstein," *Studia Polityczne* 2017, no. 3 (45), pp. 141–151.

819 A. Kahan, "A lebn unter shturem un khurbn. Lyube Bielicke-Blum (Vilna 1905 – Varshe 1973)," *Unzer tsayt* 1974, no. 1, pp. 26–30.

820 Liber Brener's date of birth is given as 1897 and 1907 in different documents. In the biography, the date is given as: I.L., "Liber Brener," *Lebns-fragn* 1986, nos. 415–416, pp. 20.

821 L. Brener, „Ruch podziemny w częstochowskim getcie. Wspomnienia," *Biuletyn Żydowskiego Instytutu Historycznego* 1963, nos 45–46, pp. 159–173; *Lebns-fragn*

Edelman Marek, aka **'Marek'** (1919[822], Homel, today Belarus – 2009 Warsaw), medical doctor, social activist, member of Skif and Tsukunft, commander of the Jewish Combat Organisation in the Warsaw Ghetto. After his mother's death on 19 November 1937, following a serious illness, Marek's family became the Bund's family. They took care of him. Young Marek attended one of the TSYSHO schools in Warsaw. Initially, he was a member of Skif, later he joined Tsukunft. He spent his summers at Skif summer camps and, at the end of the 1930s, at Tsukunft camps. Suffering from tuberculosis, he spent some time at the Vladimir Medem Sanatorium in Miedzeszyn near Warsaw. All these experiences turned him into a socialist, a belief he held for the rest of his life. In the spring of 1938 or 1939, he passed his *matura* (high school final) exams.

After the outbreak of World War II, in the autumn of 1939, Marek joined the underground Central Committee of Tsukunft, the Skif Central Committee and the Bund Central Committee as a representative of the youth organisation. In the Warsaw Ghetto, he was responsible for editing, printing and distributing the underground press. He also worked as a messenger at the Bersohn and Bauman Children's Hospital. During the Great *Aktion*, he bravely went to the Umschlagplatz and rescued people, mainly those associated with the Bund and their families. He was in favour of fighting the Germans, which is why in autumn 1942, after the Bund joined the Jewish Combat Organisation (ŻOB) he also volunteered. During the Warsaw Ghetto Uprising, he was the commander of ŻOB in the brush makers' shop district. After the suicide of Mordechai Anielewicz, he became the commander of the Uprising. When the Uprising had no chance of success, he and other fighters escaped through the ghetto sewers on 9 May 1943. In 1944, he participated in the Warsaw Uprising as a member of the ŻOB in the People's Army (AL) in the Old Town and Żoliborz. After the Uprising, he was sent to Pruszków transit camp.

After the end of the war, he initially wandered around the country in search of other Bund members in order to rebuild the party's structures. At the same

1986, nos 415–416 (p. 20: I.L., „Liber Brener"; J. Leber, „A khaver in kamf"; M. Olicki, „Mayn lerer liber"); G. Berendt, *Życie żydowskie w Polsce w latach 1950–1956. Z dziejów Towarzystwa Społeczno-Kulturalnego Żydów w Polsce*, Gdańsk 2006, p. 146; https://www.czestochowajews.org/history/yizkor-books/liber-brener/ [access: 10 September 2024].

822 One comes across different dates of Edelman's birth: 1921, 1922 and even 1924. The year 1919 is engraved on his tombstone.

time, he wrote *Getto walczy*[823] [The Ghetto Fights], which was first published in 1945 by the Central Committee of the Bund. Edelman also became a member of the Central Committee of Tsukunft. Representing Tsukunft, he participated in socialist youth conferences abroad. In 1948, upon hearing about the self-dissolution of the Bund, he almost attacked Salo Fiszgrund, the secretary of the Bund's Central Committee.

In 1951, he graduated in medicine from the Medical Academy in Łódź. In the 1960s, Edelman was denied a postdoctoral degree because of his Jewish background and was issued with negative reviews. As a doctor, he introduced a revolutionary method of treating heart disease in Poland in 1971, which involved connecting venous and arterial circulation. He did not leave Łódź or Poland, even after 1968, when his wife Alina Margolis-Edelman and their children left the country after the anti-Semitic campaign. In the mid-1970s, he joined the democratic opposition by collaborating with the Workers' Defence Committee (KOR). For Edelman, KOR was a continuation of the Bund: "The same ideals, the same values – brotherhood, social justice, the fight against dictatorship."[824] From the early 1980s, he was a member of the 'Solidarity' Independent Self-Governing Trade Union.

He was granted a Knight of the Order of the White Eagle (1998) and was awarded the St. George Medal and the Legion of Honour by the President of France (2008). He received honorary doctorates from Yale University (USA, 1989), the Université Libre de Bruxelles, the Medical Academy of Łódź (2007) and Jagiellonian University in Kraków (2009). In 1999, he was named Citizen of the Year of the City of Łódź. He was a social activist who fought for the rights of the weak and the oppressed. He emphasised that freedom is the most important thing in everyone's life. Until the very end of his life, he repeated in numerous interviews that "Zionism is a lost cause. Then and now."[825]

Falk Ignacy (Izrael), aka **Falkowski** (1904 Warsaw – 1996 Montreal), accountant by profession, activist of Tsukunft and the Bund. He graduated from the H. Wawelberg and S. Rotwand Technical School in Warsaw. Initially, he was

823 M. Edelman, *Getto walczy (Udział Bundu w obronie getta warszawskiego)*, Łódź 1945.

824 W. Bereś, K. Burnetko, *Marek Edelman*, Życie. *Po prostu*, Warsaw 2008, pp. 331–332.

825 A. Grupińska, *Ciągle po kole. Rozmowy z żołnierzami getta warszawskiego*, Warsaw 2000, p. 21. The biography is based on: M. Rusiniak-Karwat, "Marek Edelman (1919–2009). Szkic biograficzny," in: M. Edelman, *Nieznane zapiski o getcie warszawskim*, ed. M. Rusiniak-Karwat, Warsaw 2017, pp. 133–139. Information on the death of Edelman's mother: "Tsipe Edelman," *Yugnt veker* 1937, no. 26, p. 8.

associated with the Hashomer Hatsair scout organisation, then Tsukunft and then the Bund. Thanks to his excellent command of Polish, Falk delivered speeches on behalf of the Bundists, among others, at the inter-party meetings, e.g. during May Day parades. He published his political essays in *Folkstsaytung*. He was still involved with the Bund even during his military service in Białystok.

After the outbreak of World War II, Falk remained in Warsaw and co-founded the underground Bund Committee. He was a member of the Warsaw Bund Committee in the Warsaw Ghetto, and was responsible for contacts with the 'Aryan' side. He also worked for the Jewish Self-Aid and as the Joint field inspector. On 3 September 1942, he was caught by the Germans and sent to Umschlagplatz. He escaped from the train heading for the Treblinka II extermination camp. After returning to Warsaw, he took part in the organisation of the Warsaw Ghetto Uprising as well as fighting in it. He was caught yet again by the Germans during the fighting on 29 April 1943, and was sent with others to the forced labour camp in Budzyn. From August 1944, he passed through the camps in Wieliczka, Płaszów, Gross-Rosen and Brünnlitz (he worked at the Oskar Schindler's factory). On 10 May 1945, while an inmate at Brünnlitz, he was liberated by the Red Army.

After regaining his freedom, Falk returned to Warsaw and became engaged in the activities of the Bund's Central Committee. He was in favour of the party's self-dissolution and emigration from Poland. As the Bund's representative, he sat at the Presidium of the CKŻP. He also served as the head of the Organisation and Control Department of the CKŻP. When the Bund was liquidated at the end of 1948, he emigrated from Poland and in 1949 he settled in Montreal, Canada, with his family. In Canada, he continued to be active in the Bund, for example, he helped organise the Bund's World Conference in 1955. He also served as a secretary of the Canadian branch of JLC, as well as a chairman of the Municipal Committee for a while.[826]

Feiner (Löbl) Leon, see also: 'Mikołaj', 'Berezowski', 'Lasocki'; names used on the 'Aryan' side: Józef Sawicki, Józef Berezowski (1885 or 1886 Podgórze near Kraków – 1945 Lublin, buried in Warsaw), a lawyer, doctor of law; member of

---

826 AŻIH, Testimonies, ref. 301/4266 – account of Izrael Falk; AŻIH, CKŻP, WEiS, ref. 303/V/425/F 1864 and 303/V/425/F bn 673; AAN, Zachariasz, ref. 476/ vol. 29, f. 13; AIPN, ref. IPN GK 182/166, f. 76–78; Ghetto Fighters House Archives (hereinafter: GFHA), Berman Adolf – Avraham Collection, Catalog No. 5798, Israel Falk (Falkowski): six letters and a receipt; A. Lermer, *Un dokh – dem morgnroyt antkegn. Eseyen*, Tel Aviv 1999, pp. 154–156; USC Shoah Foundation, interview code 33414 – testimony of Max Falk, September 22, 1997.

the underground Bund Committee in the Warsaw Ghetto. In 1905, he was one of the founders of the Kraków-based Jewish Socialist Party (ŻPS – the so-called Galician Bund). After the end of World War I, he belonged to the party's Central Committee. He was the co-editor of *Der sotsyal-demokrat* magazine, member of the editorial office of Kraków-based *Nowe Życie* (published by the Galician Bund), *Walka*, and also an associate of *Folkstsaytung* and *Kegn shtrom*. Before the war, he lived in Kraków, where he sat on the Municipal Council on behalf of the Bund. In 1910–1911, he became close to the left wing faction of the Bund. For many years he was the chairman (or deputy chairman) of the Kraków branch and a member of the Central Committee of the Bund in Poland.

Feiner lived with his parents in Podgórze, near Kraków, where he graduated from high school. He studied law at Jagiellonian University, graduating in 1910, and later earned a doctorate in law. During his studies, he participated in strikes against Germanisation. In 1917, he was admitted to the bar. He took on many workers in his own law firm. Feiner also served as a defence lawyer in political trials. He was active in the Association of Socialist Lawyers and throughout his life, the struggle for socialism and the party were the most important to him. He was arrested on multiple occasions due to his political activities. His struggle against Polish fascism and anti-Semitism led to his imprisonment in Bereza Kartuska in June 1939. He was released in mid-August 1939, partly thanks to the help of the PPS.

After the outbreak of World War II, Feiner fled from Kraków to Równe and from there to Lvov. On 19 July 1940, he was arrested by the NKVD in Lida while attempting to cross the Soviet-German border while trying to return to the territories occupied by the Third Reich. He remained in prison until 23 June 1941 when he was released together with Salo Fiszgrund, and the two travelled to Warsaw together. After several weeks of travelling he reached his destination and – despite his miserable state, he quickly joined the underground Central Committee of the Bund and – thanks to his appearance resembling a 'Polish nobleman', he began operating on the 'Aryan' side. He only spent a few days inside the ghetto. In the autumn of 1942, he brought Jan Karski into the ghetto. It is worth noting that during the war, Feiner cared about the fate of all Jews, regardless of their political views. He would say: "This is war, a shared tragedy and a shared enemy. There is no time for disagreement as we all share the same fate."[827]

Feiner, who according to Michał Szuldenfrei was the "the soul and driving force of the underground Bund," was the link between the Bund and the

827 AŻIH, Testimonies, ref. 301/2787, speech delivered over Dr Feiner's grave, p. 3.

leadership of the Polish resistance movement. He maintained contact with the underground Polish Socialist Party (PPS). In the autumn of 1942, he became the Bund's representative in the Coordinating Commission on the 'Aryan' side. From January 1943, he was the vice-chairman, and from August 1944 the chairman of the Council to Aid to Jews, commonly known as 'Żegota'.

Feiner sent messages and documents around the world, informing about the fate of Jews in the General Government and about German crimes, as well as about underground activities of the Bund and Tsukunft – including illegal press publications. Thanks to his cooperation with the Polish resistance (also through Jan Karski), in May 1942 and on 31 August 1942 he sent reports with information on the Jewish Holocaust in occupied Poland to the Polish Government-in-Exile in London, addressed to Artur Zygielbojm, the Bund's representative in the National Council. He also asked for rescue operations to be organised.

From summer 1944, Feiner's main goal was to rebuild the Bund in the new post-war reality. He participated in the Warsaw Uprising in 1944 and after its fall, he left for Milanówek, near Warsaw. By the time of the liberation, he was already ill and bedridden in Brwinów, from where he was taken to Lublin. After arriving in Lublin, he was sent to the hospital due to cancer. Until his last days, he was involved in the reconstruction of the Bund. The first meetings and discussions about rebuilding the movement were held at his hospital bedside. To quote Dr. Michał Szuldenfrei: "Comrade Feiner arrived in Lublin at the end of January 1945. His comrades placed him in a hospital and offered him the utmost care. And in those last days – almost until his final breath – C.[omrade] Feiner never ceased to be what he had been throughout his conscious life – a devoted soldier and leader of the Jewish socialist movement."[828] He died on 22 February 1945 and was buried in Lublin. In 1947, his remains were transferred to the Jewish cemetery on Okopowa Street in Warsaw and laid to rest in the so-called Bundist quarter. In 1948, he was posthumously awarded the Knight's Cross of the Order of Polonia Restituta.[829]

---

828 M. Szuldenfrei, "Dr. Leon Fajner – 'Mikołaj' – 'Berezowski' (w drugą rocznicę śmierci)," *Głos Bundu* 1947, no. 3 (7), p. 3.

829 YIVO Archives, RG 1478, Emanuel Scherer Collection, Supplement 2, file 96; I. Aleksandrowicz, "Leon Fejner," *Unzer tsayt* 1945, no. 5, pp. 15–19; P. Szwartz, "A stoyker iz gefaln (tsum toyt fun leon fayner)," *Unzer tsayt* 1945, no. 6, pp. 29–34; L.H., "Leon fayner tsu zayn ershtn yortsayt," *Unzer tsayt* 1946, no. 2, pp. 3–4; S. Fiszgrund, "Dr leon fayner ('Mikołaj') (tsu zayn tsveytn yortsayt)," *Folkstsaytung* 1947, no. 2 (11), p. 5; "Dr Leon Feiner," *Biuletyn Żydowskiej Agencji Prasowej* 1945, no. 21/31, f. 4; M. Edelman, *Getto walczy (Udział Bundu w obronie getta warszawskiego),* Łódź 2015, p. 45; L. Oler, "Dr. Leon Feiner," in: *Doyres bundistn*, vol. II, ed.

Fiszgrund Salo (Salomon), see also: Henryk (1893 Sułkowice – 1971 Tel Aviv), came from a family of civil servants and was an accountant by profession. Initially, he was associated with the Jewish Socialist Party; after the party's merger with the Bund, he became a member of the Bund and served as secretary of the Kraków Bund Committee from 1920 to 1937, and from 1937 as the party's vice-chairman. He held this position until the outbreak of war in 1939. Fiszgrund represented the so-called leftist faction of the Bund. He was also a member of trade unions, where he held key positions.

On 3 September 1939, he fled via Lvov towards the Soviet border. He was arrested in Lida for crossing the border and for his affiliation with the Bund. He was released from prison together with Feiner after the outbreak of the German-Soviet war, in the summer of 1941. In August 1941, the two men arrived in Warsaw. Initially, Fiszgrund stayed at the Medem Sanatorium in Miedzeszyn, near Warsaw. He became a member of the underground Central Committee of the Bund organisation on the 'Aryan' side. He entered the ghetto to attend party meetings and specialised in obtaining false documents for others. He was also a member of the Jewish National Committee.

After Poland was liberated, he helped rebuild the Bund and the Jewish community. He was a strong advocate for the continuation of Bund activities in post-war Poland and he strongly opposed the emigration of Jewish children from the country. He was also involved in locating and redeeming children who had spent the war hidden with Polish families. From the earliest days after the war until his departure for Israel following the anti-Semitic campaign of 1967–1968, Fiszgrund was among those who visited former concentration camp sites and Jewish cemeteries to preserve them and commemorate the victims of the Holocaust. In 1946, he was part of a Bund delegation to New York. In 1947, he travelled to Brussels, Stockholm, and Paris in connection with the construction of a monument to the Ghetto heroes.

In the Bund, he held the position of General Secretary of the Central Committee. Representing the party, he joined the leadership of the CKŻP. In 1948, he was one of the delegates to the WJC session in Switzerland on behalf of the CKŻP. That same year, he also participated in the European Conference on Jewish Culture in Paris. In 1948, he was awarded the Knight's Cross of the Order of Polonia Restituta.

J. Sh. Hertz, Nyu york 1956, pp. 77–87; D. Klin, *Mitn malekh ha-moves untern orem. Mayne iberlebungen in poyln beys der natsi-okupatsye 1939–1945*, Tel Aviv 1968, pp. 83–85; B. Heksel, *Żydowscy adwokaci w przedwojennym Krakowie*, Kraków 2020, p. 178; "Odznaczenie za zasługi położone w walce zbrojnej z okupantem hitlerowskim. Postanowienie o odznaczeniu z dnia 19 kwietnia 1948 r.," *Monitor Polski*, M.P.1948.43.192 Individual act.

In 1949, Fiszgrund performed an act of self-criticism of the Bund and after the party's self-dissolution, he remained active in both the Jewish community and in politics. He was a member of the Main Board of the Social-Cultural Association of Jews in Poland and served as Vice Chairman of the Jewish Historical Institute in Warsaw. In 1957, he became the chairman of the Central Commission for Aid to Jews in Poland, which was funded by the Joint Distribution Committee. He joined the Polish United Workers' Party and was also a member of the Council for the Protection of Struggle and Martyrdom Sites.

Following the anti-Semitic campaign of 1967–1968, Fiszgrund and his wife, Gustawa, left Poland, despite his previous negative attitude towards emigration and Israel. These events took a toll on his health. After moving to Israel in March 1973, he was entered on a list of undesirable persons in the People's Republic of Poland. His death was met with silence in the pages of *Unzer tsayt*.[830]

Fogel (Fogiel) Gershon Mordka (1915, Krośniewice – ?), an upholsterer by trade and a Bund activist. Fogel was orphaned at the age of one, and he studied in a yeshiva until the age of 15, before becoming a labourer. From 1934 until the outbreak of World War II, he was an active member of the Łódź Bund Committee.

During the war, he was first imprisoned in the Litzmannstadt Ghetto, where he was also involved in the underground Bund Committee. From 1944 to 1945, he was a prisoner of KL Auschwitz.

After the war, he returned to Łódź where, from 1946, he served as chairman of the Łódź Bund Committee. He was also a member of the Central Committee of the Bund. During this time, he wrote articles for *Folkstsaytung*, *Głos Bundu*, and *Dos naye lebn*. Fogel opposed the merger of the Bund with the PPR. In 1949, he illegally left Poland for France and later settled in New York.[831]

830 AIPN Warsaw, ref. IPN BU 1268/19262, vols. I–II, passport file of Salo Fiszgrund; ref. IPN BU 01264/264, note made on the basis of personal files and investigation material. Warsaw, December 1952, f. 14–16; ref. IPN BU 0722/1 vol. V, Files of various Jews. Jews showing a pro-Israel stance, f. 67–77; AIPN Łódź, ref. IPN Ld PF10/668, f. 145; AIPN Kraków, ref. IPN Kr 056/18/16, f. 114; YVA. Testimonies, ref. O.3/3559 – account of Gustawa Fiszgrund (Dinstadt); S. Fiszgrund (Henryk), "Rok przed zbrojnym powstaniem warszawskiego ghetta," *Głos Bundu* 1947, no. 2 (6), p. 4; "Odznaczenie za zasługi położone w walce zbrojnej z okupantem hitlerowskim. Postanowienie o odznaczeniu z dnia 19 kwietnia 1948 r.," *Monitor Polski*, M.P.1948.43.192 Individual act; USC Shoah Foundation, interview code 7970 – testimony of Hanna Gdalewicz-Nielsen, January 14, 1996.

831 AIPN Łódź, ref. IPN Ld PF10/668, f. 44, 145; ref. IPN Ld PF10/690 vol. I, p. 2, f. 324, 327; https://congressforjewishculture.org/people/1940/Gershon,%20(Mortkhe)%20(June%2028,%201915%E2%80%93) [access: 10 September 2024].

Goldstein Bernard (Berl) (see also: **Goldsztein, Goldsztajn**), Comrade Bernard (1889 Siedlce – 1959 New York), barber by profession; one of the founders and leading activists of the Bund in Poland after 1918.

Goldstein came from a proletarian family. He joined the Bund at the age of 16. Due to his political activities, he was arrested multiple times prior to 1917, serving part of his sentence in Siberia (Russia). In 1917, he participated in the October Revolution. During the inter-war period, he lived and worked in Warsaw. He was a member of the Warsaw Bund Committee and also organised and commanded the Bund's self-defence units (the so-called Bund militia). He was part of the leadership of the Morgnshtern sports organisation in Warsaw.

After the outbreak of World War II, he fled to eastern Poland in September but returned to Warsaw on 3 October 1939. He was one of the founders and leaders of the underground Central Committee of the Bund, and was involved with the Red Cross and the Sanatorium Committee in the Warsaw Committee of the (Organisation) Bund. In the spring of 1940, Bernard organised a self-defence unit during a pogrom in Warsaw that lasted several days. He was a co-founder of the ŻOB and, after crossing to the 'Aryan' side in the late 1942, he became the Bund's representative on the 'Aryan' side.

"He had a cheerful personality, quick reflexes and a strong temperament. He was courageous and kept a cool head. [...] He helped some fighters and political activists survive the difficult times during the war both mentally and physically."[832]

In 1945, after the war had ended, he travelled to Prague on a Czech passport issued under the name Malinowski to avoid arrest, and from there, he travelled to New York at the invitation of the Jewish Labor Committee, where he remained active in the Bundist community. He is the author of the wartime memoirs: *Finef yor in varshever geto* (New York, 1947), translated into English as *Five Years in the Warsaw Ghetto* (translated and edited by Leonard Shatzkin, New York, 1961), as well as *Tsvantsik yor in varshever 'bund': 1919–1939* (New York, 1960), translated into English as *Twenty Years with the Jewish Labour Bund: A Memoir of Interwar Poland* (translated and edited by M. S. Zuckerman, Indiana, 2016).[833]

---

832 M. Edelman, *I była miłość w getcie*, noted by P. Sawicka, Warsaw 2011, pp. 47–49.

833 YIVO Archives, RG 1400 Bund Archives, M_9/155; YIVO Archives RG 1455 Bernard Goldstein Collection, files 47, 65; M. Edelman, *Getto walczy*, pp. 14–15; B. Goldstein, *Five Years in the Warsaw Ghetto*, tr. and ed. L. Shatzkin, New York 1961, *passim*; E. Scherer, "Bernard Goldstein," *Unzer tsayt* 1959, no. 12, pp. 1, 4–6; "Di leviye khaver bernard," *Unzer tsayt* 1959, no. 12, pp. 6, 45; J. Sh. Hertz, *Di geshikhte*

Herszenhorn Shlomo, Dr (1888 Lublin – 1953 Melbourne), doctor of medicine, dermatologist; one of the leaders of the Bund in Lublin. He came from a family of well-known printers from Lublin. He studied in Lublin's cheders and yeshivas (his brother Dovid was a well-known Zionist). From 1903, he was involved with the Bund in his hometown. In 1904, he moved to Puławy, where he completed high school, and then studied medicine in Wrocław, Heidelberg and Prague (where he received his medical degree in 1918). As a doctor, he participated in the 1920 Polish-Bolshevik War. In 1921, Herszenhorn returned to Lublin, and continued his work with the Bund, and became one of the party's leaders. In 1927, he became a member of the City Council as vice-chairman and a representative of the Bund. He was also a member of the Board of the Jewish Religious Community. During the Second Polish Republic, he fought for the rights of the Jewish poor in Lublin. He was active in the Lublin branch of the Society for the Protection of Jewish Public Health. He also worked with the ORT, among others. Herszenhorn was a good speaker and political and social agitator. He collaborated with local and national Jewish press, including the Bundist newspapers *Lubliner shtime* and *Naye folkstsaytung*. He worked as a doctor throughout his life, often providing free medical assistance to the poor, which is why he was called the 'Judym of Lublin'.

After the outbreak of World War II, Herszenhorn found himself in Lithuania, where he was associated with the Joint and ORT. Following the outbreak of the German-Soviet war in June 1941, he moved deeper into the USSR to Chelyabinsk. There, in the autumn of 1942, during a wave of arrests of Bund members, he was also detained and arrested for 10 months.[834] In 1943, he was released and appointed as the medical chief of the Tadeusz Kościuszko 1st Infantry Division. He returned to his hometown at the end of July 1944 with the rank of major of the 1st Polish Army. He immediately became involved in rebuilding the life of the Jewish community. On 8 August 1944, he took the position of head of the Independent Unit for the Aid to Jewish Population at the Presidium of the PKWN. He was one of the leading figures in the Bund, and he became the vice-chairman of the Central Committee and, on behalf of the Bund, vice-chairman of the CKŻP, a member of the Presidium of CKŻP, chairman of the Child Welfare Department

---

fun a yugnt. Der kleyner bund – yugnt-bund tsukunft in poyln, Nyu york, 1946, *passim.*

834 According to Kalman Goldwaser – Herszenhorn was arrested in May 1941 in Kovno and sentenced to 8 years in prison. See: K. Goldwaser, *Fun der vaysl bizn taykh kizl-su. Iberlebungen bays der yorn fun der tsveyter velt-milkhome*, Pariz 1972, p. 98.

and chairman of the TOZ (from October 1945) and ORT, therefore he frequently travelled to Western Europe and America.

When the decision was made to dissolve the Bund, he left Poland illegally in 1948, via Czechoslovakia, initially heading to Israel, and from there in 1950 to Melbourne, Australia. There, he also became active in the Bund, working for the Bundist publication *Unzer gedank* and for the Jewish Health Union.[835]

Hurwicz (Gurwicz, Górwicz) Shmuel (Samuel) (1913 Vilna[836] – 1994 Haifa), a doctor before 1939, and a lawyer after the war, a member of the Bund. During World War II, he was arrested in Sokółka in September 1939. From June 1940, he was held in Soviet prisoner-of-war camps, including in Griazovets (Vologda Oblast) and Yukhnov (Smolensk Oblast). After the war, he returned to Poland and settled in Łódź, where he became active in the Bund, serving as the secretary of the party's Łódź Committee. After moving to Warsaw, Hurwicz worked in the Presidium of the Central Committee. He supported cooperation between the Bund and the PPR, and later advocated for the dissolution of the Bund and its merger with the PPR/PZPR. He was also active in the CKŻP, where he worked in the Department of Culture and Propaganda. After the dissolution of the Bund, he joined the PZPR. He was also a member of the Board of the TSKŻ. In 1969, he emigrated to Israel, settling in Kiryat Haim near Haifa. There, he continued working as a lawyer and also taught Yiddish at a high school.[837]

Jaszuński Grzegorz (Grisha) (1910 Leningrad, today St. Petersburg, Russia – 2001 Warsaw), a lawyer and journalist, came from an assimilated Bundist family. The family spoke Polish at home. He was the son of Józef and Zofia (née Waserdam) Jaszuński. In 1932, he graduated in law from the University of Warsaw. During his studies, he was a member of the 'Ringen' (Yid., 'link') Bundist student

835 "Wznowienie działalności Towarzystwa Ochrony Zdrowia (TOZ)," *Biuletyn Żydowskiej Agencji Prasowej* 1945, no. 92/102, f. 4; J. Sh. Hertz, "Dr. Shlomo Hershenhorn," in: *Doyres bundistn*, vol. II, Nyu york 1956, pp. 99–103; A. Kopciowski, "Herszenhorn Szloma," in: *Sylwetki Żydów lubelskich. Leksykon*, eds. A. Kopciowski, A. Trzciński, S. J. Żurek, M. Adamczyk-Garbowska, Lublin 2019, pp. 126–128.

836 In his post-war biography, Hurwicz used "1906 Warsaw" as his date and place of birth, profession: lawyer. In the student records at the University of Warsaw, there are no documents to the name Hurewicz/Gurewicz, born on that date in this place.

837 AŻIH, ref. 303/V/425/G bn 6908 Gurwicz-Hurwicz Samuel; ref. 303/V/425/G 18 470 Gurwicz-Hurwicz Samuel; AIPN, ref. IPN BU 00231/205, vol. 5, *passim*; Gurwicz Samuel, in: https://indeksrepresjonowanych.pl/szczegoly/bc567d78-f7fc-41a8-bf20-afc3010002ba [access: 10 September 2024]; I. Draznik, "Shmuel Hurwicz," *Lebns-fragn* 1994, nos 509–510, p. 18.

organisation. After graduating, he worked as a judicial trainee at the court and as an official at the Western Bank. He was an active member of the Bund.

After the outbreak of World War II, together with other Bundists, he fled from Warsaw to Vilna where he initially worked for the Jewish Committee of the Union of Refugees. In the years 1941–1944, he was imprisoned in the Vilna Ghetto, where he was as a member of the Judenrat. From 1944, he was a member of the Union of Polish Patriots.

In the autumn of 1944, Jaszuński arrived in Lublin. He was part of the group of members of the Central Committee of the Bund. He was also a member of the Polish Socialist Party. He opposed Jewish emigration from Poland. He represented the Bund at socialist conferences in Paris and London and he worked as a lawyer and journalist, contributing to publications such as *Dos naye lebn*, the PPS press organ *Robotnik* and later, from 1949 to 1981, *Życie Warszawy* (including as a foreign correspondent). After the Bund's dissolution, Jaszuński refused to join the Polish United Workers' Party (PZPR).

His first wife was the Bundist activist Irena (Leyka) Jaszuńska, his second wife was Zofia Kuratowska. He is the author of several books, including *Życie i śmierć Johna Kennedy'ego* (1967), *Hiszpański happy end* (1979), *Meksykańskie fascynacje* (1981), and *Kawał* świata… (1993, co-authored with Zofia Kuratowska).[838]

Kahan Avreml (Abraham, Arkadiusz; in the USA – Arcadius Kahan), prof. (1920 Vilna – 1982 Chicago), an economist, hailed from a Bundist family. His father was Virgili Kahan. He was born and spent his early years in Vilna, where he was active in Skif and later in Tsukunft. Before 1939, he began studying history at Stefan Batory University in Vilna. After the outbreak of World War II and the Soviet occupation of the city, Kahan moved to Minsk, Belarus. From there, he travelled to Moscow where he demanded the release of arrested Bund leaders, which led to his own imprisonment and deportation to a gulag camp.

In 1941, he was released under the Sikorski-Mayski agreement and made his way to Uzbekistan. In 1945, he joined Berling's Army. He returned to Poland in early 1946 and appeared at the Bund committee in his Polish Navy officer's uniform. He settled in Łódź, where he worked for Bundist organisations and joined the leadership of the Central Committee of Tsukunft. He was chairman of the Łódź Special Commission at the CKŻP, representing the Bund.

838 AŻIH, CKŻP, WEiS, ref. 303/V/425/I-J 3279; AIPN, ref. IPN BU 00231/205, vol. 5, f. 16; ref. IPN BU 1005/2780 – Grzegorz Jaszuński's passport file; R. Pragier, *Żydzi czy Polacy*, Warsaw 2016, pp. 60–68.

In September 1948, he and others left Poland illegally. Initially, he stayed in a displaced persons camp in Germany. In 1950, he arrived in the United States, where he remained active in the Bund, serving as director of the Bund Archives. He collaborated with YIVO. In 1954, he completed his studies and, in 1958, he earned a doctorate in economics from Rutgers University. From 1955, he was affiliated with the University of Chicago, where he worked as a professor of economics, specialising in the economic history of the Soviet Union.[839]

Kersz (Kiersz) Yudl (Yehuda Yakov) (1909 or 1910 Brzeziny – 1980 Holon), involved in Bundist organisations for children and youth from an early age. He graduated from the Medem School in Łódź and later continued his education at the Teacher's Seminary in Vilna. After returning to Łódź, he worked in the secretariat of the Clothing Workers' Trade Union and at the Medem School. He dedicated most of his time to working for Skif.

After the outbreak of World War II, he found himself in the eastern territories, from where he was exiled to the Ural region with his wife and daughter.

In 1945, the three of them returned to Poland and settled in Łódź. Kersz continued to be active in Tsukunft, serving on the Central Committee of the youth organisation and chairing Skif. After the Bund was dissolved, he worked as a teacher of Jewish history and literature at the I.L. Peretz School in Łódź. In the late 1950s, he emigrated with his family to Australia and later to Israel.[840]

Klin David, aka **Bronek,** after the war: **Bronisław Marczak** (1905 Kalisz[841] – 1973 Paris), a trade unionist, Bund and PPS activist. Before the war, he was a member of Tsukunft in Kalisz and later joined the Bund in: Kalisz, Grodno, Częstochowa (from 1935) and Warsaw (from 1938) where he also took up the position of General Secretary of the Union of Socialist Craftsmen and member of the Presidium of the National Council of Class Trade Unions. He wrote for Bund newspapers, including *Folkstsaytung.* He was an excellent speaker.

After the outbreak of World War II, he helped hide the Bund's Medem Library in Częstochowa. From the very beginning, he joined the Bund's underground activities in Warsaw. In the first years of the war, he worked as a secretary in the supply department of the Joint Distribution Committee and was also active in the Jewish Social Self-Aid organisation.

839 Sh. Redlich, *Life in Transit. Jews in Postwar Lodz, 1945–1950,* Boston 2010, pp. 83, 180, 193–194; Binjamin, M. Szafran, "Abraham Kahan," *Unzer tsayt* 1982, nos 3–4, pp. 29–31; "Di letste teg fun avreml kahan," *Lebns-fragn* 1982, nos 361–362, p. 7.

840 L.B., „Jehuda Kersz," *Lebns-fragn* 1980, nos 343–344. p. 21.

841 Many biographical notes erroneously point to Łask as his place of birth.

He served as an emissary between the underground Central Committee of the Bund and committees operating in other ghettos, as well as between the Bund and the PPS. He was responsible for distributing the underground press. In 1942, he crossed over to the 'Aryan' side. His apartment became a meeting place for clandestine Bundist gatherings. On the 'Aryan' side, he operated under the name **Bronisław Marczak**. In 1944, he participated in the Warsaw Uprising alongside the PPS. His wartime memoirs were originally published in Yiddish under the title *Mitn malekh ha-moves untern orem. Mayne iberlebungen in poyln beys der natsi-okupatsye 1939–1945* (Tel Aviv, 1968). In 2017, they were translated into French as *À cache-cache avec la mort. Un résistant juif à Varsovie de 1939 à 1945*, with an introduction by Jean-Charles Szurek (Paris).

After the end of World War II, he retained his 'Aryan' identity and went by the name Bronisław Marczak. He settled in Łódź, where he remained active in the Bund and PPS while working for *Kurier Popularny*. On 29 September 1947, he was arrested and charged, among other things, with illegal possession of weapons. On 28 April 1948, the Military District Court in Łódź sentenced him to three years in prison. After his release, he left for Paris in May 1956, where he continued his activities within the Bund and collaborated with the Paris-based *Unzer shtime*.[842]

Kosovsky Vladimir (Włodzimierz), real name: **Nachum Mendel Lewinson** (ca 1867 – 19 October 1941 New York), socialist, one of the founders of the Bund, member of the party's Central Committee and editor of the Polish-language *Głos Robotniczy*. From 1900, Kosovsky lived abroad and was active as a member of the Bund's Overseas Committee. From 1930–1939 he lived in Warsaw, where he was a member of the *Folkstsaytung* editorial team. Following the outbreak of the Second World War, like many other members of the Bund, he found himself in Vilna in the autumn of 1939, and later travelled – via the USSR and Japan – to New York, where he arrived in 1941 and passed away soon after.[843]

Kusznir Motl (Motek), aka **Mietek** (1915 Częstochowa – 1960 Tel Aviv), an accountant by profession, came from a Bundist family. From 1926, he was involved

---

842 AIPN Łódź, ref. IPN Ld PF12/3107, IPN Ld 137/1397; M. Kusznir, *Di telikeyt fun "bund" in der tsayt fun der hitleristisher okupatsye in tschenstochov*, a collection of documents, b.a., *In di yorn fun yidishn khurvn. Di shtim fun untererdishn bund*, Nyu york 1948, pp. 309–311; N.K., "David Klin," *Unzer tsayt* 1974, no. 4, pp. 37–38; "Kh. dovid klin gekumen tsu forn fun poyln," *Lebns-fragn* 1956, no. 59, p. 15; L.B., "Baym frishn keyver fun dowid klin," *Lebns-fragn* 1974, nos 262–263, pp. 14–15.

843 J. Sh. Hertz, "Vladimir Kosovski," in: *Doyres bundistn*, vol. I, Nyu york 1956, pp. 11–67.

with Skif, where he served as secretary, and from 1931 with Tsukunft (also as secretary), later becoming active in the Bund in Częstochowa. He was a member of the Youth Section of the Trade Unions and, while already a member of Tsukunft, he continued to work with young Skif members in Częstochowa.

After the outbreak of World War II, he helped hide the party's archives and banners to prevent them from falling into German hands. He was a member of the Bund's underground organisation and worked for TOZ. Kusznir was one of the distributors of illegal Bund literature and a leader of resistance groups in the Częstochowa Ghetto. He also printed the underground newspaper *Rasta*. In 1941, he was arrested by the Gestapo in Częstochowa for his political activities and spent three months in prison. After his release, he continued his illegal political work inside the ghetto and, from 1943, in the Hasag forced labour camp in Częstochowa. In 1945, he was imprisoned in the Buchenwald concentration camp and later transferred to Bergen-Belsen, where he was liberated on 27 April 1945.

In July 1945, he returned to Częstochowa and became active in the Częstochowa Bund Committee, where he served as secretary. He also worked for the Central Jewish Historical Commission. After the dissolution of the Bund, he assisted former party members in leaving Poland. In November 1956, he arrived in Israel with his wife, Rivka. From the very beginning, he was active in the Bundist organisation there, serving as technical secretary and a member of the Bund's national committee. He also sat on the organisation's presidium.[844]

Lederman Moses, Moshek Hersh (1895 Częstochowa – 1964 Częstochowa), a shoemaker; Bund and trade union activist. Lederman was already involved with the Bund during World War I. In the inter-war period, he was one of the main activists of this party in Częstochowa. In 1927, as a representative of the Bund, he was elected to the Częstochowa Municipal Council, where he was a member of the art and culture commission. He resigned from his councillor position in 1929. In 1935 or 1937, Lederman moved to Łódź where he continued his activities in the Bund. During World War II, he was a member of the Underground Bund in the Litzmannstadt Ghetto. From there, he was deported to KL Auschwitz.

After the war, he returned to Częstochowa where he became chairman of the Częstochowa Bund Committee. He supported the Bund joining the PPR. After

844 AŻIH, WEiS, ref. 303/V/425/K 21 477, Kusznir Motek; L. Brener, "Ruch podziemny w częstochowskim getcie. Wspomnienia," *Biuletyn Żydowskiego Instytutu Historycznego* 1963, nos 45–46, p. 160; "Fun organizatsye lebn," *Lebns-fragn* 1957, nos 66–67, p. 23; "Motl kushnir iz nishto!," *Lebns-fragn* 1960, no. 104, pp. 3–4; N. Blumental, "Oyfn keyver fun a noentn fraynd," *Lebns-fragn* 1960, no. 104, p. 4.

1950, he was active in the Częstochowa branch of the Social-Cultural Association of Jews in Poland (TSKŻ), where he chaired the cultural and educational committee and oversaw the Janusz Korczak children's and youth club. Lederman was also a member of the Union of Fighters for Freedom and Democracy (ZBoWiD).[845]

Muszkat Zdzisław, see also **Zygmunt Dobrowolski** (1878 Warsaw – 1960 Warsaw), an economist by profession; Bund and Trade Union activist. He came from an assimilated Jewish family, hence Muszkat was raised in the Polish culture and grew up speaking Polish. He learnt Yiddish to understand it but did not speak it fluently. From an early age, he was involved in the socialist movement, initially in the Social Democracy of the Kingdom of Poland and Lithuania (SDKPiL) and after 1902 in the Bund. He was one of the leading Bund activists in Poland even before 1918. Due to his political activities, he was arrested several times, including in 1918, when he was imprisoned in the Modlin Fortress. At the end of 1917, he was elected to the first Central Committee of the Bund in Poland. During the Second Republic, he was one of the main organisers of the trade union and cooperative movement, serving as chairman of the Central Board of the Trade Union of Commercial, Industrial and Office Workers in Poland. He was also involved in educational activities and contributed to the publication of the Bund's Polish-language press. However, he preferred to work without publicity, avoiding public speeches at large gatherings and congresses. Although he was a member of the Bund's Central Committee, he remained relatively unknown to the masses.

After the outbreak of World War II, in the autumn of 1939, he refused to leave Warsaw with other Bund leaders. He became a member of the underground Central Committee of the Bund, established in October 1939, and joined the Party Council. He was also a member of the Warsaw Bund Committee, as well as the Sanatorium Committee. In the summer of 1940, he was appointed as director of the Medem Sanatorium in Miedzeszyn, near Warsaw. Having crossed to the 'Aryan' side, he remained part of the underground Central Committee of the Bund outside of the ghetto. Muszkat continued to carry out his work while

---

845 AŻIH, WEiS, ref. 303/V/425/L bn 1021, Lederman Mojżesz; AŻIH, Bernard Mark's Legacy, ref. S/333/76; R. Federman, "Moshe Lederman," *Lebns-fragn* 1964, no. 152, p. 18; J. Sh. Hertz, "Der algemeyner yidisher arbeter-bund," in: *Tschenstochover yidn*, ed. R. Mahler, Nyu york 1947, pp. 123–144; J. Sętowski, W. Paszkowski, "Lederman," in: *Żydzi częstochowscy. Słownik biograficzny*, ed. J. Sętowski, Częstochowa 2020, pp. 292–293 (I would like to thank Mr Adam Gliksman for helping me locate the book).

remaining in the shadow of others. He managed the Bund's finances, keeping records of expenditures from funds obtained from the Bund in America. He was responsible for sending reports to London about the situation of the Jewish population in the ghettos, as well as the author of the financial report on the Bund's underground activities, which was sent on 15 November 1943. Additionally, he helped to edit the party's Polish-language press. His apartment in Żoliborz served as a meeting place for activists operating on the 'Aryan' side.

After the war, he helped rebuild the Bund in Poland, even though – as he wrote to his comrades in the American Representation of the Bund – he struggled to adapt to the post-war reality and felt alienated. In 1947, he represented the Polish Bund at the First World Conference of the Bund's Coordinating Committee in Brussels. Despite his age and wartime experiences, he was still in great physical shape, even if somewhat psychologically 'bruised'. Spiritually, he was still the same person as before the war – warm, friendly and reluctant to talk about himself. As an opponent of the Bund's self-dissolution and merger with the PPR and later the PZPR, he withdrew from active life within the Jewish community in Poland after 1949.[846]

Portnoy Yekutiel, see also: **Noyekh, Comrade Józef** (1872 – 27 IX 1941 New York), social activist, teacher, one of the founders and activists of the Bund. In 1902, he was elected to the party's Central Committee. From 1917, he was chairman of the Central Committee of the Bund in Poland. In 1939, under pressure from other party members, he left Warsaw and reached New York via Vilna, the USSR and Japan. He died there soon afterwards.[847]

Pudłowski Leyb (Layb, Leybl) (1905 Bełchatów – 1972 Israel), a weaver, from 1921 member of the Trade Unions, from 1927 member of the Bund. During World War II, he fought in the Białystok region in the partisan units of 'Foroys' (Yid., 'Forward'). After the war he lived in Łódź where he continued to be active in the Bund. He was vice-chairman of the Łódź Bund Committee and member of the party's Central Committee. He represented the so-called 'leftist faction' and was in favour of cooperation with the PPR. In 1948, he fled to Germany and

846 YIVO Archives, RG 1478, Scherer, Supplement 2, file 71: Muszkat's letter from 25 October 1945; "Grus tsum khaver zdzislav mushkat," *Unzer tsayt* 1960, nos 4–5, p. 37–38; E. Scherer, "Zdzislaw Muszkat," in: *Doyres bundistn*, ed. J. Sh. Hertz, vol. III, Nyu york 1968, pp. 50–56; M. Fuks, *Muszkat Zdzisław*, in: *Polski Słownik Biograficzny*, vol. 22 (1977), pp. 297–298.

847 Kh. Sh. Kazdan, "Yekutiel Portnoy (Noyekh)," in: *Doyres bundistn*, vol. I, ed. J. Sh. Hertz, Nyu york 1956, pp. 68–122.

from there to France. He eventually settled in Israel where he continued to be active in the Bund.[848]

Samsonowicz Ignacy (Icchak) (1902 Częstochowa – 1956 Warsaw), a journalist and teacher, Bund activist. Samsonowicz was associated with the Bund in Częstochowa from 1922, where he worked as a journalist for the weekly *Arbeter tsaytung* and the daily *Der ploretaryer* from February 1923. He later moved to Piotrków Trybunalski where he worked as a teacher at the TSYSHO school, was the editor of *Pietrkoveriker*, remained active in the party and served on the Municipal Council as a Bund representative. There he also became a secretary in the presidium of the Piotrków Magistrate. During this time, he also worked with the *Folkstsaytung* and was a member of the Central Committee of the Bund in Poland. In Piotrków in 1928, he married Chaya Muszkes, a fellow teacher at the TSYSHO school (she died in 1942 together with their 10-year-old son).

During World War II, he initially stayed in Piotrków Trybunalski, where he was active in the underground Bund committee and served as the head of the Judenrat office. Due to his illegal activities, he was arrested by the Gestapo along with other Bundists. Luckily, he managed to escape and went to Warsaw where he joined the underground Central Committee of the Bund on the 'Aryan' side. He used false documents in the name of **Tadeusz Leszczyński**. As part of his party activities, he edited the Bund's underground press, including the *Biuletyn W.B.* from February 1944. He also acted as a representative of the Jewish Combat Organisation (ŻOB) on the 'Aryan' side and collaborated with the 'Żegota' Council for Aid to Jews. From January 1943 until the outbreak of the Warsaw Uprising, he was hidden by **Eugenia Wąsowska**.

After the end of World War II, he helped rebuild the Bund in Poland. He joined the Central Committee of the Bund and was the editor of *Głos Bundu*. He also wrote for *Folkstsaytung*. After the Bund's self-dissolution, he carried out an act of self-criticism and joined the PPR, later becoming a member of the PZPR. He collaborated with the pro-communist *Folks shtime*, writing about international affairs. Two years before his death, he fell ill with neurosis. The illness may have been a consequence of his wartime experiences, and a nervous breakdown related to his inability to reconcile with the political situation. This shows how hard it was for Samsonowicz to 'betray' his youthful ideals and act against his own conscience. His death was ignored by the New York-based *Unzer tsayt* where obituaries of deceased Bundists, including those who had remained

848 AIPN Łódź, ref. IPN Ld PF10/690 vol. 1 p. 2, f. 77, 82; *Lebns-fragn* 1972, nos 244–245, p. 28 [obituary].

in Poland usually appeared. His biography was not included in any volume of *Doyres bundistn*.[849]

Sobol Abraham (1905 Teklinów, n. Żyrardów – 1982 Montreal), a tailor by profession. He was involved with the Bund from an early age. During the inter-war period, he was initially one of the leaders of the party's committee in Mszczonów and one of the founders of the local people's library. He was later associated with the Bund in Żyrardów and Warsaw. He was deported to the USSR during the war (he spent time, i.a., in Magnitogorsk and Sverdlovsk). After returning to Poland in May 1946, he settled in Szczecin where he led the local Bund Committee and worked at the Tailors' Cooperative. He also served as vice-chairman of the Provincial Jewish Committee in Szczecin. After the Bund was dissolved, he emigrated to Stockholm and from there to Montreal, where he co-founded the Victor Alter and Henryk Erlich Circle at the Arbeter Ring. Sobol remained active in the Bundist community throughout his life.[850]

Szechatow Shaya (Szychatow) (1896 Równe – 1987 Los Angeles), a Bundist. Until 1939, he worked for the Health Insurance Fund at the Municipal Council, as well as for the local branch of the Joint Distribution Committee in Równe, among others. He was a member of the Bund from a young age. In 1937, he was sent to Bereza Kartuska internment camp for his political activities, and later spent eight months in prison in Równe. After his release, he moved to Warsaw, where he worked for the newspaper *Der Moment* and was a member of the Central Board of TSYSHO until the outbreak of World War II. Szechatow and his family spent the war deep in the USSR, from where he returned to Warsaw in early 1946 as part of the repatriation programme. While in Poland, he remained active in the Bund as well as in the CKŻP. In 1948, unwilling to accept the dissolution of the Bund, he and his wife illegally left Poland for Stockholm, where he continued his Bundist activities. In 1951, he moved to Canada and actively involved in the Arbeter Ring. Eventually, he settled in Los Angeles where he was a member of the Bund Committee and the JLC. He was also involved in publishing *Doyres*

849 AAN, A collection of underground and uprising press, *Yugnt shitme*, ref. 356/1–3; AŻIH, Ringelblum Archive, ref. Ring I/685; AIPN, ref. IPN Kr 056/18/16, f. 114; "Icchak Samsonowicz," in: *Tschenstochov. Nayer tsugob materyal tsum bukh „Tschenstochover yidn" / Tschenstochov. A New Supplement to the Book „Tschenstochover yidn"*, ed. S. D. Singer, New York 1958, pp. 146–147.

850 AIPN Szczecin, ref. IPN Sz 009/622 vol. II, f. 28, 67–69; A. Zimler, "Abraham Sobol," *Unzer tsayt* 1983, no. 2, pp. 34–35.

bundistn. He published his memoirs about his time in the USSR and post-war Poland under the title *Yorn fun kamf un gerangl* (Ramat Gan, 1973).[851]

Szuldenfrei Michał, Dr (1887 Częstochowa – 1965 Warsaw), a lawyer lived in Kraków until the outbreak of World War II. In 1910, he completed his studies at the Faculty of Law at Jagiellonian University, defending doctorate in law in 1911. He ran his own law firm until September 1939. Between 1930 and 1938, he was a member of the Kraków Bar Association. In 1905, he was one of the founders of the Jewish Socialist Party in Galicia (the so-called Galician Bund). He was among the most active members of the Bund in Kraków and served as its chairman for a time. Regarded as a Bund theorist, he was well-known and respected both within the Bundist movement and beyond. He maintained close contact with the Bund leaders in Warsaw.

After the outbreak of the war in September 1939, he and others left Kraków and stayed in Lvov until June 1940, from where he was deported as part of the third wave of deportations to the Mari ASSR in the Soviet Union, to Yoshkar-Ola, where he stayed until 1944. He was a member of the Union of Polish Patriots (ZPP). In 1944, he arrived in Lublin, where he became the director of the Legal Bureau at the Presidium of the PKWN, and later at the Presidium of the Council of Ministers. During the General Board meeting of the Union of Polish Patriots in the USSR in Moscow on 25 July 1944, he was elected to the State National Council. From August 1944, he served as a member of the State National Council as part of the Polish Socialist Party list, and later as a member of the Legislative Sejm. Szuldenfrei continued to support the Bund in post-war Poland, becoming the first chairman of the party's Central Committee. He published in the *Folkstsaytung* under his own name and under the pen-name 'Marianer' In 1946, he visited the United States as part of a Bund delegation. Between 1946 and 1948, he attended several Bund conferences in Switzerland and Belgium, including the first Conference of the Coordinating Committee. Throughout the post-war period, he was in favour of compromise in the Bund's political activities and opposed capitulation and self-dissolution. After the party was dissolved, he withdrew from political life and did not join the PZPR.

After 1950, he worked at the Council of Ministers' Office and taught maritime and aviation law at the School of Foreign Service.

Throughout his life, Szuldenfrei was not only a socialist but also a lawyer. He was often a defence lawyer in criminal cases, particularly in political trials before

851 YIVO Archives, ref. RG 1400, ME 40, Files 82, 83; J. Perlsztejn, *Araynfir*, in: Szychatow, *Yorn fun kamf un gerangl*, Ramat–Gan 1973, pp. 9–12.

1939 and after the war. His death was noted and commemorated in all Bundist centres outside Poland. Obituaries and biographical articles were published, and memorial services were organised. The funeral ceremonies were attended by crowds of people, including government representatives, such as the Prime Minister Józef Cyrankiewicz.[852]

Temczyn Sioma (Stefan) (1905 Pińsk – 1956 New York), a bookkeeper. He came from a Bundist family and was appointed chairman of Tsukunft in Pińsk at the age of 16–17, and later he was a member of the youth movement in Warsaw.

After the outbreak of war in September 1939, he left Warsaw for Pinsk with his wife and child. There he was arrested by the NKVD in March 1941 and sent to Siberia. In 1944, he joined Berling's Army and arrived in Lublin as a soldier, where he and others began to rebuild Bund cells. He settled in Warsaw, wrote for *Folkstsaytung* and actively participated in the life of the party. As a representative of Tsukunft, he participated in a socialist youth conference in London. He refused to accept the dissolution of the Bund and the accession to the PZPR, and left Poland with his wife and son. Initially, he spent several years in Displaced Persons camps in Germany. He then moved to New York, where he continued to be actively involved in Bundist life within workers' circles and remained active in the Pinsk branch of the Bund. He worked as a bookkeeper until his death.[853]

Winer (Wiener) Bono (Symkha-Bunim, Symkha-Binem) (1920 Łódź – 1995 Montreal, buried in Melbourne), a socialist and advocate for Yiddishkeit, came from a Bundist family. From an early age, he was involved with Skif and later with Tsukunft in Łódź. He completed his education at the Medem school in Łódź. During World War II, he and his family were in the Litzmannstadt Ghetto,

852 YIVO Archives, The Bund Archive, ref. RG 1400, ME 40, Folder 163; AAN, KRN 342, personal files of Michał Szuldenfrei; AIPN Warsaw, ref. IPN (Passport files) AP 2087304; ref. IPN BU 1264/264, Note prepared on the basis of personal and investigation files in December 1952, f. 17–18; *Stosunki polsko-izraelskie (1945–1967). Wybór dokumentów*, eds. Sz. Rudnicki, M. Silber, Warsaw 2009, p. 185; "Geshtorbn dr. Michał Szuldenfrei," *Unzer shtime* 1965, no. 132 (8514), p. 1; E. Scherer, "Tsum ondenk… Dr. Michał Szuldenfrei," *Unzer tsayt* 1965, pp. 36–38; "Matseyve oyf keyver fun khaver Michał Szuldenfrei," *Unzer tsayt* 1967, no. 1, p. 47; "Dr Michał Szuldenfrei," *Lebns-fragn* 1965, nos 162–163, p. 18; "M. Szuldenfrei," *Głos Wybrzeża* 02 July 1965; E. Scherer, "Dr. Michał Szuldenfrei," in: *Doyres bundistn*, vol. III, Nyu york 1968, pp. 103–108.

853 "Żydowska delegacja z Polski na Międzynarodowy Zjazd Młodzieży," *Biuletyn Żydowskiej Agencji Prasowej* 1945, no 94/104, f. 1; L. Lewin, "Syome temtchin," *Unzer tsayt* 1957, no. 1 (183), pp. 43–44.

where he was active in the underground Tsukunft committee. He possessed an illegal radio in the ghetto and kept a diary in which he described Tsukunft's underground activities. During the liquidation of the ghetto in August 1944, he was sent to Auschwitz concentration camp, then to KL Mauthausen and KL Gusen. After liberation, he returned to his hometown of Łódź and worked towards rebuilding the Jewish community in post-war Poland. He was actively involved in the re-establishment and restoration of Bundist organisations in Łódź, including work with children and youth. He was a member of the Central Committee of Tsukunft. He organised material aid for Bundists and their families. In September 1948, unable to accept the dissolution of the Bund and Tsukunft, he left Poland illegally with others (including his brother Pinkas Winer). He initially ended up in a DP camp in Germany. In 1950, he settled in Australia, where he remained active in Bundist organisations, worked to promote Yiddishkeit (including Jewish schools with Yiddish as a language of instruction) and became a member of the Australian Labour Party. He also worked in the Coordinating Committee of the Bund in New York, frequently travelling around the world to visit Bundist organisations. He was a founding member and co-president of the Jewish Holocaust Centre (JHC) in Australia. He passed away in Montreal during a visit to his friend Chava Rosenfarb.[854]

Wołkowicz Pinkus (Pinchas) (1907, Włocławek – 1976, Montreal) a tailor by profession, was associated with Tsukunft and later with the Bund in Włocławek. From 1935, he was a member of the Warsaw Bund Committee and the Central Committee of Tsukunft. Following the outbreak of World War II, Wołkowicz fled to the eastern territories of the Second Republic, from where he was deported to Siberia. He returned to Poland as part of the repatriation programme and settled in Łódź. He believed in the possibility of rebuilding Jewish life in post-war Poland. He was a member of the Central Committee and Warsaw Committee of Tsukunft as well as of the Łódź Bund Committee. He was in favour of merging the Bund and the PPS. He represented the Bund in the Provincial Jewish Committee in Łódź. In late September 1948, he fled to Canada with his wife Mina

854 J. Frajnd, "Bono viner. Anshtot a bliml oyf zayn frishn keyver," *Lebns-fragn* 1995, nos 519–520, p. 12; "Lodzher geto-arkhiv fun bono viner," *Lebns-fragn* 1996, nos 535–536, p. 14; M. Zelmanowicz, "Bono viner iz nishto mer mit undz," *Unzer tsayt* 1995, no. 9, pp. 32–34; S. Marks, *Obituary Bono Wiener, https://collections.ajhs.com.au/Detail/objects/53363* [access: 20 September 2024]; https://www.monash.edu/arts/acjc/yiddish-melbourne/biographies/bono-wiener [access: 20 September 2024].

and children. He remained active in the Bundist circles and in the Arbeter Ring in Montreal.[855]

Zygielbojm Shmul Mordechai, codename **Artur** (1895 Borowica near Lublin – 1943 London, buried on Long Island), political and trade union activist. Zygielbojm came from an impoverished Jewish family. He lived with his family in Krasnystaw from 1899 and attended cheder until he turned 10. After that, he was sent to a carpenter's workshop where he was to be an apprentice. After he lost two fingers, he began working as a baker's assistant. In 1907, he went to Warsaw where he learned the trade of glove-making. In 1914, after returning to his family, he became involved with the Bund in Chełm and soon became one of its most active members. In 1917, he was sent as a delegate to the First Congress of the Bund (under German and Austrian occupation) in Lublin. During this period, he made up for his lack of education and learnt, among other things the Polish language.

In 1920, Zygielbojm moved to Warsaw. He was elected secretary of the Jewish Metalworkers' Union and became a member of the Warsaw Bund Committee. He quickly became one of the most popular Bundists and representatives of the labour unions. He was widely known as 'Comrade Artur'. He was known as an excellent speaker and labour activist. In 1924, he was elected a member of the Central Committee of the Bund. He was also a member of the Jewish Section of the Central Commission of Trade Unions in Poland. From 1927, he served as a Warsaw councillor on behalf of the Bund. He also wrote for the Bund press, including *Folkstsaytung*, where he signed his articles with his real name and the penname 'Z. Artur'. Until 1930, he was the editor of *Arbeter fragn*. In 1936, Zygielbojm moved to Łódź where, although he officially held the post of a secretary, he effectively led the party committee. Towards the end of 1938, he was elected a city councillor at the Municipal Council.

After the outbreak of the war in September 1939, Zygielbojm fled to Warsaw to escape the German occupation, where he organised Jewish self-defence units in the capital. After the Germans entered the city, he was arrested as one of the 'hostages'. For a short time, he was a member of the Warsaw Judenrat. He belonged to the leadership of the underground Central Committee of the Bund, and he attempted to establish cooperation with the Polish socialists. Using the platform of the Warsaw Jewish Community, he called for resistance against the efforts to establish a ghetto in Warsaw.

---

855 AIPN Łódź, ref. IPN Ld PF10/690, vol. I, p. 2, k. 48–49; I.H., "Pinkus Wolkowicz," *Unzer tsayt* 1976, no. 5, p. 34–35; H. Hirszbejn, "Pinchas Wolkowicz," *Lebns-fragn* 1976, nos 290–291, p. 23.

At the end of 1939, he left Poland illegally, as he was wanted by the Germans, and travelled to Brussels, and from there to France. After the capitulation of France, he fled again to the USA in September 1940. In New York, he was active in the Representation of the Polish Bund in America. He earned a living as a glove maker. During public speeches and in press articles, he informed the world about the situation of Jews in Poland.

In the spring of 1942, on the orders of the Representation of the Polish Bund in America, Zygielbojm moved to London where he represented and advocated for the Jewish community in the National Council of the Polish Government-in-Exile. He tried to inform the world about the extermination of Polish Jews in Nazi death camps and the conditions in the ghettos. He tried to pressure the Polish Government-in-Exile to prioritise helping Polish Jews and publicising their extermination. He unsuccessfully appealed for help to Roosevelt and Churchill, among others.

Upon hearing of the defeat of the Warsaw Ghetto Uprising and the death of his beloved second wife, Mania Rozen Zygielbojm (an activist in the underground Bund) and their 16-year-old son Tuvia, Zygielbojm, in protest against – the world's indifference to Nazi crimes, – committed suicide on the night of 11 to 12 May 1943, aware of his own powerlessness. He left two letters addressed to the Polish President-in-Exile, Władysław Raczkiewicz, and the Prime Minister of the Polish government, General Władysław Sikorski. His death was reported in the press of many Western countries.

After the war, the Bund in Poland made efforts to bring Shmul Zygielbojm's ashes to Warsaw so that they could be laid to rest in the Jewish cemetery on Okopowa Street alongside the ashes of his fellow comrades. However, the Bund in America opposed this, arguing that the party had practically ceased to exist in Poland. Zygielbojm's ashes were finally brought to New York in May 1961. In September of that same year, after a solemn funeral ceremony at Carnegie Hall, they were laid to rest at the New Mount Carmel Jewish Cemetery on Long Island.[856]

Żeleznikow Avreml (Abram) (1924 Vilna, today Vilnius in Lithuania – 2013 Melbourne), an electrician, came from a Bundist family. Before 1939, he was an active member of Tsukunft in Vilna. During World War II, he was in the Vilna

856 D. Blatman, *For Our Freedom and Yours, The Jewish Labour Bund in Poland 1939–1949,* London-Portland 2003, pp. 128–150; A. Rowiński, *Zygielbojma śmierć i życie,* Warsaw 2004; *Zygelboym-bukh,* introduced and edited by I. Sz. Szwartz, Nyu york 1947.

Ghetto where he belonged to the Fareynigte Partizaner Organizatsye (FPO – United Partisan Organisation). He later joined the Soviet partisans in the 'Vilno' Brigade.

After the war, he mainly lived in Łódź, where he was the chairman of Tsukunft. He helped to establish youth organisations in post-war Poland. In September 1948, he and his wife Masha Żeleznikow, illegally emigrated from Poland because they did not agree with the self-dissolution of the Tsukunft and the Bund. They initially stayed in France, before emigrating to Australia in 1951. Avreml remained connected to the Bund in Australia for the rest of his life. Among other things, he taught Yiddish at the Sholem Aleichem Sunday School. He and Masha ran the famous Cafe Scheherazade in Melbourne.[857]

857 AIPN Łódź, ref. IPN Ld PF10/668, f. 55, 128; J. Zeleznikow, "Life at the end of the world: a Jewish Partisan in Melbourne," *Holocaust Studies: a journal of culture and history* 2011, no. 16 (3), pp. 11–32; https://www.monash.edu/arts/acjc/yiddish-melbourne/biographies/avram-zeleznikow [access: 10 December 2018].

Abbreviations

AAN – Archiwum Akt Nowych / Archives of Modern Records
AIPN – Archiwum Instytutu Pamięci Narodowej / Archives of the Institute of National Remembrance
AL – Armia Ludowa / People's Army
AP Wrocław – Archiwum Państwowe we Wrocławiu / State Archives in Wrocław
AŻIH – Archiwum Żydowskiego Instytutu Historycznego / Archives of the Jewish Historical Institute
CKŻP – Centralny Komitet Żydów w Polsce / Central Committee of Jews in Poland
CSW – Centrala Spółdzielni Wytwórczych „Solidarność" / Central Association of Manufacturing Cooperatives „Solidarity"
CŻKH – Centralna Żydowska Komisja Historyczna / Central Jewish Historical Commission
Files n. – unsorted files
FPO – Fareynigte Partizaner Organizatsye / United Partisan Organisation
IPN – Instytut Pamięci Narodowej / Institute of National Remembrance
JLC – Jewish Labor Committee
Joint – American Jewish Joint Distribution Committee
KPP – Komunistyczna Partia Polski / Communist Party of Poland
KRN – Krajowa Rada Narodowa / State National Council
MO – Milicja Obywatelska / Citizens' Militia
MRN – Miejska Rada Narodowa / Municipal National Council
NKVD – Narodnyy komissariat vnutriennikh del / People's Commissariat for Internal Affairs
NSZ – Narodowe Siły Zbrojne / National Armed Forces
OM TUR – Organizacji Młodzieży Towarzystwa Uniwersytetu Robotniczego / Youth Organization of the Workers' University Society
ORT – Organizacja Rozwoju Twórczości Przemysłowej, Rzemieślniczej i Rolniczej wśród Ludności Żydowskiej / Organisation for the Development of Industry, Crafts and Agriculture among the Jewish Population
PKWN – Polski Komitet Wyzwolenia Narodowego / Polish Committee of National Liberation
PPR – Polska Partia Robotnicza / Polish Workers' Party
PPS – Polska Partia Socjalistyczna / Polish Socialist Party
PPS-WRN – Polska Partia Socjalistyczna – Wolność, Równość, Niepodległość / Polish Socialist Party-'Freedom-Equality-Independence'

PRL – Polska Rzeczpospolita Ludowa / People's Republic of Poland
PSL – Polskie Stronnictwo Ludowe / Polish People's Party's
PZPR – Polska Zjednoczona Partia Robotnicza / Polish United Workers' Party
SD – Stronnictwo Demokratyczne / Democratic Party
SL – Stronnictwo Ludowe / People's Party
TOZ – Towarzystwo Ochrony Zdrowia przy CKŻP / Society for the Protection of Health at the CKŻP
TSKŻ – Towarzystwo Społeczno-Kulturalne Żydów w Polsce / Social-Cultural Association of Jews in Poland
TSYSHO – Tsentrale yidishe shul-organizatsye / Central Jewish School Organisation
UNRRA – United Nations Relief and Rehabilitation Administration
USSR – Soyuz Sovetskikh Sotsialisticheskikh Respublik / Union of Soviet Socialist Republics, commonly known as the Soviet Union
WBC – Warsaw Bund Committee
WJC – World Jewish Congress
WKŻ – Wojewódzki Komitet Żydowski / Provincial Jewish Committee
YIVO – Yidisher visnshaftlekher institut / Jewish Scientific Institute
YIVO Archives – YIVO Institute for Jewish Research Archives
YVA – Yad Vashem Archives
ŻIH – Żydowski Instytut Historyczny / Jewish Historical Institute
ŻOB – Żydowska Organizacja Bojowa / Jewish Combat Organisation
ZPP – Związek Patriotów Polskich / Union of Polish Patriots
ŻPS – Żydowska Partia Socjalistyczna / Jewish Socialist Party
ZWM – Związek Walki Młodych / Union of Youth Struggle
ŻZW – Żydowski Związek Wojskowy / Jewish Military Union

Bibliography

ARCHIVAL SOURCES

Archives of the Jewish Historical Institute, Warsaw (AŻIH)

- Testimonies (Zbiór relacji Żydów ocalałych z Zagłady), ref. 301/.
- Archives of the Presidium and Secretariat of the Central Committee of Jews in Poland 1945–1950 (Archiwum Prezydium i Sekretariatu Centralnego Komitetu Żydów w Polsce. 1945–1950), ref. 303/I/.
- Archive of the Personnel Department of the Central Committee of Jews in Poland (1945) 1946–1950 (Archiwum Wydziału Personalnego Centralnego Komitetu Żydów w Polsce. (1945) 1946–1950), ref. 303/III/.
- Department of Records and Statistics. Registration Cards of Jewish Survivors of the Holocaust (Wydział Ewidencji i Statystyki. Karty Rejestracyjne Żydów Ocalałych z Zagłady. 1945–1951; WEiS), ref. 303/V/425/.
- Central Committee of Jews in Poland: Presidium, Culture and Propaganda Department. 1944–1950, (CKŻP: Prezydium, Wydział Kultury i Propagandy), ref. 303/XIII/.
- Central Jewish Historical Commission at the Central Committee of Jews in Poland (CŻKH) (Centralna Żydowska Komisja Historyczna przy Centralnym Komitecie Żydów w Polsce. 1944–1947), ref. 303/XX/.
- the Bund collection, unsorted files. (Bund. 1945–1949), ref. 334/.
- American Jewish Joint Distribution Committee. 1945–1949, ref. 350/.
- Provincial Jewish Committee in Warsaw. 1945–1949 (Wojewódzki Komitet Żydowski w Warszawie. 1945–1949), ref. 352/.
- Ringelblum Archive (Archiwum Ringelbluma), ref. Ring I/.
- Bernard Mark's Legacy (Spuścizna: Bernard Mark), ref. S/333/.

Documentation Department of the Jewish Historical Institute, Warsaw

- Photographs related to the Bund, 1918–1948.

The Archives of Modern Records, Warsaw (AAN)

- General Jewish Labour Bund in Poland. Central Committee (the Bund) (Ogólno-Żydowski Związek Robotniczy Bund w Polsce. Centralny Komitet, 1939–1944), ref. 30/III/.
- General Jewish Labour Bund in Poland. Central Committee (the Bund) (Ogólno-Żydowski Związek Robotniczy Bund w Polsce. Centralny Komitet, 1945–1948), ref. 30/IV/.
- State National Council (Krajowa Rada Narodowa; KRN), ref. 342.
- Polish Committee of National Liberation. Presidium (Polski Komitet Wyzwolenia Narodowego. Prezydium; PKWN), ref. I/.
- Polish Workers' Party. Central Committee. Secretariat (Polska Partia Robotnicza. Komitet Centralny. Sekretariat), ref. 295/VII/.
- Szymon Zachariasz Legacy (Spuścizna Szymona Zachariasza; Zachariasz), ref. 476/.
- Zbiór Prasy Konspiracyjnej i Powstańczej (The Collection of the Underground and Insurgent Press).

State Archives in Wrocław (AP Wrocław)

- All-Jewish Union Bund in Poland, Provincial Committee in Wrocław (Bund) (Ogólno-Żydowski Związek Bund w Polsce KW we Wrocławiu), ref. 79/.
- Provincial Committee of the PZPR in Wrocław: Provincial Revision Commission Department (Komitet Wojewódzki Polskiej Zjednoczonej Partii Robotniczej we Wrocławiu. Wydział Wojewódzka Komisja Rewizyjna), ref. 75/V/.

Archives of the Institute of National Remembrance in Katowice (AIPN Katowice)

- ref. IPN Ka, D I 5263.
- ref. IPN D I 6587.

Archives of the Institute of National Remembrance in Kraków (AIPN Kraków)

- ref. IPN Kr 07/1694.
- ref. IPN Kr 056/18/16.
- ref. IPN Kr 075/214.

Archives of the Institute of National Remembrance in Łódź (AIPN Łódź)

- ref. IPN Ld PF10/668.
- ref. IPN Ld PF10/690.
- ref. IPN Ld PF12/3107.
- ref. IPN Ld 137/1397.

Archives of the Institute of National Remembrance in Szczecin (AIPN Szczecin)

- ref. IPN Sz, ref. 009/622.

Archives of the Institute of National Remembrance in Warsaw (AIPN Warsaw)

- ref. IPN 00231/205.
- ref. IPN AP 2087304.
- ref. IPN BU 00231/205.
- ref. IPN BU 01264/264.
- ref. IPN BU 0722/1.
- ref. IPN BU 1005/2780.
- ref. IPN BU 1268/19262.
- ref. IPN BU 1572/3529.
- ref. IPN GK 182/166.

Archives of the Institute of National Remembrance in Wrocław (AIPN Wrocław)

- ref. IPN Wr 032/75.
- ref. IPN Wr 032/249.
- ref. IPN Wr 032/403.

YIVO Archives, New York

- ref. RG 1400, The Bund Archive, ME 40, files 82, 83, 163; M_9/155.
- ref. RG 1452, Bono Wiener Collection.
- ref. RG 1455, Bernard Goldstein Collection.
- ref. RG 1458, Lucjan Blit Collection.
- ref. RG 1476, Roman Blit Collection.
- ref. RG 1478, Emanuel Scherer Collection, Supplement 2.

Yad Vashem Archive, Jerusalem (YVA)

- Testimonies, ref. O.3/.
- Wolf Yasni Collection, ref. P-5/.

Ghetto Fighters House Archives, Kibbutz Lohamei Haghetaot (GFHA)

- Berman Adolf–Avraham Collection, Catalog No. 5798.

National Archives, London

- Foreign Office, ref FO 371/.

ORAL HISTORY

Dina Schein, née Hiziger-Tajtelbaum, interviewed by the author in May 2008 in Rishon Letsiyon (Israel).

Mendel Schein, interviewed by the author in May 2008 in Rishon Letsiyon (Israel).

Icchak Luden, interviewed by the author in July 2006 in Tel Aviv (Israel).

Marek Edelman, interviewed by the author in April 2007 in Łódź (Poland).

USC Shoah Foundation, interview code 7970 – testimony of Hanna Gdalewicz-Nielsen, January 14, 1996.

USC Shoah Foundation, interview code 33414 – testimony of Max Falk, September 22, 1997.

MUSIC AND FILMS

In Love and in Struggle. The Musical Legacy of the Jewish Labor Bund (CD released by the Workmen's Circle/Arbeter Ring, New York).

The Last Fighters, Israel 2006, realised by R. Zaretzky, Y. Kipper-Zaretzky.

PUBLISHED SOURCES

Primary Sources

Archiwum Ringelbluma. Konspiracyjne Archiwum Getta Warszawy. vol. XVI: *Prasa getta warszawskiego: „Bund" i „Cukunft"*, part I: *„Bund"*, intr. and ed.,

Martyna Rusiniak-Karwat, part II: „*Cukunft*”, intr. and ed., Alicja Jarkowska-Natkaniec, Warsaw 2016.

En Direct du Ghetto. La presse clandestine juive dans le ghetto de Varsovie, ed. Daniel Blatman, Paris 2005.

Grüss Noe, **Grünbaum Diana**, *Rok pracy Centralnej Żydowskiej Komisji Historycznej*, Łódź 1946.

Historisher Zamlbukh. Materialn un dokumentn tsushteyer tsu der geshikhte fun algemeynem yidishn arbeter-bund, Varshe 1948.

Instrukcje dla badania przeżyć dzieci żydowskich w okresie okupacji niemieckiej, ed. Noe Grüss, Genia Silkes, Łódź 1945.

Instrukcje dla zbierania materiałów etnograficznych w okresie okupacji niemieckiej, ed. Nachman Blumental, Łódź 1945.

Instrukcje dla zbierania materiałów historycznych z okresu okupacji niemieckiej, ed. Józef Kermisz, Łódź 1945.

'Itonut ha-mahteret ha-yehudit be-varsha (*The Jewish Underground Press in Warsaw*), ed., intr. and annot., Y. Kermish, vol. I, Jerusalem 1979–1980.

Jewish Labor Bund. 1897–1957. Published by the International Jewish Labor Bund, New York 1958.

Mahler Rafael, *Bundishe ideologie in a nayer oyflage (an entfer tsu Moshe Katz)*, Nyu york 1954.

Metodologiczne wskazówki dla badania zagłady żydostwa polskiego (w jidysz), Łódź 1945.

Monitor Polski 1948.

Ostatnie pokolenie. Autobiografie polskiej młodzieży żydowskiej okresu międzywojennego ze zbiorów YIVO Institute for Jewish Research w Nowym Jorku, intr. and ed., Alina Cała, Warsaw 2003.

Pat Jacob, *Ash un fayer. Iber di khurves fun poyln*, Nyu york 1946; English version: *Ashes and Fire*, transl. L. Steinberg, New York 1947.

Pragier Ruta, *Żydzi czy Polacy*, Warsaw 2016.

Scherer Emanuel, *The Future of Jews*, London 1947.

Sprawozdania stenograficzne z posiedzeń Krajowej Rady Narodowej, Warsaw 1946.

Stosunki polsko-izraelskie (1945–1967). Wybór dokumentów, selected and edited by Szymon Rudnicki, Marcos Silber, Warsaw 2009.

Sznajderman Sh. L., *Tsvishn shrek un hofenung (a rayze iber dem nayem poyln)*, Buenos Aires 1947.

Szoskes Henry, *Poyln – 1946 (Ayndrukn fun a rayze)*, Buenos Aires 1946.

Yid, mensh, sotsyalist. I. Artuski ondenk-bukh, Tel Aviv 1976.

Zarys działalności Centralnego Komitetu Żydów w Polsce. Za okres od 1 stycznia do 30 czerwca 1946 r., Warsaw 1947.

Zygelboym-bukh, introduced and edited by I. Sz. Szwartz, Nyu york 1947.

Żydowski Instytut Naukowy, jego cele i badania, Vilna 1930.

Diaries, Memoirs, Interviews

Bereś Witold, Burnetko Krzysztof, *Marek Edelman, Życie. Po prostu*, Warsaw 2008.

Bono Wiener Remembered / Dos bono viner gedenkbukh, publ. Ch. Rosenfarb, Montreal 1997.

Brener Liber, "Ruch podziemny w częstochowskim getcie. Wspomnienia," *Biuletyn Żydowskiego Instytutu Historycznego* 1963, nos 45–46.

Brener Liber, "Tschenstochover geto," in: *In di yorn fun yidishn khurvn. Di shtim fun untererdishn bund*, Nyu york 1948.

Edelman Marek, *Getto walczy (Udział Bundu w obronie getta warszawskiego)*, Łódź 2015 (1st edition: Łódź 1945).

Edelman Marek, *I była miłość w getcie*, noted by Paula Sawicka, Warsaw 2011.

Edelman Marek, *Prosto się mówi, jak się wie*, texts selected and edited by Paula Sawicka, Krzysztof Burnetko, Warsaw 2013.

Federman Rafael, "Der 'Bund' in Tschenstochov in di yorn nokh der tsveyter velt-milkhome", in: *Tschenstochov. Nayer tsugob materyal tsum bukh 'Tschenstochover yidn'/Tschenstochov. A New Supplement to the Book 'Tschenstochover yidn'*, ed. S. D. Singer, New York 1958.

Goldstein Bernard, *Finf yor in varshever geto*, Nyu york 1947; English version: *Five Years in the Warsaw Ghetto*, tr. and ed. Leonard Shatzkin, New York 1961.

Goldstein Bernard, *Twenty Years with the Jewish Labor Bund. A Memoir of Interwar Poland*, tr., ed. Marvin S. Zuckerman, Indiana 2016 (title of the original: *Tsvantsik yor in varshever 'bund': 1919–1939*, New York 1960).

Goldwaser Kalman, *Fun der vaysl bizn taykh kizl-su. Iberlebungen bays der yorn fun der tsveyter velt-milkhome*, Pariz 1972.

Grupińska Anka, *Ciągle po kole. Rozmowy z żołnierzami getta warszawskiego*, Warsaw 2000.

Grynblat Jona, „Kopniak życia," in: *Losy żydowskie. Świadectwo żywych*, vol. III, ed. Marian Turski, Warsaw 1996.

Hecht Pinkus, "Serce zostało w Piotrkowie," in: *Losy żydowskie. Świadectwo żywych*, vol. III, ed. Marian Turski, Warsaw 1996.

Khurbn tschenstochov, ed. R. Mahler, *Tschenstochover yidn*, Nyu york 1947.

Klin David, *Mitn malekh ha-moves untern orem. Mayne iberlebungen in poyln beys der natsi-okupatsye 1939–1945*, Tel Aviv 1968.

Kuryk Eliasz, „W kilku postaciach," in: *Losy żydowskie. Świadectwo żywych*, vol. III, ed. Marian Turski, Warsaw 1996.

Kusznir Motl, "Di tetikeyt fun 'bund' in der tsayt fun der hitleristisher okupatsye in tschenstochov," in: *In di yorn fun yidishn khurvn. Di shtim fun untererdishn bund*, Nyu york 1948.

Lasman Noach, *Wspomnienia z Polski*, Warsaw 1997.

Lermer Artur, *Un dokh – dem morgnroyt antkegn. Eseyen*, Tel Aviv 1999.

Libman Hersch, *Of der grenetz fun tzaitn*, Buenos Aires 1952.

Pat Emanuel, *In gerangl. Yakov Pat un zayn dor*, Nyu york 1971.

Rosenfarb Chava, *An Oak Has Fallen*, in: *Bono Wiener Remembered / Dos bono viner gedenkbukh*, Montreal 1997.

Rusiniak-Karwat Martyna, „Powojenna Polska a działacze Bundu. Zapiski rozmów z Marianem Feldmanen," *Słowo Żydowskie* 2012, no. 11 (489).

Szer Włodzimierz, *Do naszych dzieci. Wspomnienia*, Warsaw 2013.

Szychatow Szaje, *Yorn fun kamf un gerangl*, Ramat–Gan 1973.

Temkin-Berman Basia, *Dziennik z podziemia*, introduction, edited and annotated by Anka Grupińska, Paweł Szapiro, Warsaw 2000.

Tsanin Mordechai, *Grenetsn biz tsum himl*, Tel Aviv 1969.

Tsanin Mordechai, *Iber shteyn un shtok. A rayze iber hundert khoyrev-gevorene kehiles in poyln*, Tel Aviv 1952: Polish edition of the book: Canin Mordechaj, *Przez ruiny i zgliszcza. Podróż po stu zgładzonych gminach żydowskich w Polsce*, tr. Monika Adamczyk-Garbowska, Warsaw 2018.

Tschenstochov. Nayer tsugob materyal tsum bukh „Tschenstochover yidn" / Tschenstochov. A New Supplement to the Book „Tschenstochover yidn", ed. S. D. Singer, New York 1958.

Tschenstochover yidn, ed. Rafael Mahler, Nyu york 1947.

PRESS ORGANS

Biuletyn Bundu (Yiddish version: *Byuletin fun bund – oysgabe fun tsentral komitet fun bund in poyln*) 1945.

Biuletyn Żydowskiej Agencji Prasowej 1945–1949.

Byuletin fun der historisher komisye baym ts. k. fun bund in poyln 1946–1947.

Byuletin. Yediyes vegn algemeynem yidishn arbeter-bund (››bund‹‹) in poyln 1946.

Di Tsukunft / The Future 1946.

Dos naye lebn 1945–1948.

Folkstsaytung 1946–1949.

Głos Bundu 1946–1948.

Głos Wybrzeża 1965.

Lebns-fragn 1956, 1957, 1960, 1964–1965, 1972–1976, 1980, 1982, 1986, 1994–1996.

Naprzód Dolnośląski (Dziennik WK Polskiej Partii Socjalistycznej Dolnego Śląska) 1946.

Nasze Słowo. Organ zjednoczonej żydowskiej partii syjonistycznej Poalej Syjon 1946–1948.

Nowe Życie. Trybuna Wojewódzkiego Komitetu Żydów (WKŻ) na Dolnym Śląsku 1947

Oyfgang 1947.

The Jewish Labor Bund Bulletin 1947–1949.

Tygodnik Informacyjny. Organ Wojewódzkiego Komitetu Żydów Polskich w Szczecinie 1946–1948.

Unzer shtime (Paris) 1946–1949, 1965.

Unzer tsayt 1941–1960, 1965–1967, 1971–1974, 1976, 1982–1986, 1995.

Yediyes. Prese byuletyn fun tsentral komitet fun poylishe yidn 1946–1948.

Yidishe nayes fun poyln. Vekhntlekher informatsye-byuletin 1945–1947.

Yugnt veker 1937.

Yugnt veker 1946–1948.

Za Waszą i Naszą Wolność 1946.

SECONDARY SOURCES

Adelson Józef, „W Polsce zwanej Ludową," in: *Najnowsze dzieje Żydów w Polsce w zarysie (do 1950 roku)*, ed. Jerzy Tomaszewski, Warsaw 1993.

Aleksiun Natalia, „Bund a syjoniści w Polsce po drugiej wojnie światowej," in: *Bund. 100 lat historii. 1897–1997*, ed. F. Tych, J. Hensel, Warsaw 2000.

Aleksiun Natalia, *Dokąd dalej? Ruch syjonistyczny w Polsce (1944–1950)*, Warsaw 2002.

Aleksiun Natalia, "The Vicious Circle: Jews in Communist Poland, 1944–1956," *Studies in Contemporary Jewry* 2003, t. XIX.

Aleksiun Natalia, "Where was there a Future for Polish Jewry? Bundist and Zionist Polemics in Post-World War II Poland," in: *Jewish Politics in Eastern Europe: The Bund at 100,* ed. J. Jacobs, foreword by Feliks Tych New York 2001.

Aleksiun-Mądrzak Natalia, "Nielegalna emigracja Żydów z Polski w latach 1945–1947 (part I, II and III)," *Biuletyn Żydowskiego Instytutu Historycznego*" 1995, nos 2–3 (175–176); 1996, no. 3 (179); no. 4 (180).

Anti-Zionism and Antisemitism in the Contemporary World, ed. Robert S. Wistrich, London 1990

Bauer Yehuda, *Flight and Rescue. Brichah, The Organised Escape of Jewish Survivors of Eastern Europe, 1944–1948*, New York 1970.

Bauer Yehuda, *Out of Ashes. The Impact of American Jews on Post-Holocaust European Jewry*, Pergamon Press 1989.

Bażanowska Noemi, *To był mój dom. Żydowski Dom Dziecka w Krakowie w latach 1945–1957*, Kraków 2011.

Berendt Grzegorz, „Starania organizacji działających w Polsce o przystąpienie do Światowego Kongresu Żydowskiego (1945–1961)," in: Grzegorz Berendt, August Grabski, Albert Stankowski, *Studia z historii Żydów w Polsce po 1945 roku*, Warsaw 2000.

Berendt Grzegorz, „Zjednoczenie Syjonistów Demokratów 'Ichud' – 'z biało-niebieskimi sztandarami w morzu czerwonych sztandarów'," in: *Między emigracją a trwaniem. Syjoniści i komuniści żydowscy w Polsce po Holocauście,* ed. August Grabski, Grzegorz Berendt, Warsaw 2003.

Berendt Grzegorz, "Życie od nowa. Instytucje i organizacje żydowskie (1944–1950)," in: *Następstwa zagłady Żydów. Polska 1944–2010,* ed. Feliks Tych, Monika Adamczyk-Garbowska, Lublin, 2012.

Berendt Grzegorz, *Życie żydowskie w Polsce w latach 1950–1956. Z dziejów Towarzystwa Społeczno-Kulturalnego Żydów w Polsce*, Gdańsk 2006.

Berendt Grzegorz, *Żydzi na gdańskim rozdrożu* (1945–1950), Gdańsk 2000.

Bergman Stefan, "Przyczynki do historii Bundu," *Biuletyn Żydowskiego Instytutu Historycznego* 1992, nos 2–3 (162–163).

Białostocki Izrael, „Wojewódzki Komitet Żydów Polskich w Szczecinie (1946–1950)," *Biuletyn Żydowskiego Instytutu Historycznego* 1969, nos 71–72.

Biblyografye fun oysgabes aroysgebn durkh di arbeter-parteyen in poyln in di yorn 1918–1939, ed. Izrael Szajn, Varshe 1963.

Blatman Daniel, *For Our Freedom and Yours. The Jewish Labour Bund in Poland 1939–1949*, London–Portland 2003.

Blatman Daniel, "The Bund at the Beginning of the German Occupation of Poland," *Gal-Ed* 1993, vol. XIII.

Blomqvist Håkan, *Socialism på jiddisch: judiska Arbeter Bund i Sverige*, Stockholm 2020 (English version: *Socialism in Yiddish: The Jewish Labor Bund in Sweden*, tr. H. Blomquist, P (H.) Glasser, Södertörn 2022.)

Bronsztejn Szyja, „Ludność żydowska Dolnego Śląska – ostatnia fotografia," in: *Z dziejów ludności żydowskiej na Dolnym Śląsku*, ed. K. Matwijowski, Wrocław 1991.

Bronsztejn Szyja, „Uwagi o ludności żydowskiej na Dolnym Śląsku w pierwszych latach po wyzwoleniu," *Biuletyn Żydowskiego Instytutu Historycznego* 1970, no. 3 (75).

Brumberg Abraham, „On Reading the Bundist Press," *East European Jewish Affairs* 2003, vol. XXXIII, no. 1.

Bund amol un haynt, Tel Aviv 1992.

Bund. 100 lat historii 1897–1997, ed. Feliks Tych, Jürgen Hensel, Warsaw 2000.

Bundist Legacy after the Second World War "Real" Place versus "Displaced" Time, Series: Free Ebrei, Vol. 1, ed. Vincenzo Pinto, Leiden–Boston 2018.

Cała Alina, *Ochrona bezpieczeństwa fizycznego Żydów w Polsce powojennej. Komisje Specjalne przy Centralnym Komitecie Żydów w Polsce*, Warsaw 2014.

Cała Alina, **Grabski August**, „Provincial Jewish Committe of Warsaw (WKZ) (1944–1949)," in: *Żydzi Warszawy*, ed. Eleonora Bergman, Olga Zienkiewicz, Warsaw 2000.

Cesariani David, "The Perdition Affair," in: *Anti-Zionism and Antisemitism in the Contemporary World*, ed. Robert S. Wistrich, London 1990.

Chajn Michał, „Stosunek rządów polskich do powstania żydowskiej siedziby narodowej w Palestynie w latach 1945–1948," *Biuletyn Żydowskiego Instytutu Historycznego* 2000, no. 3.

Checinski Michal, *Poland. Communism. Nationalism. Anti Semitism*, New York 1982.

Chomsky Noam, *Hegemony or Survival. America's Quest for Global Dominance*, Metropolitan Books, 2003.

Datner Helena, *Po Zagładzie. Społeczna historia żydowskich domów dziecka, szkół, kół studentów w dokumentach Centralnego Komitetu Żydów w Polsce*, Warsaw 2016.

Datner Helena, „Szkoły Centralnego Komitetu Żydów w Polsce w latach 1944–1949," *Biuletyn Żydowskiego Instytutu Historycznego* 1994, nos 1–3 (169–171).

Datner-Śpiewak Helena, „Instytucje opieki nad dzieckiem i szkoły powszechne Centralnego Komitetu Żydów Polskich w latach 1945–1946," *Biuletyn Żydowskiego Instytutu Historycznego* 1981, no. 3 (119).

de Bollardière Constance Pâris, "The Jewish Labor Committee's Bundist Relief Network in France, 1945–1948," *Kwartalnik Historii Żydów* 2013, no. 2 (246).

Di geshikhte fun bund, vols. I–III, ed. G. Aronson, S. Dubnov-Erlich, J. Sh. Hertz, E. Nowogrodzki, Kh. Sh. Kazdan, E. Scherer, Nyu york 1960–1966.

Di geshikhte fun bund, vol. IV, ed. S. Dubnov-Erlich, J. Sh. Hertz, Kh. Sh. Kazdan, E. Scherer, Nyu york 1972.

Di geshikhte fun bund, vol. V, Nyu york 1981.

Dobroszycki Lucjan, *Survivors of the Holocaust in Poland. A Portrait Based on Jewish Community Records 1944–1947*, New York 1994.

Dobroszycki Lucjan, „Zaginiona prasa konspiracyjna z lat 1939–1945," *Najnowsze Dzieje Polski 1939–1945*, 1963, vol. VII.

Doyres bundistin, ed. Jacob Sholem Hertz, vol. I–III, Nyu york 1956–1968.

Engel David, „Bund po Holocauście; pomiędzy odnową a samolikwidacją," in: *Bund. 100 lat historii. 1897–1997*, ed. Feliks Tych, Jürgen Hensel, Warsaw 2000.

Engel David, "The Bund after the Holocaust: Between Renewal and Self-Liquidation," in: *Jewish Politics in Eastern Europe: The Bund at 100,* ed. Jack Jacobs, foreword by Feliks Tych, New York 2001.

Engel David, "Patterns of Anti-Jewish Violence in Poland, 1944–1946," *Yad Vashem Studies* 1997, no. 26.

Engel David, "The Reconstruction of Jewish Communal Institutions in Postwar Poland: The Origins of the Central Committee of Polish Jews, 1944–1945," *East European Politics Societies*, 1996, vol. X, no. 1.

Fiction and Truth. A Reply to the Attacks of the Jewsih Bundists on the Jewish Conference and Zionism, USA.

Finkelstein Norman G., *Beyond Hutzpah. On the Misuse of Anti-Semitism and the Abuse of History*, Verso Books 2008.

Flisiak Dominik, *Działalność syjonistów-rewizjonistów w Polsce w latach 1944/1945–1950,* Lublin 2020.

Frankel Jonathan, *The Soviet Regime and Anti-Zionism: An Analysis*, Jerusalem 1984.

Friedgut Theodore H., *Soviet Anti-Zionism: Origins, Forms and Development*, Jerusalem 1984.

Fuks Marian, *Muszkat Zdzisław,* in: *Polski Słownik Biograficzny*, vol. 22 (1977).

Fuks Marian, „Prasa żydowska w Polsce XIX i pierwszej połowy XX wieku (do końca II wojny światowej)," *Rocznik Historii Czasopiśmiennictwa Polskiego* 1977, vol. XII, n. 1.

Gechtman Roni, "Socialist Mass Politics Through Sport: The Bund's Morgnshtern in Poland, 1926–1939," *Journal of Sport History* 1999, no. 2, vol. XXVI.

Gechtman Roni, "The Debates on the National and Jewish Question in the Second International and the Jewish Labor Bund, 1889–1914," in: *Rebels Against Zion. Studies on the Jewish Left Anti-Zionism*, ed. A. Grabski, Warsaw 2011.

Gechtman Roni, „The Rise as Reflected in the *Naye Folkstsaytung* 1935–1936," *Gal-Ed* 2000, vol. XVII.

Gorny Yosef, *Converging Alternatives. The Bund and the Zionist Labor Movement, 1897–1985*, New York 2006.

Grabski August, *Centralny Komitet Żydów w Polsce (1944–1950). Historia polityczna,* Warsaw 2015.

Grabski August, „Działalność Frakcji PPR w CKŻP (jesień 1944 r. – czerwiec 1946 r.," in: August Grabski, Grzegorz Berendt, *Między emigracją a trwaniem. Syjoniści i komuniści żydowscy w Polsce po Holocauście*, Warsaw 2003.

Grabski August, *Działalność komunistów wśród Żydów w Polsce (1944–1949)*, Warsaw 2004.

Grabski August, "Jews and Political Life in Poland from 1944 to 1949," in: *Jewish Presence in Absence. The Aftermath of the Holocaust in Poland, 1944–2010,* eds. Feliks Tych. Monika Adamczyk-Garbowska, tr. G. Dąbkowski, J. Taylor-Kucia, Jerusalem 2014.

Grabski August, *Lewica przeciwko Izraelowi. Studia o żydowskim lewicowym antysyjonizmie*, Warsaw 2008.

Grabski August, „Wiktor Szulman," *Polski Słownik Biograficzny*, n. 201 (vol. 49/2), 2013.

Grabski August, *Żydowski ruch kombatancki w Polsce w latach 1944–1949*, Warsaw 2002.

Grabski August, *„Żydzi a polskie życie polityczne (1944–1949),"* in: *Następstwa zagłady Żydów. Polska 1944–2010*, eds. Feliks Tych, Monika Adamczyk-Garbowska, Lublin 2012.

Grabski August, **Rusiniak Martyna**, "Jewish Communists after the Holocaust and the Languages of Polish Jewry," in: *Under the Red Banner. Yiddish Culture in the Communist Countries in the Postwar Era*, eds. Elvira Grözinger, Magdalena Ruta, Wiesbaden 2008.

Grabski August, **Rusiniak Martyna**, „Język żydowski jako przedmiot sporów politycznych wśród polskich Żydów (1944–1949)," in: *Jidyszland – polskie przestrzenie*, eds. Ewa Geller, Monika Polit, Warsaw 2008.

Grabski August, **Rusiniak Martyna**, „*Żydowscy komuniści po Holokauście wobec języków polskiego żydostwa*," in: *Nusech Pojln. Studia z dziejów kultury jidysz w powojennej Polsce*, ed. Magdalena Ruta, Kraków–Budapest 2008.

Grabski August, Wójcicki Maciej, *Żydowski Związek Wojskowy – historia przywrócona*, Warsaw 2008.

Grądzka-Rejak Martyna, „'Zbierać informacje o akcji przygotowawczej i sytuacji w organizacji…'. Działalność 'referenta do spraw żydowskich' przy WUPB w Krakowie w latach 1947–1950," *Pamięć i Sprawiedliwość* 2021, no. 2 (38).

Grużlewska Anna, *Polska Jerozolima. Fenomen żydowskiego osiedla w powiecie dzierżoniowskim. 1945–1950 / Polish Jerusalem. The Phenomenon of the Jewish Settlement in the County of Dzierżoniów. 1945–1950*, Dzierżoniów 2019.

Grynberg Michał, "Problemy zatrudnienia ludności żydowskiej w Polsce w pierwszych latach po II wojnie światowej," *Biuletyn Żydowskiego Instytutu Historycznego* 1986, nos 1–2 (137–138).

Grynberg Michał, *Żydowska spółdzielczość pracy w Polsce w latach 1945–1949*, Warsaw 1986.

Heksel Bartosz, *Żydowscy adwokaci w przedwojennym Krakowie*, Kraków 2020.

Hertz Jacob Sholem, *Der bund in bilder. 1897–1957 / The Jewish Labour Bund. A pictorial history. 1897–1957*, Nyu york 1958.

Hertz Jacob Sholem, *Di geshikhte fun a yugnt. Der kleyner bund – yugnt-bund tsukunft in poyln*, Nyu york 1946.

Hertz Jacob Sholem, *Di geshikhte fun bund in lodzh*, Nyu york 1958.

Hertz Jacob Sholem, „*Folkstsaytung* 1918–1939," in: *Di yidishe prese vos iz geven*, eds. D. Plinker, Mordechai Canin (Tsanin), Sholem Rozenfeld, Tel Aviv 1979.

Holzer Jerzy (Pański Wacław), *Agonia PPS. Socjaliści polscy w sojuszu z PPR 1944–1948*, Warsaw 1981.

Horn Maurycy, „Działalność Żydowskiego Instytutu Historycznego w Polsce w latach 1944–1979," in: *Trzydzieści pięć lat działalności Żydowskiego Instytutu Historycznego w Polsce Ludowej (Dzieje Instytutu i jego zbiory)*, Warsaw 1980.

Hułas Magdalena, "Polskie starania o uwolnienie Wiktora Altera i Henryka Erlicha," *Kwartalnik Historii Żydów* 2020, no. 274.

Israeli Raphael, "Anti-Jewish Attitudes in the Arabic Media, 1975–1981," in: *Anti-Zionism and Antisemitism in the Contemporary World*, ed. Robert S. Wistrich, London 1990.

Jacobs Jack, "Bundist Anti-Zionism in Interwar Poland," *Tel Aviver Jahrbuch für Deutsche Geschichte* 2005, vol. 33.

Jacobs Jack, *Bundist Counterculture in Interwar Poland*, Syracuse 2009.

Jacobs Jack, "The Bund in Vilna, 1918–1939," *Polin* 2013, vol. 25.

Jewish Politics in Eastern Europe: The Bund at 100, ed. Jack Jacobs, New York 2001.

Jewish Presence in Absence. The Aftermath of the Holocaust in Poland, 1944–2010, eds. Feliks Tych. Monika Adamczyk-Garbowska, tr. G. Dąbkowski, J. Taylor-Kucia, Jerusalem 2014; Polish edition: *Następstwa zagłady Żydów. Polska 1944–2010*, eds. Feliks Tych, Monika Adamczyk-Garbowska, Lublin 2012.

Johnpoll Bernard, *The Politics of Futility. The General Jewish Workers Bund of Poland (1917–1943)*, New York 1967.

Kaczyńska Katarzyna, *"Orać zagon lepszej doli?" Żydowskie rolnictwo w Polsce w latach 1945–1950*, Warsaw 2021.

Kaliski Bartosz, „Związek nasz bratni," *Nowe Książki* 2018, no. 1.

Kawski Tomasz, „Mniejszość żydowska w województwie pomorskim (bydgoskim) w latach 1945–1956," in: *Kujawy i Pomorze w latach 1945–1956. Od zakończenia okupacji do przełomu październikowego*, eds. W. Jastrzębski, M. Krajewski, Włocławek 2001.

Kendziorek Piotr, *Program i praktyka produktywizacji Żydów polskich w działalności CKŻP*, Warsaw 2016.

Kersten Krystyna, *Polacy – Żydzi – Komunizm. Anatomia półprawd 1939–1968*, Warsaw 1992.

Kopciowski Adam, "Herszenhorn Szloma," in: *Sylwetki Żydów lubelskich. Leksykon*, eds. Adam Kopciowski, Andrzej Trzciński, Sławomir Jacek Żurek, Monika Adamczyk-Garbowska, Lublin 2019.

Korzeniowski Józef, „Bibliografia czasopism żydowskich wychodzących w PRL, 1944–1950," *Biuletyn Żydowskiego Instytutu Historycznego* 1986, nos 3–4.

Korzeniowski Józef, „'Dos Naje Lebn' – pierwsza gazeta żydowska w PRL," *Biuletyn Żydowskiego Instytutu Historycznego* 1981, no. 3 (119).

Kowalska Irena, „Kartoteka TOZ z lat 1946–1947 (Żydowskie dzieci uratowane z Holocaustu)," *Biuletyn Żydowskiego Instytutu Historycznego* 1995–1996, nos 3/95–2/96 (175–178).

Kozłowska Magdalena, *Świetlana przyszłość? Żydowski Związek Młodzieżowy Cukunft wobec wyzwań międzywojennej Polski*, Kraków 2016.

Koźmińska-Frejlak Ewa, *Po Zagładzie. Praktyki asymilacyjne Ocalałych jako strategie zadomawiania się w Polsce (1944/45–1950),* Warsaw 2022.

Koźmińska-Frejlak Ewa, „Powojenna prasa żydowska w języku polskim (1944–1950)," in: *Studia z dziejów trójjęzycznej prasy żydowskiej na ziemiach polskich (XIX–XX w.)*, ed. Joanna Nalewajko-Kulikov, Warsaw 2012.

Kwiek Julian, „Dzieje ludności żydowskiej w Tarnowie po II wojnie światowej," *Kwartalnik Historii Żydów* 2005, no. 3.

Kwiek Julian, *Żydzi, Łemkowie, Słowacy w województwie krakowskim w latach 1945–1949/1950*, Kraków 1998.

Lech Andrzej, **Radziszewska Krystyna**, **Rykała Andrzej** (ed.), *Społeczność żydowska i niemiecka w Łodzi po 1945 roku*, Łódź 2010.

Lerer-yiskor-bukh. Di umgekumene lerer fun tsysho shul in poyln, ed. Khaim Shloyme Kazdan, Nyu york 1952–1954.

Lerman Antony, "Fictive Anti-Zionism: Third World, Arab and Muslim Variations," in: *Anti-Zionism and Antisemitism in the Contemporary World*, ed. Robert S. Wistrich, London 1990.

Lewinsky Tamar, "Polish-Jewish Displaced Persons in Occupied Germany," in: *Jewish Presence in Absence. The Aftermath of the Holocaust in Poland, 1944–2010,* eds. Feliks Tych and Monika Adamczyk-Garbowska, trans. G. Dąbkowski, J. Taylor-Kucia, Jerusalem 2014.

Mieczkowski Janusz, *Między emigracją a asymilacją. Szkice o szczecińskich Żydach w latach 1945–1997,* Szczecin 1998.

Mieczkowski Janusz, *Żydzi, Niemcy i Ukraińcy na Pomorzu Zachodnim w latach 1945–1956. Liczba, położenie i działalność polityczna*, Szczecin 1994.

Mironowicz Eugeniusz, *Polityka narodowościowa PRL*, Białystok 2000.

Mironowicz Eugeniusz, „Założenia i cele polityki narodowościowej Polski Ludowej," in: *Internacjonalizm czy…?. Działania organów bezpieczeństwa państw komunistycznych wobec mniejszości narodowych (1944–1989)*, Warsaw–Wrocław 2011.

Mishkinsky Moshe, "Between the 'Old Bund and the 'Polish Bund'," *Gal-Ed* 1993, vol. XIII.

Nalewajko-Kulikov Joanna, *Obywatel Jidyszlandu. Rzecz o żydowskich komunistach w Polsce,* Warsaw 2009; English edition: *A Citizen of Yiddishland. Dovid Sfard and the Jewish Communist Milieu in Poland*, tr. Paul Glasser, Berlin 2020.

Nalewajko-Kulikov Joanna, „'Syjonistyczna z lekkim zabarwieniem PPR-owskim'. 'Dos naje lebn' (1945–1959) – gazeta Centralnego Komitetu Żydów w Polsce," in: *Żydzi a lewica. Zbiór studiów historycznych*, ed. August Grabski, Warsaw 2007.

Namysło Aleksandra, *Utracone nadzieje. Ludność żydowska w województwie śląskim/katowickim w latach 1945–1970 / Lost Hopes. Jews in the Silesian / Katowickie Voivodeship in Years 1945–1970*, Katowice 2012.

Nowogródzki Emanuel, *The Jewish Labor Bund in Poland 1915–1939. From its Emergence as an Independent Political Party Until the Beginning of World War II*, tr. Mark Nowogrodzki, Rockville 2001 (Polish edition: *Żydowska Partia Robotnicza BUND w Polsce w latach 1915–1939*, tr. P. Sawicka, Warsaw 2005).

Olejnik Leszek, *Polityka narodowościowa Polski w latach 1944–1960*, Łódź 2003.

Olejnik Leszek, „Prasa żydowska w Łodzi w latach 1945–1949," *Acta Judaica Lodziensia* 2011, no. 1.

Olejnik Leszek, "Społeczność żydowska. Struktury życia społeczno-politycznego łódzkich Żydów w latach 1945–1950," in: *Społeczność żydowska i niemiecka w Łodzi po 1945 roku*, eds. Andrzej Lech, Krystyna Radziszewska, Andrzej Rykała, Łódź 2010.

Olejnik Leszek, "Wojewódzki Komitet Żydowski w Łodzi – powstanie i główne kierunki działalności (1945–1950)," *Biuletyn Żydowskiego Instytutu Historycznego* 1998, no. 3.

Orlicki Józef, *Szkice z dziejów stosunków polsko-żydowskich 1918–1949*, Szczecin 1983.

Orlicki Józef, „Wstęp do monografii o ludności żydowskiej w latach 1945–1949 w Szczecinie," *Przegląd Zachodniopomorski* 1972, vol. XVI, no. 4.

Person Katarzyna, „'I am a Jewish DP. A Jew from the Eternal Nowhere'. Jews from Poland in Displaced Persons Camps in the Occupation Zones of West Germany: Encounters with Poles and Memories of Poland, 1945–1946," *Kwartalnik Historii Żydów* 2013, no. 2 (246).

Pickhan Gertrud, *„Gegen den Strom" der Allgemeine Jüdische Arbeiterbund „BUND" in Polen 1918–1939*, Stuttgart-München 2001, Polish edition: *Pod prąd. Powszechny Żydowski Związek Robotniczy Bund w Polsce w latach 1918–1939*, tr. Adam Peszke, ed. Joanna Nalewajko-Kulikov, Warsaw 2017.

Pickhan Getrud, „'That Incredible History of the Polish Bund Written in a Soviet Prison': The NKVD Files on Henryk Erlich and Wiktor Alter," *Polin* 1997, vol. X.

Pickhan Gertrud, "Uwagi o Bundzie," *Kwartalnik Historii Żydów* 2003, no. 1 (205).

Pisarski Maciej, „'Na żydowskiej ulicy' Szkic z dziejów żydowskiej frakcji PPR i zespołu PZPR przy CKŻP. 1945–1951," *Biuletyn Żydowskiego Instytutu Historycznego* 1997, no. 2.

Polit Monika, "Jankiew Pat. 'Żydowski brat z ziemi amerykańskiej, który jest też polskim Żydem'," *Zagłada Żydów. Studia i Materiały* 2020, no. 16.

Pogromy Żydów na ziemiach polskich w XIX i XX wieku, vol. 4: *Holokaust i powojnie (1939–1946)*, ed. August Grabski, Warsaw 2019.

Polski słownik judaistyczny, vols. I–II, eds. Zofia Borzymińska, Rafał Żebrowski, Warsaw 2003.

Prekerowa Teresa, *Konspiracyjna Rada Pomocy Żydom w Warszawie 1942–1945*, Warsaw 1982.

Propola Krystian, "Propaganda and Methods of Persuasion of Postwar Bund Circles on the Example of *The Jewish Labor Bund Bulletin*," *Piotrkowskie Zeszyty Historyczne* 2021, vol. 22, n. 3.

Rebels Against Zion. Studies on the Jewish Left Anti-Zionism, ed. August Grabski, Warsaw 2011.

Redlich Shimon, *Life in Transit. Jews in Postwar Lodz, 1945–1950*, Boston 2010.

Redlich Shimon, *War, Holocaust and Stalinism. A Documented Study of the Jewish Anti-Fascist Committee in the USSR*, Luxemburg 1995.

Rosner Anna M., *Obraz społeczności ocalałych w Centralnej Kartotece Wydziału Ewidencji i Statystyki CKŻP*, Warsaw 2018.

Rowiński Aleksander, *Zygielbojma śmierć i życie*, Warsaw 2004.

Rusiniak-Karwat Martyna, „Bund," in: *Encyklopedia getta warszawskiego. Wybrane hasła*, ed. Maria Ferenc, Warsaw 2024.

Rusiniak-Karwat Martyna, "Bundists and the issue of emigration from Poland after the Second World War," *European Spatial Research and Policy* 2021, vol. 28.

Rusiniak-Karwat Martyna, "Bundists in the Soviet Union during World War II," in: *Bundist Legacy after the Second World War "Real" Place versus "Displaced" Time*, Series: Free Ebrei, Vol. 1, ed. Vincenzo Pinto, Leiden–Boston 2018.

Rusiniak-Karwat Martyna, "Bundists under Soviet Occupation: The Case of Matwiej Bernstein," *Studia Polityczne* 2017, no. 3 (45).

Rusiniak-Karwat Martyna, „Dzieci przyszłością partii. Skif w powojennej Polsce," *Kwartalnik Historii Żydów* 2018, no. 4 (268).

Rusiniak-Karwat Martyna, „Komisja Historyczna prze Centralnym Komitecie Bundu," *Kolbojnik. Biuletyn Gminy Wyznaniowej Żydowskiej w Warszawie* 2013/5774, no. 3 (72).

Rusiniak-Karwat Martyna, „Marek Edelman – socjalista i strażnik pamięci. Narodziny legendy (1944–1949)," *Studia Polityczne* 2013, no. 32.

Rusiniak-Karwat Martyna, "Marek Edelman (1919–2009). Szkic biograficzny," in: Marek Edelman, *Nieznane zapiski o getcie warszawskim*, ed. Martyna Rusiniak-Karwat, Warsaw 2017.

Rusiniak-Karwat Martyna, *Nowe życie na zgliszczach. Bund w Polsce w latach 1944–1949*, Warsaw 2016.

Rusiniak-Karwat Martyna, „Odradzanie się społeczności żydowskiej w Polsce na przykładzie Bundu," in: *Narody i polityka, Studia ofiarowane profesorowi Jerzemu Tomaszewskiemu*, eds. August Grabski, Artur Markowski, Warsaw 2010.

Rusiniak-Karwat Martyna, „Odrodzenie Bundu w powojennej Warszawie. Życie polityczne polskich Żydów," *Słowo Żydowskie* 2011, no. 12 (478).

Rusiniak-Karwat Martyna, "The Road to Freedom. Jewish Socialists in Shanghai," *Hemispheres. Studies on Cultures and Societies* 2017, no. 4 (32).

Rusiniak-Karwat Martyna, "*Tsukunft* publishing operations in Poland after 1945," *pl.it / rassegna italiana di argomenti polacchi* 2022, no. 13.

Rusiniak-Karwat Martyna, „W imię socjalizmu – poszukiwanie miejsca na ziemi. Przypadek Leona (Libera) Gotloba," *Pamięć i Sprawiedliwość* 2022, no. 1 (30).

Rykała Andrzej, „Łódź na mapie skupisk żydowskich Polski (po 1945 r.)," in: *Społeczność żydowska i niemiecka w Łodzi po 1945 roku*, eds. Andrzej Lech, Krystyna Radziszewska, Andrzej Rykała, Łódź 2010.

Rykała Andrzej, *W reakcji na powojenną przemoc antysemicką. Samoobrona Żydów w Łodzi – uwarunkowania społeczno-polityczne i przestrzenne*, Łódź 2020.

Sakowska Ruta, *Ludzie z dzielnicy zamkniętej*, Warsaw 1993.

Samuś Paweł, "The Bund Organization in Łódź, 1898–1939," in: *Jewish Politics in Eastern Europe: The Bund at 100*, ed. Jack Jacobs, New York 2001.

Schatz Jaff, *The Generation. The Rise and Fall of Jewish Communists in Poland*, Berkeley–Los Angeles–Oxford 1991; Polish edition: *Pokolenie. Polscy Żydzi komuniści – wzlot i upadek*, intr. Piotr Osęka, tr. S. Kowalski, Warsaw 2020.

Segev Tom, *The Seventh Million: The Israelis and the Holocaust*, tr. H. Watzman, New York 2000.

Semczyszyn Magdalena, „Nielegalna emigracja Żydów z Polski 1944–1947 – kontekst międzynarodowy," *Dzieje Najnowsze* 2018, no. 1.

Semczyszyn Magdalena, "Szczecin – 'najmłodsze żydowskie osiedle w powojennej Polsce'. Miejsca związane z działalnością Żydów w mieście w latach 1945–1950," in: *Szczecin i jego miejsca. Trzecia Konferencja Edukacyjna, 10 XII 2010 r.*, ed. Katarzyna Rembacka, Szczecin 2010.

Semczyszyn Magdalena, Szaynok Bożena, „Kwestia ludności żydowskiej," in: *Aparat bezpieczeństwa wobec mniejszości narodowych w Polsce w latach 1944–1956*, ed. Jarosław Syrnyk, Warsaw 2019.

Shapiro Robert Moses, *The Polish Kehile Elections of 1936: A Revolution Re-Examined*, New York 1988.

Shlomi Hana, "The Reception and Settlement of Jewish Repatriants from the Soviet Union in Lower Silesia, 1946," *Gal-Ed* 2000, vol. XVII.

Skibińska Alina, „Powroty ocalałych," in: *Prowincja noc. Życie i zagłada Żydów w Dystrykcie Warszawskim*, eds. Barbara Engelking, Jacek Leociak, Dariusz Libionka, Warsaw 2007.

Slucki David, *The International Jewish Labor Bund after 1945. Toward a Global History*, New Brunswick–New Jersey–London 2012.

Sommer Anna, „Działalność służb bezpieczeństwa wobec środowiska żydowskiego na terenie województwa krakowskiego w latach 1949–1954, na przykładzie rozpracowania obiektowego o kryptonimie 'Jordan' i 'Zator'," *Kwartalnik Historii Żydów* 2007, no. 224.

Sommer-Schneider Anna, *Sze'erit hapleta. Ocaleni z Zagłady. Działalność American Jewish Joint Distribution Committee w Polsce w latach 1945–1989*, Kraków 2014.

Sowiński Paweł, *Komunistyczne święto. Obchody 1 maja w latach 1948–1954*, Warsaw 2000.

Staar, Richard F., *Poland 1944–1962. The Sovietization of a Captive People*, Louisiana State 1962.

Szaynok Bożena, "Bund and Jewish Fraction of the Polish Workers' Party in Poland after 1945," in: *Bundist Legacy after the Second World War "Real" Place versus "Displaced" Time*, Series: Free Ebrei, Vol. 1, ed. Vincenzo Pinto, Leiden–Boston 2018.

Szaynok Bożena, „Bund i komuniści żydowscy w Polsce po 1945 r.," in: *Bund. 100 lat historii. 1897–1997*, ed. Feliks Tych, Jürgen Hensel, Warsaw 2000.

Szaynok Bożena, "Jews in Lower Silesia 1945–1950," in: *Jews in Silesia*, eds. Marcin Wodziński, J. Spyra, Kraków 2001.

Szaynok Bożena, „Komuniści w Polsce (PPR/PZPR) wobec ludności żydowskiej (1945–1953)," *Pamięć i Sprawiedliwość* 2004, no. 2.

Szaynok Bożena, *Ludność żydowska na Dolnym Śląsku 1944–1950*, Wrocław 2000.

Szaynok Bożena, „Problematyka żydowska w PPR i PZPR (1944–1989)," in: *PZPR jako machina władzy*, eds. Dariusz Stola, Krzysztof Persak, Warsaw 2011.

Szaynok Bożena, „Sprawa Arie Lernera – nieznany fragment 'walki z syjonizmem' w Polsce w pierwszej połowie lat 50-ych," in: *Polska w podzielonym świecie po II wojnie światowej*, ed. Marian Wojciechowski, Toruń 2002.

Szaynok Bożena, „Tematyka żydowska w działalności MBP/MSW (1945–1989)," in: *Internacjonalizm czy...? Działania organów bezpieczeństwa państw komunistycznych wobec mniejszości narodowych (1944–1989)*, Warsaw–Wrocław 2011.

Szaynok Bożena, „Walka z syjonizmem w Polsce (1948–1953)," in: *Komunizm. Ideologia, system, ludzie*, ed. Tomasz Szarota, Warsaw 2001.

Szaynok Bożena, *Z historią i Moskwą w tle. Polska a Izrael 1944–1968*, Warsaw 2007.

Szaynok Bożena, „Żydzi w Dzierżoniowie (1945–1950)," in: *Dzierżoniów – wiek miniony. Materiały pokonferencyjne*, eds. Sebastian Ligarski, Tomasz Przerwa, Wrocław 2007.

Szwarz P., *Folkstsaytung*, in: *Fun noentn oyver*, vol. II: *Yidishe prese in varshe*, Nyu york 1956.

Tokarska-Bakir Joanna, *Pod klątwą. Społeczny portret pogromu kieleckiego*, 2 volumes, Warsaw 2018.

Tomaszewski Jerzy, "Niepodległa Rzeczpospolita," in: *Najnowsze dzieje Żydów w Polsce w zarysie (do 1950 roku)*, ed. Jerzy Tomaszewski, Warsaw 1993.

Trębacz Michał, „Bund – Międzynarodówka – PPS. Historia współzależności," *Biuletyn Instytutu Pamięci Narodowej* 2011, no. 7 (128).

Trębacz Michał, „Gutman – Nejman – Stupaj. Żydowskie życie w powojennej Łodzi na przykładzie wybranych biografii," in: *Druga Rzeczpospolita i nie tylko. Ludzie, środowiska, idee*, ed. J. Pietrzak, Łódź 2016.

Trębacz Michał, *Izrael Lichtenstein. Biografia żydowskiego socjalisty*, Łódź 2016.

Urzyńska Dorota, "Kontakty Adama Ciołkosza z przywódcami Bundu Wiktorem Alterem i Henrykiem Erlichem," *Biuletyn Żydowskiego Instytutu Historycznego* 1999, no. 3 (191).

Waszkiewicz Ewa, „Powstanie, rozwój i zanik skupiska Żydów na Dolnym Śląsku (1945–1968)," in: *Współcześni Żydzi – Polska i diaspora. Wybrane zagadnienia*, ed. Ewa Waszkiewicz, Wrocław 2007.

Weinstock Nathan, *Zionism: False Messiah*, London 1979.

Wieczorek Paweł, „Żydzi wałbrzyscy po II wojnie światowej," *Kwartalnik Historii Żydów* 2004, no. 3.

Wieczorek Paweł, *Żydzi w Wałbrzychu i powiecie wałbrzyskim 1945–1968*, Wrocław–Warsaw 2017.

Wierzcholska Agnieszka, *Nur Erinnerungen und Steine sind geblieben. Leben und Sterben einer polnisch-jüdischen Stadt: Tarnów 1918–1945*, Paderborn 2022, (Polish edition: *Wspomnienia i kamienie. Życie i śmierć polsko-żydowskiego miasta. Tarnów 1918–1956*, tr. Justyna Górny, Kraków–Budapest–Syrakuzy 2023).

Wistrich Robert S. (ed.), *Anti-Zionism and Antisemitism in the Contemporary World*, London 1990.

Wistrich Robert S., *Soviet Anti-Zionism and Anti-Semitism, Another Cycle*, Jerusalem 1984.

Wolff Frank, *Neue Welten in der Neuen Welt. Die transnationale Geszichte des Allgemeinen Jüdischen Arbeiterbundes 1897–1947*, Köln–Weimar–Wien 2014; English edition: *Yiddish Revolutionaries in Migration. The Transnational History of the Jewish Labour Bund*, tr. Loren Balhorn, Jan-Peter Herrmann, Leiden–Boston 2021.

Wolff Frank, "The Collateral Prisoner. A Bundist Holocaust Survivor between Nazi Perpetrators, Anti-Communism and British World Politics," *The International of Communist Studies* 2011, no. 24.

Zaremba Marcin, *Wielka trwoga. Polska 1944–1947. Ludowa reakcja na kryzys*, Kraków 2012.

Zeleznikow John, "Life at the end of the world: a Jewish Partisan in Melbourne," *Holocaust Studies: a journal of culture and history* 2011, no. 16 (3).

Zimmerman Joshua D., *Poles, Jews and the Politics of Nationality, 1892–1914*, Madison 2004.

Żbikowski Andrzej, *Sąd Społeczny przy CKŻP. Wojenne rozliczenia społeczności żydowskiej w Polsce*, Warsaw 2014.

Żydzi częstochowscy. Słownik biograficzny, ed. Juliusz Sętowski, Częstochowa 2020.

Internet:

Grużlewska Anna, „Ogólnożydowski Związek Robotniczy 'Bund' na terenie powiatu dzierżoniowskiego," *Bibliotheca Bielaviana 2015*, 2016, online https://www.academia.edu/108869609/Og%C3%B3lno%C5%BCydowski_Zwi%C4%85zek_Robotniczy_Bund_na_terenie_powiatu_dzier%C5%BConiowskiego [access: 31 January 2023].

Gurwicz Samuel, in: https://indeksrepresjonowanych.pl/szczegoly/bc567d78-f7fc-41a8-bf20-afc3010002ba [access: 10 September 2024].

Marks Stan, *Obituary Bono Wiener, https://collections.ajhs.com.au/Detail/objects/53363* [access: 20 September 2024].

Rusiniak-Karwat Martyna, *Zygielbojm Szmul Mordechaj* [online] https://sztetl.org.pl/en/biographies/4542-zygielbojm-szmul-mordechaj [access: 10 September 2024].

Stanisław Mikołajczyk [online] https://www.ipsb.nina.gov.pl/a/biografia/stanislaw-mikolajczyk-1901-1966-premier-rp-dzialacz-ludowy [access: 10 September 2024].

W. Blum, in: Yad Vashem [online] http://www.yadvashem.org/yv/en/exhibitions/otwock/histories_blum.asp [access: 20 August 2013] and [online] https://www.yadvashem.org/education/testimony-films/aviva-blum.html [access: 15 September 2024].

https://www.czestochowajews.org/history/yizkor-books/liber-brener/ [access: 10 September 2024].

https://congressforjewishculture.org/people/1940/Gershon,%20(Mortkhe)%20(June%2028,%201915%E2%80%93) [access: 10 September 2024].

https://www.monash.edu/arts/acjc/yiddish-melbourne/biographies/bono-wiener [access: 20 September 2024].

https://www.monash.edu/arts/acjc/yiddish-melbourne/biographies/avram-zeleznikow [access: 10 December 2018].

http://www.yivoarchives.org/index.php?p=collections/controlcard&id=34156 [access: 10 August 2024].

Index of Names

Illustrations

Photo 1. Łódź, July 1946. Funeral of Fishke Nejman, murdered under unexplained circumstances (from the ŻIH collection, Documentation Department)

Photo 2. Łódź, July 1946. Funeral of Fishke Nejman. In the first row, representatives of the Łódź Bund with a flag. Behind them, members of the Bund Central Committee, from L to R: Dr Shlomo Herszenhorn, Dr Michał Szuldenfrei, Salo Fiszgrund, Gershon Fogel, Ignacy Falk (from the ŻIH collection, Documentation Department)

Photo 3. Dzierżoniów 1946/1947. Dzierżoniów Bund Committee's secretariat at work. From R to L: Toyba (Tauba) Zamieczkowska (Tsukunft), Getsl Lustgartn, Brakhe Arenfeld Erder (ORT), Józef Lejst (technical secretary) (from the ŻIH collection, Documentation Department)

Photo 4. Legnica 1946/1947. The Bund kitchen staff (from the ŻIH collection, Documentation Department)

Photo 5. Wrocław 1946/1947. Representatives of the Wrocław Bund Committee. They're wearing armbands with the inscription 'Bund' in Yiddish on their left forearms. The Bund banner is visible on the left, the Tsukunft banner is on the right. In the centre, on a curtain with the inscription *Bund*, there are portraits – starting from the left. Victor Alter, Karl Marx, Henryk Erlich (from the ŻIH collection, Documentation Department)

Photo 6. Tarnów 1st May (undated). The Bundists at the May Day parade. Behind the Bund's delegation, the members of the Tsukunft (in uniforms) (from the ŻIH collection, Documentation Department)

Photo 7. The Bund Committee of Ziębice, 1947. Celebration of the party's 50th anniversary. Inscription at the top: 'Bund'. In the portraits, from the left: Józef Portnoy (Noyekh), Shmul (Artur) Zygielbojm, Vladimir Kosovsky. Between the portraits, the symbol of the Bund (3 arrows), below – the banners of the Tsukunft and the Bund, on the right – the banner of the PPS (from the ŻIH collection, Documentation Department).

Sz. tow. ....

Komitet „BUNDU"
w Szczecinie
ma zaszczyt zaprosić Was
na
URUCZYSTE OTWARCIE
nowego lokalu partyjnego
w niedzielę, 11.I.48 r. o godz. 11
przy ul. Krasińskiego 4

w programie:
1) część oficjalna
2) część artystyczna

Zaproszenie służy jako karta wstępu.

BUND

ח׳ ....
דער קאָמיטעט פון „בונד"
אין שטעטשין
האט דעם כבוד איינצולאדן
צו דער
פייערלעכער דערעפענונג
פון נייעם פארטיי־לאקאל
זונטיק דעם 11.I.48 — 11 פרי
אויף קראשינסקעגא 4
אין פראגראם:
א) אפיציעלער טייל
ב) ארטיסטישער טייל

Photo 8. Invitation to the official opening of the new party premises in Szczecin, 4 Krasińskiego Street, on 11 January 1948 (from the AŻIH collection, the Bund)

Photo 9. Dzierżoniów 1946/1947. Members of the Dzierżoniów Bund Committee in front of the entrance to the Bund headquarters. Inscription in Yiddish above the window: 'Workers' Corner' (from the ŻIH collection, Documentation Department)

Photo 10. Wrocław, February 1947. Members of the Wrocław Bund Committee. Jakub Słucki in the last row, first from the right. Chaim Wasser from the USA in the middle of the first row. Slogans on the wall: "We're still here!"; "Long live freedom, long live socialism!" (from Marian Feldman's collection)

Photo 11. Warsaw, 15 November 1947. Event at the Roma Theatre to celebrate the 50th anniversary of establishing the Bund. Seated, from the left: Ignacy Samsonowicz, Ignacy Falk, Zdzisław Muszkat, Salo Fiszgrund, speaker – Michał Szuldenfrei, unknown, unknown, Grzegorz Jaszuński, unknown, Gershon Fogel, Liber Brener; at the rear, with the new party banner, most likely three members of Tsukunft, the Bund's youth organisation (photo [?] Dąbrowiecki; from the ŻIH collection, Documentation Department)

Photo 12. Warsaw, 15 November 1947. The event at the Roma Theatre to celebrate the 50th anniversary of establishing the Bund. From the left: Ignacy Samsonowicz, Ignacy Falk, Zdzisław Muszkat, Salo Fiszgrund, Michał Szuldenfrei, unknown, unknown, Grzegorz Jaszuński, Gershon Fogel, Liber Brener, Moses Lederman (photo [?] Dąbrowiecki; from the ŻIH collection, Documentation Department)

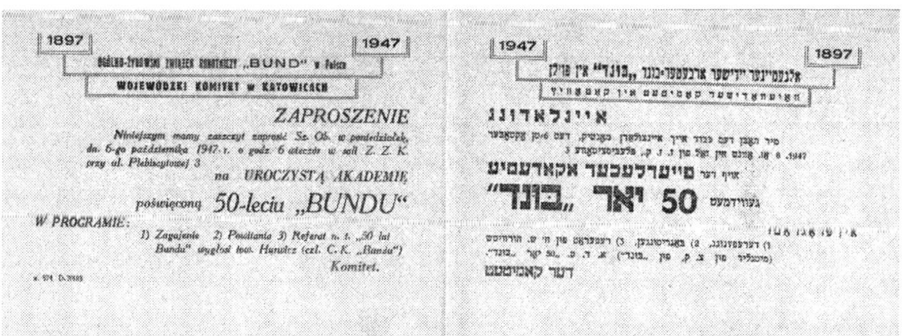

Photos 13 and 14. Katowice, 6 October 1947. Invitation to a ceremonial assembly on the occasion of the Bund's 50th anniversary (from the collection of AŻIH, the Bund)

Photo 15. Częstochowa, 29 September 1945. Celebration of the party's 48th anniversary at the Częstochowa Bund Committee. Moses Lederman is delivering a speech. First from the left, seated, is Ignacy Falk from the Central Committee of the Bund, third – Liber Brener. Over Karl Marx' portrait, a banner of Częstochowa Bund Committee (photo: Lejb Kusznir; from the ŻIH collection, Documentation Department)

Photo 16. Dzierżoniów 1947. Celebration of the party's 50th anniversary at the Dzierżoniów Bund Committee. Ignacy Samsonowicz from the Central Committee of the Bund is delivering a speech. The inscription in Yiddish reads: „Long live the Yiddish language, culture and literature" (from the ŻIH collection, Documentation Department)

Photo 17. Warsaw [undated]. Tsukunft youth attending the May Day parade. Right hands raised with clenched fist in socialist salute (from the ŻIH collection, Documentation Department)

Photo 18. Wrocław, 1946/1947. Włodzimierz Medem Children's Home run by the Bund. A slogan in Yiddish on the wall: „Yiddish is our language!" (from the ŻIH collection, Documentation Department)

Photo 19. Wałbrzych, July 1946. Employees of the 'Igła' [Needle] Bund cooperative (from the ŻIH collection, Documentation Department)

Photo 20. Duszniki-Zdrój, September 1947. Yitzhak (Ignacy) Feldman against the background of the 'Jan Kazimierz' Holiday Home (from Marian Feldman's private collection)

GŁOS BUNDU

ORGAN C. K. „BUNDU" W POLSCE

Nr podwójny 2–3 Warszawa, październik 1946 r. Cena 5 zł.

Tow. Józef Peszunj („Nojach")

W piątą rocznicę

Tow. Włodzimierz Kosowski

Photo 21. Fragment of the title page of *Głos Bundu* nos 2–3 from October 1946. On page no. 1 a commemorative article on the 5th anniversary of the passing of the fathers of the Bund in Poland: comrade Noyakh and comrade Włodzimierz Kosowski.

Opłata pocztowa uiszczona ryczałtem

Folkscajtung 4 (32) • Cena zł. 5 • 20 LUTY 1948

פאלקס-צייטונג

צענטראל־ארגאן פון „בונד" אין פוילן

שלמה מענדעלסאן

Photo 22. Fragment of the title page of *Folkstsaytung* no. 4 (32), from 20 February 1948. On page 1 photograph of the late Shlomo Mendelsohn and a commemorative article.

Photo 23. Wrocław, December 1946. Exhibition of the Historical Commission at the Bund Central Committee. Matwiej Bernstein is visible in the bottom right corner. On the wall, above the exposition, an inscription in Yiddish reads: "Unlimited loyalty". Below, i.a., posters from the subsequent post-war anniversaries of the party's establishment. Above Matwiej's head, portrait of Józef Portnoy (Noyekh) - one of the founders of the Bund in Poland (from the ŻIH collection, Documentation Department)

Photo 24. Warsaw, autumn 1947. The Bundists are laying a wreath at the first monument to the ghetto heroes. First from the right (at the back) is Marek Edelman, to his left– Maria Szuldenfrei; in the second row, second from the right (black hair, looking towards the camera) is Gershon Fogel; in the first row, holding the wreath: on the right, in front of Fogel are Grzegorz Jaszuński, Salo Fiszgrund, Ignacy Falk, Michał Szuldenfrei; at the side on the left, side profile of Sioma Temczyn (clad in a leather coat) is visible (photo: [?] Dąbrowiecki; from the ŻIH collection, Documentation Department)

Photo 25. Tarnów, autumn 1946. Chaim Wasser (fifth from the right) in front of the Beynish Michalewicz Union House, during a visit at the Tarnów Bund Committee (from the ŻIH collection, Documentation Department)

Studies in Jewish History and Memory

Edited by Lucyna Aleksandrowicz-Pędich
Sławomir Jacek Żurek

Vol. 1 Jan T. Gross (ed.): The Holocaust in Occupied Poland: New Findings and New Interpretations. 2012.

Vol. 2 Lucyna Aleksandrowicz-Pędich / Małgorzata Pakier (eds.): Reconstructing Jewish Identity in Pre- and Post-Holocaust Literature and Culture. 2012.

Vol. 3 Małgorzata Pakier: The Construction of European Holocaust Memory: German and Polish Cinema after 1989. 2013.

Vol. 4 Lucyna Aleksandrowicz-Pędich: Memory and Neigborhood: Poles and Poland in Jewish American Fiction after World War Two. 2013.

Vol. 5 Joanna Auron-Górska: Describing Who? Poland in Photographs by Jewish Artists. 2014.

Vol. 6 Lucyna Aleksandrowicz-Pędich/Jacek Partyka (eds.): Jews and Non-Jews: Memories and Interactions from the Perspective of Cultural Studies. 2015.

Vol. 7 Justyna Kowalska-Leder: Their Childhood and the Holocaust. A Child´s Perspective in Polish Documentary and Autobiographical Literature. Translated by Richard J. Reisner. 2015.

Vol. 8 Magdalena M.Wrobel Bloom: Social Networks and the Jewish Migration between Poland and Palestine, 1924-1928. 2016.

Vol. 9 Jacek Nowak / Sławomir Kapralski / Dariusz Niedźwiedzki: On the Banality of Forgetting. Tracing the Memory of Jewish Culture in Poland. 2018.

Vol. 10 Łukasz Tomasz Sroka: In the Light of Vienna. Jews in Lviv - between Tradition and Modernisation (1867-1914). 2018.

Vol. 11 Marta Cobel-Tokarska: Desert Island, Burrow, Grave - Wartime Hiding Places of Jews in Occupied Poland. 2018.

Vol. 12 Przemysław Tacik: The Freedom of Lights: Edmond Jabès and Jewish Philosophy of Modernity. 2019.

Vol. 13 Joanna Nalewajko-Kulikov: A Citizen of Yiddishland. Dovid Sfard and the Jewish Communist Milieu in Poland. Translated by Paul Glasser. 2019.

Vol. 14 Małgorzata Wójcik-Dudek: Reading (in) the Holocaust. Practices of Postmemory in Recent Polish Literature for Children and Young Adults. 2020.

Vol. 15 Krzysztof Lewalski: The Attitude of Christian Churches in the Kingdom of Poland toward Jews in 1855-1915. 2020.

Vol. 16 Alina Molisak: Jewish Warsaw - Jewish Berlin. Literary Portrayal of the City in the First Half of the 20th Century. 2021.

Vol. 17 Stanisław Krajewski: Small Numbers, Big Presence: Jews in Poland after World War II. 2024.

Vol. 18 Martyna Rusiniak-Karwat: The Rise and Fall of the Bund in Poland. 1944-1949. 2025.

www.peterlang.com

Made in the USA
Las Vegas, NV
19 September 2026

339b36cd-a608-4183-b4cf-08ee74b7cf11R01